The Faroe Islands

The Faroe Islands

THE UNIVERSITY PRESS OF KENTUCKY

Interpretations of History

JONATHAN WYLIE

Title-page illustration: Tórshavn in the 1880s (Labonne 1887).
Courtesy Harvard University Libraries.

Endpaper maps in this volume are reprinted with permission
from *The Ring of Dancers: Images of Faroese Culture* by
Jonathan Wylie and David Margolin (University of
Pennsylvania Press, 1981).

Scholarly publisher for the Commonwealth,
serving Bellarmine College, Berea College, Centre
College of Kentucky, Eastern Kentucky University,
The Filson Club, Georgetown College, Kentucky
Historical Society, Kentucky State University,
Morehead State University, Murray State University,
Northern Kentucky University, Transylvania University,
University of Kentucky, University of Louisville,
and Western Kentucky University.

Editorial and Sales Offices: Lexington, Kentucky 40506-0024

Library of Congress Cataloging-in-Publication Data
Wylie, Jonathan.
  The Faroe Islands.

  Bibliography: p.
  Includes index.
  1. Faroe Islands—History.   I. Title.
DL271.F2W95   1987   949.1'5   86-13205
ISBN 978-0-8131-6012-2

for my father

Laurence Wylie,

also a student of local history,
under whose roof this book
was written

The anthropologist who studies one of these small societies finds it far from autonomous and comes to report and analyze it in its relations, societal and cultural, to state and civilization.

—Redfield (1960:59)

Contents

Figures and Tables

Acknowledgments

🕱 Researching and writing this book have been fitted around work on other projects over a number of years. Bits and pieces of it have thus been more or less unwittingly supported, at various times, by the Comparative International Program (Department of Social Relations, Harvard University), the Foreign Area Fellowship Program, the Program in Marine Policy and Ocean Management at the Woods Hole Oceanographic Institution, a Senior Research Fellowship from the Fulbright Program in the Sosial-antropologisk Institutt at the University of Bergen, the Danish Marshall Fund, and the American Council of Learned Societies.

Criticism and encouragement of several sorts have been offered by, among others, Jeremy Boissevain, William A. Christian, Jr., Gail Filion, Davydd Greenwood, Guðmundur Hálfdanarson, Steven Kaplan, David Maybury-Lewis, Jóhan Henrik W. Poulsen, Gail Ringel, Harald Tambs-Lyche, Þórhallur Þórhallsson, Anthony F. C. Wallace, and John Weiss, and by several unusually conscientious readers (including Wayne O'Neill) for sundry presses. Dennis Gaffin, Sanford Gifford, and Søren Rønø have figured prominently in the imagined audience seated patiently by my type-writer. I have particularly valued the help of Jóan Pauli Joensen and David Margolin, and immodestly hope that they may find a few new things in these pages. I must also thank David Margolin for his meticulous copy editing, which saved this book from more errors than I like to contemplate. It goes without saying that the remaining errors and misapprehensions are entirely my own.

Parts of Chapter One and scattered passages elsewhere are adapted from my doctoral dissertation (Wylie 1974). A preliminary version of Chapter Five was delivered at the American Ethnological Society meetings, held in March 1982 in Lexington, Kentucky, on the theme of plural societies. At Jeremy Boissevain's kind invitation, an early version of part of Chapter Two was delivered at the Anthropologisch-Sociologisch Centrum at the University of Amsterdam (Wylie 1978). My translation, in Chapter Seven, of Christian Matras's poem "Neytakonur" is published by kind permission of the author. I am also grateful for their help in securing illustrations to Tove F. Hayeem of the Danish Information Office in New York, Louis A. Pitschmann of the Fiske Icelandic Collection at Cornell University, Svanhild Eriksen of the Photo Department of the Historisk Museum at the University of Bergen, and especially Ólavur Øster of the Føroya Fornminnisavn in Tórshavn.

Terra Incognita

▨ In these days of travel, when the world seems too small for the inexhaustible globe-trotter and every spot that is at all accessible is overrun with excursior ts, it is refreshing to find a remote corner in Europe that has up to the present been spared the desecrating foot of the tourist, and still remains a *terra incognita*. To those who would diverge from the beaten track, and enter the confines of [the] mysterious North . . . , Iceland offers a fair field, and the Faröe Islands should be included, as they are on a direct route. [Anon. 1899:385]

The author of these lines was far from the first tourist to visit the Faroes, and far from the last to imagine them a *terra incognita*. In fact, in some fields the Faroes have long enjoyed a substantial claim to fame: among ornithologists for their stupendous birdcliffs, among folklorists for their balladry, among epidemiologists for Ludvig Panum's classic work on measles (Panum 1940 [1846]), and among linguists for the remarkable survival and renaissance of the Faroese language. But among anthropologists, "excursionists" par excellence, the Faroes are practically unknown; and in historians' knowledge there tends to be a gap a millennium long between a footnote about the Viking settlement "on the way to Iceland" and a footnote about the attainment of home rule in 1948.

Such ignorance is not surprising. The Faroes are an obscure corner of Scandinavia and, apart from Lapland, Scandinavia is perhaps the most obscure corner of the world, ethnographically speaking. At least outside Scandinavia, historians and others have generally found themselves by turns bedazzled by the Viking past and bemused by the modern "Nordic enigma": "Our concern should be to see whether the Nordic world is indeed distinctive, whether it differs significantly from a world called Europe, or another called America. Beyond that, we need to see whether the five countries of this region, for all their substantial similarities, are not also significantly different" (Graubard 1984:ix). But little is known, or can be known, about the Faroes' Norse settlement in the early ninth century, and their situation today is even more enigmatic than that of the North's "five countries." They are a Danish dependency, but internally self-governing and culturally distinct.

This book, then, is for readers who like genuinely remote corners: neither the Viking past nor the present, for our story does not really begin until the Reformation, in about 1540, and it ends in about 1920; neither a nation-state nor a province; neither an utterly isolated place nor one in the

1

West European mainstream. It concerns how, and why, and to what extent the Faroese have maintained their cultural distinctiveness—a matter of great consequence to them and of considerable comparative interest as well.[1]

My own discovery of the Faroe Islands began in 1970. I was a graduate student in social anthropology. Casting about for a place to do fieldwork, I was heartened by the very short shelf of literature I thought I should have to master in order to write a standard sort of village study. This pleasant expectation began to founder when I visited the Faroes that summer. My first discovery was the well-stocked shelves of H.N. Jacobsen's bookstore in Tórshavn, the Faroes' capital. There were a number of books and journals of anthropological interest, if not actually in anthropology.[2] Moreover, there were a great many literary and historical works. Literature and historiography were evidently thriving in the Faroes; so much so, that although I could not hope to master either (even assuming that my professors would approve such an eclectic course!), I was clearly going to have to find out something about these areas that were so important to Faroese.

The importance of the past in modern Faroese culture struck me in a rather different way in the village where I began doing fieldwork the next year. For one of the first things I was told (and told repeatedly) was the story of how the village had been founded in 1833 (Wylie 1982). I did not think this any more remarkable, to begin with, than that at festivals people danced to ballads relating events of the Viking Age. But somehow I did find it remarkable that, when an American friend wrote to ask me about Magnús Heinason (a sixteenth-century coastguard and freebooter whom Ibsen had once contemplated writing a play about), my principal informant in matters genealogical, admittedly a man exceptionally interested in such things, told me in great detail about Heinason, his parentage, and his descendants.

Increasingly it has seemed to me that although anthropologists' debate about the validity of historical materials for understanding living cultures had pretty much beaten itself into the ground, a crucial fact has often been overlooked. No people is without a past; but different peoples remember it more or less well, attribute more or less significance to it, and recall it in different ways and for different reasons. The Faroese find themselves at one end of the spectrum. Their remembered past is secularly construed, a touchstone of their collective identity, and immensely long. In legends and ballads it runs back a thousand years or more—not, to be sure, without thin spots and breaks and shadings off toward myth, but on the whole fairly continuously since the late sixteenth century. Oral transmission is fading, but it has been supplanted by schoolbooks and meticulous scholarly historiography. Similarly, the Faroes' rich folk literature has been supplemented by such modern genres as lyric poetry, plays, and novels. One may suggest in a general way that for the Faroese (and perhaps for other

Scandinavian peoples as well), historiographic and literary affairs are as important as, say, kinship is among the peoples anthropologists usually study. It is quite certain that the survival of a distinctively Faroese culture through the great social changes of the late nineteenth and early twentieth centuries depended upon the reformulation of an acute literary and historical self-consciousness.

I have made a second discovery more slowly, a discovery that is not only my own, and that does not concern only the Faroes. It has long been a commonplace in peasant studies that villages are not social, cultural, economic, or political isolates. Nonetheless, the Dutch anthropologist Jeremy Boissevain (Boissevain and Friedl 1975:11) has complained: "Trained on literature dealing with comparatively slowly changing, isolated, undifferentiated non-Western societies, anthropologists are often ill-equipped for the complexity of Europe. This complexity, and, increasingly, that of the rest of the world, cannot be handled adequately with traditional anthropological concepts. . . . Nor is the traditional anthropological technique of participant observer alone any longer sufficient. . . . Consequently many [anthropologists] have sought refuge in villages, which they proceed to treat as isolated entities. They have tribalized Europe." Boissevain exaggerates, perhaps. Europeanists as well as others are increasingly working their way from single communities seen in timeless isolation toward changing patterns of relations between communities, from local levels of social and cultural organization toward regional and national ones, and from out-of-the-way parts of the world toward its centers in Western Europe and elsewhere. He is right, however, in saying that participant observation is no longer enough, and that our traditional concepts must be modified.[3]

So far as my own work is concerned (for "my" village has been modernizing rapidly, and its relations to the rest of the Faroes and the rest of the world have been growing more complex), all this means that the present work is a kind of prologue to a proper ethnography. It is an attempt to define the historical and sociopolitical setting in which "my" villagers live. But I hope this work may have a wider interest, since it approaches the still unsettled matter of what a national culture is and how it originates—not in isolation, but in interaction with (in this case) Denmark.

The Faroes are an attractive field for such a study. Faroese society is both small enough and complex enough to combine features of tribal and rural societies, on the one hand, and nation-states, on the other; until about 1800 there were fewer than five thousand Faroese, and today there are only about forty-five thousand. The islands' geographical isolation simplifies questions of contact, while their association with politically superordinate peoples has been unbroken since the eleventh century. Their own records are good (and in many cases published) from the late sixteenth century on, and continental conditions are well known. In short, we may trace both internal developments and patterns of external contact with greater confidence, over greater time, and in greater detail than among most rural or tribal peoples.

This book is thus mainly descriptive. I hope, however, that it may interest anyone (historians in particular) who wonders how at least one anthropologist navigates on an excursion into unfamiliar territory: more or less by the seat of one's pants, to be frank about it, but not without a certain perspective on things. For if anthropologists have lately been exploring historians' traditional stamping grounds (nations, ideologies, public figures, affairs of state, literary cultures, historiography itself), historians have returned the compliment by invading "our" territory of small communities, parochial affairs, and ordinary folk doing ordinary things. One suspects, however, that historians often find that the basic tools of anthropological thinking lie awkwardly in the hand. (Professing much interest in "what anthropology has to offer," a distinguished historian acquainted with the latest twists in poststructuralism recently told me that he found "promising" the notion that culture is learned.) My approach has been simple. In perusing such sources as folktales, parliamentary records, tourist writings, poetry, old newspapers, and data on land tenure, I have looked for evidence of how a people's life is organized and how its distinctiveness is defined. How does a group articulate its own identity, and how is it understood by others?

In this light the Faroes are interesting in that their social organization has changed and their identity has been redefined by formally establishing their cultural distinctiveness as a claim to recognition as a separate political entity. Here the anthropological and, indeed, the general reader may need a word of warning. We easily assume that a separate political status follows (or should follow) inevitably from a statement of cultural distinctiveness, and so entertain a "whig" interpretation of culture akin to the "whig interpretation of history" attacked by Herbert Butterfield (1973:17) in the 1930s: to interpret "the past with reference to the present," and so "to write on the side of the Protestants and Whigs, to praise revolutions provided they have been successful, to emphasize certain principles of progress in the past and to produce a story which is the ratification if not the glorification of the present" (1973:9). Now Faroese history has clearly been used to ratify a progressive present. That is the raison d'être of most Faroese historiography as well as a guiding principle in other areas of scholarship and in the fine and literary arts. We may sympathize, for in contrast to most of the peoples we study, the Faroese have been singularly fortunate in preserving cultural continuity over a period of deep social change. Our present concern, however, is not to celebrate this achievement but to understand how it became possible.

Finally, this book is addressed to students of Faroese history, society, and culture—a select group, to be sure. They will find that I have hurried past some well-studied events and periods and have treated others in an unconventional way. In Chapter 1, for example, I have failed to treat *Fær-*

eyinga saga in depth, and in Chapter 5 I have stressed the Danishness of the national-cultural ideology that was eventually domesticated by Faroese. More important, I have thought it worthwhile to investigate several topics that have been slighted in the literature and to suggest others deserving greater attention than I have paid them in these pages. The eighteenth century awaits deeper study, for example, as do the political sociology of the late nineteenth and early twentieth centuries, the operation of village economies after 1856, and the rise of evangelical and temperance movements a generation later. Surely it is no coincidence that these movements arose simultaneously with the deep-water fishery. I assume that the general problem, here as elsewhere in Scandinavia, is the sociology of divisiveness in a formally unified culture. The specific problem is blind spots produced by the role of Faroese historiography and social science as agents of formal unification.[4]

This history has two parts. The first runs from the Faroes' Norse settlement, in the early ninth century, to the establishment of a royal Danish trade monopoly, in 1709. The second runs from 1709 until about 1920, covering a century of near stagnation followed by one of increasingly rapid socioeconomic change.

In the first part, Chapter 1 treats the erratically documented period from the Norse settlement to the Reformation, in about 1540. It is chiefly concerned with the Faroes' political institutions and political and commercial relations with Norway and Denmark.

Chapter 2 considers the Reformation and its bleak but well documented aftermath in the seventeenth century. The Faroese extension of the continental Reformation involved substituting Lutheranism for Catholicism. The Faroese Reformation, however, entrenched an archaic system of land tenure, forestalled the growth of a native middle class, and reduced Faroese (a West Scandinavian tongue most closely akin to Icelandic and the western dialects of Norwegian) to a spoken language only. The Reformation also fixed the Faroes' ecclesiastical, commercial, and political dependence on Denmark. In doing so, it created a shell of official Danishness, within which Faroese culture retained a somewhat precarious integrity. Its most notable expressions were the vernacular itself, which gradually developed into a language of its own without being written, and such works of language as legends, ballads, and folktales.

Chapter 3 considers several such legends, particularly one about a mid-seventeenth-century outlaw named Snæbjørn and his illegitimate son Jákup. I argue that the legend's imagery, semisupernatural elements, and distortions of historical fact are the interpretive framework through which Faroese understood their past and their place in the world. I conclude that the tale reflects an attempt to maintain the integrity of Faroese culture, at a time when Faroese lost control over their relations with the outside,

Danish world, by asserting control over relations with the local, natural world.

In the second part, Chapter 4 takes up the eighteenth century, a period when nothing much seems to have happened. However, tenurial data and the contorted fate of a proposal for agricultural reform suggest that Faroese society was slowly evolving to a critical point: the upper limit of the traditional economy's ability to support the population.

In Chapter 5 the scene shifts to Denmark, with which the Faroes became more closely integrated between 1814 and 1851. Here I consider the application to the Faroes of National Romantic ideology, the creation of a satisfactory Faroese orthography, and, in general, the development of the notion that formal demonstrations of cultural distinctiveness constitute a claim to separate political status. Language and works of language were held to be prime symbols of what was then called "nationality."

Returning to the Faroes, Chapter 6 outlines the social and cultural changes attendant upon demographic growth, the rise of an export fishery, and the abolition of the trade monopoly in 1856.

Chapter 7 describes the further socioeconomic changes of the period from 1890 to 1920 and relates how, in this changing context, the National Romantic ideology was domesticated as a movement to preserve and honor the language and was at last politicized. The result, by about 1920, was the establishment of a national culture—a selective version of the old local culture, whose new institutions embodied and expressed symbols of a political existence separate from Denmark. In a sense, the national culture represents a local extension of the intellectual movements that had contributed to the revolution of 1848-49 in Denmark; at the same time, it represents an extension of the local version of the Reformation, a means for Faroese to reassert control over their relations with the outside world.

Just as the national culture mediates between the Faroes' home world and its international setting, the final chapter looks abroad to the Faroes' closest neighbors, Iceland and Shetland, and back to the way local life has been appreciated in modern literary and historical works. Here I review in a comparative light the main social, economic, and political factors shaping the creation of a formal sense of cultural continuity during changing times; and I look briefly at how such a sense is expressed in Faroese literary and historiographic practice.

I have relegated to an appendix a number of tedious details about the Faroes' governance, especially in the seventeenth and eighteenth centuries.

All translations are my own, unless otherwise noted. Full English translations of the most important medieval documents concerning the Faroes will be found in Young (1979:139-70).

 Norse Settlement to Danish Monopoly

CHAPTER ONE

Another Set of Small Islands
The Faroes in the Norse World, circa 800-1550

At Aix-la-Chapelle in the year 825, the Irish monk and scholar Dicuil composed an essay called *Liber de mensura orbis terræ,* "The Book of the Measurement of the Earth," in which he reckoned the world's extent by piecing together estimates of distances between known points. Dicuil drew most of his data from ancient sources, but occasionally he added something fresh. Thus, having noted that around Britain islands "abound mostly to the north-west and north," he went on: "Among these I have lived in some, and have visited others; some I have only glimpsed, while others I have read about." Still others he had heard about from Irishmen who had visited them.

There are many other islands in the ocean north of Britain which can be reached from the northern islands of Britain [i.e., the Orkneys and Hebrides] in a direct voyage of two days and nights with sails filled in a continuously favorable wind. A devout priest told me that in two summer days and the intervening night he sailed in a two-benched boat and entered one of them.

There is another set of small islands, nearly all separated by narrow stretches of water; in these for nearly a hundred years hermits sailing from our own country, Ireland, have lived. But just as they were always deserted from the beginning of the world, so now because of the Northman pirates they are emptied of anchorites, and filled with countless sheep and very many diverse kinds of sea-birds. I have never found these islands mentioned in the authorities.[1]

This "set of small islands" was surely the Faroes. The "Northman pirates" were Vikings, the Norse warriors, explorers, pioneers, freebooters, and traders who were then launching their great push out around the North Atlantic rim to Markland and Vinland and down along the populous coasts and waterways of Britain and continental Europe, while eastward, across the Baltic, they pioneered commercial routes to Byzantium and beyond.

It is still tempting to imagine as you approach the Faroes that you see them as the Vikings first did, or to recall Beowulf's famous landfall (though that was in Denmark): "after the curl-prowed ship had gone on another day's time the seafarers saw land, the sea cliffs shine, the steep hills, the wide ocean headlands; then the water was crossed, the voyage ended." Rising steeply from the sea, the islands, as Dicuil was told, are "nearly all separated by narrow stretches of water." The treeless land seems bleak until one grows accustomed to the subtle greens and browns of its upland pasturage, seamed with gray outcroppings. Light and mist play about the peaks and the sea cliffs, where birds whirl so high up they seem like gnat swarms against the sky. The villages are small, nearly hidden at sea level. Today the houses are brightly painted, but not so long ago they were built of fieldstone and black-tarred wood and roofed with sod. They were nearly invisible from the sea. All this will seem especially true, of course, if you are lucky enough to reach the Faroes in good weather. For as often as not, the weather is foul: seldom cold but never hot and, as a rule, windy and rainy.

It is fitting to begin an account of the modern development of Faroese culture with the islands' Viking discovery, because as this heroic legacy has been recalled in modern times and as it was shared with other nations of the North, it proved a crucial element in the process of redefining the Faroes' place in the world. So did the intimate but austere landscape, and the "very many diverse kinds of sea-birds" an Irishman found remarkable twelve hundred years ago. But we must not be led astray by the romance of the North. The ninth century was a long time ago. Already in the eleventh century the Viking impulse waned, with the political coalescence of Scandinavia and its conversion to Christianity. The western colonies settled into an increasingly isolated and impoverished existence; or they passed into non-Scandinavian hands. Vinland was forgotten except in the sagas. The Hebrides and Man passed to Scotland in 1266. Greenland, poor and distant, was more and more left to its fate. Norway itself was slowly drawn back into a more Baltic orbit. In the 1380s it lost its political independence and, along with its island dependencies, was subsumed under a joint Danish-Norwegian crown. The most important of these dependencies was Iceland, which had given up its freedom in 1262. The Faroese had already been subject to the Norwegian crown for over two hundred years. Orkney became Scottish in 1468, Shetland in 1472.

By the time of the Reformation, in the middle of the sixteenth century, the Faroes were a small and rather unimportant part of an already much diminished Norse world, whose society had developed a good deal over seven hundred years. We must begin by setting this stage, furnishing it with the characters and institutions that accumulated between the days of the Irish monk Dicuil and the German monk Luther.

Very little is known of early Faroese society. Dicuil's comments and scattered archeological, literary, and linguistic evidence suggest that Norsemen began raiding here in the early ninth century; that settlers followed quickly; and that they came partly from western Norway and partly, perhaps in greater numbers, by way of the Scottish islands. They built homesteads at defensible spots near the sea, and high up in the hills they built structures that appear to have been outbuildings for looking after cattle or sheep in the summer.[2] At Kvívík, where a Viking Age homestead has been excavated, part of their diet "is revealed by finds of the bones of sheep, cows, pigs, seals and pilot whales, guillemots, razor bills, cormorants, sea-gulls, and, of course, cod. It is uncertain whether they ate horse, but bones tell us that they certainly had them, and we know that they gave toy horses to their children" (S. Dahl 1970b:69). Finds of spindle whorls and loom weights suggest that spinning and weaving were major occupations. Woolens were probably important in trade as well as for domestic use. Certainly the Faroese traded with both Norway and the British Isles and perhaps farther afield as well, "for such necessities as corn, soapstone and timber, and for such luxury goods as glass, amber beads and hazel nuts" (S. Dahl 1970b:71).

Probably well before the late tenth century, the Faroes formed a political unit whose principal parliament or high court (Old Norse *þing*) met at Tórshavn on a rocky spit called the Tinganes, "Parliament Headland." Tórshavn itself was most likely sparsely inhabited, if at all, like the meeting places of other Norse parliaments (see S. Petersen 1972). As in Iceland, the Faroese parliament was "apparently presided over by a *løgsǫgumaðr*, 'law speaker,'" although later this official was called the *løgmaður* (Foote and Wilson 1970:91; see also Foote 1970:174). It met once a year, in late spring or early summer. The central parliament may at one time have been a popular assembly, to which all free men might come; but men probably attended less on their own behalf than as followers of regionally powerful chieftains. In historical times, it has been called the Løgting. In addition, the islands were probably divided early on into districts, each of which had what was later called a "spring parliament" (*várting*).

Our picture of Faroese society in these early, pagan days is unfortunately rather foggy; for our principal source, an Icelandic saga that was not composed until around 1200, is in many respects inaccurate and anachronistic. Nevertheless, there is no reason to doubt that *Færeyinga saga*'s central episode is true enough, in a general sort of way.[3]

The saga's two main figures are Tróndur í Gøtu and Sigmundur, the former a pagan chieftain, the latter a Christian who, it is said, pledged himself to carry out in the Faroes the twin policies of Ólaf Tryggvason, who had made himself king in Norway: conversion to Christianity and the further unification of the realm. In about 998, according to the saga, Sigmundur contrived to baptize Tróndur by force and so overcame the initial strong opposition to Christianity. Two years later the new religion was formally accepted by Faroese. This did not at once bring peace, however, and in 1005 Sigmundur met his death escaping an attack by Tróndur. Tróndur, Sigmundur's grandson Leivur Øssurarson, and a third chieftain then divided up the Faroes. Resistance to Norwegian influence ceased, and it is said that when Tróndur died, in 1035, Leivur received the Faroes as a fief from King Magnús the Good.

This makes a good story, but among its less reliable details is the success ascribed to Ólaf Tryggvason in converting the Faroes. "In the course of time he was given credit for Christianizing Norway (which is an exaggeration), the Shetlands and Faroes (about which little is known), Iceland (which is overgenerous), and Greenland (which is wrong). He stands before posterity as one who in his day and place was Christ's best hatchet-man, and the Icelandic retailers of his life approved the role" (G. Jones 1968a:135; 1968b:30). His brief reign ended violently, in 1000. His twin policies of unification and Christianization were, however, pursued rather more successfully by his successors. Whatever happened in detail, there is no reason to doubt that the early eleventh century saw the Faroese become both Christian and tributary to Norway.

Toward the end of the century, the Faroes were made a separate bishopric. The first few bishops were surely more missionaries than anything else. It was probably the third whose name we know, Guðmundur, who sometime around 1120 established the episcopal residence at Kirkjubøur, a favorably situated farmstead across the ridge from Tórshavn. After 1152, the Faroe diocese was part of the archdiocese of Nidaros (modern Trondheim). The bishops were chosen, mostly from among their own number, by the canons of the cathedral minster in Bergen. Except perhaps for Hilarius, who held office in the late fifteenth and early sixteenth centuries, the Faroes' bishops were all foreigners, although the priesthood may have been largely Faroese (Øssursson 1963; P.M. Rasmussen 1978).

Until the Reformation, Kirkjubøur also had a school where candidates for the priesthood were educated. This school's most famous alumnus (or dropout) was a certain Sverri, a Norwegian-born child brought up there by Bishop Rói. Sverri decided not to become a priest but, claiming to be King Sigurd's natural son, found his way to Norway, where he made himself king, in 1184, after a long civil war.

The Faroes' most notable bishop was Erlendur, who was consecrated in 1269. Erlendur is credited with undertaking construction of a stone cathedral in Kirkjubøur. According to legend, the taxes he raised proved too burdensome and provoked something like a civil war, in which he was killed. In fact he died in Bergen in 1308, though quite possibly he had been driven out of the Faroes when his attempt to increase the power of the Faroese Church was violently opposed.[4] At any rate, the cathedral was never finished. Still unroofed, it is now one of the Faroes' principal tourist attractions.

The exact nature of the ties between the Faroes and the crown in the eleventh and twelfth centuries is unclear, but "it is likely that . . . the king left the superintendence of his interests to some individual leader from one of the traditionally important families in the islands, a man who would doubtless be a member of his hird and under vows of personal loyalty to him" (Foote and Wilson 1970:132). Sometime before 1200, in an attempt to regularize the administration of his scattered realms, the king began appointing an important man in each district to represent him and his law. This official was first called the sheriff, and in 1273 King Magnús Hákonarson decreed that "the sheriff shall have no more officers than two."[5] Later on, the number of officials and the names by which they were called changed. The king's chief representative in the islands came to be called the bailiff (*fúti*). Six sheriffs (*sýslumenn*) stood under him, one for each of the Faroes' six districts (*sýslur*). The sheriffs were Faroese and as a rule lived in the districts they administered. Their duties included collecting taxes locally and bringing transgressions of the law to court. The bailiff was a foreigner. At times in the Middle Ages, "the Faroes were bestowed as a fief, and often the feudal lord then also had the bailiff's powers" (L. Zachariasen 1961:325). As the system developed, the bailiff would come out to the Faroes with the first trading vessel in the spring. In the fall he returned to the continent. During the winter he was represented by a "winter-bailiff" (*vetrarfúti*), who was a local man. The bailiff's principal duties included collecting taxes and prosecuting cases before the Løgting. Then at some point (probably around the Reformation) he also began appointing the representatives (*løgrættumenn*) to the spring parliaments and the Løgting. At about the same time, the king assumed the privilege of confirming the election of the Løgting's foreman, the *løgmaður*.

One more official must be mentioned, though his post was not formally established until well after the Reformation. We have no proof, but it is likely that the Løgting had long been in the habit of keeping records of its judgments. The early recording clerks may have been literate members of the Løgting, perhaps "closely associated with the church" (L. Zachariasen 1961:332). The earliest indication of a recording secretary dates from 1584. The post was officially established in Norway in 1591, probably somewhat later in the Faroes. In 1634 the *sorinskrivari,* as he came to be called in Faroese, was given judicial functions in Norway; by the middle of the seventeenth century in the Faroes, he had likewise taken over from the *løgmaður* the role of sitting as circuit judge for the spring parliaments.

Until the late thirteenth century, the Løgting probably both made the law and interpreted it in cases brought before it. It was thus a legislative as well as a judicial body, serving in the latter capacity as a court of appeal from the spring parliaments. The Løgting's independence, however, was greatly curtailed in the last quarter of the thirteenth century. In 1273 King Magnús wrote: "we want all men to know, that we have agreed to confirm for you, according to your request and according to the advice of all the

Figure 1.   Institutions and officials of the Faroes' commerce, government, and Church, through the early seventeenth century.

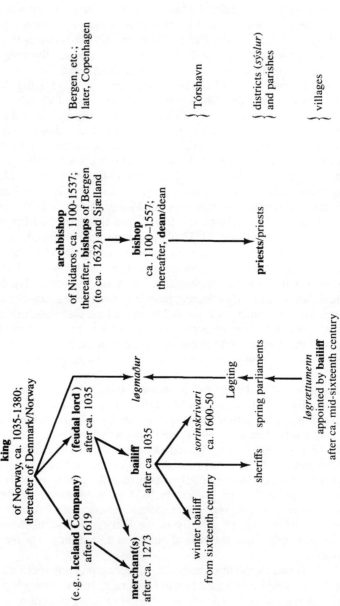

Note: Non-Faroese are shown in **boldface type**. Arrows indicate, as the context requires, membership or powers of election, appointment, or confirmation. Not all such relationships are shown. After the Reformation, the **bishop** was chosen or confirmed by the **king**, and the **dean** became an ex officio member of the Løgting.

Names in parentheses indicate institutions or officials not always present.

best men, that such laws shall be valid here as are valid in the whole Gulating district [in southwestern Norway], except that the chapter of laws concerning the land shall still stand according to what your own book already witnesses" (Jakobsen 1907:23-24). The Løgting complied. The Seyðabræv, or "Sheep-Letter," followed in 1298.[6] The Seyðabræv codified earlier Faroese land laws, which the crown thus recognized as acceptable local variations from continental practices. It is still the basis of Faroese land laws. Following these legal reforms, the Løgting ceased to be a legislative body. Except for the land laws, Faroese law was the same as that on the continent, and the king was recognized as the final arbiter and giver of law for the Faroes. The Løgting's judicial independence was also lost, since its judgments could be overturned upon appeal to the king.

In all this, and particularly in the Seyðabræv, one discerns not only the increasing power of the crown but also the heavy hand of Bishop Erlendur. Although Erlendur is mentioned in the Seyðabræv, there is no reference to a Faroese løgmaður, only to Shetland's løgmaður, Sigurd. This is generally taken to mean that at that time the Faroes came under Shetland's jurisdiction. It has been argued that Bishop Erlendur had promoted such an arrangement in order to give himself a freer hand in increasing his own power and that of the Faroese church. How long the Faroes remained in this subordinate status is unclear, but we find that in 1412 they once again had their own løgmaður (Jakobsen 1907:xxii).

All in all, then, the system was as follows in the late Middle Ages (see Figure 1). It undoubtedly incorporated many ancient features. There were thirty-six representatives, or løgrættumenn, six from each of the Faroes' six districts; the groups of six met to form the Faroes' spring parliaments. Two løgrættumenn from each district met together in Tórshavn to form the Løgting, which thus had twelve ordinary members. The Løgting chose its own foreman, the løgmaður. He was the islands' chief justice, acting upon the advice of the Løgting's ordinary members. Until the middle of the seventeenth century, the løgmaður also served as the circuit judge for the spring parliaments, attending each in turn. Thereafter the sorinskrivari assumed this function. It is not clear just how the løgrættumenn were chosen, or what their term of office was. It is possible that in about 1400, emissaries from each district would meet each year in Tórshavn to elect them, usually from among themselves (Jakobsen 1907:27). By the Reformation, although the løgrættumenn may still have been elected, they served long—probably life—terms. So did the løgmaður. At about the time of the Reformation, the løgrættumenn began to be appointed by the bailiff. The king confirmed the løgmaður's election.

Bishop Erlendur's plans may have gone awry, but the Faroese Church nevertheless became an important temporal institution. For one thing, it was far and away the greatest landowner in the islands. At the Reformation, it owned about half the land in the Faroes. Some holdings it had surely come by honestly enough, as lands were piously bequeathed to it or were given over in lieu of the tithe; but other acquisitions were not so proper. The rapaciousness of a certain priest named Kálvur is legendary: "He was villainously greedy in character, a mocker and an utterly intractable man."[7] The legends call him "the last Catholic priest on Sandoy," but he was almost certainly Sandoy's priest toward the end of the fourteenth century; or so it seems from a letter dated 1412, in which Bishop Jóan and Kálvur's son Harald (who was løgmaður) agree out of court to divide between themselves some land that the current priest on Sandoy had mortgaged illegally. Presumably this private compromise was in order because Kálvur had acquired the land by dubious means.

It should be pointed out that around 1400 the Faroese population was probably not yet fully recovered from the ravages of the Black Death, which swept the islands in about 1350. It has been estimated that in 1327 the population had stood at about four thousand; here, as elsewhere in Scandinavia, mortality might have been on the order of 70 percent.[8] Legends recall that whole villages were wiped out (there is also a suggestion that the Faroes may have been partially resettled from Norway) and it may have been possible for the survivors to amass immense private holdings in land. Eventually these must have been split apart by inheritance, but the Church's holdings were more permanent. Some were the priests' and the bishop's livings, but the rest were large leaseholds. Tenant farmers were thus better off than freeholders, since their holdings were impartible.

The Church's power was also moral, and the workings of ecclesiastical law may have contributed to the relative impoverishment of freeholders. We do not know what ecclesiastical law was in the Faroes before the Reformation; only that in 1584 the Løgting complied with Frederik II's request that a compilation of late thirteenth-century Icelandic ecclesiastical law called the Stóridómur continue to be valid in the Faroes. Among other things, the Stóridómur set the bounds within which kinsmen were forbidden to marry; since marriage between cousins was held to be incestuous, lands divided by inheritance could not easily be recombined. After the Reformation, the Stóridómur was supplemented by secular laws prescribing harsh punishments for bearing or fathering children out of wedlock (death, if the parents were cousins) and allowing couples to marry only if they had a certain amount of land. Similar restrictions on marriage were in effect earlier as well. It could hardly be otherwise in so ecologically precarious a land, where overpopulation was always a threat. Thus the Seyðabræv had "established certain requirements for a man if he was to be able to marry and set up his own house": none could do so without being able to support at least three cows.[9] In effect, the poor were forbidden to marry.

Some of the Faroes' most important ties with the continent were commercial. In this as in other respects, their main point of contact was Bergen.

The sagas tell us that Bergen was founded in 1070 by Ólaf Haralds-son, called Ólaf Kyrri, "the Peaceful." Ólaf's father, Harald Harðráði, had been slain with most of his army at Stamford Bridge, a convenient if somewhat arbitrary marker for the end of the Viking Age as well as the conquest of England by the Norsemen's Norman descendants. Sparing Ólaf, the English hurried south to Hastings. He returned to Norway to undertake what was to prove a long, peaceful, and poorly remembered reign that lasted until 1093.

Before Ólaf's time, Bergen had evidently been a fishing village of no particular importance. But as a commercial center, it held magnificent potential. The harbor itself was large and defensible. Well sheltered at the end of a modest fjord, it was easily accessible from the open sea, at the crossroads of several important trade routes. Iceland and the other island colonies lay west across the Atlantic, and England, an increasingly im-portant trading partner, lay over the North Sea. North along the coast lay the archepiscopal town and trading center of Nidaros; beyond that stretched the pasturages and hunting and fishing grounds of North Norway. Moreover, bypassing Norway's mountainous interior, one might sail down the coast and around to the Vik (the Oslofjord region) and into the Baltic, a voyage both safer and more usual now that "the west-coast magnates had given up piracy and gone in for land and trade" (Foote and Wilson 1970:48).

Tourists today may find Bergen a distant place, "in the heart of the fjord country" if it is in the heart of anything at all. But wandering along its still busy quays, through the churches and the great hall inaugurated by Hákon Hákonarson in 1261, and visiting, nearby, the wonderful modern museum, one also realizes that in the late Middle Ages this was one of the most important cities in the northern world.

Norway, like Flanders, was a country which depended on other countries for most of its food supply, and, moreover, had no wool and cloth and hardly any metals. It relied largely on imports, and in return supplied an inexhaustible supply of fish. *Sverri's Saga* [the history of the same Sverri who had been raised at Kirkjubøur] has preserved the speech of one of its kings in 1186 on the relative merits of different countries who came to the port of Bergen. We desire, he says, to thank the Englishmen who have brought hither linen and flax, wax and cauldrons, and the men of the Orkneys, Shetland and the Faroes, who have brought hither such things as made the land richer, which we cannot do without. [Power 1941:58]

As Christianity spread along the southern shore of the Baltic, as the Han-seatic towns grew, and as the Church promulgated stricter fasting laws, Norway was beginning to trade great quantities of salted and dried cod out of Bergen. The Faroese may have contributed to the Norwegian export fishery, but they could hardly compete with Lofoten's more plentiful and convenient cod or, later, with English catches from around Iceland or on the Grand Banks (Foote and Wilson 1970:202; A. Jensen 1972:53ff.). Faroese exports perhaps also included some feathers, tallow, and train oil,

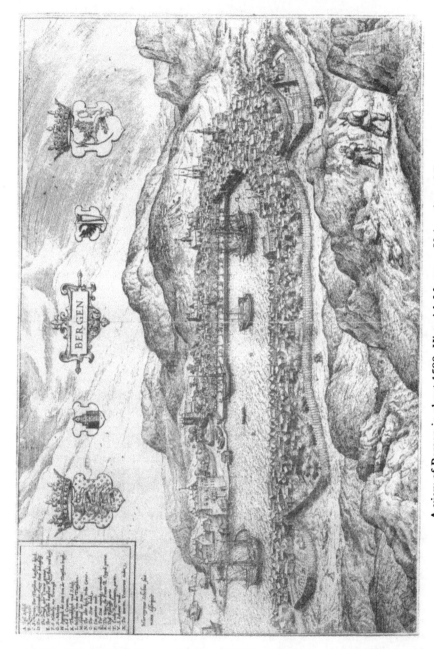

A view of Bergen in about 1580. Historisk Museum, Universitetet i Bergen.

but until well into the nineteenth century their main exports were wool and woolens. In return they received grain, timber, salt, metals, and a few luxury items.

In earlier times, judging from the saga evidence, the more important farmers owned ships capable of crossing the sea, while foreign merchants also called in the Faroes from time to time. *Færeyinga saga* relates that, in an ill-fated move, Tróndur í Gøtu paid a merchant from Novgorod to take away the young cousins Sigmundur and Torir; they spent the winter in Tønsberg, in the Norwegian Vik. But as has been said of the Icelanders, "had they kept up the character of sea-rovers in a land almost destitute of raw materials for ships, theirs would have been a remarkable achievement" (Carus-Wilson 1954:101; cf. Gelsinger 1981:108-15). By the end of the thirteenth century, and perhaps well over a century before, the Faroese were unable to carry out on their own the trade upon which their survival depended. Its management fell into foreign hands.

These hands were first and foremost the king's, who undertook in the late thirteenth and early fourteenth centuries to regularize the North Atlantic trade and to share in such profits as could be made from it. When Iceland gave up its independence, in 1262, the king agreed to have six ships a year sailing between Iceland and Norway. Much the same agreement was reached with the Faroese. In the same letter in which King Magnús extended the law of the Gulating to the Faroes, he said, "We also promise you, that those two ships which are most useful to you, shall go between Norway and the Faroes each year."[10] This suggests that trade with Iceland and the Faroes needed some artificial encouragement.

From the continental point of view, Magnús's letter is symptomatic of how Bergen's place in the world was changing. Until the mid-thirteenth century, "Norwegian expansion was largely westward, in an effort to maintain the viking hold on the islands off Great Britain and to assert sovereignty over Iceland and Greenland" (Haugen 1976:181). Greenland came under the Norwegian crown in 1261, Iceland the year after. But this was the high-water mark of Norwegian expansion. In 1266 the Hebrides and Man passed to Scotland, while Norway's own center of gravity was rapidly shifting south and east. Economically, it was drawn that way by the Hanse, whose merchants dominated the commercial life of Bergen after about 1300. "The development of Norwegian trade relations with the ports of Northern Germany went hand-in-hand with a growing preoccupation with inter-Scandinavian politics. . . . The 1250's saw the origin of the south- and east-oriented policy that gradually turned Norwegian foreign interest away from the traditional connection with the British Isles, and led her into the Scandinavian unions of the later middle ages" (Helle 1968:113). In 1299 the capital and royal chancellery were moved from Bergen to Oslo. Less than a century later, by the treaty of Kalmar (1397), Norway was formally united with Sweden and Denmark, under Margaret of Denmark. The union with Sweden proved short-lived, but that with Denmark lasted until 1814.

From the Faroese point of view, the most important result of this shift was that they became a more peripheral part of the realm, increasingly different from their rulers and the foreigners with whom they came in contact by way of trade. In 1294 Hanseatic merchants were forbidden to trade with the Faroes. This prohibition was renewed in 1302 and again in 1348, until, in 1361, "they received the same rights to sail to the taxed lands [Iceland, the Faroes, Shetland, etc.] as the native merchants in Bergen" (Joensen, Mortensen, and Petersen 1955:8). Trading rights were granted by the Norwegian king (or the Danish-Norwegian king, with more and more emphasis on the "Danish"), who rented them out to interested merchants. These merchants were often Hanseatic, but they were also Norwegian, and from time to time, English or Dutch.

By the sixteenth century, the usual system was that the king rented out exclusive trading rights for a fixed sum for a fixed period. The merchant was sometimes the Faroes' feudal overlord as well, and was thus also engaged with tax collecting. In 1524, for example, on the eve of the Reformation, the bailiff of Bergen, Jørgen Hansen, received the Faroes as a fief and was granted exclusive trading rights. He was succeeded in 1529 by the Hamburger Thomas Koppen. Koppen died in 1553, and for three years the Faroe trade was open to all Danish or Norwegian merchants. The king himself managed it from 1556 until 1569. In 1558 a Copenhagen man, Anders Jude, had been made both the Faroes' bailiff and the king's merchant. In 1569 Jude and a colleague were granted exclusive trading rights.

As matters continued in this somewhat erratic way during the sixteenth century, control over the Faroe trade shifted gradually away from Norwegian and Hanseatic merchants to Danes, and from Bergen to Copenhagen; around the turn of the sixteenth century, however, it was managed by a Bergen consortium. This trend culminated in 1619, when Christian IV chartered the Iceland, Faroe, and Northern Norway Company. The "Iceland Company," as it is commonly called, was based in Copenhagen, which now finally supplanted Bergen as the Faroes' commercial link to the continent.

First settled by Norsemen in the early ninth century, the Faroes became a Christian colony of Norway in the early eleventh century. They retained their ancient judicial institutions, but these were increasingly hedged about by an officialdom headed by the bailiff, originally a tax collector, who was a foreigner and a royal appointee. Ecclesiastically, the Faroes were a separate bishopric, but the bishop was likewise chosen abroad. The Church was the greatest landowner in the Faroes. Commercially, as well as politically and ecclesiastically, the Faroes were most directly linked to Bergen. Bergen itself, however, was now less Norway's central point than an outpost (albeit a vitally important one) of a Baltic and coastwise trade. Copenhagen was definitely the capital of the Norwegian-Danish kingdom.

CHAPTER TWO

Church, King, Company, and Country
The Reformation and Its Aftermath, 1540-1709

⬛ In January 1523, with Sweden in revolt and a Lübeck fleet harrying the Danish coast, a group of Jutland noblemen renounced their allegiance to Christian II. Civil war broke out. In March, Christian's uncle, Duke Frederik of Holstein-Gottorp, was formally elected king. Christian fled to Holland in April. He made a disastrous attempt to invade Denmark in 1531 and was imprisoned by Frederik.

Frederik died two years later. Civil war broke out again, lasting until the triumphant entry into Copenhagen in 1536 of his eldest son, Christian III, a convinced Lutheran whose victory assured the success of the Reformation in Denmark. In 1537 Christian III abolished the office of archbishop and took over the governance of the church. Piously and in order to fill the depleted royal coffers, he appropriated the third of the tithe that had previously gone to the bishops and the lands belonging to the Church, at least a third of all the cultivable land in the realm.

Such, in brief, was the Danish version of the clash of great Northern interests we call the Reformation. There were rival claimants to the throne: Frederik and the two Christians, and Christian III's brother Hans, who was supported by a Catholic faction. There were rival commercial, national, and regional interests: Denmark and Sweden, Holland and the Holy Roman Empire, Jutland and Holstein, and Copenhagen, Lübeck, and Hamburg. There were rival classes: the Danish nobility favored Frederik, commoners and the growing middle class mostly favored Christian II and Christian III. And there were rival faiths: Christian II sympathized with Lutheranism while he was king, but after being deposed he sought support wherever he could; Frederik was Catholic, but he could not oppose Lutheranism lest he alienate the townsfolk among whom it was rapidly gaining ground in the late 1520s; and Christian III made the new faith as obligatory as the old.

Taking a longer view, we find the Danish Reformation carrying on a story as old as the history of Christianity in Scandinavia: at the end of the Viking Age, the rulers of the North had likewise used the new faith to help unify and control their emergent kingdoms. The next 125 years or so saw two intertwined trends in the course of events in Denmark. Internal affairs were marked by a growing opposition between the crown and the nobility; foreign affairs were marked by commercial and military rivalry

The siege of Copenhagen in 1536, from a contemporary woodcut. Det Kongelige Bibliotek, Copenhagen.

among the powers of the Baltic and the North Sea. Particularly in the seventeenth century, war threatened constantly. These trends led to the establishment of a strictly hereditary monarchy and the assumption of absolute powers between 1660 and 1665 by Christian III's great-grandson Frederik III.

In 1657 Denmark was drawn into an ill-advised war with Sweden. The kingdom was saved only by a desperate defense of Copenhagen in 1658-59, Dutch aid, the intercession of France, England, and Holland, and the sudden death of Charles X of Sweden, in 1660. The Danish economy was a shambles. When the Estates met that year, commoners and clergy wanted to break the power of the nobility by requiring that noblemen pay taxes and by making the kingship hereditary. Hitherto the king had been elected by the nobility, ruling, technically at their pleasure, within the limits of a charter (*håndfesting*) signed at the inauguration of his reign. In demanding a hereditary kingship, commoners and clergy naturally had the tacit support of Frederik and the more open support of his ministers, prominent among whom was the treasurer, Christoffer von Gabel. The nobility having been forced to submit, the king was released from his charter and was publicly acclaimed a hereditary monarch. The Estates were dissolved.

The next year Denmark's citizenry got more than it bargained for: a constitution making the king a monarch more absolute, at least on paper, than any other in Western Europe, whose rule was to be exercised through a streamlined system of councils and ministries. The old aristocracy lost out in all this, while over the next decades much of the peasantry was virtually reduced to serfdom. The middle classes, whose prosperity was based largely on international and colonial trade, benefited, as did the state bureaucracy they increasingly staffed. Trade revived, and no further wars were fought on Danish soil until the nineteenth century. In practice, however, the king's powers were checked, so that his rule never became as absolute as, for example, the theoretically less absolute monarchy of France under Louis XIV.

Students of Danish history will rightly protest that this account of the period from 1523 to 1655 has overlooked the glories of Christian IV's reign; the question of the depth of Frederik III's complicity in the plot (if it was a plot) to make the crown hereditary; the rewards and difficulties inherent in Copenhagen's position as both mistress of the long Norwegian coast and gatekeeper and tollmaster for the Baltic; the subtleties of relations with the rival seafaring Protestant powers of Holland and England; the call to empire in the Indies east and west; the dissolution of the union with Sweden; and Denmark's awkward place between a united Sweden and a fragmented Germany. But this is a Faroese history, and although the Faroes' fortunes depended on the turn of events in Denmark, they were a distant and peculiar part of the kingdom. Why Denmark went to war or avoided it was less important than the effect on prices of grain or the market for woolen stockings in Holland. Why Christoffer von Gabel rose to power was less important than the simple fact that he did so, or that, as a Faroese schoolbook says, he and his son Frederik "thought more of getting a profit from the Faroes than of doing good for Faroese" (Djurhuus 1963:38). In short, like other movements reaching the Faroes from the continent, the Reformation had different consequences as it was refracted through local conditions.

Unlike Denmark, the Faroes had no nobility or middle class to begin with, and the bureaucracy was almost entirely concentrated in the person of the bailiff. After the Reformation, the inherently small capacities of the land and the crown's increasing restrictions on the marginally profitable Faroe trade isolated the islands further, forestalling economic growth and the rise of a native middle class. The Faroese remained free peasants, whose way of life changed little until the nineteenth century. This was not just a matter of oppression from abroad, although that was part of it, along with such factors as pirate raids and a worsening climate. Rather, a distinctively Faroese way of life survived because local interests coincided with the crown's: both wanted to maintain the tenurial and mercantile systems upon which it was based. This coincidence masked, however, a radical difference between local and Danish views of the crown's place in Faroese society, which did not really come to light until the nineteenth century.

As an ecclesiastical event, the Faroese Reformation passed quickly.[1] In 1533, the incumbent bishop having died, a certain Ámundur, a canon in the cathedral at Bergen, was chosen bishop, perhaps (exceptionally) by the Faroese clergy themselves. Ámundur's election was confirmed by Frederik I, in accordance with his ruling of 1526 forbidding bishops to seek confirmation in Rome. Then in 1535 the Løgting "recognized the Reformation" (Zachariasen 1961:11). Except in implying allegiance to Christian III, it is not clear just what this means; indeed in general "we know very little of how the process of spreading the Reformation among Faroese went on" (Degn 1933:70). An unknown number of churches and chapels were destroyed or passed out of use, however, and this may have triggered some protests. As late as 1551, we find the king ordering parishioners to attend services.

In about 1538, Christian III, now victorious on the continent, advised Ámundur of his intention to take over the possessions of the Church. Ámundur protested and was removed from office.

He was replaced, in about 1540, by Jens Gregersøn Riber, a Dane who had served in the Bergen cathedral. Riber was the Faroes' first and only Lutheran bishop. In 1541 the king ordered a survey of Faroese church lands, and went on to appropriate two-thirds of them, perhaps in the following year. He took over the remaining lands in 1557. The Church had owned about half of all the land in the Faroes. The crown thus became the greatest landowner in the Faroes; this was perhaps the single most important consequence of the Reformation.

Riber did not remain long in the Faroes. He left some time before 1557, when the Faroese Church was reduced to a deanery, under the diocese of Bergen (J. Dahl 1938). The Faroes' first dean was a Norwegian priest called Heini Jónsson, nicknamed Heini "Shipwreck" because, according to legend, he had been storm-blown from Bergen. His boat fetched up on the beach at Húsavík, where he married the girl who nursed him back to life. She was from a prominent local family (their son, Jón Heinason, became løgmaður in 1573). She died young, and Heini "Shipwreck" married again, this time a Norwegian woman, his old girlfriend, they say, who had married someone else when Heini was believed lost at sea, but was now widowed (see Heilskov 1915:251). Their son Magnús Heinason became a trader, freebooter, and sometime coastguard. In 1579 the king granted him a monopoly over the Faroe trade on condition that he clear the sea of the Barbary pirates, whose raids, which for some years had troubled the Faroes, were probably one reason Bishop Riber had left.

The episcopal church at Kirkjubøur passed out of use, though a new church was not built until 1609, in Tórshavn. In about 1620, the Faroe deanery was transferred to the Sjælland diocese, thus cutting the Faroese Church's ancient connection with Bergen. The priesthood, meanwhile, became increasingly Danish. The records are poor before the end of the sixteenth century, and not always definite afterwards, but it seems likely that of the Faroes' seven "priests" (*prestar*), as they are still called, three were Danes in 1590, four in 1620, and five in 1660 (Øssursson 1963). Thereafter, many were second-generation Faroese, sons following their fathers' calling.

Of course the Faroese Reformation was no more simply an ecclesiastical event than the Danish Reformation was. Among other things, it had profound linguistic consequences.

Until then the Faroese vernacular evidently differed little from Icelandic and the western dialects of Norwegian, despite a modest amount of phonological divergence and, in all likelihood, some internal phonological dialect diversification as well (Hamre 1944; Sørlie 1965). As elsewhere in the Catholic world, the primary liturgical language was Latin. Latin and the "old Language" were evidently used as late as 1673 at a feast following the annual session of the Løgting (Debes 1676:283-86). But otherwise Danish replaced both Latin in the Church and the vernacular for law and commerce during the second half of the sixteenth century. Thus by 1600, "the old Faroese language of the Middle Ages had . . . passed out of use in all documents, and the understanding of this language had begun to fade among Faroese" (L. Zachariasen 1961:320). When Danish was established as the liturgical language in the Faroes and Norway in 1607, no attempt was made to produce a vernacular Bible. (The first satisfactory Danish Bible dates from 1550.) This was not so surprising in Norway, whose written language was already virtually identical with Danish. The Icelanders, however, had produced their own translation of the Bible in 1584; there the liturgical language became, and remained, Icelandic. Meanwhile, as we have seen, the episcopal school at Kirkjubøur, which had probably fostered an independent writing tradition in Faroese, had closed down in 1538. It was replaced, after a fashion, by a "Latin school," founded in Tórshavn in 1547, "in the same way as in all Danish market towns at that time, and in the seventeenth century a so-called 'Danish school' was also founded in Tórshavn" (J.P. Heinesen 1966:49).

This is not to say that the Faroese language died out, or that it diverged immediately from Icelandic. Jón Indíafari, an Icelandic mariner who visited the Faroes in 1616, commented that a Faroese farmer read two Icelandic books easily, "for there was no great difference between their tongue and ours, and it was the same in many ways with their cus-toms." But, he went on, "Danish manners have come in there, both in churches and outside it, with common Danish speech" (Blöndal 1908:121; Phillpotts 1923:143). Nonetheless, like Icelandic but unlike Norwegian, Faroese proved resistant to Danish influence, although (unlike Icelandic) it failed to survive as a written language. It developed on its own, in increasing isolation from the remnants of the old Bergen-based North At-lantic confederacy. A small token of this is the fact that the Icelandic hymns composed after 1609 never became known in the Faroes. The new hymns were in Danish (L. Zachariasen 1961:13). Danish likewise became the language of Faroese law. The earliest extant records of the Løgting's deliberations, from 1615, are written in Danish, and the Seyðabræv itself was translated into Danish in 1637.

As the Faroes' ecclesiastical link with Bergen was broken in about 1620, so their trading link was broken in 1619.

The crown had begun to oversee the Faroe trade in the late thirteenth century, granting trading privileges to interested merchants. The trade passed through many hands in the sixteenth and early seventeenth centu-ries. In 1529 the Hamburg merchant Thomas Koppen became the Faroes' merchant and feudal overlord, but in 1534, during the confusion following Frederik I's death, a group of Bergen merchants briefly gained control. The Faroes' løgmaður, Andras Guttormsson, wrote to them how glad he was that "this land, the Faroes, shall no longer be under Hamburgers or any other foreigners, but under the crown of the realm of Norway, as it was in old times" (Degn 1938a:26; see also L. Zachariasen 1961:172). Just how seriously he meant this is open to question, for Guttormsson, who may have been Norwegian-born himself (Young 1979:86), had a tal-ent for opportune alignments. He and Bishop Ámundur seem at first to have supported Joachim Wullenweber, Koppen's rival and erstwhile col-league and sometime bailiff of the Faroes, who, though also a Hamburger, was more closely associated with the party of Lübeck and Christian II. But soon the bishop and the løgmaður had a falling out, and Guttormsson expeditiously found himself on the side of Koppen and Christian III. He was eventually granted the tenancy of a large farm in Kirkjubøur that had previously belonged to the bishopric.

Koppen died in 1553. For three years the Faroe trade was open to any Norwegian or Dane. For the period 1556-69, it was granted to the Copen-hagen merchant (and the Faroes' bailiff) Anders Jude and his Hamburg colleague, Mads Lampe. But Faroese protested their management, and after another brief period of free trade it passed to the Hamburger Joachim Thim (1573-78), briefly became a royal monopoly again, and then was granted to Magnús Heinason. When Heinason fell from favor (he was executed on a piracy charge in 1589, but was pardoned posthumously, the next year, by Christian IV), the Faroe trade was again briefly a royal monopoly; between 1586 and 1597, it was managed by a Hamburg merchant and a Copenhagen merchant in partnership. A consortium of Bergen merchants managed it until 1619.

In that year Christian IV chartered the Iceland, Faroe, and Northern Norway Company. Like many of the individual merchants before it, the Iceland company collected the Faroes' taxes. Unlike them, it was based in Copenhagen. Its privileges "represent an explicit version of [those] the previous merchant companies had received, except only for the necessary change that the Company did not have its seat in Bergen, but distinctly in Copenhagen. Thus the bailiff no longer moved to and from Bergen, but to and from Copenhagen" (Joensen, Mortensen, and Petersen 1955:16).

Thus by 1620, the Faroes' political, commercial, and ecclesiastical links to the continent were moved from Bergen to Copenhagen. From a Danish point of view, the Faroes must increasingly have resembled a Danish province. The official language was Danish, as was the Church. The people's loyalty to the king was unquestioned. Tórshavn, like many a Danish market town, housed a marketplace and a fort (built in Magnús Heinason's day) to guard it, the meeting place of a regional assembly, schools, and the principal church. The "marketplace," however, was the Company store and warehouses, and Faroese were forbidden to trade elsewhere. Economic and geographical conditions, not to mention cultural ones, made the Faroes in reality a very un-Danish sort of place.

The Faroes had two economies. The first was a highly diversified, domestic, or internal subsistence, economy. Men fowled, went whaling, cut peat for fuel, raised some barley (which, because of the short growing season, had to be reaped green and dried over peat fires), and kept sheep and cattle. But perhaps their most important pursuit was fishing: "more than the keeping of sheep or cows, fishing seems to have determined whether the times were good or bad" (L. Zachariasen 1961:87). Yet these pursuits alone could not sustain the population. Imports were needed, especially of grain and of timber for building houses and boats. The internal economy was thus supplemented by an export economy. The merchant bought some tallow, feathers, sheepskins, butter, train oil, and dried fish; but by far the most important item in the export trade was wool, which was increasingly sold in the form of stockings, for which Faroese received a better price than unworked wool.

Both economies were virtually cashless. A crucial part of the Company's charter was a price schedule that fixed the rate of exchange between imported and exported goods. The price schedule could not be changed, a provision designed to insulate Faroese from potentially disastrous fluctuations in the international market, but one that by the same token left the Company in a risky position. War or shipwreck or bad weather might trim away its profits. Moreover, Holland and England were the markets

Details from an eighteenth-century map illustrate the diversified subsistence activities of the Faroes, including fowling, fishing, haying, and whaling. Det Kongelige Søkort Arkiv, Copenhagen.

for the Faroese woolens it bought; in order to make a profit, the Company had to insist on dealing only in goods of high quality.

The whole system was terribly precarious. The Faroes' survival depended on the weather, on good fishing, on economic and political factors beyond anyone's control. And in the early seventeenth century, it threatened to collapse entirely: the weather worsened, the fishing failed repeatedly, and war disrupted markets and made grain scarce and expensive.

Perhaps the worst years were those between 1629 and 1633. The fishing failed utterly in 1629-30, and many sheep died over the terrible winter of 1632-33. In a raid on Hvalba, on Suðuroy, Barbary pirates carried off thirty people as slaves. Denmark's economy had not recovered from the brief but disastrous involvement in the Thirty Years War, from 1624 to 1628. Even more desperately than in so many years around this time, Faroese complained that the Company was failing to ship enough food to Tórshavn, "wherefore we poor people have had to consume whatever bad fish we had gotten from the sea, which we otherwise could have had to pay our rents. Moreover, the greatest part of all our sheep perished the previous winter as well as hundreds of cows, so that there has never been such a pitiable state here in the country as any person now can recall. So God help us poor folk" (N. Andersen 1895:41). The merchant replied that so much grain and flour had in fact been imported, that "he could not have believed it would have been sold in an entire year, let alone in one winter. But that the grain [i.e., locally grown barley] failed for the poor people the previous fall could not be the Company's fault, but if our Lord had given them grain, then they would not have bought half of what lay in stock the previous fall" (N. Andersen 1895:45). The Faroese often complained as well that the Company was rejecting the stockings they had to sell. The merchant insisted that he could afford to take only top-quality goods. In 1631, for example, when the Faroese protested that the merchant had refused to buy the few stockings they had, "though they had nothing else," he answered that he was rejecting only those that "are worth little or nothing," for "God knows that the Company must buy at the highest price whatever goods and wares they send here to the country, [and] at the very least the inhabitants ought to make good stockings, since the fishing has failed here for several years' time" (N. Andersen, 1895: 44-45).

Ideally, the monopoly system insured the Faroese a market for their products and guaranteed that some imports would arrive. Their complaints, therefore, were not directed at the system itself, much less at the king, but at its management. In 1619, for example, Strange Madssøn, a dishonest type who doubled as the Faroes' bailiff and was a shareholder in the Bergen consortium that had carried out the Faroe trade, was removed from office, preparatory to the founding of the Iceland Company. The following year, the new bailiff, Mads Christensøn, threatened to crack down on smuggling. The Løgting, whose members were no less involved in smuggling than other prominent and not-so-prominent Faroese, immediately resolved to appeal to the king to "forgive them their great offence." The Løgting assured the king that it was not trying "to win freer trade provisions for the country"; nor, evidently, did the king want to be troubled by a case the Løgting had threatened to bring against Madssøn and the Bergen consortium (L. Zachariasen 1961:146; E. Joensen 1953:135-36). A quiet compromise seems to have been reached. The Løgting would not press its suit against Madssøn, Christensøn would not press his attack on smuggling, and the trade would be better managed.

The Iceland Company was indeed an improvement, but the persistence of smuggling suggests how precarious both the Faroes' situation and the Company's were. The "smuggling trade" was an illegal barter system. A foreign ship, usually British or Dutch, would call at an isolated settlement (meaning just about anywhere but Tórshavn), where people would exchange stockings or other goods for flour or whatever else the ship was willing to part with. In this way Faroese could "undoubtedly get almost the same price for bad goods as they got for good ones at the [Company] store and warehouse" (L. Zachariasen 1961:154).

Practically everyone smuggled. A well-known story recounts the adventures of a Dutch vessel, in 1636. The Dutchman first visited Vágar, where the Danish chaplain, Oluf Bottelsen Gullandsfar, traded him a few stockings "for some little bread and beer for household needs on account of hunger." Then he sailed to Hvalba, where, as the sheriff of Suðuroy later reported,

"some poor people have, out of the distress of great hunger, come to the same ship and asked the skipper, that he for God's sake help them in their great distress of hunger with a cask of flour, and there were twenty poor wretches to buy a cask of flour, so that the people had hardly a thing to give him for the same flour; a part of them took the stockings from their legs and gave them to him in payment, so that the skipper saw their great hunger and wretchedness more than any payment he got for it, and did not lie out the night there, and ran thence to Iceland."[N. Andersen 1895:54; E. Joensen 1953:286-87]

This is a somewhat curious story. No one was convicted of smuggling, and in any case the Company warehouse was not out of flour that year. But in 1636 the fishing was bad on Vágar and Suðuroy, and "it must be remembered that Suðuroy was very badly placed to get goods from Tórshavn by boat in the winter" (L. Zachariasen 1961:78, 148).

Even such fleeting contact with foreigners was illegal, since it threatened the merchant's profits and hence the interests of the crown. One of the most significant expressions of the crown's relatively narrow, essentially economic interest in the Faroes, and of the ultimately divergent perceptions of Faroese society by Faroese and the Danish government, was the negotiation of a "sea limit" around the Faroes, the year before the Iceland Company was founded.[2] The Faroese, alarmed at the depredations of foreign fishermen in "their" waters, asked the king to help them. The king, alarmed at the smuggling, complied.

British fishermen evidently began to fish heavily in Faroese waters whenever there was good fishing in the late sixteenth and early seventeenth centuries. In 1617, a good fishing year, for once, the Løgting complained to Christian IV that for the past two or three years, "a great crowd of Scottish ships" had gathered

"under Your Grace's land and islands and with their small ships sail or row through the land and into all the fjords and harbors, fish and harrow within the fjords and outside them the poor livelihood which we poor folk with our small boats are able to attend to in such places just as on all our fishing hills and banks (*fiskeklakke og grunde*). As soon as they see us in our small boats sitting and fishing thus, at once they run out in great numbers, and there right close against us they take away our poor livelihood, which the Almighty God is thus pleased to allow us poor folk; for they all have nets with which they catch herring, and they use the same herring as bait for their hooks, upon which the fish run; but we poor folk have no herring. Wherefore they can fish, but we lie near them and get nothing at all, whereat this poor land, if this shall be for a long time, will in time come upon the very greatest wretchedness, so that we cannot buy anything for our domestic needs and are unable to pay our rents and taxes."[L. Zachariasen 1961:133; E. Joensen 1953:39-40]

This is a complicated argument.

It rests, first, on customary Faroese conceptions of the sea. As the letter suggests, Faroese conceived of fishing grounds as extensions of the land: they were protesting that the Scots were sailing "through the land" to work "fishing hills and banks." Faroese held, moreover, that the sea was divided "as if it were outfield" (J.S. Hansen 1966:158), each village customarily claiming exclusive rights over particular grounds, just as each village had an exclusive right to pasture sheep over particular stretches of outfield. Thus they were arguing that the king, an important landowner as well as the Faroes' sovereign, ought to prevent the Scots' criminal trespass, just as his law prohibited trespass on outfields.[3] By the same token, just as foreigners had been forbidden since 1566 to acquire Faroese lands, they should not be able to fish Faroese waters.

Second, Faroese were appealing to the king's self-interest. He should protect the local fishery so that they could buy goods and "pay our rents and taxes."

Third, although they were well aware of the Scots' superior technology, they did *not* propose to improve their own. They were not asking the king to provide them with nets or the materials to make them with. As Lucas Debes was to write in 1673, the Faroese were "so minded in general that they will not change their ways" (1676:257).

In short, the Faroese were asking Christian IV to safeguard their way of life. He should protect the basis of their internal economy, fishing, just as his laws preserved the system of land tenure. Christian's interests were narrower. He was moved only to protect the Faroe trade. In 1615, when Faroese had also complained about foreign fishermen, the "quite remarkable" reply, perhaps dictated by Strange Madssøn, was a prohibition against smuggling (L. Zachariasen 1961:144). Meanwhile, however, he had begun corresponding with his brother-in-law James VI of Scotland (James I of England), representing the Faroes' case in terms of fishing rights and international law. His negotiations were successful; in 1618 James forbade his subjects "to fische within sight of land of the Ile of Fara" (P. Petersen 1968:89). "Within sight of land" came to be defined as four miles, or sixteen sea miles as we now reckon it.

Of course the "sea limit" was not regularly patrolled; although in 1698, for example, a Dutch fishing vessel was seized (D. Nolsøe 1963:115). So far as the king was concerned, the main point of the limit was that it gave him and his agents grounds for prosecuting not only smuggling ships but also such Faroese as had anything to do with them. While the Faroese recognized this, they continued to smuggle anyway, and in good sea-lawyerly fashion, professed themselves astonished that the king would not allow them to trade freely even out of sight of land. The *løgmaður* wrote in 1647 that "he was astounded that the king forbade the Faroese to have anything to do with foreigners even when they were out fishing . . . 16-24 miles from land. It is obvious that the *løgmaður* is thinking here of the sea from the sea limit outward, which he believes lies outside all jurisdiction" (L. Zachariasen 1961:155-57).

Crown, Company, and country may finally have entertained different conceptions of Faroese society. But if by "country" we understand prominent Faroese, then all three parties had an interest in maintaining the land-based economy and the production of wool for export. The ancient system of land tenure was preserved and simplified after the Reformation. This, together with the Faroes' isolation, ensured that Faroese culture remained highly resistant to danicization. Rather, it survived relatively unchanged within a Danish shell.

The basic unit of value in land was (and is) the "mark" (*mørk*, pl. *merkur*).[4] There are about 2400 *merkur* of land in the Faroes by the traditional reckoning.

Land may be either infield (*bøur*) or outfield (*hagi*). The village is clustered in the infield, which is divided into plots and used for crops, hay, and winter grazing. A stone wall surrounds the infield. The outfield is uncultivated, except in isolated enclosures called *traðir*. It is used for summer grazing.

The basic principle of land use is that ownership or leasehold of each *mørk* of outfield entails proportional rights over certain plots of infield, and to similar rights over sections of the shore and the bird cliffs.

All land is classified according to how it is held. Some is reserved as priests' livings (*prestajørð*). The rest is either freehold or leasehold.

Until 1632 there were about 108 *merkur* of "priests' land." Then the priests complained that their parishioners would not give them offerings;

rather than divide the tithe in thirds, as the law required, they were persisting in the traditional practice of dividing it into four parts, "of which four parts they withhold one for themselves on the pretext that they distribute and divide it among the poor." The priests said they were so poor that they could not support their "poor wives and children," and had to "drink *Vand og Bland,*" water and watered ale (*Tillæg,* p. 25). The king obliged them by increasing the priests' land to 151½ *merkur,* which gave them average livings of about 22 *merkur.* Priests were very rich men by local standards. Like other prosperous farmers, they kept large establishments with many hired hands.

At the Reformation, perhaps a third of the Faroes' land was freehold. Freeholdings might be bought and sold and—most important—had to be divided among their owners' heirs. Freeholdings were thus small and scattered, and "it must have been rare to find a man who owned a whole *mørk,* and rarer still a man who owned a whole *mørk* together" (P. Petersen 1968:116).

Foreign noblemen and, for example, the cathedral minster in Bergen also owned some land in the Faroes, which they leased to local farmers. In the seventeenth century, some of this passed through the hands of the Iceland Company, but eventually it all became locally owned or controlled. In the 1670s and 1680s, Faroese bought up about 276 *merkur* as freehold. The king himself had owned about 120 to 130 *merkur* before the Reformation, land he had come by in various ways. According to the laws of Magnus Lagabøter, for example, land appropriated as fines in criminal cases went to the king (L. Zachariasen 1961:285).

When the crown took over the Church's lands, its holdings increased about tenfold. We find that in 1584, it owned 1288 *merkur.* (Not all of this had belonged to the Church. Some the king already owned, some was bought. In 1566 the king forbade Faroese to sell land to anyone but the crown or, of course, each other.) These 1288 *merkur* did not belong to the king personally, but to the crown—*ad nostram dominationem jure regio pertinere,* as the Latin legal phrase had it (P. Petersen 1968:105). The danicism *festi* became the current local term, a significant exception to the general rule that Danish terms concerning agriculture did not replace local ones (P. Petersen 1968:138).

Tenant farmers have been called "king's farmers" (*kongsbøndur*) since the Reformation. It seems from the Seyðabræv that leases were technically held only from year to year, but by custom they were probably held for much longer periods, perhaps for life. After the Reformation, the king's chief representative in the islands, the bailiff, was charged with renewing leases as well as collecting rents and taxes. This quickly led to corruption. As early as 1559, in response to Faroese complaints that the bailiff was evicting them from their farms "without good reason," Frederik II proclaimed that for the betterment of "our land Faroe" and the well-being of his subjects, "when any of our Crown's farmers and servants in the Faroes receives a leasehold of any farm from our bailiff who is in command in that place, then he shall have, enjoy, use, and retain it while and so long as he builds, improves, and remains in control over it, and pays his rent [*landsgildi*] at the proper time; and in all respects behaves as a true subject should do" (*Tillæg*, p. 22). Even assuring farmers of lifelong leaseholds eventually proved inadequate. A century later, at the beginning of "the Gabels' time," the bailiff was in effect selling tenancies to the highest bidder when they fell vacant. In 1673, following a royal commission's investigation into this and other abuses, what had probably long been customary was made law: crown tenancies passed from a father to his eldest son. Priests' sons were given preference if a farmer died without male heirs, or if for some other reason the tenancy fell vacant.

All in all, then, the century or so following the Reformation saw the simplification of the system of land tenure and the establishment of (roughly speaking) two classes of Faroese. At the top were what West (1972:16) has called the "privileged class" of priests and king's farmers, who enjoyed large, compact, impartible holdings. King's farmers payed modest yearly rents, on the order of perhaps 8 percent of the assessed value of their lands and livestock. At the bottom were freeholders, who shaded off into a loose class of paupers who might survive by laboring for priests or king's farmers, but who could not in general marry. These "class" distinctions seem to have become more pronounced in the first two decades of the seventeenth century.[5]

We should not exaggerate these distinctions, important though they were within the Faroes. The gap between rich and poor was modest by continental standards and, as Debes wrote in 1673, "the riches of the Inhabitants doth consist in their Sheep, for those that have many of them, though few grow rich thereby, those means being very casual; for when there cometh a hard Winter and Sheep dye, they are almost all equally rich" (1676:133-34). Moreover, the differences between rich and poor were finely graded. The Faroes had neither serfs nor nobles, and the distribution of substantial holdings varied a good deal from island to island. Nor were all king's farmers wealthy: "During the seventeenth and eighteenth centuries there were about 300 substantial farmers, mostly crown tenants, who farmed 2 to 8 marks, but occasionally as much as 30 or even 50 marks" (West 1972:16). And the "privileged class" was relatively large. Assuming, roughly, that each "substantial farmer" had four dependents in his family (see Mortensen 1954:34*n*), then perhaps fifteen hundred of the Faroes' four thousand or so inhabitants were members of "privileged" families. On the other hand, since land was the source of all wealth and the economy was virtually cashless, landholdings were the only investment prosperous men might make. Priests and well-to-do farmers bought up freeholdings to provide for their heirs, thereby consolidating their position (P. Petersen 1968:116). The heirs were sometimes numerous. Clement Follerup, Sandoy's priest from 1648 to 1688, is remembered both for his twenty-three children and his rapacity for land. At his death he owned 46 *merkur* in freehold.[6]

Assured of substantial livings and marrying into "the most prosperous Faroese lineages" (L. Zachariasen 1961:313), the Danish priests who entered Faroese society after the Reformation were quickly ensnarled in the web of Faroese kinship. Committed to the system of land tenure upon which their own prosperity and the fortunes of their heirs were based, they did not significantly danicize the Faroes. Fecundity aside, Follerup was typical enough. He married one of the daughters of his predecessor, the Danish priest Jens Skive. (It was customary at the time for an incoming priest to marry his predecessor's widow.) She was descended on her mother's side from the prominent Sandoy family that Heini "Shipwreck" had married into a century before. When she died, Follerup married her sister. A third sister, Maren Jensdatter, married another Danish priest, Oluf Bottelsen Gullandsfar, whose first wife's family had provided most of the Faroes' *løgmenn* since the Reformation.[7]

The intermarriage of prominent Faroese and Danes continued in an exceedingly complex fashion in the next generations. Follerup's sons, for example, included Peder Clemensen, who succeeded him as priest of Sandoy from 1658 to 1719, and Jens Clemensen, who was priest of Suðuroy from 1679 until his death, in 1697. Jens's own son, Clement Jensen, was priest of the Norðoyar from 1706 until 1766 and dean from 1730 to 1746; his widow (who was the daughter of Peder Hellesen Viborg, the Danish priest of Eysturoy from 1642 to 1679 and also dean from 1675 to 1679, and of the Danish sister of Lucas Debes, who was South Streymoy's priest from 1652 to 1675 and dean from 1670 to 1675) married his Faroese successor, Søren Johannesen. One of Debes's step-daughters—for his wife was the widow of his predecessor, the second-generation Faroese priest Hans Rasmussen—married the Faroese Niels Jacobsen, who served a brief term as *sorinskrivari* in 1622 and 1623; another married the sometime winter-bailiff, Christen Hanssøn; and a third married another Danish priest, Jacob Christensøn Klinte, who was priest of Suðuroy from 1656 to 1679 and then priest of Eysturoy and dean until 1700.

Similarly, Follerup's brother-in-law Oluf Bottelsen Gullandsfar was a Dane who served as priest of Vágar from 1641 to 1681. Oluf's son Rasmus succeeded him there from 1681 to 1702, while a daughter married the Faroese Joen Poulsen, who was sheriff of the Norðoyar from 1646 to 1661 and then *løgmaður* until 1677. This was a more politically prominent branch of the family. Joen's son Jacob followed him as *løgmaður,* having previously been the sheriff of Sandoy. He was married to one of Follerup's daughters. Jacob himself was removed from office in 1679 for shady dealings in land, but one of his sisters was married to his successor as *løgmaður,* the second-generation Faroese J. H. Weyhe. (Weyhe's parents were the Danish commandant Johann Weyhe and the infamous Christoffer von Gabel's sister Margrethe.) Weyhe proved a most able and conscientious *løgmaður,* serving until 1706. Meanwhile, Jacob's brother's wife (whose sister was married to the Faroese *sorinskrivari* from 1695 to 1705, Morten Mortensen) was a daughter of the Faroese priest of North Streymoy from 1650 to 1666, Jónas Mikkelsen. Jónas was a son of the legendary Mikkjal Jónsson. Mikkjal, a third-generation Faroese (his father was Joen Heinesen, who was *løgmaður* from 1572 to 1583 and his grandfather was Heini "Shipwreck") served as sheriff of Eysturoy from 1622 to 1640. We shall meet him more closely in a moment.

A few priests, like Follerup, are badly remembered in legend; but several priests and priests' sons, though they are little, if at all, remembered in legend, contributed greatly to the more formal side of Faroese culture. We owe our first full account of Faroese life to Lucas Debes, who, as dean from 1670 to 1675, earned the Gabel's enmity by protesting the corruption of the bailiff and the oppression of the poor in Tórshavn. Another description of the Faroes was written by Debes's student, T. J. Tarnovius, son of the Danish priest on Suðuroy from 1656 to 1679, Jacob Christensen Klinte, and his German wife, Karen Tarnovius (Tarnovius 1950). In the next century, Jens Christian Svabo, who also described the Faroes at length, and who in addition collected ballads and wrote a Faroese-Danish-Latin dictionary, was the son of the priest on Vágar, Hans Christophersen Svabo.[8]

A further reason the Faroes were not danicized was that the margin of survival was narrow; immigrants had to adopt the local way of doing things. This is illustrated dramatically in an episode in "Óli Jarnheysur," a legend some of whose other episodes are datable to around 1620. The hero, Óli, is working for Mikkjal Jónsson, whom we met briefly a moment ago. Mikkjal, it seems, had decided one fall to keep a yearling ram over the winter instead of slaughtering it, as would have been usual. Óli, who is said to have "stood in such esteem that he was almost the farmer on the farm (the farm at Lamba was thirty *merkur*)," epitomizes the legendary stock figure of the indispensable hired hand. But figures like him must also have been common in fact, as they saw to it that even a Danish priest's estate was run by tried and true methods. On this occasion, Óli protested that keeping the ram

would make the cows short of fodder later—there was too little hay. But the farmer thought it made no difference for all the cows of Lamba: the lamb should be kept. Óli submitted, but about two days afterward he went outside the walls to the shed where the lamb stood, and killed it. As well might be, he said nothing of this to the farmer. Later he went in to Strendur; there he cooked and ate the lamb. Óli looked after the cows in the winter, and each day when he took them their hay he took a handful of hay and carried it out to the shed to that blessed lamb which he had killed. The spring came and was bad, so that the farmer was short of hay. After Holy-Rood Day [3 May] a great deal of snow lay on the ground; three days came when people had to stay indoors, and the farmer's hay was used up. "The cows must be killed," he maintains. Then Óli says that if, now, the yearling ram had not been kept, there would have been so much hay that the cows could be helped with it. The farmer still maintains, as before, that it would not have made a big difference. Óli asks him then to come out to the shed and look at the yearling ram. When the door is opened, he tells the farmer that now he will tell him the truth: he killed the yearling ram in the fall, but he had kept in the shed the hay that was intended for it; he now asks him to tell him if it made no difference. This hay was so much, that it saved all the cows of Lamba that year. Óli should not have dealt so quickly with the lamb. But the farmer was so pleased that he gave Óli the cured carcass of a fat old ewe in payment. [Jakobsen 1898-1901:98-99]

There is a final, legal aspect of Faroese society's conservatism after the Reformation, a reflection of both its perennially precarious ecological base and the increasing power of the Danish crown.

Faroese law had a triple foundation: King Magnus Lagabøter's codification of 1273, the Seyðabræv of 1298, and the ecclesiastical law known as the Stóridómur, which in 1584 had been confirmed by the Løgting at the king's request. In 1604 Christian IV promulgated a modified version of King Magnus's laws. It is not clear just how or when this "Norwegian Law" was applied to the Faroes. Some special provisions were made; in 1606, for example, Faroese were allowed to retain the Bergen system of weights and measures to which they were accustomed. It appears that a rather uncertain mixture of Faroese, Norwegian, and Danish law may have been used until 1687-88, when Christian V issued a new version of the Norwegian Law (L. Zachariasen 1961:320). The Seyðabræv and the Stóridómur remained in force, however, the former being translated into Danish in 1637, the latter in 1682. They were incorporated with minor changes into Christian V's Norwegian law of 1688, the most important consequence of which, so far as the Faroes were concerned, was further to diminish the independence of the Faroese judicial system. It officially established the *sorinskrivari* as the judge for most cases brought before the spring parliaments, and increased the number of *løgrættumenn* from six to ten for each district. Nor was it now "permitted for farmers to be appointed year after year; all had to take their turn. Hence few men built up any great legal experience. In the end, the Løgting became a mere shadow of its former self" (West 1972:23-24).

Among the ancient provisions that were preserved and even elaborated during this period were ones that insured the primacy of farmers like Mikkjal and made it all but impossible for the likes of Óli to marry. The intention of these provisions was to check population growth. An unintended result was to insure that the basic unit of the Faroese economic and social systems was the farmstead, worked by the farmer and his wife and children, along with a number of men and women hired hands.

Secular law, the Seyðabræv and its descendants, insured a low birth rate by setting "requirements for a man who wished to marry and set up his own household. The average age at marriage was apparently quite high" (Guttesen 1971:36; see also R. Rasmussen 1968). According to the Seyðabræv, as we have seen, a man had to have enough land to support three cows; according to the last version of this sort of regulation, an ordinance of 1777 that we shall consider in detail in Chapter 4, couples could not marry "unless they had half a *mørk* of land, freehold or lease-hold, or could earn a living as blacksmiths or carpenters, and in any case both boys and girls had to have served a farmer for at least four years and to have received a good recommendation from him" (J. S. Hansen 1966:115).

Ecclesiastical law and its secular embodiment in the Norwegian Law of 1688 helped check population growth by prescribing punishments for bearing or fathering illegitimate children. The punishments were harsh: incestuous parents could be put to death. Several such executions occurred (the last was in 1706), but a heavy fine was more usual. In 1636, for example, the first cousins Peder Hermandsøn and Marion Hansdatter were tried for having had a child together. The bailiff demanded "the death sentence or suitable judgment," but the Løgting, interpreting the law more leniently, fined them and banished Peder from his home island (L. Za-chariasen 1961:35-36; E. Joensen 1953:287-88). Sometimes, particularly when priests were involved, leniency went even farther. Toward the end of the century, three of Clement Follerup's sons married three daughters of P. H. Viborg, who was priest of Eysturoy and dean. As Zachariasen says, "this seems to sort badly with the Stóridómur," but of course nothing was done about it (L. Zachariasen 1961:349). But these were exceptions, and not surprisingly by far the greatest number of cases brought before the Løgting in the early seventeenth century involved fathering or bearing children out of wedlock (L. Zachariasen 1961:55-64).

In a sense all Faroese benefited from population control. The most immediate beneficiaries, however, were the priests and tenant farmers. They could afford to marry, and their lands could not be fragmented by inheritance. The rich got richer (or at least no poorer), and the poor were forbidden to have children.

In 1655, in return for a payment of 1000 *rigsdaler* a year, Frederik III made his treasurer Christoffer von Gabel the Faroes' overlord for life. The year before, probably at Gabel's urging and certainly against the wishes of the Løgting, Frederik had installed a foreigner, Baltzer Jacobsen, as *løgmaður*. Jacobsen was removed from office in 1661, more for habitual drunkenness than anything else. In the same year, Frederik III granted all the Faroes' income to Gabel and his son Frederik to follow him. The Iceland Company closed in 1662, ruined by high wartime prices for grain and a decline in the woolens market in Holland. In the same year, the Løgting followed the rest of Denmark in swearing the oath of allegiance to the king.

"The Gabels' time" (*Gablatíðin*), as the period through 1708 is

called, is one of the bleakest in Faroese history. The times were bad anyway, Gabel's appointees were inexperienced or corrupt or both, and Gabel
himself insisted on wringing a profit from the islands. It was almost impossible to get word of the Faroes' plight to the king, since Gabel's charter
included the requirement that petitions be written "in such a style and form
as cannot be contrary to our land's laws and our servants," and the merchant was no longer obliged, as he had been in the days of the Bergen
consortium and the Iceland Company, to give passage to anyone wishing
to petition the king directly (N. Andersen 1895:82,85).

The worst period lasted from 1661 to 1672. As well as virtually selling tenancies, Gabel's bailiff engaged in many smaller rackets. In 1672,
for example, he required the inhabitants of Tórshavn to sell him cows,
oxen, and sheep, which he resold at a considerable profit to a Dutch fleet
that was lying off shore (N. Andersen 1895:90). The merchant, for his
part, failed to import "what, for a people whose chief means of livelihood
is fishing, is just as necessary as grain, namely timber for boats" (N.
Andersen 1895:79). Such grain as did arrive was expensive, since its price
had been temporarily raised, partly because Europe was in turmoil and
Denmark, having allied herself with Holland, was girding for war with
France and Sweden. A local echo of these preparations was the rebuilding
of the fortifications guarding the company store in Tórshavn. This work,
which was undertaken in 1666, was paid for by doubling the defense tax,
which fell more heavily on freeholders than on king's farmers.

The Faroes' dean, Lucas Debes, took it upon himself to get word of
the Faroes' distress to Denmark, but for the better part of two years, he
was unable to get away (see S. av Skarði 1921). He finally reached Copenhagen in August 1672, with two other emissaries, the sheriffs of
Suðuroy and the Norðoyar. Early the next year, the merchant's records
were destroyed in a great fire that seems to have broken out in his office.

Meanwhile, Christoffer von Gabel had fallen from favor after Frederik
III's death, in 1670. He lived on until 1673, but his son Frederik effectively became the Faroes' ruler. Defending his father's "great consideration for the country" before the royal commission charged with investi-
gating the Faroese complaints, and accusing Debes of a "noisy and
rebellious disposition" (N. Andersen 1895:102), Frederik nonetheless
took steps to check his subordinates' abuses. But times were still bad.
There was famine when the fishing failed and sheep died over the winters
of 1673/74, 1680/81, and 1684/85. War broke out in 1675, and in 1677
the French sacked Tórshavn. Trade continued unprofitable. Faroese kept
complaining that the merchants were rejecting stockings and that if the
merchants lost money it was their own fault (N. Andersen 1895:115). Like
many a merchant before him, Frederik von Gabel replied that the Faroese
themselves were to blame. He went so far as to accuse them of effemi-
nacy:

In the old days there came almost all [unworked] wool to the warehouse, for 1 Gl. per wey, and very few stockings. Then the inhabitants had more life than they have now, both for exploiting the fishing and for other industriousness; and then the country and the company had good relations, so long as they undertook manly work. But now they have forsaken the fishing, taken up womanly pursuits and jobs and become stocking knitters and learned to use grinding mills to fill their bellies. They think to lose their lives immediately if they go [to the company store] with a little bit of wool for their profit and advantage, although they are offered 4 Gl. instead of 1 for it. [N. Andersen 1895:156]

Finally, in 1691, a new and more satisfactory price schedule was agreed upon. The price of imports was raised, but so were those for sheepskins and better grade wool and woolens, while the merchant undertook to buy unworked wool for 6 *gyllin* per wey (about 40 pounds). Except that in 1723 this was lowered to the "more realistic figure" of 3 *gyllin,* the new price schedule lasted, little changed, until 1790.[9]

Frederik von Gabel died in 1708. The following year, the Faroe trade became a royal monopoly, which endured until the introduction of free trade, in 1856. Faroese might still justly complain that the goods they received were shoddy and insufficient, but until the nineteenth century, few if any proposed its abolition; quite the contrary. For one thing, the royal monopoly operated on the premise that the company existed to serve the country, not, as under the Gabels, the other way around. Its retention meant, however, that Faroese remained fixed in their ways.

The period from 1540 to 1709 saw the substitution of Lutheranism for Catholicism, the Faroes' ancient connection with Bergen broken, their increasing subordination to agents of the Danish crown, the development of the monopoly trade system, the deterioration of the climate, and the preservation of the old tenurial system and elements of pre-Reformation ecclesiastical law. The critical years in this period came between 1540 and 1557, when the crown became the largest landowner in the Faroes and the old Faroese bishopric was reduced to a deanery; between 1604 and 1620, when the climate took a turn for the worse, Danish became the official language of the Church as it was also the language of trade and government, oversight of the Faroe deanery moved from Bergen to Copenhagen, the Iceland Company was founded, Christian IV's Norwegian Law was promulgated, and the "sea limit" was set; and between 1655 and 1672, when Christoffer von Gabel virtually ruled the Faroes. Thereafter the crown consolidated its control over the Faroes with the promulgation of Christian IV's Norwegian Law (1687-88), the establishment of a new price schedule (1691), and the foundation of the royal trade monopoly (1709). The result was to perpetuate an already old-fashioned culture, which was to remain little changed for another century and a half.

In order, now, to give a more complete picture of Faroese culture, we must adopt a different perspective on the period following the Reformation, whose events and circumstances were long retained in popular memory in the form of legends (*sagnir*). In them we find the local world and its past seen differently—not in terms of royal ordinances or formal complaints to the king about the quality of imported grain, but in terms of rich farmers and canny hired hands, peril at sea, elvish *huldufólk,* and brilliantly conceived details, at once homely and heroic.

Outside the Wall
Seventeenth-Century Society in Legend

🖎 Especially in the long, dark, stormy winter evenings, when the day's work was done, families and hired hands would gather in the kitchen to card, spin, knit, and do other indoor chores. These evening gatherings, called *kvøldsetur,* were economically productive occasions; as Lucas Debes remarked, Faroese "are not accustomed to pass the time idly or in vain jollity" (1963 [1673]:118). *Kvøldsetur* also provided the main occasion for recounting folktales and legends and for reciting the old ballads, though these were more closely associated with dancing at festival times.[1] *Kvøldsetur* were thus a primary institution of remembrance. They remained an established feature of Faroese life until the late nineteenth century, when economic change rendered them obsolete.

The kitchen, or *roykstova* (literally, "smoke room"), was the most important room in the house. Sometimes it was the only room.

The houses of the poorest folk consist of only one room, which serves at the same time as kitchen, living-room, sleeping apartment, place for keeping chickens, and so on. The only door of this room, which is not lined with boards, is about four feet high; the floor is of earth; there are no windows at all, but a quadrangular hole in the roof, which may be closed by a shutter, serves at once for entrance of light and exit of smoke. The beds are arranged like berths, lengthwise around the walls, and beside them there is commonly a bench. An apartment thus arranged is justly called a "røgstue" [in Danish], for it is usually so full of peat-smoke that it is often difficult to understand how human beings can breathe in such an atmosphere. [Panum 1940(1846):26-27]

Wealthier farmers' *roykstovur* were larger, wood-panelled, and, as Dr. Panum says, "furnished with a sort of chimney" above the hearth. Panum, a rather fastidious Danish physician, did not think much of Faroese living arrangements ("I was not seldom obliged to rush outside to draw breath before I could finish seeing and examining . . . patients") but he was right that the *roykstova* was "an indispensible part of every Faroese dwelling." It was in a sense the center of the Faroese world. In its close, almost troglodytic atmosphere, people ate and slept, callers were received, women cooked, and both men and women did their indoor work.

The best known description of a *kvøldseta* is Hammershaimb's, published in 1891 in a series of vignettes of traditional Faroese life in his *Færøsk Anthologi.* "Now the spinning wheels whirl, the cards swish, the needles jingle, and work has begun for everyone. But the proverb says, 'silent rowing is hard'—so all labor is hard when there is nothing delightful therein to shorten the time of it. So it is not silent in the kitchen on winter evenings." Someone sings a ballad. When it is over,

all fell silent, both the man who had led the ballad, and the men and women who took up the refrain on each verse. Then the old woman on the little bench by the hearth caught hold and began to tell stories; here was something to listen to for fun; but when giants, trolls, ghosts and other frightful beings appeared to the imagination in the telling, fear struck the young, the cards went less quickly than before, the needles stopped jingling, and often it was asked in wonderment and impatience: "what happened then, love?" [1891,1:390; cf. Holm 1855:32; 1860: 96-100]

Hammershaimb's description is romanticized, reflecting both a child's memory of occasions when in fact most of the audience was adult and not all the stories were spooky or even fanciful and the nineteenth-century conviction that, like other peasant ways, the kvøldseta had something noble about it. Niels Winther wrote that "the legend, which lives in the memory of Faroese, casts a poetic glow over his whole life, and prevents him from sinking down into dull materialism" (1875:490; cf. Holm 1855:32). Be this as it may, the legends certainly drew meaning from and gave meaning to the intimate geography of the Faroese world, reaching out from the woman by the hearth to the upland pasturages, the bird cliffs, and the sea from which men drew a living, and then on to the storied realms of courts and kings.

Kvøldsetur were a vitally important cultural institution. Jakobsen comments in the introduction to the great collection of legends and folktales he made in the 1890s, "It is scarcely an exaggeration to say that Faroese popular culture [almues kultur] and spiritual life . . . were chiefly conditioned and borne up by these gatherings on winter evenings" (1898-1901:xxxiv). For one thing, the institutionalized telling of tales insured the survival of Faroese as a literary language and, since much of Faroese oral literature dealt with the past, kvøldsetur lent a ritual importance to its recollection. Kvøldsetur were, moreover, everyday (or every-evening) events, in which all participated by telling stories and listening to them. The local past was thus both universally accessible and actively and collectively recalled. Some individuals were better storytellers than others, but otherwise historical knowledge was neither esoteric nor the property of specialists.

By the same token, the past (which was very like the present anyway) was illuminated by the ordinary circumstances of everyday life. Faroese sang and danced to the ballads at special times, of course, but the Faroese identity, insofar as it differed from that of "other Danes," was not entirely driven back, like that of so many colonial peoples, to nonverbal expression in music and dance. Nor did it find a home in a religion different from

Denmark's; the Faroese Church was simply a branch of the established Danish Church, and the Faroese were a God-fearing, observant people. Faroese identity was not expressed through an alternative or parallel political system, either; the Faroes' old judicial and political institutions were increasingly integrated with and eventually more or less absorbed by the Danish administration. Rather, a peculiarly Faroese identity was bound up with everyday life, with the vernacular, with domestic activities, the varied pursuits of farming and seafaring, local scenes and the local past. Insofar as it was ritually expressed, not just lived out, it was literary as well as historical.

Traditional Faroese oral literature has four main genres, two verse and two prose. The verse genres are the famous heroic ballads (*kvæðir*) and the satiric ballads called *tættir*. The former deal mostly with the distant past, sometimes at terrific length. They reach back through the Viking Age and the Faroes' conversion to Christianity (*Sigmundarkvæði*) to the Charlemagne cycle (*Rólantskvæði*) and Germanic myth (*Sjúrðarkvæði*, about Sigurd the Dragon-Slayer). Most are based on written sources and seem to have been composed in the late Middle Ages. Some were composed later, however, and almost all evidently date, in their present form, from the eighteenth and nineteenth centuries.[2] *Tættir* deal mostly with local figures in a satirical vein; sung and danced to at festival times in the same way as the *kvæðir*, they are still being composed, and have modern analogues in, for example, radio skits (Wylie and Margolin 1981:76).

The prose genres are similarly divided between distant (or unspecific) settings and local ones. The folktales proper (*ævintýr*) resemble other Scandinavian and European "fairy tales." They include, for example, versions of "Beauty and the Beast" and "Ashlad." *Ævintýr* took on peculiarly local meanings from the Faroese context of their telling, but they do not purport to describe the local scene directly (see Wylie and Margolin 1981:46-72).

Legends (*sagnir*) are markedly different from *ævintýr*. Matter-of-fact in tone and richly and realistically detailed in content, they concern named local characters in specific local settings. If they contain folktale, mythic, or quasi-supernatural elements, these are fully assimilated to the local scene.

Legends are often made up of one or two central episodes, to which others have been attached. They thus have a highly episodic, almost anecdotal structure. This episodic effect is partly the result of the way in which Dr. Jakobsen collated associated and variant tales; dubious as such editing is by modern standards, it surely lends them in their written form something of the air of collective composition they must have had when people took turns telling them around the hearth.

Legends contain a number of standard elements, themes, and characters. Most specify at the beginning where the action is to take place, and give a brief genealogy of the principal character. Most give further genealogical and tenurial details. As a result, many distinct legends complement one another; characters from one show up or are referred to in others. Many legends include an episode in which a character's reputation is fixed by his (or her) acquisition of a nickname, and some tell how parts of the landscape were named. Many are built around a memorable phrase, often a boast or prediction fulfilled in an unanticipated way.

Legends are not easily divided into types or subgenres. Although it resists strict definition, perhaps the clearest type, so far as Jakobsen's collection is concerned, is what he called *huldusagnir,* or elf legends, in which the elvish *huldufólk,* a gray, pagan, half-magical people of the outfields play a role. In discussing the elf legends, Jakobsen notes that, curiously enough, these apparently less realistic and less firmly datable tales tend to derive from a more recent period than do many of the seemingly more realistic ones, all of whose characters are human (1898-1901:xv).

We may take this observation as a starting point for an investigation of popular recollection in the Faroes. Why do many of the more recent (chiefly late seventeenth- and eighteenth-century) legends seem less realistic than older ones? More generally: In what sense does a legend collected in the late nineteenth century represent an accurate account of, say, events that took place in the seventeenth century?

Sometimes, as in the episode of "Óli Jarnheysur" quoted in the previous chapter, the accuracy is of a direct but simple sort, perhaps surprising after some 270 years of oral transmission. Yes, there was a prosperous Eysturoy farmer named Mikkjal. Yes, his "farm at Lamba" had 30 *merkur,* or pretty close to it, anyway: it actually had comprised 29 *merkur* until 1764, when it was divided in half; these halves were themselves halved in 1820-21 (Degn 1945:175). And yes, the winters were often long and harsh in Mikkjal's day. One lamb more or less might well have made the difference for "all the cows of Lamba."

Like most legends, however, "Óli Jarnheysur" also has a timelessness about it. Some of this quality is due to the relatively unchanging character of Faroese life. "Óli Jarnheysur's" most immediate inspiration was perhaps the late springs and shortages of hay in 1891 and 1892 (*Føringatíðindi,* May 1892). The legends' timelessness is also due to the fact that they seldom date themselves explicitly. Some contain phrases like "Before the Black Death came and devastated the Faroes," meaning before about 1350 (Jakobsen 1898-1901:46), but none like "In the reign of Christian IV," or "When So-and-so was *løgmaður.*" Most legends are therefore datable only from internal evidence and by comparison with documentary sources. Here and there one finds mention of earlier times, including what appear to be references to the Irish, but the oldest seem to derive from the thirteenth century, and they provide nothing like a continuous history until the late sixteenth or early seventeenth century; and even then they cover the ground only in patches. Those in Jakobsen's collection by and large end with the eighteenth century. More recent events are recalled both in other written renderings of oral tales and in tales still commonly told in Faroese communities. When I was doing fieldwork, I was often told the story of the village's founding. Two basic versions of the story were extant, and people sometimes took pains not only to dismiss the rival version, but also to correct what published sources have to say. The village was founded in 1833-34, but a fixed date was rarely included in the tale (Wylie 1982).

Accurate though they are in some respects, the legends thus construe the past in more oblique and inexplicit ways than we are accustomed to in scholarly histories, eschewing, for example, such niceties as dates. In approaching them as a kind of history as well as a kind of literature, we must therefore distinguish legendary historiography from the scholarly sort of historiography we have engaged in so far. A scholarly historian collects records of events, organizes them more or less chronologically, and uses them as examples to illustrate general statements about political and social trends. The "facts" give color to explicit, abstractly statable meanings of a course of events. This meaning may naturally be bound up with modern cultural and political concerns. For instance, writing at a time when Faroese were reintroducing themselves to the world and rekindling their culture, Símun av Skarði (1923:189) says: "In the period after the Reformation, the Faroese were barred from contact with other peoples as they never had been before. . . . The little we know about the period . . . all points the same direction and shows the same tendency: then over the Faroes and the Faroese people sank the heavy, dark and long night, which came close to extinguishing all these islands' sparks."

Legendary histories (or at least the Faroese *sagnir*) proceed by a rather different route to a rather different end. They also seize upon actual events and organize them into stories, usually around a few notable characters' notable deeds. Since they are told to entertain as well as instruct, character, plotting, and familiar settings are more important than in scholarly accounts. But the legends generally stop short of pointing a moral or otherwise making explicit sense of the events they describe. In this respect they differ both from scholarly histories and from such religiously construed accounts as Bible stories, in which the course of events is said to illustrate some divine plan. By the same token, they resemble fiction, since much of their consistency lies behind the sequence of episodes in the implicit logic of their plotting, the elaboration of incidental details, and the accretion of improbable or "unrealistic" figures and events.

From this point of view, if we were to treat "Óli Jarnheysur" as a kind of half-finished scholarly work, as "examples" without "conclusions," we should find it a study of, among other things, the relations between hired hands and prosperous farmers in the early seventeenth century, "arguing" through repeated variations that hired hands were indispensible to an estate's prosperity. In the episode following the one already quoted, for example, Mikkjal's crew embarks on a pilot-whale hunt. The chase fails, but Mikkjal tells Óli to spear a whale. Óli does so, when suddenly another whale entangles itself in the line. Óli holds on, bracing his feet against the prow of the boat. "The farmer called and told Óli to let go, but Óli said no, '*bóndin hevði biðið hann stinga stórt—nú hevði hann fingið stórt*'": the farmer had ordered him to strike a great blow—now he had gotten a great catch. Mikkjal threatens to cut the line, but Óli will not let him. Finally both whales are killed. In the next episode, Óli tricks Mikkjal, "who was always urging his hired hands to go to sea," into the boat. Óli takes the tiller; Mikkjal pulls at an oar. A blizzard overtakes them at sea. Óli is seaman enough to save both boat and crew when they come to shore, although Mikkjal has told the men "to save themselves and pay no heed to the boat, even though it might break up."

The episode with the whales suggests another way in which legendary historiography operates in a fictionalizing manner. It is clearly based on a case that came before the Løgting in 1619. The prosperous farmer Ólavur Larvasson (he is said wrongly, in the legend, to be Óli's father; the real-life Óli was more likely Mikkjal's sister's son) captured two pilot whales at sea after a hunt had failed. It may have been a tricky case, since the hunting and particularly the distribution of pilot whales are governed by elaborate regulations. The Løgting ruled that Ólavur Larvasson owned the whales without having to pay the tithe (E. Joensen 1953:111; L. Zachariasen 1961:27, 88n).

In the legend, now, the capture has been transferred to Óli, his reputed son. This minor change is well in keeping with the legend's general focus on Mikkjal and Óli, and on relations between farmers and hired hands. A more telling change is that in the legend the hunt resumes afterwards. Mikkjal's men take part again, and it turns out successfully. But when it is over, "they owned both these whales apart"—apart, that is, from the division of the rest of the school (including tithing). In other words, the legend both recapitulates the Løgting's judgment and, by adding a fictional sequel to the real story, generalizes the legal point and makes it clearer: pilot whales taken at sea are legally whales "apart," so long as they are not taken when the hunt is actually in progress.[3]

Concern with fine points of law is as much a central theme in "Óli Jarnheysur" as are relations between farmers and hired hands. It is likewise expressed in repeated variations, beginning with the opening episode:

Ólavur Larvasson lived in Øravík on Suðuroy. One day when the Øravíkingar were out fishing they came across a blue whale, which was lying floating in the water. They cut blubber off it as it lay there, but were careful not to come to the meat. When they went away again, Ólavur Larvasson took his ax and struck so hard in the whale's back that it swam off to the north, and they did not see it again. Later it drifted in to Kolbeinargjógv westward to Raktangi on Eysturoy.

The ax stood in its back, and Ólavur's name on the shaft.—In those days it was the custom, that girls came to the spring court to choose themselves men. The Eysturoy spring court then met in Selatrað, and a girl in Sjógv who had come there chose for herself that man who owned this ax. Thus it happened that Ólavur Larvasson came to Sjógv. There he came to stand in great esteem and took over the sheriff's position on Eysturoy. [Jakobsen 1898-1901:97-98]

The legal point illustrated here is that, according to the laws of Magnus Lagabøter, men finding a whale at sea had rights to a certain amount of blubber, but not meat. Hints and references here and there reinforce the tale's preoccupation with the law. We are told, for example, that Selatrað was where the Eysturoy spring court met; though we are not told so, the Suðuroy spring court met at Øravík. Ólavur Larvasson is clearly a man who knows the king's law; it is fitting that he should become the sheriff of Eysturoy. This promotion, however, is another bit of fiction. The real-life Ólavur was a *løgrættumaður*, but he never became sheriff. It was Mikkjal who was sheriff of Eysturoy from 1622 to 1640. Such distortions and outright fictions are in a sense the tale's interpretive elements, the analogues of scholarly "conclusions," since they lend events a thematic coherence. Ólavur is the sort of person one would like to have as sheriff, while Mikkjal (who actually was sheriff) is, with his unruly henchman Óli, the sort who is forever testing legal and natural limits.[4]

The teller of this tale and his (or her) audience must have been aware of its legal theme, just as they appreciated the delicacy of the relationship between farmers and hired hands both in the tale and in their own lives. It was common knowledge that Øravík and Selatrað were court sites, and of course everyone knew that the spring sometimes came late. Fishermen could tell you what set of the currents would have brought the blue whale from the Øravíkingar's customary fishing grounds to Kolbeinargjógv and Raktangi. Common knowledge of this sort, esoteric though it must seem to outsiders, surely formed the basis for such interpretation as there was. It must likewise inform our own explication of the tale.[5]

Some factors shaping the legends cannot have been conscious, though it is correspondingly difficult to know what to make of them. Jakobsen comments rightly that the opening episode of "Óli Jarnheysur" is "mythically colored" (1898-1901:488); so is the rest of the legend. Ólavur Larvasson's striking a great sea beast with his ax; its swimming off; Óli's bracing his feet in Mikkjal's boat; Mikkjal's threats to cut Óli's line and to slaughter his own cattle; and another episode in which, upon coming ashore, Óli acquires the nickname "Iron Skull" by drinking dry a great iron pot all confusedly echo the famous myth of Thor and Hymir. Disguised as a youth, Thor offers to go fishing with the sea giant Hymir. For bait, he fetches the head of the largest ox in Hymir's special herd. The World Serpent takes the bait, and Thor heaves so hard on the line that his foot goes through the bottom of the boat. He is just about to strike the Serpent with his hammer when Hymir, terrified, cuts the line. The Serpent swims off. In a related version of the myth, Thor had eaten two of Hymir's oxen before setting out, and upon returning to land, throws Hymir's most precious cup at him, shattering it against the giant's skull. Then he takes away a cauldron in which ale for the gods was brewed.

A more hidden connection between Ólavur Larvasson and Thor is that, as we happen to know from the account of the Icelandic mariner Jón Indíafari, who visited him (it was Ólavur who could read the Icelandic books), Ólavur was an accomplished smith, having learned the craft at Trondheim, in Norway. Trondheim had once been the site of a temple to Thor, whose symbol was a hammer or ax. The cathedral there now housed the relics of St. Olaf, whose symbol was also an ax.

"Óli Jarnheysur" thus almost appears to be a highly refracted version of a pagan myth in which, indeed, some of the same themes appear—the question, for example, of whether the boat's owner or the crewman is really in charge. Surely, however, the relationship between "Óli Jarnheysur" and pagan myth is rather distant and second-hand. It most likely derives from the accretion of associated seventeenth-century items and episodes to ones which were themselves associated in fading transmutations of the original myth.

In any case, by whatever process the myth was rendered merely legendary and local, its refraction into episodes confirms our impression that legends characteristically operate on their raw materials by splitting them into thematically associated vignettes. They work by repetition, their wealth of circumstantial detail and the seeming disjunction of their episodes being an essential part of their historiographic technique. Thus our problem in translating them into scholarly terms is partly a matter of stating their themes explicitly.

A final characteristic of legendary historiography is its sifting out of foreign connections and nonlocal figures, even when these played a considerable part in the events upon which the legends are based.

"Óli Jarnheysur" is exceptional in this respect; from court records and other documentary sources, we happen to know a good deal about the real-life models for its characters. Mikkjal was a contentious man with large holdings that he was forever trying to increase. As well as freeholdings and the tenancy at Lamba, he held four other tenancies on Eysturoy, amounting to 28⅝ *merkur* (Degn 1945:155,173,175,177). He got on so poorly with his wife, Magdalena, a litigious personality herself, that their vexed relations were often brought to the Løgting's attention and even to that of the Danish court. From Jón Indíafari's account we know something of Mikkjal's household and something of Ólavur's too. Both men were of the last generation of Faroese to have had extensive contacts abroad. Mikkjal probably met Magdalena when he studied in Bergen as a youth. She was the young, widowed daughter of a Norwegian priest.[6] Ólavur Larvasson had made a trading trip to North Norway as a young man; it was probably on this trip that he learned smithing in Trondheim. He was from Eysturoy, but for a time lived in Øravík, on Suðuroy, with his sister Marjun. Marjun is a legendary figure in her own right, one of the very few, in fact, whose travels are recounted in legend. It is said that she and her sister went to North Norway, presumably accompanying Ólavur, and though her sister died there of "Finnish magic," she herself learned it.

Both the trip and the magic are exceptional. The horizons of most legends are drawn in to the Faroes themselves, while their characters' foreign connections have been edited out. Legendary characters are almost exclusively local figures, often, like Óli himself, lowly members of Faroese society. Prominent people like Mikkjal or Danish priests generally play supporting, sometimes villainous roles, or, like Marjun, are ambiguously characterized. Smugglers and pirate bands sometimes make brief, faceless appearances. While "the king" is a stock figure in the *ævintýr,* the real king appears very rarely in legend. Christoffer von Gabel's single appearance in Jakobsen's collection is an exception proving the rule that oral tradition tends to exclude named foreign figures. It occurs in a sequence of three legends Jakobsen put together from a collection written in Danish by a Svínoy farmer in 1849, and supplemented by the farmer's son, who was a teacher (Jakobsen 1898-1901:155, 501-2).

Huldufólk, trolls, and the like are a rather different matter. Although they clearly belong to a different order of reality from that of families and farmhands gathered round the hearth of a winter's evening, they are not so fanciful as they may seem. Whether *huldufólk* actually exist is not our concern. I have never seen one myself, but several of my Faroese friends believe they have, and (more to the point) their existence was apparently not questioned until quite recently. In the late seventeenth century, Lucas Debes collected some elaborate first-hand accounts of encounters with them (1933 [1673]:150-77). *Huldufólk* thus are (or were) established features of the local scene; they were far more immediately real than, say, the king in Copenhagen or the princes and princesses abounding in the *ævintýr.* We will find in considering the legend of Snæbjørn that, like other departures from or additions to documentable reality, *huldufólk* and their doings may be seen as interpretive figures, figures of thought, as it were.

Faroese *sagnir* thus straddle history and literature as we know these fields. Like the former, they draw on actual events and are (or were) believed to be factual accounts; indeed, given the inherent vagaries of oral transmission, they are sometimes remarkably accurate ones. But they interpret the past in literary ways. Most obviously, they are told for entertainment's sake, and as well as concerning themselves with character, plot, and setting, they may draw on folkloric, mythic, or otherwise unrealistic or at least undocumentable sources. In addition, there are three characteristic, overlapping techniques of legendary historiography: the *repeated variation* of themes in vast amounts of circumstantial detail and in series of seemingly disjointed episodes; the *elaboration* of these themes in the distortion of actual events and the invention of others; and both the *exclusion* of real but nonlocal elements and the *inclusion* of unreal (or undocumentable) but local ones.

In giving legends a scholarly sense, then, our task is not just to reconcile legendary and documentary accounts at their shared factual foundation, but to respect the way in which generations of anonymous authors have worked up their material. That is, we must try to make more explicit sense of what a legend says *about* events, whether "historical" or not, in terms that seem congruent with the principles by which its authors have already undertaken to organize experience.

This means, for example, that apparent flights of fancy will prove more important than "sticking to the facts"; that precise dating, with which legends are little concerned, will be less important than the geographical details that do abound in them; and that the decisions of courts and kings will be less important than the actions of *huldufólk*. For as well as a kind of history, the legends are a kind of literature; a sort of tower, as J.R.R. Tolkien said some years ago of the Anglo-Saxon epic *Beowulf*, from whose top one might "look out upon the sea" (1963[1936]:59). But the *sagnir* are an altogether more homely edifice. In them we find ourselves beside the hearth, while the pounding sea a few steps away marks the edge of the Faroese world.

The legend of Snæbjørn (Jakobsen 1898-1901:29-34) offers an illuminating commentary on Faroese circumstances in the mid-seventeenth century. Also, since it is composed of two distinct episodes, the second of which is an elf legend, "Snæbjørn" suggests why elf legends are later in origin than many purely human ones.

Snæbjørn

The farmer Jákup við Neyst in Hvalba had a hired hand who was both deft and daring and an exceptional man at going fowling on the cliffs. He was named Snæbjørn (Snæbi, Snábi). The farmer had two byres, one at home við Neyst, and the other west in the village, at á Heyggi. He kept his cows in the home byre in the latter part of the winter. He had a woman working for him who was from Mykines; she tended the cows, but because it was a rather long way for her to go to the western byre, she mostly lived in that byre while the cows stayed there. For this they called her "the byre woman," and Snæbjørn was her lover.

So it happened one year that the great men came south to Suðuroy to hold court, and they came to Hvalba. The judge was a guest at Jákup við Neyst's house and got rock-dove fledglings for a meal. These tender young birds pleased him greatly, and he asked the farmer where he had gotten them. The farmer answered that Snæbjørn had caught them in a hollow in the cliff, but it was so dangerous getting to where the birds lived that no man in the village dared to go to them except Snæbjørn.

The next year the judge again stayed at Jákup við Neyst's house. He asks the farmer to send Snæbjørn out to the dove hole to take some fledgling doves. The farmer asked Snæbjørn to go, but he refused to do it, because he was angry that the judge did not come to him himself and ask him to do him a service, but wanted

The "judge" sentences Snæbjørn. Bárður Jákupsson. Courtesy of the artist.

to have the farmer send him off just like a dog. So Snæbjørn didn't go at all, but the judge bore him a grudge because of this.

Some time after this a Dutch ship came to Suðuroy. It had many fine things to sell, but no one dared to buy because the king had rented out to some merchants the right to have the islands' trade. Snæbjørn quietly got himself four scarves from this ship, and two of them he gave to his girl, the byre woman. This became known, and Snæbjørn was summoned to meet at the Øravík court to hear sentence passed on him for unlawful purchase. The court was held in the court vale "Up Between the Rooms," below Øravík. Snæbjørn knew that the judge felt hostile toward him and expected a harsh sentence, but he came to court nonetheless. He had a good iron-shod staff with him. The judge and the bailiff both sat below the bluff called "The Court Table." The judge reads the sentence to Snæbjørn and condemns him to work in iron chains for four years at Bremerholm. Snæbjørn calls this a harsh and unjust sentence, swings his staff above his head, and means to strike the judge down cold; but the judge throws himself aside and down onto the bailiff's lap. The staff struck the bailiff in the head, so that he dropped down dead. Then a cry went up to grab Snæbjørn because he had killed the bailiff; but Snæbjørn took to his heels at once and fled, and he was so swift of foot that no one could catch up with him. He headed for the mountain, up Klovningar, through Øraskarð and up on Fjallið Mikla. Many in the crowd of men headed after him, but there was a fog up on the mountain, so they quickly lost sight of him. There is a mound on the west side of Fjallið Mikla, called Snavalsheyggjur; there one of the men heard Snæbjørn's iron-shod staff ring on the stones and called, "He was here! I heard his staff clatter!" "You heard it now, but you won't hear it again," Snæbjørn answered from the fog above and turned his staff around, tip up and knob [top] down. The crowd of men gave up pursuing him, because they lost him again and the day was waning. Snæbjørn went south through the island and into the cliff ledges that are called Snæbjarnarrøkur after him (in Gjógvaráfjall in Vágur on the west side, a little north of the border with Fámjin). In the middle ledge there is a hollow forming a cave beneath the overhanging cliff. He lived for a long time in this cave, breaking into pantries at night and stealing. He had a sister in á Teigum in Fámjin; he went secretly to her and got himself food, fire, and a pot. Stones are still standing in a half-circle in against the cliff in Snæbjarnarhelli, and ashes are found in the middle. But when there was a south wind, it was so very damp for him on the ledges, and therefore he determined to get himself another hiding place. In the fall he took an ox from Lopransdalur, killed and skinned it; he had the meat for food, but he cut the hide into strips and then moved north to Hvalba. Outside Tjørnunes, south near Vatns-dalur, is a steep ridge; there Snæbjørn climbed down as far as he could get, onto a grassy place in the cliff wall, hammered a stake in, and tied to it the rope of hide strips he had with him. So he lowered himself down into the dove hole, which is named Snæbjarnarhol after him. But no one went so far down from the top of the cliff that they saw the rope, because the footing is so bad here. He was here when there was a south wind, and at night went to the byre at á Heyggi to his girl the byre woman, who was with child by him. He got food, fire, and a pot from her. He was in Snæbjarnarhol when there was a south wind, and stole mostly in the southern parts of the island; but when there was a north wind, he was south in Vágur in Snæbjarnarrøkur and then stole mostly to the north. So three years passed in this way.

Snæbjørn was well acquainted with an old man of í Smillum in Vágur, who had three sons. One night when the men of Vágur were out fishing, they saw a fire in Snæbjarnarrøkur and began to talk together about this. They thought Snæ-bjørn might be there. When the fishermen came back, the old man of í Smillum went to Snæbjørn and told him that now he was discovered and would be captured tonight if he didn't move. So Snæbjørn threw out the pot and everything else off the ledges, fled, and did not come back to Snæbjarnarrøkur. Shortly afterward, a ship came into Hvalba in the evening and was gone in the morning. At the same time, a boat was missing from Skálamøl in Hvalba, and nothing more was known of Snæbjørn. But the story is that later he turned up in Shetland.

The son of Snæbjørn and the byre woman grew up with his mother, in the byre at á Heyggi, and she was so secretive about it that no one knew that the maidservant at við Neyst had a child before the boy was so big that he came down onto the beach to play with the other kids. They asked him who he was, but he answered that he was his mother's son; otherwise he knew nothing else to say. So the byre woman was asked and had to admit that he was hers. Afterward, Jákup

Snæbjarnarson, who was called "the byre child," grew up on the farm at við Neyst and became the shepherd for the [outfield called] Hamrahagi, beyond Tjørnunes. One day, when he had been in the outfield driving sheep, he was sitting and sewing himself shoes from thick oxhide. He wonders if it would be possible for a person to walk so far in one day that he wore a hole in it. Men thought that would be impossible. Before day, he headed back into the outfield, so that birds should not disturb the sheep. When he had come a good mile from the settlement, he saw a man coming toward him, but at first he paid no attention to him. The stranger had a dog with him just as Jákup did, and as soon as they met, the dogs attacked each other. Jákup's dog killed the other, but then the heathen—for it was a *huldumaður*—came at Jákup and they both began to fight. The church was out of sight and nothing could be seen of the village. One time the Christian fell and called out: "Jesus!" Then the heathen's strength was diminished by half, so that Jákup got back on his feet and managed to shove the other so far up the hill that the church came into view. Then the *huldumaður* lost his strength and lay underneath. He asked the Christian not to kill him and promised him three good things each year. A big whale with one eye would come to Hvalba each year so long as his descendants lived; a tree with roots on the end would drift ashore to Hvalba from the west, and a bird would come to live on the land he inherited. But no one should make fun of any one of these three things or be dissatisfied with it, for then it would not come back. On this condition Jákup released the *huldumaður,* and when he came home to við Neyst, the shoes he sewed himself from the hide were all worn out.

Soon after this a tree came drifting ashore to Hvalba, and then one like it each year; but then people made fun of the tree—it was so gnarled, waterlogged, and so forth—and so it ceased. The bottle-nosed whale, however, still comes to Hvalba as before. The gannet came too, but because the land Jákup Snæbjarnarson inherited was on Mykines, the gannet went there to live, and there it still is.

It is impossible to date "Snæbjørn" exactly, since it does not appear to be based directly on any documented events. No bailiff was ever killed after pronouncing judgment, for example. Still, several details in the part of the legend dealing with Snæbjørn himself allow us to date it in a general sort of way to the mid-1640s; the second part, dealing with Jákup Snæbjarnarson and the *huldumaður,* is thus roughly datable to about twenty years later, or the beginning of "the Gabels' time," in the mid-1660s.[7]

The "judge's" host on Suðuroy, Jákup við Neyst, is surely Jákup Hálvdansson, who lived at the farmstead called við Neyst and became sheriff of Suðuroy in 1630; it was he who wrote the report about the Dutch smuggling ship, in 1636. He was removed from office in 1648, for having conspired with the *løgrættumenn* to deprive the priest of certain lands that should have been reapportioned to him.

The legal arrangements pictured in "Snæbjørn" are rather strange. The bailiff never took part in the proceedings of the spring courts, and "judge" (*dómari*) is a peculiar term that was never used in the Faroes. It must nonetheless refer to the *sorinskrivari,* who probably around mid-century replaced the *løgmaður* as circuit judge for the spring courts. Indeed, in another version of the legend, Snæbjørn is said to kill the

løgmaður (Jakobsen 1898-1901:470-71). The legend thus most likely re-
calls the poorly documented transitional time between the *løgmaður*'s and
the *sorinskrivari*'s eras. The use of *"dómari"* rather than *"sorinskrivari"*
further suggests that this official was not Faroese; in fact, from 1641 to
1645, the *sorinskrivari* was one Jacob Willemsøn Hannemand, a Dane.
Some previous *sorinskrivarar* had also been foreigners, but from 1645
until about 1770, the office was almost always filled by Faroese. When
the bailiff died in Copenhagen, over the winter of 1644/45, Hannemand
tried to take over the post, or at least he anticipated what he hoped would
be his own appointment to it. Among other things, he wrote to the sheriffs
in the bailiff's name. This was illegal, and he was removed from office
when the Løgting met in 1645.

It seems likely that in "Snæbjørn" the distortion of mid-seventeenth
century Faroese judicial arrangements both reflects the historical pattern
of shifting and conflicting authority (the *sorinskrivari*'s replacement of the
løgmaður as circuit judge, Jákup Hálvdansson's run-in with the priest,
Hannemand's exceeding his authority, Gabel's rise to power) and makes
the pattern neater, by aligning it with a distinction between Faroese and
Danish authorities. Thus the (Faroese) *løgmaður* becomes the (Danish)
bailiff, while the *sorinskrivari* (who actually was a Dane in the early
1640s, though his successors were Faroese) acquires the anomalous title
of "judge." Furthermore, as if to emphasize the point that the central
theme of "Snæbjørn" is authority over Faroese life, the king makes one of
his rare appearances in the legendary corpus: "the king had rented out to
some merchants the right to have the islands' trade." Taken out of context,
this statement could refer to almost any period from the late thirteenth
century until the founding of the royal trade monopoly, in 1709; here,
however, it clearly stresses the growing distance between the Faroes and
the crown in the seventeenth century, and thus the increased authority of
non-Faroese intermediary officials, principally the bailiff and the merchant.

Historical speculations must end here. It would be misleading to try
to date "Snæbjørn" too exactly, or to tie it too firmly to particular events.
It is obviously largely invented, which suggests that it interprets the past
rather abstractly. In approaching it more closely, we may begin with a
general statement.

Faroese society is perennially balanced between Denmark, on the one
hand, and the land and the sea, on the other. That is, like all rural peoples,
the Faroese have found themselves looking two ways at once: toward a
metropolitan society that very largely controls their economic and political
relations with the outside world, and toward the local environment from
which a living must be made. "Snæbjørn" both reflects and reflects upon
the readjustment of the Faroes' relations with Denmark in the seventeenth
century, and in consequence the rearticulation of the relationship between
Faroese society and its natural environment. The forced renegotiation of

the contract with Denmark entailed renegotiating the contract with nature. This general theme is carried in the tale not only by the techniques of legendary historiography (particularly, in the second part of the tale, by the inclusion of the local but "unreal" *huldumaður*), but also, fittingly enough, by an allegorical treatment of the Faroes' human geography.

"Snæbjørn's" principal characters and events are carefully placed in space and society. The space is for the most part *uttangarðs*, that is, "outside the wall" surrounding the village, the church, and the infield.

There are three main areas "outside the wall": the outfield, the cliffs, and the sea. Both in the legend and in everyday life, this geographical progression is associated with parallel progressions in useful animal life (and hence in economic pursuits) and also in institutions, officials, and levels of political organization. Sheep live in the outfields; birds live on the cliffs; fish live in the sea. Shepherds go out to tend the sheep; fowlers go out to harvest birds and eggs on the cliffs; fishermen go to sea. They all bring back the fruits of their labors for collective use in the village. Each Faroese village was (and still is) the center of its world, a social place in an economic and natural setting.

Faroese legal and political institutions also have geographical connotations, and to some extent seasonal ones. In the spring, at lambing time, local courts for each district (*sýsla*) met in the outfield; the Løgting for all the Faroes met in Tórshavn in summer on a rocky spit called the Tinganes; the royal court met "down there" (as people say), in Copenhagen. All of these places were peripheral to village-centered society although, paradoxically, they were politically central. Faroese did not live there, but only visited them. The spring courts met in bowls in the hills, attended by each district's sheriff and *løgrættumenn*, by the *løgmaður* (later the *sorinskrivari*), and by other interested parties from the district's scattered villages. The Tinganes, the political equivalent of a cliff or seaside, was the realm of the *løgmaður* and the bailiff, and, in ecclesiastical affairs, of the dean. It was also the site of the company store and warehouses.

Figure 2 offers a kind of map of Faroese society "outside the wall," and of the action of "Snæbjørn" as well. The outfields, where sheep live, are the level of the Faroes' several districts and their officials and institutions; the cliffs are the level of bird life, of the Faroes as a whole, and of Tórshavn and its intermediary officials and institutions, which were increasingly Danish; the sea is the level of fish, of Denmark, and of a foreign officialdom.

The first sentence of the legend establishes Snæbjørn as the epitome of a *bakkamaður* ("fowler," literally "cliff man"): he is "both deft and daring and an exceptional man at going fowling on the cliffs" (*til bakkagøngu*, literally "at cliff-walking"). At the same time, it establishes him socially as a hired hand; like Óli Jarnheysur and many another legendary hero, he is one of those indispensable servants of well-to-do farmers. The

Figure 2.   The Faroes "outside the wall" (*uttangarðs*)

Geography	Animals	Areas	Courts	Sites	Political Officials	Ecclesiastical Officials	Trade
sea	fish	Denmark	royal court	Copenhagen	king, etc.	king, bishop, etc.	Iceland Co., Gabels', etc.
cliffs	birds	Faroes	Løgting	Tinganes (Tórshavn)	*Løgmaður,* bailiff	dean	warehouse in Tórshavn
outfield	sheep	districts (*sýslur*)	spring parliaments	traditional sites	*løgrættu-menn,* sheriff	priest	
(stone wall)..							

question is, what happens when this delicate relationship is upset, when something or someone attempts to turn to his own advantage Snæbjørn's mastery of the cliffs and his relationship with his employer, Jákup við Neyst?

The legend poses the question by having the "judge" ask Jákup við Neyst to tell Snæbjørn to get him fledgling rock doves from the cliff. Snæbjørn is angry, and rightly so; for as our "map" suggests, Snæbjørn is actually a cut above the *sorinskrivari.* He complains, indeed, that he is being treated like a dog—not even a shepherd, but a shepherd's animal.

The "judge" bears Snæbjørn a grudge because of this.

Snæbjørn is the only person in the village who dares trade with a Dutch ship that has put in at Hvalba. Again he is acting in accordance with his high, cliff-level position. Unfortunately, however, "the king had rented out" trading rights. This brings Snæbjørn into conflict with the king's subordinates, by whose lights such dealings were smuggling, as much transgressions against their own mastery of the importation of goods from abroad as, from Snæbjørn's point of view, the "judge's" request to get him more rock-dove nestlings was a transgression against his own mastery of the "importation" of food from the cliffs.

So Snæbjørn is brought to court. The Suðuroy spring court met outside Øravík, toward the middle of the island, near where the modern road from Øravík to Fámjin switchbacks over a saddle called Øraskarð. He brings with him an iron-shod staff, a rather ambiguous token, since it may be used both in the outfields and on the cliffs. The "judge" sentences him to banishment in Bremerholm, virtually a death sentence. Finding the sentence too harsh, Snæbjørn strikes out at the "judge," who takes refuge in his superior's lap. So, appropriately enough, Snæbjørn kills the bailiff instead, his own cliff-level equal. This, however, is murder, an antisocial act by everyone's reckoning. The hue and cry is raised, and Snæbjørn takes to his heels. He flees through the outfields, nearly losing his pursuers in a fog. He is almost caught when his staff clatters on the stones. Again turning his staff to an antisocial use in the interests of self-preservation, he reverses it. The chase is abandoned.

Snæbjørn goes to live in the cliffs, where his life becomes as topsy-turvy as his staff. Both literally and figuratively, socially and geographically, his position is precarious. He lives alone between the land and the sea, an outlaw, taking things away to the cliffs instead of bringing them in to the village. His dwellings are not houses but caves, where nature is so poorly kept at bay that he must move whenever the wind shifts. His sister in Fámjin and his lover in Hvalba both give him "food, fire, and a pot," but these relationships are personal, not social. He has a friend in Vágur who warns him that his hiding place has been discovered. He must flee again; as the old proverb says, "Follow the land's custom or flee the land" (Hammershaimb 1891, 1:317). The only sign of his departure is something amiss on the shore.

Snæbjørn is a markedly peripheral man. Geographically, he is at home, so to speak, on the cliffs; politically, by extension, he is at home where the foreign and the Faroese meet. His lover, the byre woman, is a markedly peripheral woman, which means, in the Faroese scheme of things, that she is estranged from a woman's position closer to home and the hearth (Wylie and Margolin 1981:54-56). She lives in a sort of house, but alone, with cattle, in a crude barn well outside the village. Looking after cows was indeed largely women's work (men looked after the sheep), but they would go out in groups to the outfields in the summer to milk them. They did not spend the night there. The byre woman is also peripheral in that she comes from another island, Mykines. Women commonly moved more often than men, but they did so either to work in someone else's house or to set up their own when they married. The byre woman does not live in Jákup við Neyst's house; nor is she married. Rather, her relationship with Snæbjørn transposes the usual relations between men and women to the world "outside the wall." This implies that they are unmarried, since the church lies within the wall. But all too naturally it does not prevent their having a child.

The first part of "Snæbjørn" thus suggests the consequences of two crucial developments in the early and mid-seventeenth century. The first was the tightening of the monopoly system. The company store on the Tinganes was the only place where Faroese could trade legally. Trade elsewhere, and with non-Danes, was criminal. Our "map" thus has a blank, which it was Snæbjørn's unhappy fate to try to fill, by trading with the Dutchman at Hvalba. Interestingly enough, the blank was actually partly filled at about that time by a Hanseatic or Dutch smugglers' storehouse near the present site of Tvøroyri (R. Jensen 1952:56-57; Trap 1968:339).

The second, related development was increasing Danish control over Tórshavn and its institutions and the establishment of the *sorinskrivari* as the circuit judge for the spring courts. In terms of our "map," this meant a partial dissolution of the boundary between Faroese and Danes, as Danish control intruded upon the borders of the local world. The legend stresses this by unrealistically having the Danish bailiff present at the spring court and by giving the *sorinskrivari* the curious title of "judge." As a practical matter, Faroese of course acquiesced in greater Danish hegemony, but culturally it posed a problem. As the legend suggests in recounting Snæbjørn's doomed resistance to political and economic change, the counterbalancing distinction between Faroese society and the natural order likewise threatened to dissolve. If Faroese were treated like dogs, how might they remain men?

The second part of the legend addresses this problem, proposes its temporary resolution, and suggests a more satisfactory one that was finally arrived at in the late nineteenth century. The temporary resolution was to people the natural boundaries of the home world with *huldufólk* and the like and to control them in oral literature. The later solution was to erect political institutions and a written literature between the Faroes and Denmark.

Jákup Snæbjarnarson takes after his mother. He first shows up on the very shore where his father had disappeared, but "he was his mother's son; otherwise he knew nothing else to say." She acknowledges him publicly, and he is nicknamed the "byre child" after her, thereby acquiring a social identity.[8] He lives at við Neyst, finding his place in village society at a level appropriate to his parentage, as a shepherd charged with looking after the sheep on a stretch of outfield.

One morning, having been driving sheep the day before on a stretch of outfield near where his father had hidden out, young Jákup sets forth before daybreak to make sure that birds are not troubling the flock.[9] He is wearing new oxhide shoes, which he had wondered if it would ever be possible to wear out in a day. This stock motif in Faroese folklore anticipates some event so exceptional that the shoes will be worn out. It also occurs, for example, in a Sandoy tale about a man named Eirikur who, although he boasted he could not wear out his new shoes in a day, lost his way in a blizzard between Skopun and Sandur; he was later found dead, his shoes full of holes, on top of the mountain named Eiriksfjall, after him. So it comes as no surprise that Jákup should meet a *huldumaður,* for his musing at the shoe he is sewing has introduced a complementary level of reality into the story, a reality composed of folkloric conventions and motifs, and supernatural or semisupernatural beings.

The story of Jákup and the *huldumaður* also contains some muted mythic elements. On the Christian side, there is of course the story of another herdsman named Jacob, who at daybreak wrestled with an angel in the wilderness (Genesis 32:24-32), while on the old Norse side, the one-eyed whale, the tree, and the bird (though it is a gannet, not an eagle) suggest Odin. But this part of the story is more closely linked to a well-known Mykines tale that hovers between legend and myth (Hammershaimb 1891, 1:348-51). "Once upon a time a giant named Mighty Tórur lived in Gásadalur on Vágar, and at the same time a man named Mighty Óli lived on Mykines." Tórur coveted Óli's island and came over to kill him for it. They fought, but Óli got the giant down, putting out his eye. In return for his life, Tórur gave Óli "three rare things": a whale each year, a driftwood tree, and a bird that lived nowhere else in the Faroes, on condition that no one make fun of these gifts. The giant and the man became fast friends, and they are buried near each other, on Mykines. The whale came each year, but people made fun of it because it had only one eye, and they found fault with it because it sickened them to eat the meat. (Bottle-nosed whales, which do not make good eating, reputedly have only one eye.) So the whale no longer comes. The tree came each spring, but it was too crooked and gnarled to be of much use in rebuilding the chapel, which blew down each spring. So the tree no longer comes. The birds, gannets, still live on Mykineshólmur, and people are careful not to make fun of them.

This Mykines story clearly has very ancient roots and seems to have served as a kind of model for the story about Jákup Snæbjarnarson and the *huldumaður*. In fact, the stories complement each other: Jákup's story has the gannets go from Hvalba to Mykines, while according to one version of the Mykines story, the yearly whale did not disappear entirely, but went from Mykines to Hvalba. Another thing these two stories share is a fight between a man and a nonhuman being.

The general significance of the folkloric fights is plain. As our investigation of geographical metaphors in the first part of "Snæbjørn" leads us to suspect, the issue is who controls the land in the Faroes, the giant or the man? The *huldumaður* or the farmer? Danes or Faroese? The answer is mixed. Faroese may own the land, but without excluding (in the tales' terms, killing) such beings as the giant and the *huldumaður*. Moreover, these beings retain a certain power to grant or withhold useful items from outside the Faroes, useful items, but only barely so. On a rather obvious level, the parallel with the Faroes' mercantile situation is inescapable: the "certain merchants" controlling the Faroe trade often import shoddy goods, but complaining does not make them any better.

"Snæbjørn" treats the question of who controls the land more deeply and in greater detail. The first part of the legend has posed the question as a legal and political matter. The second part follows from the first, in that its hero is the son of Snæbjørn and the byre woman, and in depicting a more intrusive challenge to the integrity of Faroese life: Snæbjørn was driven from the cliffs; will Jákup be driven from the outfields? It differs from the first part, however, in that the consequences of Snæbjørn's exile are seen to involve Faroese relations with the natural and supernatural worlds, not those of politics and the law. Snæbjørn assaults the judge; Jákup wrestles a *huldumaður*.

Huldufólk are one of a number of supernatural or semisupernatural beings Faroese have believed in. Each kind is generally associated with a particular part of the landscape. Thus *vættrar,* a sort of pixie, or sprite, "live in good people's houses," while trolls live in or under mountains. *Huldufólk* live in the outfields: "They are large in size, their clothes are all gray, their hair black; their dwelling place is in caves, they are also called 'elves.' . . . They live like other people, go fishing, keep sheep and cattle, which mingle [often invisibly] with other cattle in the outfields" (Hammershaimb 1891, 1-327). Except that *huldufólk* are not Christian, being called "heathens" and living literally as well as figuratively out of sight of a church, their society mirrors that of Faroese. Although you must treat cautiously with *huldufólk,* their relations with humans are sometimes amicable enough and, like Faroese, they are punctilious about keeping promises and returning favors. Like Snæbjørn's relationship with the byre woman, *huldufólk* represent a transposition of Faroese ways to the world "outside the wall." They are intermediate between the village world and the natural one.

Structurally, then, this *huldumaður* is a fitting opponent for Jákup, the illegitimate byre child; he is no doubt abroad in the outfield with his dog on much the same business as Jákup and his dog. Their fight echoes Snæbjørn's with the "judge," which also took place in the outfield. Neither Jákup nor Snæbjørn has sought to fight; they have been driven to it by non-Faroese subordinates, the bailiff's underling the "judge" and the *huldumaður*'s dog. But like the "judge" and the dog, the bailiff and the *huldumaður* are opposite sorts of non-Faroese. The bailiff is human, but at best marginally local. The *huldumaður* is local, but at best marginally human. This opposition determines the outcome of the fights.

When Snæbjørn kills the bailiff, he is driven into exile by a popular hue and cry: he too becomes marked as human but only marginally local. Forfeiting his membership in village society, he retains only personal relations with other people. In outwrestling the *huldumaður,* young Jákup demonstrates both his own humanity and his membership in village society. Personally, indeed, Jákup is outmatched: the *huldumaður* throws him. The "heathen's" strength is halved when Jákup calls out Jesus' name, but only halved, since Jesus, like Jákup, is after all only an individual. The *huldumaður* loses all his strength only when Jákup wrestles him to within sight of Hvalba's church, which, like most Faroese churches, lies on the outskirts of the village proper, though well within the infield. In other words, Jákup's strength derives from his membership in village society, defined as a spiritual community.

The tale's conclusion stresses the opposition between Snæbjørn's individualism and Jákup's social identity. Both Snæbjørn and Jákup have acquired fine things, for example. Near the start of the tale, Snæbjørn traded for scarves with the Dutch smugglers, while at the end, Jákup gets "three good things" from the *huldumaður.* Both acts of acquisition have involved defying authority, in Snæbjørn's case that of "the great men" and in Jákup's case the *huldumaður's*. But Snæbjørn has acquired cultural items for individual use, which led to his murder of the bailiff, his banishment from village life, and his exile from the Faroes. Jákup lets the *huldumaður* live, thereby acquiring natural items for collective use; when he moves, it is only to another island, where he has inherited land.[10]

Logically this is a neat enough conclusion, but it suggests how precarious Faroese identity was. Foreigners have a right to govern the Faroes and to control their intercourse with the outside world. *Huldufólk* have a right to use the outfield, too. The Church is a branch of the Danish Church, but local churches belong to the villages.[11] The problem is that the integrity of Faroese life depended on the existence of mediating, or intermediary, figures, who are not themselves Faroese: in politics, the bailiff; in trade, the merchant; in religion, the dean; and in nature, such beings as *huldufólk*. In what sense, then, were the Faroes Faroese? How did a peculiarly local culture survive economic and political domination from abroad? In part, as we suggested in Chapter Two, it survived because the Reformation preserved an archaic economic system. But our analysis of "Snæbjørn" suggests that this was not the whole story.

Faroese society finds itself balanced between Danish society, on the one hand, and the natural environment, on the other. These twin externalities serve as negative symbols for local self-identification: we are non-Danes, but we are also non-natural. The first part of "Snæbjørn" reflects upon the fact that, by the middle of the seventeenth century, Faroese had for all practical purposes lost control of their economic and political relations with Denmark and the outside world; they were less and less clearly non-Danes, their land becoming, as the *løgmaður* called it a hundred years later, "a province within the realm" (*en indenrigs Provints*) (H. Debes 1769:38). This entailed a further question: If Faroese were to remain non-Danes, how could they also remain non-natural? The second part of the legend suggests that they might do so by continuing to people the natural world with figures as outlandish as agents of the Danish state and who, like Danes, are not subject to Faroese control: *huldufólk*, trolls, *vættrar*, and the like.

Lucas Debes (1676:376ff.) was thus not so wide of the mark when he argued that what he believed were "Specters and Illusions of Satan in Feroe" were evidence both of a reaction against God's true word and of the devil's persistence in a land so long uninhabited and so recently made Christian (and even more recently delivered from popery). I would argue, however, that the reaction was not satanic but cultural, and pagan only in the term's root sense of "countrified." This is also why, as we have followed Dr. Jakobsen in wondering, a disproportionate number of elf legends apparently date from the seventeenth and eighteenth centuries: *huldufólk* counterbalanced Danes, being as necessary as Danish authorities were intrusive.

Moreover, Faroese acquiescence in the increased exercise of Danish sovereignty created a relatively changeless social and economic order. This in turn meant that the crucial matter of cultural concern was not the past construed as a "historical" record of passing events, so much as the more timeless, almost mythic, treatment of people in their habitat. Since the persistent presence of figures like himself required it, perhaps Debes should not have been so surprised at "how stedfastly some keep their old Traditions and superstitious customs, which they do secretly and diligently observe" (1676:381). Nor should he have "blame[d] in our people of *Feroe,* that almost all of them know the most part of the old Gyants Ballads; not only those that are Printed in the Danish Book of Ballads, but also many more of the Champions of *Norway,* that may be are forgotten elsewhere, here [remain] in fresh memory, being usually Sung in their Dances" (1676:337-38; original italics).

Still, this was obviously a precarious solution. The greatest danger was that the intermediaries between the Faroes and the outside world might disappear or fail in their functions. What would happen if the monopoly system were abolished? What if the Danish government really began to treat the Faroes like a part of Denmark?

This danger was realized tentatively in the eighteenth century and acutely in the nineteenth century. The Faroese reaction verifies our analysis of "Snæbjørn." The first reaction, as we shall see in the next chapter, was to try to preserve Faroese society's precarious stability by protesting government proposals to abolish the royal trade monopoly. Abolition seemed as much a cultural danger as an economic one. The *løgmaður* Hans Debes (1769:33) wrote, in 1766, that free trade would further threaten a culture already affected by too much contact with others: "Nowadays the Faroes are greatly changed from former times. The continual contact with Danes and several foreigners who live in the land causes foreign fashions to be affected, both in costume, food, drink, and other matters. Indeed, if the opportunity were like the will, truly the Faroes would be as vain a nation as any other." If Faroese were to regain the "lost freedom to trade with their own ships," it "would only give a few rich men occasion to bleed white the poor commonality," thereby destroying the equality his granduncle Lucas Debes also found appealing about the Faroese (1769:32).

But radical change was unavoidable by the middle of the nineteenth century. The Faroese reaction is again instructive. Our analysis of "Snæbjørn" implies that if, in fact, the Faroese did in some measure control the borders of their world, it was through literature. Legends, ballads, and folktales were, after all, where everything was put in its proper place: Vikings in the past, Danes across the sea or in Tórshavn, trolls in the mountains, *huldufólk* in the outfields, the village in the middle. So long as village society and domestic institutions like the *kvøldseta* remained intact, it did not matter much that the Faroes were more closely integrated

with Denmark in 1816, with the abolition of the Løgting and their reduc-
tion to a Danish county (*amt*). The old techniques of folk-literary self-
defense could still be used. The first decades of the nineteenth century
thus saw a final flowering of traditional ballad composition.

The Faroese were, however, forced onto the offensive after the abolition of the Monopoly, in 1856, and the industrialization and urbanization
of local society after the late 1880s. What they did was to reinstitutionalize
their literature on a higher level, in written form and as an explicit representation of their separate identity. The collection of folk literature was
part of this movement, but at the same time "a Faroese poetry of modern
form arose. It is especially lyric poetry, songs, and hymns" (Jakobsen
1904:15). In these first works of modern Faroese literature, mostly lyric
poems written in Copenhagen in the 1870s and 1880s, we find ennobled
precisely those aspects and areas of the natural world through which
Snæbjørn and Jákup the byre child moved, those rural institutions the
Reformation had left most untouched, and the very language in which
these are described. Frederik Petersen's hymn to the Faroese language,
"Føroyska málið," contains these verses:

> Hear the surf roar on the shore!
> Hear the storm sing in the mountains!
> That's the Faroes' language.
> Hear the waterfall play on the cliffs!
> Hear the dwarves talk on the bluffs!
> That's the Faroes' language.
>
> Hear the merry lambs bleat!
> Hear birds sing in the outfield!
> That's the Faroes' language.
> Hear, in thanks for a good trip,
> the psalm sound from the boats!
> That's the Faroes' language.
>
> Hear the dancing in the room!
> Hear the long ballads about heroes!
> That's the Faroes' language.
> Hear the old man by the hearth
> gather children about old stories!
> That's the Faroes' language.
>
> [Hammershaimb 1969 (1891):310-11]

Much of this poetry was recited at open-air political meetings in the outfields in the 1890s. Thus, symbolically as well as in political practice, the
Faroese reclaimed the outfields and the cliffs; recently they have extended
their claims for further separation from Denmark, on the grounds that they
should control the seas about them. The modern nationalist poet Steinbjörn Jacobsen has written:

This land and these grounds were the springs of all life.
The great sea drove, drove upon these shores.
With much art and courage they got life from all of this.
But from outside—from other lands—came men with great vessels.
These men usurped the grounds and made themselves more and
    more obtrusive.
Finally they thought they owned everything—right up to the
    sea cliff itself.
. . . .

Let us lay claim to the land anew. Take our old grounds.
Expropriate our own property.

[S. Jacobsen 1974:50, 52]

So politicized and so loftily represented, literature, language, the landscape, and the past continue to identify Faroese culture for its bearers,
while now also betokening its new-found dignity.

All of which has gotten us ahead of our story. Before turning to the reformulation of Faroese culture in the nineteenth century, we must consider
its evolution (or lack of it) in the period from 1709 to 1816. How stable
was Faroese society? How were the Faroes governed, and how did the
government's policies (or the lack of any one consistent policy contribute
to the preservation of what a later generation would call the Faroes' "folkishness"?

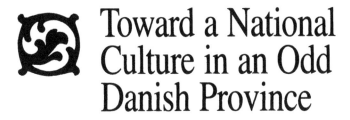

PART TWO

Toward a National Culture in an Odd Danish Province

CHAPTER FOUR

A Great Deal of Fuss for an Omelet
A Precarious Stability, 1709-1816

Frederik von Gabel died on 21 June 1708. His heirs briefly retained the Faroe trade, but the following May it was taken over by a department of the Exchequer (Rentekammer), which was responsible to the king.[1] In the same year, the Faroes were administratively incorporated in Sjælland province, to which they were returned after a long stretch during which they were combined in a single province with Iceland (1720-75).

From 1771 on, several administrative changes were likewise made in the management of the Faroe trade. In 1774, for example, it was combined with the Finmark and Iceland trade, and in 1781 with the Greenland trade, as well. The royal monopoly for Iceland was abolished five years later, and in 1790 the Faroese monopoly was made a separate entity.

In the Faroes it made little practical difference which office in Copenhagen did the paperwork. Commerce and the collection of rents and taxes were no longer grounds for personal enrichment, as they had been under the Gabels. Imports came more regularly, if not always in sufficient quantity. In a *tættir* composed around 1800, the hero, Páll, arrives in Tórshavn from his home in Leirvík, and the bookkeeper gives him credit for the socks he has to sell. Páll says:

> "Write me down some lumber,
> tobacco and blue dye";
> the bookkeeper shakes his head:
> "It can't be gotten here."

> "Write me down a pot of brandy,
> hemp and some birchbark";
> the bookkeeper shakes his head:
> "It's not here, my man."

This irked Leirvík-Páll,
he wasn't used to giving way:
"Shame and blame upon the brains
who manage this trade."
. . . .
Páll whirls through the warehouse door
in a wicked temper:
"Is there any leftover rye bread
inside the warehouse here?"

The stockboy grasps a barrel
to look down inside it,
sees a few leftover crumbs
lying down on the bottom.

Half of it was mouse dung
that Páll might rake about in:
"What will Nimfur the merchant
take for mouse droppings?"

A Tórshavn woman answered this
(she mostly lives on flour):
"Páll didn't get the first crap
that was sold in the warehouse."
[Djurhuus and Matras 1951-72, 6:353]

Smuggling fell off, though it did not disappear. In 1770, for example, the priest of Suðuroy was convicted for one hundred eleven pairs of stockings his wife had sent to the skipper of a ship that was lying disabled in Hvalba (Degn 1945:253-54). According to Hans Debes, the *løgmaður* between 1750 and 1769, a Danish frigate had captured a number of Dutch vessels with Icelandic and Faroese goods on board, in 1741. Representations were subsequently made to the Dutch government, "which earnestly forbade these fishermen to carry out trade with the inhabitants. With this prohibition their trickery ended wholly, so that one has almost never seen them since" (1769:30). The decline of smuggling may have been a mixed blessing for the Monopoly. Debes went on to say that "this is a principal reason, why the land at present requires more provisioning than in former times, since this hidden channel has been wholly stopped" (1769:30).

Though more flexible than the Gabels, the Exchequer was of course not oblivious to profit and loss. At first the Monopoly operated in the red, finding no market abroad for the stockings it was bound to buy so dear in the Faroes. A revision of the price schedule, in 1723, rectified this fault, and until 1777 the Monopoly showed a profit.[2] Thereafter it again ran at a loss, for despite a rise in Faroese exports (mostly stockings) from around 20,000 *gyllin* in the early part of the century to around 30,000 *gyllin* after the mid-1760s, grain was becoming more expensive on the continent, while the Faroes' demand for it was also rising (Svabo 1959:289-91; see also Degn 1929:98ff.).

Not surprisingly, the Monopoly's abolition was officially proposed in 1789. The bailiff, Wenzel Hammershaimb, and the commandant of the Tórshavn garrison, Christian Born, were summoned to Copenhagen for consultations. They carried with them a letter signed by twenty-eight Eysturoy farmers, pleading that the Monopoly be retained. Hammershaimb and Born nonetheless recommended abolishing it within a few years and revising the price schedule in the meantime.

Abolition was duly scheduled for 1796, but because of the increasingly unsettled state of European politics, it was not carried out. This was undoubtedly to the Faroes' advantage. The price schedule was revised in 1790. Such changes as were made encouraged the continued production of stockings, and thus discouraged what eventually proved to be the key to the Faroes' economic development, the commercial exploitation of the sea. Fishing is, of course, a notoriously uncertain business, and these were bad fishing years. Moreover, as J.C. Svabo had noted presciently several years before,

On account of the great uncertainty the Faroese fishery must be considered more a household than a commercial fishery. . . . It always remains true that while farmers in the Faroes, or those who have farms, great or small, or else are *bønamenn*, i.e., poor landless men, who are engaged for pay to perform all a farmer's outdoor work, are fishermen as well; and since agriculture is never so uneven as fishing, so the latter must always be *subordinated* to agriculture. . . . I dare say that agriculture and fishing would be carried out to greater perfection if the farmer were not a fisherman, and the fisherman not a farmer, but the Faroes' present underpopulation does not seem to permit these pursuits to be separated. [1959:110-11; his emphasis]

By Svabo's reckoning, the Faroese population was 4409.

In 1807 the British seizure of Copenhagen forced Denmark into an ultimately disastrous alliance with France. The following summer, a British brig, the *Clio,* took Tórshavn. A few weeks later, Tórshavn was ransacked by a privateer, Baron von Hompesch. The hijinks of von Hompesch and the Commandant (and acting *amtmand*) Løbner of the Tórshavn garrison, and the heroic attempts by Nólsoyar Páll to keep the Faroes provisioned (until his death at sea, at the end of 1808), provide the Faroes' own dim version of the great dramas of Napoleonic Europe.[3] A special arrangement with Britain was worked out in 1810, and thereafter the Faroes were spared the famine that had threatened from 1807 to 1809.

Denmark capitulated in 1814. By the Treaty of Kiel, it was stripped of Norway, which passed to Sweden, but retained Greenland, Iceland, and the Faroes. In 1816 the Løgting was abolished and the Faroes were made a Danish county (*amt*). As John West (1972:76) points out, "There have subsequently been many regrets over the passing of the ancient Løgting. At the time there were few or none, for it had long been a mere shadow of its former self." It had little or no real power, its functions having been increasingly bypassed, as more regular communications with Copenhagen facilitated appeals to higher authority there. In fact, it was no longer a purely Faroese institution. Since 1769 its chief officer, the *løgmaður*, had been a Danish or Norwegian appointee.

Between 1766 and 1788, the Faroes had felt another muted reverberation of world events. High British tariffs being as unwelcome in many parts of Britain as they were in what were soon to become the United States, a Copenhagen merchant named Niels Ryberg hit upon the idea of setting up a base in the Faroes for smuggling rum, tea, and tobacco into Britain, thereby circumventing British customs and turning a handsome profit for himself. In 1763 he applied to the General Customs Bureau (Generaltoldkammer) for permission to open a station for "transshipping" such goods. Acting to protect its own interests in the Faroe trade, the Exchequer insisted on several conditions. Wares from Copenhagen or the West Indies should be brought on Danish ships, and Ryberg "must not sell anything to the inhabitants of the islands, and thereby infringe on the royal trade monopoly"; nor could he provision his ships and men from the Monopoly store in Tórshavn, because this "would be too expensive for the trade" (Rasch 1964:170). Accepting these conditions, Ryberg began operations in Tórshavn in 1767, although his "station" did not really open until the next year, when a warehouse was built there. It remained in existence until 1788, when the end of the American Revolution and the revision of British tax laws made the enterprise unprofitable.

In the long run, the Ryberg Company's effect on the Faroes was minimal. Its warehouse in Tórshavn was enlarged in 1781. A wharf, the Faroes' first, was built the next year, and out on Nólsoy a kind of lighthouse was set up, also the Faroes' first. For a while, as Svabo described in 1781, Tórshavn almost bustled, its harbor sometimes filled with as many as twelve or fourteen boats—Ryberg's ships and small craft loading goods to smuggle into Britain. The "station" employed a fairly large personnel, "namely one or two 'procureurs' or superintendents together with the necessary office workers. Then came 16-18 coopers, both Scots and Danes and some Faroese, and finally it had some workers from Tórshavn employed at the station, some full time, some for daily wages. Finally there were a pilot and two tobacco-twisters, who had some Faroese boys in training" (Rasch 1964:172; cf. Svabo 1959:298). A few men's horizons may have been broadened by all this. Nólsoyar Páll, for example, sailed on Ryberg's as well as the Monopoly's ships; but there was not enough steady work to promote the establishment of a laboring or artisan class. In 1775 a porter, a cooper, a joiner, a pilot (who was a retired Danish skipper), and two carpenters employed in all only nine men and seven women; and the sheriff of Streymoy considered, in addition, that five men who worked for Ryberg were to be numbered among Tórshavn's "loose and idle persons, who without employment lie idle and have no proper means of support and are in addition able to work, etc." (*Tillæg*, pp. 139-40).

A potentially more important economic innovation failed. Ryberg had been interested in Faroese fish as early as 1768, and a few Faroese were trained to manufacture klipfish (dry-salted cod). But the 1770s were bad fishing years, and nothing came of this. Between 1767 and 1776, 96.9 percent of Faroese exports by value were wool, woolens, tallow, and lambskins (Degn 1929:142).

At first glance, the Faroese eighteenth century offers the historian little food for thought. Nothing much seems to have happened. We may only hear echoes and see portents, the raids of 1808 recalling the French attack of 1677, when the fort at Tórshavn also surrendered without a shot fired, and Ryberg's station and Nólsoyar Páll's trading ventures anticipating free trade. But some matters do promise greater interest, although, significantly enough, they seem merely unaccountable by the lights of modern separatist historiography. Joensen, Mortensen, and Petersen (1955:52) preface as follows, for example, the text of the Eysturoy farmers' appeal to retain the Monopoly: "Some might think that such a proposal to remove the royal monopoly would have been gladly received by Faroese. Now conditions might be thought to be dawning on better times. But where do we find words of such gladness? Nowhere. On the contrary, there is a protest on record which shows how little interest in progress some Faroese had—unfortunately." Similarly, J.S. Hansen cannot really account for the fact that, in 1774, faced with a rising demand for increasingly expensive grain, a committee of prominent Faroese "found the remedy that would work: Just to hinder people from getting married!! Thus they tried their best to diminish the growth of the population, for it went more easily at that time to enact a prohibition against marriage than to raise the price of grain by a few cents" (1966:115). In fact, as we shall see, this was not so much the committee's recommendation as the *løgmaður*'s; but more stringent restrictions on marriage did become law in 1777.

With such evidence in mind, we may interpret the Faroese eighteenth century as follows.

First, practically all witnesses agree that natural conditions offered little hope for economic development. The weather was perhaps less awful than in the early seventeenth century, but the barley crop often failed, sheep and cows sometimes died of disease or had to be slaughtered when hay was scarce, fishing was erratic, and few pilot whales were taken. In the twenty-six years from 1755 to 1780, only two saw whale slaughters (Müller 1883b:15; see also Joensen and Zachariassen 1982). *Løgmaður* Hveding was whistling in the dark in 1774, when he opined that, "It is very possible, that in half a century's time the Faroes may be able to support by their own husbandry all the inhabitants there are now, and more" (*Tillæg*, p. 105).

Second, trends set in motion during the previous century were tending slowly but inexorably toward the creation of an internally dynamic society. The most obvious trend was demographic. It is next to impossible to know

the Faroes' population before the late eighteenth century. As we have
seen, Degn (1932) reckons that in 1327 it may have been about 4000.
According to Arnbjørn Mortensen's careful scrutiny of the rent rolls of
1584 and his rather conservative calculations, the population at that time
was about 3180 (Mortensen 1954), but other estimates place it as high as
4185 in 1614 (N. Andersen 1895:37). Andersen estimates that in 1715,
the population was about the same, 4149. Thereafter we find ourselves on
firmer ground. The 1769 census figure of 4773 is generally accepted as
reasonably accurate, although according to Svabo's calculations, the population had dipped to 4409 by 1782 (Svabo 1959:166-67). According to
the meticulous census of 1801, the Faroese population was 5265. The
essential point is that a population of about 4500 was evidently near the
upper limit that could be supported without increased imports of grain.
Moreover, the population was quite healthy, except in times of epidemic
or famine. Rolf Guttesen (1971:36) has estimated that between 1770 and
1780, the death rate was "as low as 19 per thousand," an extremely low
level by contemporary standards. It was essential, then, that the birthrate
be kept equally low.

Seen in this light, the connection between the price of grain on the
continent and marriage regulations in the Faroes is not so surprising as
Hansen makes it seem. Grain was dear; the Monopoly was barely able to
show a profit anyway; the Faroese population was at the point where—
barring a suddenly improved climate, the return of pilot whales or good
fishing, or a radical change in the system of land tenure—it needed more
imports than it could pay for; and there was a tradition going back to the
late thirteenth century of controlling population growth by restricting marriage. Faroese and Danish authorities reacted conservatively to the growing population pressure by extending this tradition. I shall suggest, however, that they failed to understand the underlying causes of population
growth.

Third, the general conservatism of Faroese in the late eighteenth century, a time of enlightened reform in Denmark, cannot be traced wholly
to an ingrained reluctance to try new ways of doing things. This does seem
to be the only way to account for the failure to take up growing potatoes,
which had been suggested as early as 1780 (Tillæg, p. 84). In 1789 an
English visitor, James Wright, was told "The Potato grows well in Faroe,
but has not yet come into general use" (West 1970b:53), and though the
priest of Suðuroy, J.H. Schrøter, promoted potatoes later on, they were
not widely grown until "a generation" after 1811 (West 1972:69). Some
Faroese conservatism was perfectly well considered. Farmers rejected the
plow, whose use was repeatedly and hobbyhorsically proposed. It is un-
suited to Faroese soils and requires not only as much labor as spading but
also a horse to pull it—and horses eat hay. But not all innovations were
rejected out of hand. An improved keel invented by Nólsoyar Páll was
"rapidly adopted throughout Faroe" (West 1972:51), and Wright was told

that "Barley is separated from the straw by stripping it through the Fingers or by an Iron comb, which last is new, & likely to become the general practice" (West 1970b:49; cf. Svabo 1959:340-42).

These were small matters. In larger ones, Faroese conservatism and the unchangingness of Faroese society may be traced in part to the convergent self-interest of the largest farmers, who profited by cheap and subservient labor (this was one aim of the ordinance restricting marriage) and of smaller ones who were in effect subsidized by the state through the Monopoly.

Faroese conservatism may also be traced to a multiple cultural and political discordance. Despite all the proposals made to improve the Faroes' lot, "nothing came of it" is the century's refrain. On the one hand, the enlightened ideals of agricultural and administrative reform adhered to at the highest levels in Copenhagen were pursued only intermittently and with mixed results in the Faroes. The ordinance of 1777 is a prime example of official good intentions turned upside down by the local Danish officialdom. On the other hand, the few natives who entertained progressive ideas found no hearing in influential circles in Copenhagen and had no popular following at home. J.C. Svabo had trouble even getting paid for the research he carried out for the Danish government; and, while he favored progress, he considered that it would lead to the extinction of much of Faroese culture, including the language. It was another generation's ideals, more widely shared in Tórshavn as well as Copenhagen, that were placed in the nineteenth century at the service of a now urgently needed and popularly acceptable reformulation of Faroese culture.

Most of the data necessary for a detailed study of population growth in the eighteenth century await excavation in the Danish and Faroese archives. Still, a few general causes are clear enough. Denmark was at peace after 1722; grain was not too dear until the 1770s; and the royal monopoly was far more ably and beneficently managed than the Gabels'. Thus, despite a smallpox epidemic in 1709-10, for example, and the hunger reported in 1720, the Faroes were more secure and prosperous than they had been in the seventeenth century. Hans Debes wrote, in 1766:

For as old people in the country relate both what happened in their youth and also what they have heard from their forefathers, and which old documents also confirm, in the time when others [besides the king] had the country's commerce, supplies were so bad, especially in times of war, that the inhabitants suffered the greatest want of foodstuffs, so that they even had to still their hunger with seaweed, boiled lambskins, roots from the fields, bark and other [such things]. But since the time that commerce has been carried out on His Royal Majesty's account, they have seldom and almost never suffered any important want. [1769:22]

A more fundamental cause of population growth was a small but decisive shift in the predominant pattern of land tenure: the rise of what

Figure 3. Distribution of leaseholds, 1584-1884

A. Number of leaseholds by size of holding

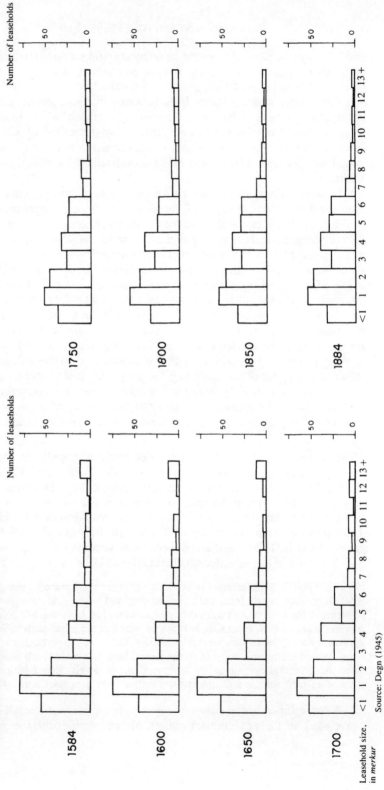

Source: Degn (1945)

B. Total lands in leasehold, by size of holding

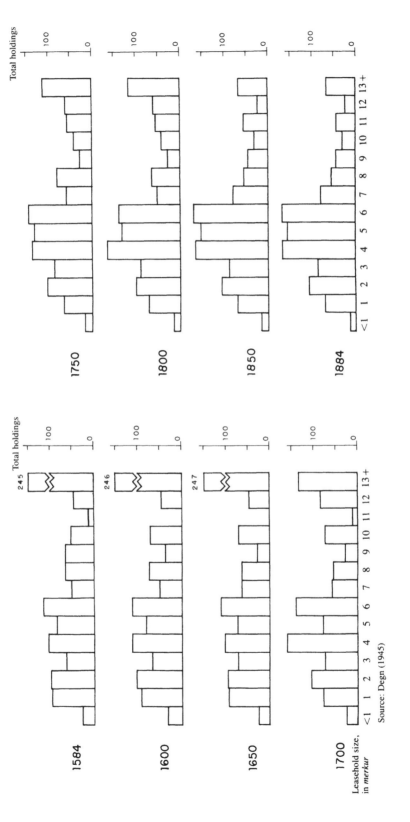

Source: Degn (1945)

might be called the "family farm." This is suggested by an analysis of the data on tenancies provided by Degn (1945) and in turn suggests why, in 1774, there was a paradoxical concern that the population was too large, but labor was in short supply.

The total number of tenancies and the total amount of land held in tenancies varied little between 1584 and 1884. There were about three hundred tenancies comprising in all just over 1100 *merkur*.[4] The average holding thus scarcely varied over three hundred years, ranging only between 3.6 *merkur* in 1584 and 1700 and 3.9 *merkur* in 1750 and 1800. This continuity masks, however, significant changes in the distribution of tenancies (see Figure 3).

The general trend, most pronounced during the Gabels' time but continuing through the eighteenth century and into the nineteenth, was toward the division of the largest estates and the combination of the smallest ones, with a resulting rise in tenancies of middling size, particularly those of 4-6 *merkur*. In 1600, tenancies of 4-6 *merkur* had made up about one-fifth of all tenancies; in 1700, they made up about one-quarter; and in 1850, they made up nearly one-third. The proportion of all leasehold land held in tenancies of this size likewise rose, from 27 percent in 1600, to 34 percent in 1700, and then to 43 percent in 1850.

It is not entirely clear why this trend began in the late seventeenth century. Changes at the low end of the scale presumably reflect a desire to combine the smallest estates in the interests of greater efficiency and profitability; changes at the high end presumably reflect the pressure to provide for one's heirs. Since it was not easy to combine or divide estates, both must have been facilitated or encouraged by corrupt or political motivations in the Gabels' time. Nor were very large estates so profitable as they might have been, since the price schedule favored the production of finished goods, mainly socks, rather than the raw wool they could produce more efficiently.

The results are not entirely clear either. That is, the available evidence does not allow them to be given with numerical precision, and we have practically no data on freeholdings. But they are obvious enough, in a general sort of way.

Most important was the growing number of estates that might be worked by family labor. Various evidence suggests that a holding of 4-6 *merkur*, and even up to 8 *merkur*, was of an efficient but critical size. It could be worked by four or five able-bodied people: two or three men and two or three women.[5] In other words, in most cases and at most points in the domestic cycle, a farm of up to 6 *merkur* would very seldom need hired hands. It could be worked by the farmer and his wife and a son or two and a daughter or two, or by any one of a number of other frequently occurring family arrangements. In Sandur in 1775, for example, Peder Clemensen, who had 4¾ *merkur* of king's land, had working for him his

Figure 4.   Two Fugloy households, 1801

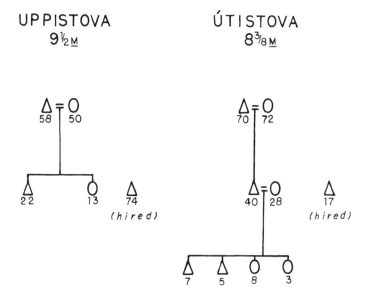

Source: Hansen (1971: 126, 133)

son, 19, and his two daughters, 21 and 16; across the fjord, on Skúvoy, Joen Hansen worked 5½ merkur of king's land with his son, 28, his daughter, 30, and two sisters whose ages are not given.[6]

Even slightly larger farms would only sometimes need hired hands. Thus on Skúvoy, in 1775, there were two men with 8 merkur of king's land plus some freehold. One seems to have gotten by without hired hands; the other had his son and his son's wife working for him, but he also hired a girl, 16, and a boy, 14 (Tillæg, p. 135; Degn 1945:238-42). Similarly, the only two servants on the island of Fugloy in 1801 worked on the only two farms of more than 8 merkur; and one of these men was getting on in years (see Figure 4). Only holdings of over 8 merkur regularly required hired hands. In 1775, on Stóra Dímun (one farm of 13 merkur), according to the sheriff, "At the home of Ole Thomassen . . . are found 8 men, of whom 5 can be considered servants fit to work; one of great age bedridden for many years; 1 about 60 years, almost a cripple, and also one who is well on in age, who must always look after the cows so that they do not fall over the cliff. 9 women, of whom four to five are mostly bedridden on account of age and other infirmity, and partly not altogether able to work" (*Tillæg*, p. 136). The number of aged and infirm people on Stóra Dímun, while exceptional, gives some idea of how, among a long-lived people, those no longer able to work were cared for.

We may surmise, therefore, that the redistribution of holdings at the end of the seventeenth century and, at a less dramatic pace, on through the eighteenth, had a somewhat paradoxical result.[7] On the one hand, breaking up the largest estates decreased the need for hired labor, while the larger number of middling "family farms" meant that more couples could have a few more children. The population could thus rise slightly. On the other hand, the larger number of "family farms" meant that more of the working population was absorbed at home, and was thus not free for hire. In short, while the population grew, the number of available hired hands shrank even below the level of a decreased need for them.

We must not exaggerate; the numbers involved must have been small, both absolutely and relatively, and scattered evidence suggests that these general demographic trends were quite complex in detail. Fertility varied by class, for example. At the low end of the scale, servants were forbidden to marry. In 1775, according to the sheriffs' reports, only seven servants in the Sandoy, Streymoy, and Vágar districts were married.[8] Near the middle of the scale, as James Wright was told in 1789, "tho' they differ in the Time of Marriage [from island to island] they agree perfectly in scarce ever having more than 2 Children in a family, which is perfectly unac-countable. In the Villiage of *Survaag* [Sørvágur] on the west end of the Island of Waggoe [Vágar], which contains about 6 Families, & from time immemorial—no one couple has produced more than 2 children" (West 1970:52). At the high end of the scale, the six women who were priests' wives in 1770 had borne or were to bear a total of thirty-one children who survived infancy, or about five apiece (Degn 1945). Overall, however, it is undeniable that the population was growing. In a place with such lim-ited resources, at a time when the population was evidently near the upper limit that the traditional way of life could support, even small changes might prove critical.

The largest farmers felt the labor shortage most. The *løgmaður*'s, bailiff's, and *sorinskrivari*'s report to the *amtmand* in 1774 indirectly sup-ports our contention that the shortage arose partly because more labor was absorbed at home. These worthies proposed a law forbidding people to "keep their grown children at home, but as soon as they have reached their sixteenth year [should] annually give their names to the sheriff of each place during his circuit [of the district], so that when anyone announced himself needing workers he could choose them from amongst these. . . . Even less should any of them be allowed to keep any [persons] at home as undertenants or workers who are required by farmers as servants or maids" (*Tillæg*, p. 105). We must come back to this report, and to the *løgmaður* himself. He was perfectly obsessed with the servant problem, whose severity he exaggerated.

We have little direct evidence, but a further result of the shift in patterns of land tenure must have been greater pressure on freeholdings, both from tenants' younger sons seeking a chance to set up house on their own, and from the poor. Some of the latter went to Tórshavn to seek what work they could find, while some, both there and in the country, lived by "wool beggary and vagabondage." Jacob Eisenberg, the priest of Sandoy, wrote in 1774 of the "all too frequent vagabondage and wool begging, which has increased not only among a part of Tórshavn's inhabitants, but even among the country people themselves, who will not know anything of proper subordination or command, but, as soon as they are rebuked in service because of neglect of diligence or some such, they rush together in marriage, strain themselves to pay rent for lands from freeholders, maybe more dearly than is customary, wherewith they can get fodder for a cow to live from, and for the rest beg wool, etc., from other people in the parish, who have somewhat greater means" (*Tillæg*, p. 120). C.R. Müller, the priest of Suðuroy, who took a slightly more lenient view of things, wrote that the labor shortage was due partly to some farmers' working their servants too hard and paying them too poorly. But it also arose, he said, because "the young and idle people, who were most diligent in husbandry all too frequently run together in marriage with few possessions or none at all; and when they beget children, then they remove to Tórshavn to be near the store and get grain, so they stand in need of life's sustenance; this they cannot get in the country, for each needs his own for his own house's sustenance; partly, too, a number of young persons remove from the country to Tórshavn in order to get easier service and less onerous work—the last of which it would be desirable not to allow" (*Tillæg*, p. 124).

These strictures must be taken with a grain of salt. The following year, the sheriff of Sandoy reported that in his district only four more maidservants were needed, and found only four or five "idle" people. The sheriff of Streymoy found in all only about forty "loose and idle" people in Tórshavn, including adults with part-time work and children, less than 1 percent of the Faroese population. Still, the priests' fears were perhaps not groundless. What threatened to develop was an impoverished underclass of "urban" poor and rural subtenants, surviving partly by charity and partly from tiny plots of rented freehold.[9]

This brings us to the official inquiry of 1774, and to the royal ordinance of 1777 that grew out of it. They offer a particularly clear picture of the state of Faroese society in the late eighteenth century and (perhaps more important) of the somewhat haphazard way the Faroes were governed. The eighteenth century saw a gradual decline in the old estate system, a gradual rise in "family farms," and a growth of the population as well. The results seem paradoxical. In 1774 some priests and officials could complain both that the population (especially of the virtually landless poor) was too large, and that labor was in short supply. The obvious remedy, although it addressed only the symptoms of the problem, was to check population growth by making marriage a more restricted privilege, and to enforce the subservience of labor. Well might some Copenhagen bureaucrat wonder acidly whether it was "quite conceivable, especially in a land where the lack of people is complained of, and that with justice, to forbid or hinder marriage" (*Tillæg*, p. 141).

The Danish background to the inquiry of 1774 is interesting, because perhaps at no other period has the course of events in the Faroes been so tenuously related to those on the continent. Although the Faroes shared Denmark's government by civil service, this rather hindered than promoted the movement for agricultural and economic reform that marked Danish affairs.

Christian VII was insane. During the first part of his long reign (1766-1808), the kingdom, in theory an absolute monarchy, was actually governed by his ministers. After Crown Prince Frederik established a regency by a peaceful coup d'état, in 1784, it was governed by the prince regent and his ministers in concert. Denmark's most pressing need was neutrality, brilliantly achieved by the foreign minister J.H.E. Bernstorff from 1751 to 1770, and by his nephew Andreas Bernstorff from 1773 to 1780 and from 1784 until his death, in 1797.[10]

The government's chief domestic preoccupation was agricultural reform, including freeing the tenantry—which in Denmark, unlike in the Faroes, was poor—from the restrictions of adscription (*stavnsbånd*), a form of villeinage. Reforms would surely have come sooner or later. Enlightened opinion was in the ascendant, and was eventually represented in the highest circles of government by the younger Bernstorff, his friend and colleague Christian Reventlow (Minister of the Exchequer after 1784), and by Crown Prince Frederik himself. The waters had been muddied, however, by the king's physician (and the queen's lover) J.F. Struensee, who, having gained control over the king, ousted J.H.E. Bernstorff in 1770 and for ten months in 1771-72 exercised nearly dictatorial powers. Struensee was himself a reformer par excellence, but so precipitous in his zeal and so devoted, in pursuit of economy and efficiency, to attacking vested interests in the civil service, that a reaction in internal affairs set in during the succeeding ministry of Ove Høegh-Guldberg (to 1784). The most important agricultural reforms were not enacted until the early years of Frederik's regency, from 1786 on.

Although the Faroes were far removed from these high-level ministerial machinations in Copenhagen, their condition did not escape official notice. In the early 1770s, officials at less exalted levels of the civil service proposed several well-intentioned schemes. But perhaps partly because of Struensee's disruptions, they were only intermittently pursued, and many were not especially appropriate in the first place. Moreover, a long run of bad fishing years and the failure of whaling left only agriculture as the unpromising foundation for any economic development.[11] Nothing came of them. In 1772, for example, the Exchequer, having briefly been abolished by Struensee, regained management of the Faroe trade. The manager proposed that an "Economic Society" be founded in the Faroes and the office of *løgmaður* abolished. The society would assume the *løgmaður*'s functions. Steigagarður, the large (24 *merkur*) estate in Sandavágur that went with the office, should be sold. The proceeds should be used to aid its buyer in carrying out agricultural experiments. The Chancellery (Danske Kancelli) did not object to abolishing the *løgmaður*'s office, but for some reason the whole scheme was laid aside. Two years later a more modest one was undertaken. A Norwegian farmer was sent to Steigagarður to experiment with various innovations, including the use of the plow. Two Faroese were sent to Norway and Denmark on similar missions. Two more were sent in 1778. Nothing came of this rudimentary agricultural exchange program, unless it was to demonstrate the impracticability of plowing.

Meanwhile, the falling profits of the Faroe trade had inspired a more comprehensive attack on the problem of agricultural productivity in the Faroes. Something did come of this, though not quite what anyone had intended.[12]

On 5 April 1774, Andreas Bang of the provincial governor's office, in Copenhagen, sent out an official letter of inquiry to sound out Faroese opinion on the trade's profits and other matters. On 28 May, apparently in the form of a questionnaire, the letter was forwarded to the Faroes' priests by the dean, Christen Jensen Djurhuus. Bang seems to have asked four main questions: (1) Why has the importation of grain products to the Faroes increased? (2) Has agriculture declined in the Faroes, and if so why? (3) Are farmers in the Faroes in want of servants for the maintenance and further development of agriculture? (4) What are the necessary means to remedy these faults? Perhaps because he himself was concerned about them, or because they were also troubling the local government, Djurhuus asked the priests two further questions. Why were young men and women coming "so frequently" to Tórshavn to seek work? Could something be done to eradicate vagabondage and wool begging, "especially in Tórshavn"? Except that the priest of South Streymoy put off answering until late July, when the Løgting met, the replies came back promptly.

Opinions were mixed. The priest of Vágar, Samuel Christopher Svabo, offered what was to prove the official interpretation. Some places once cultivated no longer were; this was due to a shortage of servants; this in turn was due to young people's going to Tórshavn. The Sandoy priest's answer, which we have already quoted, was vehement but confused. The Norðoyar priest's was vague. The priests of North Streymoy, South Streymoy, and Suðuroy (who was seconded by his chaplain) said that in their parishes there was now *more* agriculture than formerly. The dean, who was also the priest of Eysturoy, said that agriculture had declined in his parish; but his son and chaplain, Andreas Djurhuus, thought it had increased.

The priests mostly agreed that imports of grain had risen because of some combination of hay shortages, the failure of fishing and whaling, uncertain harvests, bad weather, and the death of sheep. The elder Djurhuus added that "the population's growth does something too." His son noted succinctly, "more mouths, more bread."

Most thought Tórshavn too big and too attractive to young people. They decried beggary and vagabondage, but did not think much could be done about them and were unwilling to proscribe the charity of householders who gave wool to the poor. The younger Djurhuus, among others, pointed out how difficult it was to distinguish "shameless beggars" from the "true poor."[13]

The priests of Sandoy, Suðuroy, and Vágar said there was a shortage of servants, and the priests of South Streymoy said that "some farmers may fairly complain of a lack of servants." But from Eysturoy, both Djurhuuses maintained that only those farmers who were bad masters had anything to complain of.

The priests suggested few remedies. The chaplain on Suðuroy allowed that some workers were needed in Tórshavn "when ships come," but wanted to prohibit from keeping servants those inhabitants who did not have a craft.[14] Only Andreas Djurhuus showed much imagination. He favored breaking up the largest estates and developing other industries, for example weaving or flax spinning. He said he was experimenting with home-grown flax.

When the Løgting met, in late July and early August, the sheriffs were asked a shorter series of questions: How many servants were needed in their districts? What might be done about wool begging? (They were also asked a question about horses.) Their replies suggest that perhaps only a few dozen servants were needed in all the Faroes: four on Vágar, four on Sandoy, one on South Streymoy (the sheriff did not know about North Streymoy), and "some" on Eysturoy, Suðuroy, and the Norðoyar. In other words, there was a labor shortage, but it was not acute; and certainly it was hardly so bad as to be the cause of the alleged decline of agriculture.

So far as beggary was concerned, the sheriffs all insisted, in various ways, on distinguishing the deserving poor from those who could work but would not. Some suggested licensing the former and requiring the latter to take work as servants.

So far so good. A fair reading of all the evidence might have been that agriculture was not seriously in decline; that increased imports of grain were unavoidable and were due to population growth and uncertain weather conditions; and that beggary, while troublesome and perhaps growing, was not out of hand. What the Faroes needed was not more or better agriculture so much as something else to turn to. Unfortunately, there was only the sea, which was producing poorly.

A fair reading was exactly what these reports did not get. As so often happens in even the best-intentioned development schemes, local coordination of the preliminary survey was left in the hands of someone who not only knew the least about local conditions, but had his own ax to grind as well. This was Jacob Hveding, a Norwegian who had been appointed *løgmaður* in 1772. Hveding rapidly made himself a poor reputation, especially on Vágar where, in 1774, he began a legal battle with five men in Sandavágur over rights to 8 *merkur* of infield there.[15] His management of Steigagarður and the visiting Norwegian's plowing experiments did nothing to enhance the farm's profits or his own reputation. In 1775 Hveding requested a yearly salary of 100 *rigsdaler,* claiming that there was no income to be had from the farm. However, at the same time, the sheriff of Vágar, Anders Jacobsen, wrote that "this year's grain fields on the *løgmaður*'s farm are no greater in length and across than ½ or ⅓ of what the former *løgmaður* had in his fields." A plow, Jacobsen said, was no easier to use than a spade, and the *løgmaður*'s crops were, if anything, poorer than other farmers'. He begged that Faroese be spared such unproven techniques, "for our poor circumstances will not allow us to make such expenditures for uncertain advantages as have already been devoted to the present plow, etc." Jacobsen added that "no one in the district has yet taken instruction from the aforementioned Norwegian farmer" (Degn 1945:201).

Jacobsen's observations seem fair enough, and he was supported by the sheriffs of Eysturoy and the Norðoyar. But it was the *løgmaður* who enjoyed the government's confidence. It was also Hveding who, of all those asked, was most inclined to trace the alleged decline of Faroese agriculture to a shortage of labor and the insubordination of such servants as could be found.

Hveding sent Copenhagen his own report on 8 August, which was also signed by the bailiff and the *sorinskrivari.* It said nothing directly about imported grain or the decline of agriculture, but was devoted to the labor shortage and beggary, and proposed measures to deal with them rather more extreme, as it turned out, than the authorities in Copenhagen were willing to endorse. The report begins by painting a dark picture of the consequences of the "all too frequent marriage among young persons of the commonality": "after they have married and, most often, begotten children, [they] cannot be taken on as servants" but live poorly, and pass on to their children an affection for this "pinched way of life." As we have seen, the report goes on to propose forbidding children to be kept at home after their sixteenth birthday and forbidding marriage unless both bride and groom have served an apprenticeship of six years and have gotten good recommendations.

Hveding's report then addressed the problem of beggary, recommending a scheme whereby poor people who were unable to work would be licensed to beg, while those who could work would be registered and required to serve farmers needing hands. Moreover, the poor should be sold wool collected in tithes, from which they would knit stockings to be sold to the Monopoly.[16] The idea here was that farmers spent too much time knitting, which would be a more profitable occupation for the poor.

The report then injected a new concern: the manner of paying servants. It is worth quoting in full on this point, though it is written, sometimes with elephantine irony, in some of the most opaque prose imaginable. Reflecting the attitude of someone who had trouble keeping both his servants and his good name in local society, it gives some idea of traditional conditions of labor in the Faroes' intimate and nearly cashless economy. Servants worked mostly for food and clothing, and, while theirs was not an enviable lot, they maintained a certain measure of control over their circumstances by gossipping about their employers and by virtue of employers' competition for their hire.

The usual way of paying servants is not too suitable. This consists in giving a little in cash, the rest in clothes, and food in superabundance. All that a [male] hired hand gets in money is one *krone*, which is here called "above the wage." In addition there is given yearly a woolen jacket or a wool sweater of coarse homespun, an undershirt of finer ditto, and a pair of dark homespun trousers,—all valued according to the old price schedule [?*landepris*] at 2 *Gylden* 4 *Skind*, but now most often regarded as 2 *Gylden* 10 *Skind*, and ½ a cowhide [valued] at 10 *Skind*. The rest consists in food, whereof a hired hand gets each festival day about ¼ of a lamb carcass, dried; and when haying, etc. [and] heavier work occurs, double or triple rations are given. These are real expenses to the farmer without being of any use to the servants; for when such receipts fall *peu à peu*, so either they [i.e., the servants] are given away to their acquaintances who are dwelling in and most often related by kinship in the settlement and (as commonly happens) are abusers of [the farmer's] household, or they are leased out to such people for a trifle. By this trade workers are given the greatest inducement to run from house to house behind the back of the farmer, the farmer's wife, and others. Thus it will be easily understood, what greater disorders and infidelities such occasions can lead to. To this some add a sheep and other such extra income. In a word: a hired hand serves only for one *krone;* and it will be easily understood what incentive this wage can give people rather to be ordered about as servants for hard work than to live by their own hand with the easy stocking work. But if the following most necessary ordinances were made, there would be fewer who could complain of the wage, to the extent that it would be more certain, and the farmer and his wife as well as servants and girls would all see at once their duties to each other, without ill-intentioned people being able, as easily as now, to entice serving-people from each other by offering them better conditions which nonetheless they are not intending to keep.

So Hveding and his colleagues proposed limiting servants' wages and requiring that they be paid as much as possible in cash. A man would receive 7 *gylden* a year, from which half would be taken out for his clothing. A woman would receive 5 *gylden,* "out of which she should nonetheless receive the customary clothing *in natura*" (i.e., the raw materials for clothes). Servants could not be given more food than their regular board. Finally, Hveding's report proposed policing regulations, which would be largely the sheriffs' responsibility.

Apparently having gotten wind of this report, Sheriff Jacobsen wrote an additional memorandum, dated 5 October, in which he came back to the question of grain imports. He mostly reiterated the observations of his ecclesiastical brethren (local crops often failed; Tórshavn was too big and its population too unproductive; servants were sometimes hard to find, even ones paid by the day) but he particularly stressed that some estates were unproductive because their farmers did not live on them. This was clearly a thinly veiled criticism of Hveding and the likes of the *sorinskrivari,* Peder Samuelsen.[17]

Matters hung fire for a year and a half. Then, in March of 1776, the governor in Copenhagen prepared a long report, in which he summarized the results of the inquiry and proposed in draft form what he thought were appropriate laws to deal with the Faroes' problems. He generally followed Hveding's recommendations, concluding that

The chief reason for the greater demand for grain lies especially in the decline and neglect of agriculture; this in turn has its good reasons partly in the farmers' neglect, but also partly and especially in the lack of servingpeople for the farmers, and this lack arises partly because those persons fit for service in the country frequently run to Tórshavn to live by wool beggary and idleness, partly because of a lack of good order and mutual respect [*Politi*] between the farmer and the servant, partly because of the faulty way of paying wages, and finally also partly because of young people's all too early but untimely marriages.

The *amtmand* forwarded the relevant documents to the West Indian and Guinean Exchequer and General Customs Bureau.

Another year passed while officials in this office and the Chancellery (which was responsible for writing bills for the royal signature) exchanged memoranda. A few changes were made in the governor's draft, and on 21 May 1777, Christian VII signed the result into law. By now the original concern with the Faroes' balance of trade had been almost utterly obscured: "Know all men by these presents, that We, Christian the Seventh, by God's grace King of Denmark and Norway and of the Wends and the Goths, Duke of Slesvig, Holsten, Stormarn, and Dytmersken, Count of Oldenborg and Delmenhorst, have learned of various disorders rampant in our land Faroe, particularly the now so prevalent wool beggary and vagabondage, and also wherefore abundant idleness and lack of servingpeople in the country, which again has lately occasioned greatly increased want of grain and the decline and neglect of agriculture in the land." The law has twelve articles: (1) each year the sheriff should make an inventory of grain fields, and action can be taken against farmers who grew less than they could (this provision was apparently the governor's inspiration); (2) farmers may punish servants for insubordination; (3) servants who quit their jobs unlawfully may likewise be punished; (4) masters who mistreat or refuse to pay their servants may likewise be fined and otherwise punished by law; (5) each farmer shall give his servants a recommendation when they leave his employ; (6) sheriffs will in the first instance mediate disputes between servants and masters, and false charges may be punished; (7) farmers may not give servants more food than their meals, and must "give their servants in cash the wage agreed upon between them, and the customary clothing *in natura*"; (8) "common people" wishing to marry must demonstrate to the priest that they have ½ to 1 *mørk* of land, freehold or leasehold, and both must have worked four years as servants and received good recommendations (the language here follows Hveding's, but the term of service is reduced from the six years he had proposed); (9) the bailiff shall require young men who, in his determination, are not "required by their parents" to go into the country to work, or else be pilloried or jailed on bread and water; (10) none may come to Tórshavn or take up service there without the sheriff's and the bailiff's permission; (11) sheriffs shall each year make lists of servants and of children over sixteen years of age living with their parents and see to it that farmers wanting servants get them from this pool; and (12) beggars must be licensed: idle people without begging licenses must go into service if required, while both unlicensed beggars and those who give them anything can be punished. The first of these provisions remained in force until the twentieth century; the one governing marriage remained in force until 1846, and the one concerning beggary until 1860. The rest were repealed in 1856.

On the whole, the ordinance was reactionary by both Faroese and Danish standards. From the Faroese point of view, the manner of its drafting and its extensive policing clauses further bypassed the Løgting. Its restriction on marriage recalled and strengthened those anciently embodied in the Seyðabræv. Based as they were on a biased reading of the priests' and sheriffs' replies to the inquiry of 1774, its provisions concerning beggary and agricultural labor served only the interests of farmers with large estates, if they served any local interest at all. From the Danish point of view, the ordinance was reactionary in that it reduced the freedom of agricultural labor at a time when enlightened opinion was tending in the opposite direction. Nor did it embody the single suggestion of Hveding's that might have proved progressive: a state-supported knitting and weaving industry, using the Tórshavn poor for labor and tithe wool for raw materials.[18]

It would be fitting to conclude with some notice of the effect this ordinance had on Faroese life. But there is little evidence that it had much effect at all, which is not surprising, since it addressed the Faroes' problems obliquely and in a piecemeal fashion. It most likely checked beggary and the growth of Tórshavn, and perhaps also the threatened rise of an impoverished underclass. So far as marriage is concerned, it was certainly "intolerably oppressive . . . when extramarital relations remained a criminal offence" (West 1972:55), and by promoting late marriages among "the commonality," it may have slowed population growth somewhat. Despite the requirement that servants be paid in cash, the Faroese internal economy remained chiefly based on barter and on exchanged labor, in such pursuits as sheep driving and haying. It had little or no effect on grain imports; the year it came into effect, the Monopoly slipped into the red and remained there.

Perhaps most important, from our point of view, the ordinance betokens both the growing prominence at the end of the eighteenth century of such intermediaries between Faroese society and the Danish state as the bailiff, the *løgmaður,* and the Copenhagen officialdom (Korsgaard 1982), and the fact that whatever their motivations and intentions, these authorities actually affected the day-to-day life of Faroese very little. Culturally, the Faroese remained essentially unchanged, curiously out of touch with the continent. In the seventeenth century, government policy had actively preserved a quasi-medieval society; in the eighteenth century, government policy continued to preserve it by haphazardness and earnest indirection. We might almost leave the last word to a Chancellery officer named Luxdorph: "It seems to me that this is *beaucoup de bruit pour une omelette,* and that it becomes a long-winded decree about small things, including in its provisions a quantity of forceful measures where matters will not be put in good order by force. Still, it might as well come to pass, since all concerned desire it" (*Tillæg,* p. 141).

"Since all concerned desire it." Luxdorph's phrase is perhaps the key to the ordinance's curious nature and to the general problem of the unchangingness of Faroese society in the late eighteenth century.

Luxdorph meant, of course, his colleagues in the Chancellery and their opposite numbers in the Exchequer and the West Indian and Guinean Exchequer and General Customs Bureau, as well as more lowly civil servants like the *amtmand* and *Løgmaður* Hveding. The Faroes' priests and sheriffs were little heeded, despite the elaborate inquiry, and no one seems to have consulted the Løgting, let alone the poor of Tórshavn. But at least in Copenhagen, "all concerned" with Faroese affairs do not seem to have been particularly ill-willed, short-sighted, or intransigent men. (Hveding in the Faroes is another story.) Rather, they were only distantly and intermittently concerned with the welfare of this small, poor, distant part of the kingdom. In the Faroes, unlike in Denmark, they pursued no consistent policy of reform, even after the coup d'état of 1784.[19]

Meanwhile, in the Faroes, conditions did not really favor reform, since a want of natural resources severely limited the possibilities for economic growth. Moreover, even (or especially) small farmers understandably wanted to retain a monopoly system that amounted to a government subsidy of their operations and signified the king's continuing interest in his subjects. In 1789, hearing well-founded rumors that a royal commission might recommend abolishing the Monopoly, some Eysturoy farmers got up a petition that reached one of the committee members, Captain Born of the Tórshavn garrison, just before he left for Copenhagen. The petition evidently began circulating among freeholders in the northern part of the island, and then attracted support from middling tenants in the south (Degn 1945:149ff.). "Whereas it seems to us most necessary to report on the approaching free trade, which in time will concern the land of Faroe, it is advisable that all Eysturoy stand as one man and consult together to plead with the king against free trade, since we poor inhabitants cannot expect anything but misfortune to befall us if His Majesty does not cast a gracious glance upon us" (Joensen, Mortensen, and Petersen 1955:52).

After the Napoleonic Wars, when Copenhagen again proposed freeing the Faroe trade, another advisory committee "closed [its report] with the famous words: 'The Faroes are not accustomed to, and the inhabitants would not be well served by, a freed trade'" (Degn 1929:106). As West (1972:72) comments, "The signatories on this occasion included not only the Tórshavn officials like [Governor] Løbner, who would have been expected, due to timidity and personal interest, to resist change, but also the district sheriffs, all Faroemen in touch with opinion throughout the country, and even pastor Schrøter, who was later one of the staunchest advocates of opening Faroese commerce to the world."

Finally, Faroese of a progressive turn of mind (including the young Andreas Djurhuus, J.C. Svabo, and Svabo's friend the naturalist Nicolai Mohr) did not enjoy positions of much practical influence in the Faroes, must less in Copenhagen. Even West, perhaps the closest student of the late eighteenth century and the Napoleonic period, can only conclude rather lamely that these years briefly saw "windows open on the world."

Thus in the period from the founding of Rybergs Handel to the seven years' war between Denmark and England [1807-14], the people of Faroe became ever more aware of the outside world, and the ancient isolation of the islands had almost broken down. The career of Nólsoyar Páll showed the islanders that change for the better did not need to wait for a new royal ordinance or an enlightened governor from Copenhagen, but the initiative could come from within the islands themselves. The physical and social change in Faroe during the half-century which ended in 1814 was not perhaps impressive; but the psychological atmosphere had become very different. However, a final period of stagnation was yet to intervene before the great changes which Faroe experienced in the nineteenth century. [1972:69-70]

But no doors opened, and very little air seems to have come in. There is little evidence that, except at the very end of the period and except among a few men (most notably Nólsoyar Páll, the Suðuroy priest J.H. Schrøter, and, somewhat earlier, Svabo and Mohr), the "psychological atmosphere" was "very different" for very many people. And the immediate effect of these men's labors was small. Svabo's great description of the Faroes remained buried in the Danish archives for the best part of two centuries, and Nólsoyar Páll, for all his heroism and undoubted genius, gained more posthumously and symbolically than in fact and in his own time.

I do not mean that in a Danish or pan-European perspective these were not men of their times (Helgason 1931; M.A. Jacobsen 1939). In a way, Svabo and Mohr represented the Faroese Enlightenment. They were the first Faroese to study anything except theology in Denmark; Svabo studied economics and natural history, and Mohr took up medicine and botany, as well. Svabo's description of Faroese life was undertaken as part of one of several official inquiries into the possibilities of land reform, a burning question in Denmark as elsewhere in Europe. Nólsoyar Páll has something almost Napoleonic about him: a man of humble origins, he had an adventuresome genius that shone through the cracks of a suddenly crumbling old order, which, however, was soon shored up. In this limited sense, the "psychological atmosphere" of the late eighteenth and early nineteenth centuries was indeed new, for in their own provincial way, such men embodied the spirit of the Enlightenment. Nevertheless, progressive as they may have been by the standards of their time, they stand in marked contrast to the romantics and separatists of succeeding generations: they were a tiny and, more importantly, ineffective part of the Faroese population.

Faroese society thus remained largely, if not entirely, as the Gabels had left it. Patterns of land tenure were changing (slowly); the population was growing (slightly, but to a critical level); Danish governance was increasingly direct (but at best only intermittently reform-minded); and the Monopoly kept operating (in the red). The time would soon come when Faroese conditions could no longer be left to the sporadic attentions of civil servants in Copenhagen. Moreover, the Faroes' problems were increasingly to be construed in political and cultural as well as economic terms. Since these problems were foreshadowed in the eighteenth century, we may forecast their solutions in the nineteenth century.

First, there was the perennial problem of the natural base of the Faroese economy. This base was in effect immensely expanded by the development of a commercial fishery, beginning in the 1830s. Better fishing and the revival of pilot whaling permitted the Faroese to turn to the sea, but it was also encouraged by a new and more liberal generation of resident governors, who were less concerned with the year-to-year profits or losses of the Monopoly than with the modernization of the economy as a whole. Most decisively, the Monopoly itself was abolished in 1856.

Second, socioeconomic change was forced by the continuing growth of the population. The excess population was at first absorbed in fishing, which at first expanded labor-intensively as a kind of sea-going cottage industry and then, after around 1880, as a deep-sea pursuit. By the end of the century, a growing proportion of the population was absorbed in subsidiary industries such as fish processing and in the economy's growing secondary and tertiary sectors. The Faroes now had their own middle class.

Finally, the Faroes were politically, culturally, and economically more closely incorporated with "Denmark proper" after the end of the Napoleonic Wars; but their relations with Denmark were increasingly conceived as a cultural and political matter, not just an economic one. The National Romantic movement of the early and mid-nineteenth century glorified rural and old-fashioned ways, language, the landscape, and the past, and found "folkishness" to be the foundation of "nationality." First applied to the Faroes, in the 1840s, by elements of the Danish intelligentsia and by Faroese students in Copenhagen, this ideology was domesticated, after 1889, in a culturally separatist movement that became openly politicized around the turn of the century.

What Better Thing?
The Copenhagen Connection, 1814-1855

▣ So far we have been able to treat continental events as impinging intermittently on a still almost "medieval" Faroese society. Now our task becomes more difficult. On the one hand, the Faroes were more closely
integrated with Denmark after 1814; on the other hand, they acquired a
demographic and economic momentum of their own. What happened in
Denmark thus affected a less and less passive society more and more immediately, openly posing the vexed question of how greatly Denmark and
the Faroes did (and should) differ.

This chapter concentrates on the Danish side of things in the first half
of the nineteenth century, a period when Faroese themselves lacked the
intellectual and political resources to play leading roles in establishing the
framework for debate about the islands' status. Having outlined the main
course of events (the Faroes' administrative incorporation into "Denmark
proper," in 1816; their "legislative union" with Denmark, in 1851; and the
reconstitution of the Løgting, in 1852), I will consider two critical episodes in detail: the creation of an orthography for Faroese, between 1844
and 1846, and the parliamentary debates about the Faroes' constitutional
status, in 1850. These episodes not only had immediate practical consequences, but also involved the articulation of an ideology which, when it
was finally brought home, around 1890, underlay a separatist redefinition
of what it meant to be Faroese.

Greenland, Iceland, and the Faroes had anciently belonged to Norway.
Norway itself was joined with Denmark in the fourteenth century. By the
mid-seventeenth century, the Greenland colony had disappeared, while
Iceland and the Faroes became more closely ruled from Copenhagen. In
1814, Denmark came out on the losing side of the Napoleonic Wars. It
was stripped of Norway (which passed to Sweden) but retained the Atlantic island dependencies.

This final dissolution of the exiguous ties between Norway and the
Faroes has sometimes been seen as a result of ignorance, diplomatic skul-
duggery, or Sweden's lack of interest in the distant and impoverished
North Atlantic colonies. Finn Gad, the most recent student of the subject,
finds that Britain's concern for its northern flank tipped the scales in Denmark's favor. "If it was out of the question that Britain herself should hold
them, then it was preferable that they should remain in the hands of a

89

weakened Denmark. . . . Countries were later divided without ceremony and without regard to historical tradition. The British government tried to divide the lands of the Norwegian crown during the negotiations of the years 1812-1814, but only a part of this process, the retention of the Atlantic islands by Denmark, figures in the final settlement" (Gad 1979: 204-5).

The following years saw the Faroes drawn closer into the Danish state. The Norwegian *lagtings* had been dissolved in 1797, followed by the Icelandic Althing in 1801. The Faroese Løgting survived; but it decided fewer and fewer cases; and, since 1769, the *løgmaður* was no longer a local man chosen by the Løgting itself, but simply a Danish or Norwegian royal appointee. The Løgting was finally dissolved in 1816, during the postwar period of renewed absolutism and deep economic depression in Denmark. At the same time, the Faroes were made a Danish county (*amt*). Henceforth, an appointed resident governor (Da. *amtmand;* Far. *amtmaður*) would virtually rule the Faroes. His duties included administering local laws and deciding how Danish laws should be applied to the Faroes.[1]

Denmark, like the rest of Europe, underwent periods of political turmoil in 1830-31 and 1848-49. The Danish crown, however, forestalled violent revolution by granting liberal reforms, in 1831, and a new constitution, in 1849. Thus the first quasi-democratic, official forum for debate on the Faroes' relationship to "Denmark proper" was set up in 1831, when, prompted by the French Revolution of 1830, the Danish government proposed the establishment of advisory provincial assemblies. One of these, commonly called the Roskilde Assembly because it met at Roskilde, about twenty miles west of Copenhagen, was to be for the Danish islands, including Iceland and the Faroes. (Icelandic representation at Roskilde ceased when the Althing was reestablished, in 1843.) Despite the objections of Governor Frederik Tillisch, the king and his ministers decided that the Faroes should be represented at Roskilde. Like so many decisions concerning the Faroes, this one was evidently "made on a rather random basis" (Høgnesen 1966:95). The Faroes' delegates at Roskilde, who were appointed by the king, were Danish officials who had recently completed tours of duty in the Faroes: the former governors Christian Tillisch (1836-41); his brother and successor, Frederik Tillisch (1841-44); and Neils Hunderup (1844-48), who had been *sorinskrivari* from 1832 to 1841.

After the quiet Danish revolution of 1848-1849, the Roskilde Assembly was supplanted by a more important and more democratic forum, a bicameral legislature in Copenhagen, called the Rigsdag. The constitution of 1849 did not grant the Faroes a special status like Iceland's or Slesvig's; in fact, it failed to mention the Faroes at all. Thus, almost by default, and despite the objections of ex-Governor Christian Pløyen, who represented the Faroes at the constitutional convention, the Faroes formally became an integral part of Denmark. Their actual legal status remained ambiguous, however, for even the Rigsdag's dimmest member must have realized that the Faroes' "special conditions" made special laws necessary. Indeed, a special law had to be passed in order to seat Faroese representatives in the Rigsdag at all.

The government may have meant well in framing the Faroese electoral bill, which in effect enacted what the Minister of the Interior, H.M. Rosenørn, called a "legislative union" between Denmark and the Faroes.[2] As he put the case, "Nothing better can be given the Faroese than to give them a seat here in the parliament; for what better thing can one people give another, with whom it wishes to live together, than to give it a place among its own representatives?" (Ri.2.F:3074-75). The bill passed handily in both houses, but only after sharp debate explicitly posing the question of how far a separate political status should follow from cultural differences.

The next step in the government's legislative program for the Faroes was taken in 1851-52, after their representatives were seated in the Rigsdag. This step was to reconstitute the Løgting, in name if not in its old form, as an advisory assembly on the model of the Danish provincial assemblies. Debate was again long and sharp, and was confused by the presentation of two bills: the government's and one proposed by the Faroes' representative in the lower house, Niels Winther, which envisaged something very close to home rule. The result, which satisfied no one, was a compromise heavily favoring the government. The governor would enjoy practically vice-regal powers, while the Løgting would have little independent authority, particularly since it was decided, in 1855, that the Rigsdag, not the Løgting, should determine the applicability of new laws to the Faroes. The Faroes were thus denied home rule, but were granted its institutional foundation in a reconstituted Løgting.

The period from 1816 to 1855 thus saw the Faroes made an integral, if somewhat peculiar, part of the Danish state. Meanwhile, however, a new ideology had gained ground in Denmark. Romantic, nationalistic, and generally liberal, stressing language, literature, the ennobling quality of "folkishness" (*folkelighed*), and the North's heroic legacy, it set in motion a contradictory trend in Danish-Faroese relations. In a sense, modern Faroese history may be said to begin after 1844, with the application to the Faroes, following the Roskilde Assembly's debate on an educational reform bill, of the National Romantic notion that language is "the primary distinguishing feature of a people who, it was claimed, should be granted the right to political self-determination" (Oakley 1972:172-73).

Two circumstances shaped National Romanticism's application to the Faroes. The first was one of northern Europe's most pressing issues, the Slesvig-Holstein Question. Happily, since this is not a Danish history, its monstrous intricacies need not detain us. (Lord Palmerston, the British

Prime Minister, reportedly said that only three people had ever understood the matter: a German professor, who had gone mad; Prince Albert, who was dead; and himself—and he had forgotten all he knew.) Briefly, however: Denmark and Prussia (later, Germany) laid rival claims to the duchies of Slesvig and Holstein at the base of the Jutland peninsula. Denmark's claim was based partly on the fact that they had been hereditary possessions of the royal family. One complication was that Frederick VII (ruled 1848-63) had no male heir. By the 1840s, moreover, most of Holstein was commercially, socially, and linguistically essentially German, while southern Slesvig and the towns of northern Slesvig were becoming increasingly so.

In reaction to increasing German hegemony, a growing body of Danish opinion claimed that the political affiliation of Slesvig, at least, should follow its traditional linguistic one. An inconclusive war from 1848 to 1851 settled nothing. In 1864, however, Denmark was soundly defeated, and Germany acquired both duchies (northern Slesvig was restored to Denmark after World War I, however). In its more radical forms, this opinion formed part of the nativistic "pan-Scandinavian" scholarly, literary, and political movement, with which several early champions of Faroese distinctiveness were associated. More generally, Denmark's entanglement in the Slesvig-Holstein question meant that in the critical decade of the 1840s, leading Danes of all persuasions were acutely aware of linguistic symbols of nationality and equally sensitive to threats that the kingdom might be dismembered further.

The second circumstance demands closer scrutiny: nascent scholarly interest in the Faroes' language and folk literature, based in part on J.C. Svabo's research of a half-century before. The issue here was not only the "discovery" of Faroese, but also the manner in which the language was written.

Faroese had passed out of existence as a written language in the seventeenth century. Toward the end of the eighteenth century, Svabo chose to render it with a cumbersome phonetic system, using Danish spelling conventions, diacritical marks, and his own Vágar dialect as a base. His writings included a voluminous description of the Faroes in Danish, texts of ballads, and a Faroese-Danish-Latin dictionary. These remained in manuscript, but they did not go entirely unread. Jørgen Landt, a Dane who served as priest of North Streymoy from 1791 to 1799, borrowed heavily from Svabo in writing up his own description of the Faroes, which was published in Danish in 1800, and in a slightly abridged English translation in 1810. More important in the long run, however, was the notice Svabo's renderings of Faroese received in the enormously influential Icelandic grammar published in 1811 by the brilliant young Danish linguist, Rasmus Rask.

It seems scarcely credible today that such a book could be so influential; but it was Rask's contention, still popularly held, that Icelandic was essentially identical with Old Norse and was thus a living symbol of all Scandinavia's heritage and "singularity." "The prestige of [Icelandic] after Rask's work . . . was such that it formed a model for all nativistic and puristic thinking. The ease with which Icelanders could read the old literature that was now a closed book to other Scandinavians confounded even Rask into identifying it with the [Common Scandinavian] mother tongue" (Haugen 1976:401). Icelandic, too, was then generally written following Danish orthographic conventions. Rask proposed an archaizing orthography which, in his words, would "take the language as it is, but as it is in its greatest purity, singularity, and beauty; then the difference between the old and new languages will not be great" (Rask 1811:253).

Rask considered Faroese to be one of many "Nordic subdialects" of Icelandic (1811:xlvi), and lamented the fact that Icelanders, who, after all, could "still read and understand the old sagas" (1811:253), could "scarcely understand a sentence" of Faroese as Svabo transcribed it (1811:262). "The reason," he went on, was "particularly that latterly one has forgotten the old orthography, and has therefore written the language as nearly as possible according to the pronunciation." In the brief treatise on Faroese that he appended to his Icelandic grammar, he accordingly stressed how Faroese had diverged from its "Icelandic" base.

Rask was both right and wrong; wrong, as philologists soon realized, that modern Icelandic was virtually identical with the ancient tongue and that Faroese was a "subdialect" of it; but right that Svabo's phonetic orthography masked the considerable similarities between Faroese and Icelandic. In a sense, Rask's error was more important than his criticism of Svabo. For in treating Faroese as a kind of Icelandic, he not only bathed the Faroes in the light of Iceland's glory, but also suggested a politically charged sociolinguistic consequence: "In the Faroes the old language has maintained itself in a linguistic form (*Sprogart*) somewhat divergent from Icelandic. At the same time, Icelandic has fared in the Faroes as Danish has fared in Slesvig; for although the inhabitants speak Faroese with each other, the church service is not performed in the country's language, but in Danish" (1811:240). Nonetheless, until near the end of his life (he died in 1832), Rask favored an improved but still essentially phonetic orthography for Faroese.[3] Until the 1840s, then, the small but growing interest in Faroese folk literature relied on various, more or less idiosyncratic, quasi-phonetic writing systems.

This first phase of Dano-Faroese folk-literary studies began in 1817, when a young botanist named Hans Christian Lyngbye visited the Faroes to study seaweeds and became entranced by balladry (see Lyngbye 1820a, 1820b; Gade and Lyngbye 1820). His transcriptions were poor, but a fragment of the *Sjúrðarkvæði* he recorded excited the bishop, historian, and linguist P. E. Müller, who was publishing a three-volume "Saga Library." Recognizing the ballad as part of the Niebelungen cycle, Müller encouraged its publication, in 1822 (Lyngbye 1822).

Müller's requests for more and better texts, and the further encouragement of the linguist, folklorist, and antiquarian Carl Christian Rafn, inspired a trickle of native interest in the language and history of the Faroes.
Foremost among the handful of Faroese who compiled collections of the
ballads through the 1840s was Johannes Clementsen, called Jóannes í
Króki, a sheriff's son and secretary to the priest of Sandoy, who, having
written out eighteen ballads for Müller in 1819, went on, between 1824
and 1831, to collect ninety-three ballads on his own. A balladeer himself,
Jóannes was concerned that "the old ballads would be forgotten, because
young people paid them no heed" (M. A. Jacobsen 1921:25). His concern, however, was not much more comprehensible in the upper reaches
of Faroese society than among the young. Jóannes had been drawn into
collecting by the dean and Sandoy priest, Peder Hentze, whom Müller
had asked for material. One of Hentze's successors, Frederik Petersen,
later recalled with the amused condescension of a man whose own views
have triumphed, that Hentze had been taken aback by Müller's request.
For Hentze "particularly regarded the dead languages with partiality. . . .
[He] cherished such a great respect for 'the republic of letters' that a request from such a distinguished teacher at the college must have flattered
him, so that he could . . . readily encourage what for him could only be
conceived as having a scholarly purpose. For that it also, and not least,
had importance for Nordic folkishness, a character like Hentze, who by
his whole development stood bound fast to the unfolkish eighteenth century . . . could scarcely have envisaged" (quoted in M. A. Jacobsen
1921:23).

A man with greater ambitions for the language was Johan Henrik
Schrøter, the Tórshavn-born priest of Suðuroy, who had likewise been
encouraged by Müller and Rafn. He not only collected oral literature, but
also attempted a Faroese version of the gospel of Matthew (1823), translated the Icelandic *Færeyinga saga* into Faroese for Rafn (Rafn 1832), put
out a collection of documents relating to Faroese history (1836, in Danish), and wrote articles for Danish newspapers, many of them in support
of free trade.[4]

The audience of such men as Schrøter and Jóannes í Króki was more
Danish than Faroese, however, and in neither country was it a popular
audience. Eventually the image of Faroese farmers singing the old ballads
would take its place in the North's iconography of national cultures,
alongside that of Icelanders poring over the sagas. But for the moment,
the chief importance of this early Faroese folklorizing was to alert the
scholars with whom a new generation of Faroese students came into contact in Copenhagen to the existence of a distinct and lively Faroese literature. In the Faroes, even this level of appreciation was lacking; Faroese
could not conceive that the language of everyday life and the literature of
the *roykstova* could possibly be as fine as Danish. Thus the Faroese theology student V.U. Hammershaimb noted, in 1844, that Schrøter's trans-

lation of Matthew was "flat and tasteless," and offensive to Faroese, because it evoked "the lowest sphere in their *roykstovur*. When, for example, it is said in the parable in Matthew 25 that the maidens used train oil (*lysi*) in their lamps (*kòla*) it is natural that the like must offend as religious a people as the Faroese."[5]

Hammershaimb's comments appeared in an article opposing the creation of a Faroese school system, which was proposed to the Roskilde Assembly in November 1844. Debate on this issue at Roskilde catalyzed the creation of a satisfactory orthography for Faroese—in effect, the creation of a written language, and hence a prime symbol of the Faroes' "nationality." The story is "not without a certain drama" (C. Matras 1951:9); and although its sequel has been Faroese separation from Denmark, it also illustrates how, in the 1840s, the Faroes were ideologically as well as politically incorporated into the modern Danish world through the activities of a largely Danish intellectual elite.

A bill to extend the Danish compulsory primary education system to the Faroes was presented to the Roskilde Assembly on 20 November 1844. Numerous, mostly minor amendments having been proposed, mostly by Frederik Tillisch, it was immediately referred to a three-man committee including the Faroes' current delegate, Niels Hunderup, and Bishop J.P. Mynster, of Sjælland, whose see included the Faroes. On 10 December, the committee reported out the bill to the Assembly, which spent the day discussing it. After further debate, on the twentieth, it was unanimously approved for submission to the king on the twenty-first. It became law on 28 May 1845.

The bill and the debates about it reflect an honest attempt to adapt Danish laws to Faroese conditions. This was no easy task, as the bill's immense length and detail suggest. Its fifty-two articles not only covered such obvious topics as the length of the school day and the school year; but Article 10, for example, set forth which children might be excused, and by whom, and for how long, in the event of a pilot-whale hunt (Ro. 1844:1896-97).[6] The heart of the debate, however, concerned the seemingly innocuous Article 20: "The teacher should strive to bring the children thoroughly to understand and speak the Danish language, but may nonetheless make use of Faroese in addition in instruction, insofar as it is seen to be necessary for the development of the children's understanding, or to restore a full understanding of what has been recited to them" (Ro. 1844:1898-99).

Debate on this provision was initiated by the first delegate who rose to speak, Ulrik Adolph Plesner, dean of Humble on the little Danish island of Langeland and, like Bishop Mynster (whom he opposed on the issue), a delegate for the Church. Plesner was described as the very model of a country minister by a frequent visitor to his parsonage in the late 1830s: a lively, kindly man, learned but unimposing in conversation, and suffi-

ciently strict in his morals that idle games were not played at his home
(Graae 1901:26-27). His orotund objections to Article 20 also reveal an
ingrained stubbornness. Separatist historiography later saw Plesner as a
doughty champion of Faroese aspirations (Dahl-Krosslíð 1969 [1902]);
actually, his main concern was that members of the provincial assemblies
were not elected, a topic on which, in 1832, he had composed a little tract
(H.G.A. Jørgensen 1937:27ff.; see also Nedergaard 1956:603, 636-38).

Plesner raised the question that was to underlie countless speeches
over the next decades. If, as everyone agreed, "special conditions" prevailed in the Faroes, how could Danish laws be applied there? How, indeed, could local conditions be adequately known in the first place and
the Faroese people's will taken into account, when, in his words, "they
have no official organ through which they can express their opinion
. . . ?" Plesner thus anticipated the later separatist position: that the Faroes' linguistic, historical, social, and economic conditions were sufficiently different from Denmark's that the islands should at least have their
Løgting reconstituted. Plesner suggested that the matter was particularly
pressing because the Faroes' ancient isolation, which was itself a result of
Danish policy, would soon be breaking down. He reminded the Assembly
that trade with the Faroes was not free and that "no Faroese had had permission to leave the islands without posting a bond." The issue of the
government's Faroe policy was, of course, far broader than the schooling
bill actually before the Assembly. So, while lamenting the lack of "communal organs on the islands through which the inhabitants can express
themselves," Plesner hoped that "particular care . . . be taken to respect
the desire which the Faroese have to instruct their children themselves—
something which is in keeping with their whole mode of thought." He
went on, "From what I have understood, it would be acceptable that the
Danish language be used in Tórshavn, where a greater familiarity with it
is found, while on the other hand it would be most correct that round about
in the villages the Faroese language be the customary language of instruction" (Ro. 1844:3190-96).

It is not clear where Plesner picked up these accurate assessments of
Faroese opinion. Perhaps it was through some ecclesiastical grapevine,
for at least since 1796, when an educational ordinance for the Faroes had
also been bruited (nothing came of it), the Faroese priesthood had held
that "parents out in the villages insisted on teaching their own children
. . . but that it would be best if a good Danish school were founded in
Tórshavn, and also that village children should have permission to come
to Tórshavn to go to school" (Dahl-Krosslíð 1969 [1902]:43). In any
event, Plesner stubbornly insisted that Faroese should be a required language of instruction in the villages, although he admitted the truth (as well
as what proved to be the errors) propounded by Hunderup and Mynster,
who spoke in favor of the bill.[7]

Hunderup said rightly that "In the Faroes the instruction of youth has hitherto been left, as a rule, to the parents' own care, and it has thus become in a sense a fundamental opinion amongst them, to consider their children's instruction not just as a duty, but as a sacred right." Indeed, he feared that the Assembly was trying to introduce "a *Danish* education system into the Faroes," and was failing to "take as much notice of the inhabitants' mentality and outlook (*Tænkemaade og Aandsretning*) as, I am convinced, should have been deserved" (Ro.1844:3180-81; his emphasis). But the problem was, he claimed, that "The Faroese language . . . cannot well be called a language, for it is only a manner of speaking (*Mundart*), or dialect, which consists of a mixture of Icelandic and Danish. It is well known that no Faroese written language can be had, and neither, therefore, can it be made into a subject of instruction in the schools" (Ro.1844:3198). The Royal Commissioner agreed that "since the Faroese dialect is not capable of being a written language," it might be used only in a limited way to "teach children thoroughly to understand and speak the Danish language" (Ro.1844:3211).

Bishop Mynster went further. "It is undeniable," he claimed, that "the Faroese dialect bears the same relationship to Danish that Low German does to High German in Holstein, and I do not believe that anyone in Holstein has ever demanded that there, where the popular language (*Folkesproget*) is Low German, instruction should be carried out in that language." He sought to clinch his argument by referring to Schrøter's translation of Matthew. "The Bible Society several years ago had the Gospel of Matthew printed up in a Faroese translation, written by a minister in the country there. This translation was then sent up to the islands and distributed amongst the inhabitants, but found no approbation whatsoever; it appeared to them that the Holy Word ought not to ring out to them in the language which they were accustomed to use in their daily activities, so that they appear to consider Danish as a higher language" (Ro. 1844:3206).

Mynster was right, of course, that Danish was the Faroes' high language, and that the Faroese wanted to keep it that way (although he missed the point that this insured the survival of Faroese as the language of everyday life). And he had conventional wisdom on his side in assuming that what mattered was a people's high language in a standard, written form, not their everyday speech. But the analogy with Holstein was unfortunate, since it raised the whole question of Slesvig-Holstein's relationship to Denmark. Indeed, as Rask's readers knew, the more accurate, if uncomfortable, parallel was between German hegemony in Slesvig and Danish hegemony in the Faroes. Even before the education bill was passed at Roskilde, this argument found partisans in the scene to which the story now shifts: the world of scholars, students, and pamphleteers of the national-romantic left in Copenhagen. They faced two tasks: the easier one of establishing that Faroese had its own ennobling antiquity and was not a mishmash of Icelandic and Danish; and the more intractable corol-

98 TOWARD A NATIONAL CULTURE

lary of providing Faroese with a sufficiently respectable form so that it might be seen, at least potentially, as something even Plesner had admitted it could never become: "the language of the Church or the everyday language of cultured people (*de Dannedes Omgangsprog*)" (Ro.1844:3207).

The first published response to the Roskilde debates appeared on 19 December, in a letter by "A Faroese" to the editor of the Copenhagen newspaper *Kjøbenhavnsposten*.[8] Its author, V.U. Hammershaimb, "offended," he said, by the "dubious denomination of Faroese as a *dialect*," rehearsed the evidence for the language's affinity to Icelandic, quoted Rask's analogy between Danish in the Faroes and German in Slesvig, and listed what had been published in Faroese. He predicted that if the bill passed, "the Faroese people will come to the sorry realization that one intends to uproot by force such a cherished and sacred treasure as the mother tongue must be to them." He claimed that a "guardian of the language" was to be found in the Faroes' equivalent of the Icelandic sagas, "the heroic ballads and folksongs, which to this day are preserved in such great number that scarcely any people can show the equal, without ever having been published in print." Looking to the future, however, he admitted that "a small, isolated archipelago like the Faroes, with seven or eight thousand inhabitants, cannot think of fashioning any great literature for itself."

Hammershaimb concluded by suggesting that further consideration of the Faroese schooling issue should await recommendations from the "expected district superintendancies," through which Faroese opinion might find official expression. This point was hammered home on 24 January 1845, in a long letter to the radical journal *Fædrelandet* ("The Fatherland"), by the Faroese law student Niels Winther. In his polemical style, sharp even by the standards of the day, Winther argued on moral, legal, and historical grounds that the Faroes deserved their own popularly elected assembly. As so often during his troubled career, however, Winther found himself slightly out of joint with the times. Although the question of establishing a Faroese parliament had been raised at Roskilde in 1844 and was gingerly discussed again in 1846, it did not become pressing until after 1849.[9]

The initiative now passed from Faroese to Danes; in particular, to Hammershaimb's friends Svend Grundtvig and Frederik Barfod. Grundtvig had made the acquaintance of his fellow student Hammershaimb in 1843, having sought him out in pursuit of an interest in folk literature. He was a son of N.F.S. Grundtvig, the prominent scholar, democrat, and ecclesiastical and educational reformer, who cut a leading figure in Danish intellectual life. The slightly older Barfod, a childhood friend of Svend Grundtvig's, had studied philology and the law, and was now a leader of the pan-Scandinavian movement. In April Barfod argued, in two long articles in *Fædrelandet*, that the Faroese had the same "natural right" to their language that Danish-speaking Slesvigers had to theirs. Svend

Grundtvig then weighed in with a powerful, if floridly written, tract entitled *Danish in the Faroes: A Parallel with German in Slesvig*.[10]

Most of Grundtvig's tract was devoted to a devastating critique of the opinions of Faroese expressed by the Roskilde delegates. Combining Hammershaimb's more linguistic arguments with Barfod's and Winther's more legalistic ones, Grundtvig placed the Faroese question firmly in the context of the ideology that eventually evolved, or dwindled, into the received opinion of Danish liberalism.

Whoever has truly held and seized upon the idea of the North's, of Scandinavia's spiritual unity has also recognized that it is not the essence of this unity to strive either to crowd out or to master other nationalities, or to uproot the characteristics which have developed naturally and historically among the various branches of the common Scandinavian trunk, but . . . to let each of them develop according to its own nature and essence, to let them meet again in a rich and luxuriant crown wherein each twig and each leaf has its own character, but all still so alike that they could never belong to any other tree than that from which they grew. [Bekker-Nielsen 1978:14-15]

Moreover, each people, whether Faroese at home or Danish speakers in Slesvig, has a "natural right" to have its mother tongue respected. Danes, Grundtvig said, were waging a "righteous struggle to raise a rampart in Slesvig against German's invasion, and to obtain for our southernmost fellow countrymen the right and opportunity to keep their mother tongue and nationality uncorrupted" (Bekker-Nielsen 1978:16). But what about our "small, defenseless, brother people" (1978:79) in the Faroes? Would Danes play the role of "Schleswig-Holsteiners" there?[11] Or, true to their ideals, would they voice a "recognition of the value of nationality in general, a recognition . . . that nationality and the mother tongue are inseparable conditions for each people's spiritual life and development?" "Yes!" he resoundingly answered himself, although it found no echo in Danish public opinion (1978:14).

Perhaps the most striking feature of Grundtvig's argument is the alignment of "nationality" with what we would call "culture" today, its roots (to use an image he would surely have appreciated) in nature and history, and its quintessential expression in language. Not surprisingly, Faroese would eventually symbolize their separate "nationality" in works of language, evocations of natural conditions, and recollections of a past distinct from Denmark's.

Grundtvig made two further points worth stressing. First, unlike Hammershaimb, he anticipated that Faroese would someday become the language of Church, law, and politics. These aspirations for the language seem prescient in retrospect. In the context of the time, however, they suggest that Grundtvig saw the issue in a different light than did Faroese. Mindful of the parallel with Slesvig, he apparently understood the basic issue to be that Danish was to be the language of instruction in the Faroes. But Faroese evidently did not mind that Danish should be the language of instruction; it always had been, and as Hammershaimb had written in December, "Since Danish has for such a long time been the religious language of Faroese and their legal language, they have become so accustomed to this that they do not think it a complication to have a written language different from the one they speak." Rather, Faroese objected to the attack on what Hunderup had called their "sacred right" to control their children's education and to what Hammershaimb feared might follow: the introduction "into domestic life [of] the language [which] children are accustomed to speak in school" (quoted in Bekker-Nielsen 1978:86). Grundtvig misread the Faroese point of view. As Hunderup's and Hammershaimb's comments suggest, the Faroese found the education bill threatening not because Danish itself was alien, but because government-controlled, Danish-language schools threatened the distinction between official institutions and the hearth, the written language and the spoken one, book learning and local lore, the outside world and the home—in a word, the whole precarious balance of local culture (see Wylie and Margolin 1981:81-82).

Grundtvig's second point, inevitably rather condescendingly expressed, was that having been fated "to assume the guardianship, so to speak, of its little brother people," Danes were duty-bound to help Faroese by preserving Faroese literature until at last "the national sense awakens to consciousness" (Bekker-Nielsen 1978:76-77). He might indeed have been encouraging himself, for his subsequent scholarly career was devoted to collecting and editing the immense corpus of Faroese ballads. For the moment, however, he skirted the increasingly pressing practical problem of providing the language with a sufficiently respectable written form.

This orthographic question became acute in April, when Hammershaimb, Grundtvig, Barfod, and the brilliant young Icelander Jón Sigurðsson, among others, publicly proposed founding a club "to work for the continued existence and full recognition of the Faroese language and Faroese folkishness."[12] Rehearsing the claims already made for the language by Hammershaimb and Grundtvig, the club's organizers stressed that "the Faroes are the only place where Scandinavia's old sagas have been kept alive through the course of centuries without the pen's help." Noting the analogy between the Faroes and Slesvig, they hinted that Faroese literature, when properly respected, might even prove a valuable *Danish* cultural resource in the struggle against Germany. "Indeed, a single great poetical memorial of olden times like the great epic poem about Sigurd Fafnirsbane and his lineage—a poem which can in every respect be compared with the German 'Niebelungenlied'—would, when fully collected and arranged, be sufficient to underlie a legitimate claim for the preservation of the language." They hoped that eventually, "the whole holy writ may . . . appear in Faroese," so that "a Lutheran congregation with a foreign Church language" might become "a dismal memory." The club's more immediate goals were to advertise the Faroes' circumstances abroad, to establish lending libraries at home, and, in general, to "collect and publish the poetic and linguistic memorials preserved in the Faroese language, and thereby to establish a literature to which the Faroese themselves may attach themselves, and from which the outside world may learn how to treat the Faroese language in the future."

The club's organizers particularly solicited the support of the distinguished philologist N.M. Petersen, who had just assumed the University of Copenhagen's first professorship in Nordic languages. Petersen dashed their hopes by declining the invitation in a long open letter, published in *Fædrelandet* on 13 May. His letter is a key document in the Faroes' cultural history and an important one in that of Scandinavia as a whole; for it linked the linguistic and literary situations of Iceland, the Faroes, Denmark, and Norway to a clear statement of the language movement's ideological premises.

Like Hammershaimb, Petersen doubted that "a separate literature for about 7000 people can . . . be realized." Still, the "foundation" of Faroese might be "saved from destruction" by presenting it in "a form that . . . is acceptable and comprehensible" in terms of the other Scandinavian languages: "without such a support it will languish and perish, just as Danish in Slesvig would quickly disintegrate if it could not bind itself to and take refuge with an already existing and extensive Danish literature; and just as the same fate, albeit after a much longer time, inevitably awaits even Danish literature if it does not bind itself to and associate itself with Scandinavia as a whole." Petersen thus professed himself sympathetic to the goal of giving "the Faroese people their own lingusitic monument in a written form, and [making] it accessible to others."

But his main point must have struck the club's organizers as little different from Bishop Mynster's views at Roskilde: that a language which is written down is not the same as a written language. For Petersen insisted that the club merely proposed to write down Faroese as Svabo, Schrøter, and others had done; which, he said, would produce no more than "a written rendering of mere dialectal pronunciation." Referring to the Faroes' several phonetic dialects, he said that "maybe [such a rendering] is Suðuroyish, maybe it is Norðoyarish, maybe it is Tórshavnish, but it is not Faroese." A true "written language" (today we would say a standard language) is, he claimed, a good deal more: It "is what is harmonic in the dialects, taken back to the language's simple, noble, original form. When it is sundered from that it ceases to be what it should be: the common and most noble expression of a whole people's thoughts."

In theory, then, a written language should reconcile spoken, dialectal variants in a unified writing system that itself demonstrates the affinity between the written language and its noble stock. What was required in practice was an etymologically based orthography, "particularly corresponding to the Icelandic, with which the principal sounds can be expressed precisely and exactly, but only in their most noble form. . . . [Until then] each publication of writings in Faroese must remain a doubtful, tottering business, more disturbing than beneficial." Petersen thus applied a classic statement of the linguistic ideology of the 1840s to the Faroes. The worthiness of a language, however "folkish," is limited, until a unified writing system reconciles spoken variants, demonstrates the language's noble ancestry, and aligns it with kindred tongues. "In other words: a Faroese written language must be created."

Petersen's reasoning apparently baffled the club's organizers. Hammershaimb probably saw the struggle as lost. Grundtvig drafted a reply but never sent it. And from the Faroes, Schrøter replied with a confused defense of the phonetic writing system. The club never met.

Linguists understood better what Petersen was driving at. P.A. Munch, a Norwegian scholar on the "left," or Icelandicizing, wing of the movement to create a written Norwegian language (eventually called Nynorsk or Landsmål), which would transcend the multiplicitous dialects spoken in Norway, replied constructively and at length in *Den Constitutionelle,* a Christiania (Oslo) paper, in late June and early July (Munch 1845). But the decisive moment came that summer, when C.C. Rafn, who was then secretary of the Royal Scandinavian Ancient Text Society (Det Kongelige Nordiske Oldskriftselskab), received from the Faroes a collection of magical formulas written according to Svabo's phonetic system. Unwilling to publish them in that form in the Society's *Annaler,* Rafn gave the manuscript to the Icelander Jón Sigurðsson, undoubtedly on Petersen's advice. Sigurðsson quickly produced an Icelandic-looking version, which (again surely on Petersen's advice) Rafn passed on to Hammershaimb to be checked and modified where necessary. Slightly modified, the formulas were published in the 1846 number of *Annaler for Nordisk Oldkyndighed og Historie,* followed by an article in which Hammershaimb told three folktales in Faroese and in Danish translation, together with a guide to the pronunciation of Faroese (Hammershaimb 1846).[13]

Faroese thus became a "written language" one day early the next year, when the 1846 *Annaler* rolled off the presses of one J.D. Quist, a Copenhagen printer. It was, of course, a written language in which virtually nothing was written. Hammershaimb, now a convert to the writing system that has since borne his name, partly remedied this fault in the next few years by publishing further collections of Faroese oral literature (ballads, legends, epigrams, riddles), followed by a full grammar of Faroese in the 1854 *Annaler* (collected in Hammershaimb 1969; see also Schrøter 1849-51). The grammar, which incorporated a few minor changes in his original system, established written Faroese in essentially the same form that is still used today. However, little else was written in Faroese until a fresh generation of Faroese students in Copenhagen began composing lyric poetry, in the 1870s.[14]

Two points must be made about the emergence of Faroese as a written language. Both concern the increasing ambiguity of the Faroes' relationship to Denmark.

The first point is cultural and ideological. After 1846, Faroese was theoretically raised to a status more nearly equal to that of Danish or Icelandic. No one could now claim uncontradicted that "the Faroese dialect is not capable of being a written language," or that it was "a mixture of Icelandic and Danish." On the one hand, therefore, the creation of written Faroese *differentiated* Faroese and Danish culture, and did so by selectively extending the Faroes' response to the Reformation by establishing linguistic productions as formal guardians of the local culture as a whole. The difference was, of course, that the new literary symbols of the Faroes' cultural integrity were to be, in the first instance, such written renditions of oral literature as the *Sjúrðarkvæði*. On the other hand, the creation of written Faroese *integrated* Faroese and Danish culture, by bringing Faroese intellectual life into the Danish orbit; for leading Faroese came to adopt the liberal Danish view that language exemplified "nationality," a concept of political as well as cultural relevance, whose more immediate application concerned the disputed provinces of Slesvig and Holstein.

The second point is more political and sociological. These were revolutionary times in Denmark. As always happens in such periods, established political institutions lost their grip on events, whose course was more freely shaped by fragmented parties in society at large. Thus the task of correcting the Roskilde delegates' misunderstanding of the Faroes' "special conditions" fell to extraparliamentary figures concerned, as it happened, with linguistic and "national" issues. In a sense, the creation of written Faroese was a revolutionary act, plotted in the back alleys of scholarship by a defiant little mob of intellectuals. Less picturesquely put, it resulted from a partly unwitting collaboration of members of several elites: Plesner, Hunderup, Mynster, and others at Roskilde; the Faroese students Hammershaimb and Winther; their radical Danish friends Barfod and Svend Grundtvig; and such established intellectuals as Petersen and Rafn. Neither in Denmark nor in the Faroes was there any popular participation in this collaboration. One still meets educated Danes who believe that Faroese is a mixture of Icelandic and Danish; and, more to the point, it was not until the 1890s that the Faroese language movement gained substantial popular support at home.

Until then, the linguistic "revolution" of 1845-46 remained chiefly symbolic. Not only did it lack popular support at home or in Denmark, but soon a new set of official institutions asserted control over events. The most notable such institution was the Rigsdag, the bicameral legislature established under the constitution of 1849. Here men with liberal views about the Faroes, including Barfod and N.F.S. Grundtvig, were well represented, although they remained a minority; and after 1851, there were Faroese members of parliament as well. The Faroes were thus drawn into the orbit of Danish political institutions, where the still unanswered question of their relationship to Denmark at least gained a respectable hearing. Shouldn't the Faroes be accorded a political status to match their linguistic distinctiveness? This question was most thoroughly ventilated in the fall of 1850, when the Rigsdag considered a bill providing for the election of Faroese members. The bill passed, and two years later the Løgting was reconstituted. But the question went essentially unanswered. Politically, as well as ideologically, the Faroes' status remained ambiguous.

Like the Roskilde education bill, the electoral bill was simple in concept but complex in practical detail. It represented an honest and doubtless well-meant attempt to extend Danish law to the Faroes, by granting them representation in the Rigsdag despite such difficulties as redefining property qualifications for voting rights, so as to suit the Faroes' "special conditions." Unlike the Roskilde Assembly, however, the Rigsdag in 1850 was one of those rare places where many of a nation's best minds deliberate matters of real consequence and range well beyond immediate issues to take up the principles at stake. The debates involved, for example, N.F.S. Grundtvig on one side and the redoubtable chief architect of the constitution, D.G. Monrad, on the other. The fact that debate was sometimes sharp and generally at a high level, both rhetorically and in terms of substance, is due in part to the quality of its participants, in part to the peripheral nature of anything having to do with the Faroes, and in part to the still somewhat uncertain partisan lines among the members of the Rigsdag.[15] They were thus particularly free to address the bill's premise directly and at great length. Was it right (was it even constitutional?) to extend Danish law to the Faroes, and so to create a "legislative union" between the countries? Were the Faroes like Bornholm, distant but indubitably Danish? Like Iceland, culturally and historically distinct, but suffering from a lack of "civic development"? Like Slesvig? Like the Danish West Indies or Greenland? Might they even be like Canada within the British Empire?

We shall take up only a few strands of the debate.[16] Everyone agreed, at least tacitly, that conditions were different in the Faroes; that Faroese society and especially Faroese civic life were less developed than Denmark's; that the Faroes' civic, social, and economic development was both desirable and inevitable; and that sooner or later the Løgting must be reconstituted.

Led by the Minister of the Interior, H.M. Rosenørn, who introduced the bill, its supporters insisted that seating Faroese representatives in the Rigsdag, along with representatives from "the other provinces," was a necessary first step in promoting the islands' development.

Opponents of the bill doubted the constitutionality of seating Faroese representatives in the Rigsdag at all, and claimed that, in any case, the Faroes were so fundamentally different from Denmark that the first step in promoting their development must be to reconstitute the Løgting. The opposition formed two wings. The larger one, consisting of one or two members of the upper house, or Landsting, and perhaps a dozen members of the lower house, or Folketing, led by A.F. Tscherning, rested their case primarily on legal and constitutional grounds. The smaller wing, consisting of six or eight members of the Folketing, led by Barfod, stressed the Faroes' "nationality," "individuality," and "folkishness," or, as we would now say, cultural issues.

Rosenørn's introductory remarks outlined the basic argument in favor of the bill (Ri.2.L:131ff.). A number of important matters concerning the Faroes would soon have to be considered (abolishing the trade monopoly, for instance) and the government did not want them passed without Faroese representation. In general, the bill followed Danish electoral laws as closely as possible, but conditions were rather different "up there": the Faroes had no press or "communal institutions," for example, and natural conditions and the dispersed settlement pattern made it practically impossible for voters to assemble for the district-wide electoral meetings required under the constitution. Certain modifications had therefore been made, with the help of the Faroes' governor. At the bill's first reading, Rosenørn noted that in the Faroes, "civilization stands in a much less advanced state" than in Denmark proper; thus, despite the natural but anachronistic "democracy" prevailing amongst them, Faroese themselves would benefit from "a legislative attachment to Denmark" (Ri.2.L:875). Later, he remarked that although "Iceland's historical development has taken a quite different course from Denmark's," the Faroes lay much closer to "the civilized world" (Ri.2.L:1037ff.). He implied, in short, that Denmark's duty was to civilize them further.

The bill's supporters in the Folketing likewise insisted that the Faroes were essentially a Danish province, distinguished chiefly by their backwardness; and no single province should be able to accept or reject laws passed by the *whole* realm's legislature. The country was already sufficiently divided, the National Liberal clergyman Johan Wegener said; why should the Faroes be consulted any more than any other province was? No, it would be best to "bind the Faroes to us fast and well" (Ri. 2.F:2675ff.). The minister of religion, J.N. Madvig, agreed that representation in the Rigsdag could not be left to each province's whim, and at all events did not "obliterate" provincial characteristics (Ri.2.F:2609). Kristen Rovsing added that, left to its own devices, "such a little province" probably never could develop "a true social life," especially if it was sundered from "the whole of European society" to which it was "quite naturally" bound through Denmark. If the Faroes were cut off from Denmark, not only would they lose "the good things which civic life (*Statslivet*) . . . and nationality bring," but "the state itself will come to lack the contribution that it has a full right to demand from this province just as from any other. . . . And I say: Do not ask the Faroese [if they want to be represented here], for it is highly doubtful whether this Faroese people itself can reach an answer" (Ri.2.F:2620-21).

Monrad himself summed up this point of view. Goaded by Tscherning's ironic shouts of "Hear! Hear!" he acknowledged that the Faroes should have some form of provincial organization; but we ought not, he said, to cut the Faroes off from participation in the fatherland's affairs. On the contrary, it should be offered to them as quickly as possible. "If they want it!" called out Tscherning's ally, Otto Jespersen. No, Monrad answered, "they *should* want it and they must want it, if they feel themselves a part of the common fatherland, if they do not shut themselves out from the common society that embraces us all" (Ri.2.F:2647; his emphasis). Rosenørn had the last word: "What better thing can one people give another . . . than . . . a place among its own elected representatives?"

That the bill's supporters were driven back to such chauvinistic paternalism suggests how weak they must have known their legal case to be. Indeed, Rosenørn had told the Landsting that, from the government's point of view, it would be easier to administer the Faroes as a colony; but the Faroese themselves, he said, would profit more from a "legislative union" with Denmark. Nonetheless, he acknowledged his own ministry's doubts about "whether one should establish representation of the Faroes in the Danish parliament at all" (Ri.2.L:873ff.).

His doubts were constitutional ones, and they were serious. The problem was that the Faroes had never been asked to ratify the constitution, as Denmark's "other provinces" had; nor did the constitution accord them a special status like Slesvig's or Iceland's. It failed to mention the Faroes at all. It was highly questionable, therefore, whether the constitution embraced the Faroes in the first place, and thus whether a law providing for Faroese representation in the Danish legislature was constitutional.[17] Thus A.C. Ørsted, an ultraconservative Copenhagen member of the Landsting, held that "just as this group of islands, as well in its natural character as in its whole development, is very different from Denmark proper, so they have never been included in the kingdom" in the manner assumed by the bill. The Faroese probably did not come under the new constitution; and while surely they *could* be represented in Copenhagen, it seemed "necessary that the inhabitants' voice should be heard concerning the manner in which [they] should be represented" (Ri.2.Anhang B XI:78-79).

In the Folketing, the constitutional argument against the bill was broadened to include concern about how the Faroes would actually be governed. Jespersen suspected that the government would use the single Faroese representative's presence in the Folketing as an excuse to rule the Faroes as a de facto colony. "It will be said, what are you complaining about now, now you are represented just as well as all other Danes, how can you now demand greater control over your own affairs than the others have?" (Ri.2.F:2573; see also 2916). Tscherning predicted accurately that the government would respect the Faroese representatives' opinion only when it coincided with its own. Otherwise, the Folketing would have to decide whether they or the government were voicing "true" Faroese opinion (Ri.2.F:2582).

This wing of opposition to the bill generally favored a closer association between Denmark and the Faroes, but insisted that the Faroes' civic development would depend on preserving the islands' "individuality" or "nationality." This meant reconstituting the Løgting *before* Faroese were offered representation in Copenhagen. Thus Tscherning said that the bill did not summon the Faroes forth "to become an individuality, as we desire that they may become, and failing which they will never make any particular progress" (Ri.2.F:2586). Furthermore, it was the Danes themselves who "have closed the Faroes off from Europe, and to a considerable extent from ourselves" (Ri.2.F:2635); thus the first step in "awakening [the Faroes'] political life" and so making their people fit to elect representatives to the Rigsdag must be to provide them with their own representative body at home (Ri.2.F:2640). In fact, Tscherning declared, the bill rather broadened than repaired the breach between Denmark and the Faroes, because it set up electoral procedures different from Danish ones; and because it was forced upon the Faroese, it forged no "living connection" between them and the representatives they would elect (Ri.2.F:3060ff., 3068ff.).

This part of Tscherning's argument did not rest on constitutional grounds alone, but also on the slippery proposition that the Faroes' "nationality" and "individuality" were inherently different from Denmark's.

Bernhard Rée stated the difference as a simple matter of fact: "Bornholm is only geographically separated from us, but is ethically and nationally most closely kin to us, while this cannot be said to be the case with the Faroes, which form a nationality entirely for itself, in any case a nationality which is very different from our own, a society different from the development ours has taken, from the steps whereby ours has progressed, and which taken all in all in its inner condition is distinguished in every respect from our own characteristics" (Ri.2.F:2611-12). But piling on terms like "ethically . . . kin" and "inner condition" scarcely answered the underlying question: What are the outward signs of nationality, especially among a people with no government of its own?

Language was one such sign, but it now appeared that this was not enough. Rée's remarks suggest (and Rosenørn would have agreed, although he found the Faroes like Denmark in this respect) that another such sign was a distinct history. As it happened, Rée was right and Rosenørn was wrong. The Faroes' "historical development" was much more like Iceland's than like that of Denmark proper. But as matters stood, no one could correct him as tellingly as Hammershaimb and Svend Grundtvig had corrected the Roskilde delegates about the Faroese language, for the lack of written histories of the Faroes to match either Danish histories or the Icelandic sagas left their historical distinctiveness invisible. Not surprisingly, the writing of scholarly histories, the publication of documents, and the collection of legends and the sagaesque ballads later became corner-stones of the Faroese separatist movement, along with philology and literary pursuits.

For the moment, the smaller, "cultural" wing of opposition to the election bill, led by Barfod and powerfully seconded by the elder Grundt-vig, were driven to rest their case on poorly substantiated notions of "nationality" and "individuality," and on the even slipperier concepts of "folk-ishness" and what Grundtvig called a "spiritual bond" linking Denmark to the heroic past through the Faroes. Grundtvig saw the Faroese as a kind of noble peasantry, whose civic development must depend on preserving a "nationality" as distinct as possible from Denmark's. As a matter of practical politics, however, he agreed with Barfod, Rée, and others, as well as with the opposition's more constitutional wing, that the Løgting should be reconstituted before anything else was done about the Faroes.

Modern readers may find themselves in sympathy with Barfod, Rée, and Grundtvig. The Faroes' cultural distinctiveness has now been proved, we probably agree that the proof should have political consequences, and we can gloss in terms of "culture" their talk of nationality, folkishness, and ethical kinship. But in 1850, they found themselves on shaky ground. Thus at one point Barfod was sarcastically accused of contradicting him-self. How could he claim the Faroese were different from Danes when he himself was a partisan of *ultranorskhed* ("ultra-pan-Scandinvianism")? Was he not among those who held that "Norwegians, Swedes, and Danes are the same folk?" (Ri.2.F:2575-76). He replied that he had not intended to speak of these matters, but yes, of course there were differences be-tween Danes and Norwegians; and "If I have the right to speak of Danish and Norwegian folkishness in contrast to the common Nordic folkishness, so, I claim, I may also have the right to speak of *Faroese* folkishness (Rovsing: No!). . . . But even if I myself am not permitted to speak of a Faroese folkishness, both the honorable member for Naskov and the hon-orable member for Hobro must agree with me that what I permit myself to call Faroese folkishness is less a part of Danish folkishness than of the Norwegian (Grundtvig: Yes!)" (Ri.2.F:2624; his emphasis). Barfod re-minded the house that Faroese did not speak Danish as their mother tongue.

Grundtvig carried the argument a step further. He considered it "for-tunate beyond reason, that we have retained the Faroes and Iceland," whose value for Denmark itself could "be reckoned in neither money nor power." "We must not," he warned, "be tempted to deal with them in a stepmotherly fashion," for the bond between Denmark and the Faroes maintained a "spiritual" link between "us and the old North." Indeed, the Faroes were even more precious than Iceland; for "I see in Iceland much more an embalming of the old North, and in the Faroes a living continuation of it. . . . As matters stand in the Faroes, many of the old ballads and lays, which in Iceland we see only in parchment books, have been preserved to this very day on the lips of Faroese, and not preserved on their lips only, but in the whole of their life." He concluded that, in order to preserve this precious "fragment of the vigor of old times," the Faroes needed first and foremost an institution of home government (Ri.2.F:2899). In this he was seconded by Barfod, who declared, just before all debate was cut off, that "communal government" would help to preserve the Faroes' "provincial characteristics" (Ri.2.F:3078-82).

Despite such impassioned speechifying the bill passed by wide majorities in both houses, whose foreman announced, on 3 January 1851, that the king had signed it into law. Rightly or wrongly, constitutionally or unconstitutionally, the Faroes were joined with Denmark in a legislative union that still endures; for the Faroes still send representatives to Copenhagen. The union, however, was ambiguous. Not only was the extension of Danish law to the Faroes of doubtful constitutionality; but it involved giving a respectable hearing to an ideology maintaining, essentially, that formal demonstrations of cultural distinctiveness constitute valid claims to political recognition. Language was the most important area in which such demonstrations might be made. Others include history and natural, demographic, and other "special conditions." At least so far as the Faroes were concerned, the national-cultural ideology enjoyed only minority support in the Danish legislature, and the strength with which it was articulated had less to do with the Faroes than with Danish domestic politics and intellectual life. Nor, as we shall see in the following chapters, did Faroese domesticate it and turn it to the cause of separation from Denmark until the decades around the turn of the century. Even then, I shall suggest, its adoption was not a reaction to Danish hegemony so much as a response to domestic conditions: the threatened demise of the traditional way of life and the rise of a native intelligentsia and middle class.

Before turning to this later, more Faroese side of things, however, we must tie up a few loose ends on the earlier, more Danish side.

The education ordinance proved a dead letter. Faroese simply refused to obey it, and it was repealed in 1854. Repeal was followed, however, by "widespread interest in elementary education in the villages."[18] A number of village schools were founded, and in 1872 the reorganization of Danish (and Faroese) townships (*kommuner*) vindicated the Faroese desire to maintain local control over education, by making each township responsible for its children's schooling. The language of instruction was supposed to be Danish, but for practical and, increasingly, ideological reasons, teachers did more and more of their work in Faroese.

Elections for the Faroes' two seats in the Rigsdag were held in July 1851.[19] Faroese narrowly rejected the "official" candidate for the Folketing, Bailiff J.A. Lunddahl, who held moderately liberal views. Instead they chose Niels Winther. Winther's views were radical even by Copenhagen's standards, and as his narrow margin of victory suggests (he won by only 37 votes), the deciding factor was undoubtedly that Faroese simply preferred to have their own countryman representing them. To the seat in the Landsting, they elected the well-to-do farmer J.H. Weyhe, a far more plodding, conservative man than Winther, but scarcely a pawn of Danish officials. On the whole, "the election was . . . a vote of no confidence in the officials, whom until a few years previously the population had obeyed with a deference and timidity bordering on slavishness" (Steining 1953:120).

Parliament's first order of business for the Faroes was to reconstitute the Løgting. Bills to do so were introduced by Frederik Tillisch, who had replaced Rosenørn as minister of the interior, on 6 December 1851, and by Winther on the eighth. The bills' tortuous course through the Rigsdag, the long, uneasy debates about them, and the law that eventually resulted amply justified Tscherning's and Jespersen's fears that the government would continue to treat the Faroes as a de facto colony, despite (or because of) their representation in Copenhagen.[20] Essentially, Winther was out-maneuvered. He had announced his intention to present a bill earlier, but Tillisch stole a march on him by hastily presenting his own bill first. Winther chaired the committee appointed to reconcile the bills, but when his own bill's provisions were brought to the floor, as amendments to Tillisch's, they were voted down piecemeal.

Winther envisaged something very close to home rule for the Faroes. Technically the Løgting would have had no legislative power, which was constitutionally reserved to the Rigsdag. But it might propose bills to Copenhagen, and could very largely have determined the extent to which Danish laws would be applicable to the Faroes. The Løgting would elect its own chairman. The governor would be a nonvoting member. Tillisch's bill, on the other hand, made the governor ex officio chairman of the Løgting, whose recommendations he could effectively veto. To all intents and purposes, the Løgting was an advisory board he might consult at his pleasure. It was basically Tillisch's bill, somewhat watered down, that became law on 26 March 1852.[21]

The Rigsdag was not happy with either bill, or with the compromise it struck. Some members who had championed the Faroes' "individuality" the year before now shied away from granting it an institutional form. Tscherning, for example, reminded the Folketing that "When we pass laws for the Faroes at this moment, we must not only consider them as that curious combination of a colony and a separately governed country, cut off from the rest of the world." The Faroes would change, gaining an "inner life" and even "a certain measure of European importance," while in time "their population will acquire a quite different character"

(Ri.3.F:1903). But he feared that Winther's proposals would "put the Faroes on a quite different footing." "Yes, I hope so too," called out Jespersen, with whom Tscherning now found himself at odds. Well, Tscherning replied lamely, it might not be "the footing on which we might want to treat the Faroes in the future" (Ri.3.F:3704). Jespersen disagreed: "Really, we should not be so jealous of the institutions we ourselves create." Winter's proposal was "the least we can offer the Faroese with any decency" (Ri.3.F:3697).

The practical question was, of course, who should oversee the Faroes' development, the Faroese themselves, or the governor? Recalling his own days there, Tillisch maintained that such a backward province required a governor enjoying wider powers than his Danish counterparts'. However, this paternalism failed to envisage not only what might happen when the Faroese finally acquired a "quite different character," but also, as Winther pointed out (Ri.3.F:1893), that the governor and the people might ever disagree. *Then* who would have the last word?

It is an open question whether the Faroese would in fact have been capable of the degree of self-rule Winther proposed. But by stopping short of granting the Faroes any real legislative autonomy, the Rigsdag created an inherently weak system of government: an advisory Faroese parliament, with legislative power invested in the Rigsdag and executive power in the Danish administration. It made the governor legally responsible to Copenhagen, but morally responsible to the Faroese people among whom he lived. A great deal would depend on the personality of the governor; as it happened, the incumbent, Carl Emil Dahlerup, though "able and conscientious" enough, was unfortunately also stiff-necked and patronizing and "did not take kindly to sharing his authority with an elected body" (West 1972:94).[22] He immediately antagonized the Løgting, alienating even his natural ally on it, the dean. The Danish government sensibly removed him from office in 1861; but until the governorship was abolished, in 1948, the Faroes' relations with Denmark were bedevilled by local attempts to appeal to Copenhagen over the governor's head.

By the time Dahlerup left the Faroes, Winther had also removed himself from the scene. Having agitated for a revived Løgting as early as 1844, he had long been a thorn in the side of the Faroes' Danish officialdom. In 1852 he brought home a printing press and started a newspaper (written in Danish) in which he criticized the Monopoly in a way the officials found defamatory. He was fined heavily, and the paper ceased publication. In the Folketing, he continued to work for free trade, but as soon as the Monopoly was abolished, he resigned his seat. Embittered by the difficulty of getting anything done for the Faroes and by the lack of support for his programs either in Copenhagen or at home, he retired to practice law in a little town in north Jutland.

Fresh from Copenhagen's heady atmosphere, Hammershaimb returned to the Faroes in May 1855, to take up pastoral duties in Kvívík. There, in the last few hours of the Monopoly's existence, he faced one of the most poignant moments in Faroese history. On New Year's Eve, 1855, he read out the Gospel in Faroese; "people were so amazed and outraged that he never dared try it again" (C. Matras 1935:55).

The Transition from Monopoly
Social Change in the Faroes, 1856–1920

◙ Four changes define the trajectory of Faroese social history in the nineteenth century. The trade monopoly was abolished in 1856. Fish replaced wool as the main export. The population tripled, rising from 5265 in 1801 to 15,230 in 1901. And the proportion of Faroese supported by what the censuses call "agriculture" fell from over 80 percent to under 30 percent, although the absolute number remained nearly constant, at around 4400. In short, a growing population was supported by an expanding and increasingly diversified economy based on an export fishery.

Except for the abolition of the Monopoly, these were trends, not sudden events; and except that the economic importance of "agriculture" soon waned along with the eclipse of the old-fashioned style of inshore, openboat fishing, they were trends that continued into the new century. It is convenient, then, to distinguish four rough phases of socioeconomic change between 1800 and 1920. They correspond, not so coincidentally, to phases in the Faroes' cultural and political life.

Until 1856, rather tentative economic growth was accompanied, as we have seen, by some native and Danish folklorizing and the preliminary formulation, in Copenhagen, of a new sense of Faroese cultural and hence political identity. From the abolition of the Monopoly until the late 1880s, a final efflorescence of the traditional way of life was accompanied by few cultural or political events of any consequence at home; but in Denmark, the Faroese language was first turned to nontraditional uses. In the 1890s, as the deep-water fishery expanded rapidly and the population continued to grow, formal expressions of the Faroes' cultural distinctiveness, based partly on an idealization of the now clearly threatened traditional way of life, proliferated and gained wide acceptance. Finally, the first two decades of the twentieth century saw population growth peak, the economy modernize and diversify further, and a complex politicization of Faroese life accompanied by the establishment of a national culture.

The present chapter surveys social, economic, and demographic changes in the second half of the nineteenth century and the first decades of the twentieth. The next chapter will take up cultural and political developments after about 1890.

Population pressure was the most direct agency of socioeconomic change in the Faroes in the nineteenth century. Various evidence (the inquiry of

Table 1.   Population growth and urbanization in the Faroes, 1801-1980

	Population			Est. yearly growth rates (%)		
Year	All Faroes	Tórshavn	% Tórshavn	Faroes	Outside Tórshavn	Tórshavn
1801	5265	554	10.5			
1834	6928	721	10.4	0.83	0.84	0.80
1840	7314	714	9.8	0.91	1.02	−0.17
1845	7781	801	10.3	1.24	1.13	2.30
1850	8137	841	10.3	0.90	0.88	0.98
1855	8651	856	9.9	1.22	1.32	0.36
1860	8922	823	9.2	0.61	0.67	−0.78
1870	9992	918	9.2	1.13	1.13	1.09
1880	11220	984	8.8	1.16	1.20	0.70
1890	12955	1303	10.1	1.48	1.29	2.81
1901	15230	1656	10.9	1.47	1.38	2.18
1906	16349	1791	11.0	1.40	1.39	1.58
1911	18000	2097	11.7	1.92	1.76	3.16
1921	21352	2496	11.7	1.71	1.71	1.74
1925	22835	2896	12.7	1.69	1.39	3.71
1930	24200	3200	13.2	1.17	1.03	2.00
1935	25744	3611	14.0	1.24	1.05	2.40
1945	29178	4390	15.0	1.25	1.13	1.96
1950	31781	5667	17.8	1.71	1.03	5.11
1955	32505	6067	18.7	0.45	0.24	1.37
1960	34596	7447	21.5	1.24	0.53	4.89
1965	37205	9730	26.2	1.45	0.24	5.35
1970	38612	11695	30.3	0.75	−0.42	3.68
1980	43609	13757	31.5	1.22	1.04	1.63

1775, the Monopoly's perennial deficits from 1777 on, and the immediate threat of famine when imports were briefly cut off in 1807-8) suggests that, given the monopoly system, traditional agricultural and fishing techniques could support at most around 4500 people. In 1769 the population was estimated to be 4773, and as we have seen, an attempt was made in the 1770s to check further growth by restricting people's opportunity to marry. We cannot judge in detail how effective these measures were, but in all likelihood, the birth rate stood little higher than the death rate in the late eighteenth century, around 19 per thousand (Guttesen 1971:134-36).

By 1801 the population had nonetheless crept up to 5265. It rose to 6928 in 1834, representing an average growth rate of about 0.8 percent per year (see Table 1 and Figure 5). By 1855 it had risen to 8651, spurred by the birth rate's rise to about 27 per thousand between 1840 and 1859. As the death rate fell only slightly and emigration was negligible, the population as a whole was growing by about 1 percent per year. The death rate remained nearly constant into the 1880s, while the birth rate rose steadily to 31 per thousand. Thus in the 1880s, the population was growing at an annual rate of about 1.5 percent. In 1890 there were 12,955 Faroese, nearly two and a half times as many as at the turn of the century. The decades around 1900 were marked by erratically falling death rates (to about 11 per thousand between 1906 and 1920) and erratically rising birth rates (to nearly 33 per thousand between 1911 and 1915). Since there was still no emigration to speak of, the population was growing by as much as 1.9 percent per year between 1906 and 1911. By 1921, the total Faroese population was 21,352, or about four times what the traditional economy could have supported.

These observations pose two related questions. First, what factors external to Faroese society caused the vital rates to change? And second, what internal economic changes both encouraged further population growth and enabled Faroese society to accommodate its growing membership? Neither question can be answered with numerical precision. It is clear, however, that external factors played a relatively small role, and that the chief internal one was the rise of an export fishing industry.

The death rate was probably most directly affected by external factors, particularly the improvement or creation of medical, midwifery, and apothecary services from the early 1870s on (Trap 1968:133ff.). It is possible, too, that Faroese acquired greater resistance to imported diseases as contact with Danes and other foreigners became more regular after 1856. In 1860, for example, a visiting British yachtsman noted that "English and Scottish vessels frequent the islands in great numbers for the fisheries."[1]

The restrictions on marriage were repealed in 1846. There is little or no evidence that this had any effect on the birth rate, since by that time the loosening of trade restrictions and the wages men might earn from fishing, and both men and women might earn processing fish, had rendered the law a dead letter. More telling was the easing of the ecological constraints that had made the restrictions necessary in the first place, through the widespread adoption of the potato and the greater exploitation of marine resources.

The short growing season had always stunted Faroese agriculture. As the British naturalist W.C. Trevelyan noted, in 1835, "The only corn which is generally cultivated is a hardy variety of barley . . . and that does not always ripen. Oats and rye have been tried, but seldom with success."[2] Until well into the twentieth century, Faroese farmers continued to tend plots of barley or even, here and there, what a later British visitor described as "a field of rye some fifteen yards by five, the heads of irregular height and separated from each other by inches" (Edwardes 1885:124). Such cultivation was undoubtedly favored by the general warming of the climate in the northern hemisphere; but it had little economic or dietary

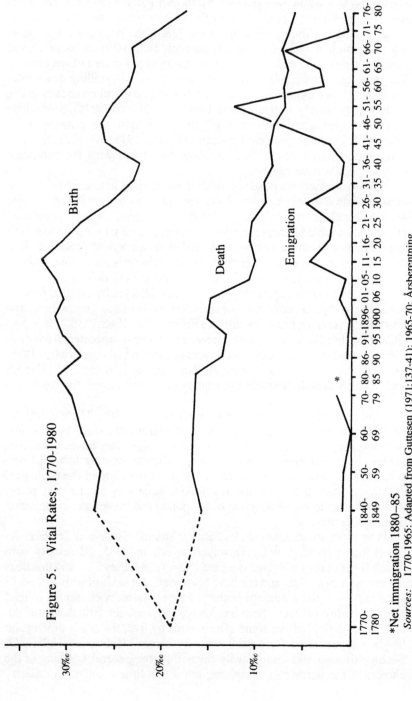

Figure 5. Vital Rates, 1770-1980

Birth

Death

Emigration

*Net immigration 1880–85
Sources: 1770-1965: Adapted from Guttesen (1971:137-41); 1965-70: Ársberentning
1972:18; 1971-80: Ársfrágreiðing 1980:53-54

1770- 1840- 50- 60- 70- 80- 86- 91- 96- 01-05- 11- 16- 21- 26- 31- 36- 41- 46- 51- 56- 61- 66- 71- 76-
1780   1849   59   69   79   85   90   95   1900 06 10   15   20   25   30   35   40   45   50   55   60   65   70   75   80

30‰

20‰

10‰

importance. For, as Trevelyan also found, "potatoes thrive well" in the Faroes, and, being a rich and relatively reliable source of carbohydrates, helped alleviate the land pressure produced by a growing population. Potatoes had in fact been introduced to the Faroes in the eighteenth century. In 1797-98, for example, the commandant of the fort at Tórshavn had an experimental plot for his men (Degn 1945:3-4; see also Dalsgaard 1964). But it was not until the 1820s and 1830s that they became widely grown; and by 1839 Governor Pløyen could remark, "There are scarcely any households in Faroe in which potatoes are not eaten at least once in the day. It is to me almost inconceivable in what manner the Faroese subsisted before the introduction of this blessed tuber" (1896:23).

Another natural limit on population growth in the eighteenth century had been the repeated failure of the fishery and the virtual disappearance of pilot whales. Undoubtedly for reasons connected with the warming of the climate, fishing improved in the first decades of the nineteenth century, and vast numbers of pilot whales reappeared in the 1840s.[3] Whale slaughters helped tide Faroese over failures of the potato crop. Thus on Christmas Eve, 1852, a Faroese correspondent (undoubtedly Schrøter) wrote Trevelyan that "the potato disease continues, and it has been worse this season. . . . As the potatoes failed, the inhabitants would have been badly off, but abundance 'of whales' having been caught last season, in some way made up for the loss" (Trevelyan 1853:380).

In the long run, however, the most important cause of population growth was the rise of an export fishing industry capable of supporting more people. Faroese had always fished, of course. It has been said that "The farmer was a fisherman-farmer," and "More than the keeping of sheep or cows the fishery seems to have determined whether the times would be good or bad" (E. Patursson 1961:15; L. Zachariasen 1961:87). But the commercial exploitation of the sea was something new. Its beginnings were encouraged by the loosening of trade restrictions, in the 1830s and 1840s, when the Monopoly reluctantly carried out several small but significant reforms at the urging of Governors Christian Tillisch (1825-30), Frederik Tillisch (1830-37), and Christian Pløyen (1837-48), and that of Nólsoyar Páll's almost equally remarkable brother Jacob Nolsøe, who managed the Monopoly store in Tórshavn between 1831 and 1850. Branch stores were opened in Tvøroyri (1836), Klaksvík (1838), and Vestmanna (1839). The Monopoly began to buy small cod in 1834; dry-salted cod (klipfish) in 1837; flatfish and ling in 1838; liver, blubber, and train oil in 1846; and, perhaps most important, fresh fish for processing in 1845. As early as 1841-50, fish and fish products accounted for nearly 40 percent of Faroese exports by value.[4]

The Monopoly's days were numbered. It was, in Governor Pløyen's striking phrase, "the great hinge upon which the whole affairs of the islands turn" (1896:15). It had effectively subsidized Faroese agriculture and had done much to preserve a highly conservative culture. In 1789 and again in 1816, Faroese had pleaded that it be retained, and in the 1830s and 1840s, the Monopoly's management in Copenhagen still argued that the Faroes' slight population and "inconsiderable" productivity would "place great dangers in the way of free trade, if this were not to come into conflict with the State's financial and commercial interests" (quoted in Joensen, Mortensen, and Petersen 1955:73). But by that time, the Monopoly was quickly losing the support it had once enjoyed in the Faroes. For one thing, the Faroes' governors, unlike the bailiffs of former times, were career civil servants who lived year-round in the Faroes and had no vested interest in the fortunes of the Faroe trade. Pløyen and the Tillisch brothers, in particular, were well-meaning men with liberal (if sometimes patronizing) views, whose program for economic reform envisaged the Monopoly's abolition.

As for the Faroese themselves, Pløyen acknowledged, in 1839, that "the bulk of [them] have hitherto been afraid of the crisis which the transition from monopoly must bring with it." Nevertheless, he went on, "the last four or five years have had a marked influence on Faroese views upon this question." He traced the change of heart to the founding of the Monopoly branch stores; or, rather, to the "disappointed expectations" that these would bring prosperity, which, he said, "have in a far greater degree than could have been foreseen called forth in the breasts of Faroese a craving for Free Trade, a craving which, especially in the younger generation, who by a superior education are more accessible to new ideas, is warm and lively" (1896:204-5).

By the 1840s it was clear to almost everyone that the Monopoly would have to go, and that the fishery promised to become prosperous enough to prevent the islands' becoming, or remaining, a charity case.[5] In 1851 the Folketing voted to free the Faroe trade "at the latest with the end of the 1852-1853 fiscal year" (Joensen, Mortensen, and Petersen 1955:73). Abolition was delayed, however, until the Faroese representatives secured guarantees that the trade would be open to merchants of all nations, that any person residing in the Faroes might become a merchant once he or she had taken out the appropriate papers, and that mercantile establishments would not be limited to Tórshavn and the three sites where branch stores already existed. The Monopoly was abolished under these conditions by a law of 21 March 1855. When it came into effect at the new year, "a new time had come" (Joensen, Mortensen, and Petersen 1955:74).

The Faroes did indeed enter upon a new age on New Year's Day, 1856. No longer living in a "closed land" (Degn 1929:1), Faroese could now trade both among themselves and directly with merchants of any nation, at home or abroad. At the same time, fish overtook wool as the Faroes' main export, and proved a vastly more profitable one. Spurred by a doubling in the price for fresh fish between 1845 and 1874, the average yearly exports of fish rose from about 200 tons in the 1840s to over 2100 tons in between 1876 and 1885 (E. Patursson 1961:5, 55). But a crucial fact must be emphasized: the new economic order did not at once destroy the old. Despite a number of economic, social, and technological changes, the chief immediate effect of the Monopoly's abolition was a long, final flowering of old-fashioned rural life.

Between 1856 and 1858, 103 men and 1 woman took out merchant's papers. Twenty-one of them lived in Tórshavn, and the rest in forty-two other communities (Joensen, Mortensen, and Petersen 1955:95-102). Their businesses varied greatly in size. At one extreme stood a handful of wholesale and import-export firms in Tórshavn, Tvøroyri, Vestmanna, and Klaksvík. At the other extreme we find, for example, that in 1857, Skopun (a fishing hamlet and port of entry for Sandoy) boasted two merchants among its nine or ten households (Clementsen 1983:21-24). But on whatever scale they operated, the merchants were the prime agency by which cash began to percolate through the Faroese economy. They not only took over the functions of the Monopoly, acting as brokers for imported goods and buying, processing, and selling wool; they also created a market for wage labor (as opposed to the salaried labor of farmers' hired hands) by paying villagers, including women and girls, to process the fish they bought from local fishermen and sold for export. Merchants served as informal bankers, as well. A savings bank, one of the first in Denmark, had been founded in Tórshavn as early as 1832. In 1833 it had 42 accounts, worth 4,608 *kroner;* by 1858 it had 393 accounts, worth over 56,000 *kroner.* But thereafter, merchants increasingly attracted people's savings by offering higher interest rates (Joensen, Mortensen, and Petersen 1955:161-63). By the 1880s, some merchants had accumulated enough capital to buy, or back the buying of, most of the fleet of fishing ships that began to come to the Faroes, and whose advent brought about "what might be called the period of the Faroese industrial revolution" (West 1972:130).

Until then fishing remained essentially a sea-faring cottage industry based in the Faroes' many villages, an intensification of the age-old style of subsistence fishing called *útróður* ("rowing out"). Carl Julian Graba, a young German who visited the Faroes in 1828, offers a fine description of what *útróður* entailed. A neglected minor classic of travel literature, Graba's *Reise nach Färö* is the first and in many ways the best account of Faroese life written by the growing number of travelers and tourists who visited in the nineteenth century.

If the Faroeman goes to sea, he dons a jacket and long trousers of thickly sewn sheepskin leather, well suited to keep out rain, wind, and seawater. Over his head he casts a kind of black woolen cloth, which covers the forehead and neck, and also protects the neck from storm and wet with a prolongation attached behind. . . .

The boats are long and narrow, sharp at both ends, and furnished with a high

stem that reaches above the planks so that one can grasp it with the hand and so
be able to stop the vessel. Two rowers sit on each bench, and so close together
that some practice is necessary lest their hands and oars disturb each other. The
oar is very light and narrow, and is stuck through a thong of whaleskin fastened
to a peg. Thus Faroemen have the advantage of being able to employ their oars
on all sides equally well backwards and forwards. . . . Rudders are used only
under sail—which seldom happens, for the sail is reckoned to be worth only two
men in moderate winds, so that an eight-man boat then needs only six men. The
sea is seldom so calm that one does not become wet through with the waves; only,
this troubles the Faroeman little, unless a wave half fills the boat. If they cannot
escape a tumbling wave or a breaking sea, then they try at once to turn the bow
and bail the water out quickly before a second wave can fill the vessel. . . .

A piece of dried meat, a barley loaf, and the full water keg accompany him
on the sea, where he often works for twenty-four hours, wet through from rain
and dashing waves, and in constant danger of being surprised by a storm, in order
to be able, perhaps, to bring home a halibut, which must then be divided among
the four fishermen (as a rule, this many go out together), the owner of the boat,
and the Church, which will have its tithe. If the catch is lucky, an individual may
earn a *thaler*—but how seldom is this the case, and how seldom does the stormy
sea permit going fishing! More than twice a week we could not easily obtain fresh
fish, and this in the best season. [Graba 1848:14, 16, 23]

Graba might almost have written these lines a century earlier—or
fifty or even a hundred years later.[6] For technological changes came
slowly. Perhaps most important was a belated, partial shift from handlines
to longlines. In 1839 Pløyen had taken several Faroese to Shetland, where
they learned of long-lining; but longlines were not used in the Faroes until
about 1850. They remained uncommon for many years, and as late as
1887, hand-liners were urging (vainly) that long-lining be banned (E. Patursson 1961:19-21). The quality of hooks and cordage improved, but
other gear remained little changed. In March of 1887, for example, it was
reported that when the only survivor of a four-man crew was rescued at
sea, clinging to his overturned boat, he was wearing rubber boots. One of
them had been worn through in his struggles to keep ahold of the keel, an
almost folkloric motif that suggests how notable such gear still was (*Dimmalætting*, 26 and 30 March 1887).

Other, more significant changes involved the size of boats used and
the practices of manning them and rewarding their crews. These and other
changes revitalized the rural economy and allowed it to support the growing population.

Population pressure was slightly relieved, at the governors' urging,
by founding or refounding settlements. Nineteen such settlements were
made between 1800 and 1850, including at least ten in the 1830s (R.
Joensen 1966). Five more were founded between 1850 and 1910. Three
of these new settlements, as well as four older ones, were later abandoned, mostly in the twentieth century; many remained small, but a few
prospered. Skopun, for example, where Governor Pløyen persuaded two

families to settle, in 1833-34, had over 200 inhabitants by the turn of the century. Today it is a prosperous fishing village with a population of 578 (Clementsen 1983:26; Ársfrágreiðing 1980:56). Tvøroyri, the Suðuroy landing place where a Monopoly branch store was set up in 1836, became an early center of "ship fishing" and was the Faroes' second-largest community by the turn of the century (see P. Nólsøe 1963–70, 2[1]:9-10).

Village populations also grew because farmers responded to the greater profits that might be made from fishing by taking on additional hired hands. In 1801, for example, only two of the six households in Hattarvík, on Fugloy, had hired hands (see Table 2). Both were men, who worked on the only two farms of over 8 *merkur* on the island. As early as 1834, there were six hired hands in Hattarvík. Four of them were men, an additional one on each of the two largest farms. By 1860, there were ten hired hands in the village, including six men. As before, four of them worked on the two largest farms, but the other two were members of the already swollen households of Innistova and Uttarstova, whose holdings of 4½ and 3¼ *merkur* were too small to need extra hands for farm work alone. Thereafter, the number of hired hands in the village dwindled, as growing families could satisfy their own labor requirements. In Hattarvík and elsewhere, some of the surplus population stayed home, fishing more heavily as the land was increasingly split apart by inheritance. The rest may have contributed to the first trickle of emigration from the Faroes, in the 1870s, and otherwise began drifting to Tórshavn and the towns where the more industrial style of "ship fishing" grew up, in the 1880s.

Another early trend was a shift toward using smaller boats, which allowed more men to earn an independent living from the sea. In 1828, Graba noted that "as a rule," four men went out together. In fact, four-man boats had customarily been used chiefly for summer fishing, when the sea was calmer. Eight-, ten-, or twelve-man boats were used in the spring and fall. But between 1810 and 1858, in the Norðoyar (and surely elsewhere in the Faroes, as well) the number of larger boats remained nearly constant, while the number of four-man boats grew by over half (see Table 3). Using smaller boats was perilous, as the March drownings mentioned above suggest; but in part because the smaller boats were less expensive, it undoubtedly allowed village fisheries to support more individuals.

Meanwhile, customs of distributing the catch and the profits from its sale were modified to meet changing conditions. The general rule under the old system was first to take out a few fixed shares and a few species (called *sjálvsdráttarfiskar*) reckoned to be the property of the man who caught them, then to set aside one-tenth of the remainder for the tithe (abolished in 1892), and to divide the rest so that each man and the boat received a share (Svabo 1959:100). These customs were extended from the catch itself to the profits from whatever portion of it was sold, with additional shares provided for such new, collectively used gear as long-

Table 2.   Population of Hattarvík (Fugloy), 1801-90, showing hired hands

	Holding in 1801[a]	1801	1834	1840	1850	1855	1860	1870	1880	1890
Útistova	9m 8gl									
Population		9	9	9	9	9	9	10	11	12
Total hired hands		1	2	2	1	4	4	3	1	2
Male hired hands		1	2	2	1	2	3	2	1	1
Uppistova[b]	8m 6gl									
Population		5	8	8	6 / 5	9 / 7	9 / 4	7 / 5	6 / 5	5 / 5
Total hired hands		1	3	2	3 / 1	3 / 1	2 / 1	– / 1	– / 1	– / 2
Male hired hands		1	2	1	2 / 1	2 / –	1 / –	– / –	– / –	– / 1
Keldhúsið	1m									
Population		4	3	5	5	?	4	10	4	3
Total hired hands		–	–	–	–	?	–	–	–	–
Male hired hands		–	–	–	–	?	–	–	–	–
Innistova	4m 8gl									
Population		3	6	5	8	9	9	8	3	7
Total hired hands		–	–	–	–	1	1	–	–	2
Male hired hands		–	–	–	–	1	1	–	–	1
Uttarstova[c]	3m 4gl									
Population		4	7	7	5	6	8	4	6 / 2	9 / 2
Total hired hands		–	–	–	1	1	2	–	– / –	– / –
Male hired hands		–	–	–	1	–	1	–	– / –	– / –
Suðurstova	2m 13½gl									
Population		2	5	7	6	7	8	6	6	5
Total hired hands		–	–	–	–	–	–	1	2	1
Male hired hands		–	–	–	–	–	–	–	1	–
Total										
Population		27	38	41	44	(47)	51	50	43	48
Total hired hands		2	6	5	6	(10)	10	5	6	7
Male hired hands		2	4	3	5	(5)	6	2	2	3

Source: J.S. Hansen (1971:118-62)

[a] In *merkur* and *gyllin*

[b] Uppistova comprised two distinct households in 1850, and was divided into two homesteads the following year

[c] Uttarstova was divided in two in 1873 or shortly thereafter

Table 3. Types of boats in Hattarvík and the Norðoyar, 1782-1905

Year	10-man	8-man	6-man	4-man	Total
		Hattarvík, 1801-58			
1801[a]	0	2[b]	1	2	5
1855[c]	0	1	0	4	5
1858	0	1	0	4	5[d]
		The Norðoyar, 1782-1905[e]			
1782	?	15	7	?	(22)
1810	0	24	14	45	83
1858	3	22	13	68	106
1905	0	35	62	135	232

Source: J.S. Hansen (1966:121-24, 143–44)

[a]There were eight adult men in Hattarvík in 1801

[b]One at Uppistova, one shared by Innistova, Uttarstova, and Suðurstova; these were used in alternate years

[c]There were fifteen adult men in Hattarvík in 1855

[d]In addition, one 8-man boat used in the winter; also a 4-man boat used "sometimes"

[e]According to E. Patursson (1961:10, 73), there appear to have been about 2000 boats altogether in the Faroes throughout the nineteenth century

lines. For the most part, however, fishing had simply been one of the many chores required of hired hands, who "received no special pay for it" (E. Patursson 1961:15). That is, an employer received his crewmen's shares. Moreover, substantial farmers had long been required to maintain large boats that were manned not only by their hired hands, but also by men from other households who had the right (and the duty) to "hold a thwart" (eiga sess) in them. This law was repealed in 1865, "the year of liberation" for landless and boatless men (J.S. Hansen 1966:16-17), accentuating the trend toward more and smaller boats, allowing more men to profit from fishing, and probably diminishing the economic distinction between king's farmers and freeholders. Degn suggests (1929:9) that these trends had gotten under way as early as the hungry years between 1807 and 1814, no doubt because of population pressure and the resulting shortage of "thwarts" in established boats. The growing popularity of small, independently owned boats and the fact that "the boat" continued to receive only a single share suggest that the level of capital investment needed to start and maintain a household fishery remained modest, and in keeping with fishing's gradually increasing profitability.

Finally, we may surmise that this more "democratic" style of fishing reinforced the integrity of village life, by increasing the importance of kinship in local social organization. Graba notes that "The Faroeman works gladly and diligently, but without seeking work; this his pride will not allow"; but, he adds, "whoever wants to go out fishing must seek out his mates (*Gehülfsen*) and ask to go out with them for a portion of the catch" (Graba 1848:24). This paradox still characterizes relations between skippers and crewmen in the Faroes.[7] The way out of it is (and presumably was) to secure crewmen or a place on a crew by exploiting social ties of sufficient intimacy that an indirect approach can easily be made to a potential skipper, crewman, or "mate." The formal properties of the kinship system and scattered, admittedly more recent evidence suggest that such ties tend to follow connections of kinship and are particularly strong between brothers (*beiggjar, brøður*), fathers and sons (collectively, *feðgar*), and brothers-in-law (*svágir: svágur* is either wife's brother or sister's husband; the term may also refer to daughter's husband), who customarily exchange labors and favors in other pursuits, as well. It is likely that, as well as making kinship a more important factor in the village economy, the use of smaller boats by more men tended to raise the already high social position of women, since it was they who enlarged a man's field of potential "mates" by providing him with brothers- and sons-in-law.

We may also suggest that by reinforcing informally sanctioned relationships of trust, kinship allowed an economy based on credit to be superimposed on one based on the exchange of labors and favors. At least in the village where I have done fieldwork, the local economy remained virtually cashless until the Second World War. Women bought on credit in the shops, and the debt was paid off when men brought back their earnings from the Iceland fishery. I know of no data bearing on the period before the rise of the distant-water fishery. But the smooth operation of such a system clearly depended on a willingness to extend credit, a willingness doubtless founded on the traditional Faroese punctiliousness about repaying nonmonetary debts. The elaboration of norms governing such traditional credit relationships was presumably reinforced by an elaboration of those governing relationships among kinfolk. The result was both to ease the introduction of a money economy (if not, strictly speaking, a cash economy) and to buffer its effects.

In sum, between (roughly) 1830 and 1890, the Faroese economy acquired an infinitely larger base, as fishing became a commercial as well as a subsistence pursuit. Villages absorbed the growing population, and village fisheries supported it (see Tables 4 and 5). Tórshavn, the Faroes' only "city," actually lost population between 1855 and 1860; as late as 1880, it still contained only 8.8 percent of the total population, as opposed to about 10 percent before 1855 (see Table 1, above).

I have suggested several reasons why the advent of commercial fishing did not seriously disrupt Faroese society. It was village-based and technologically conservative, and it depended on the labor of hired hands and then on the widening use of smaller boats; and it rested rather on the

Table 4.   Means of support of the population of the Norðoyar, 1802-70

Year	The land[a]		The sea		Total
1801	652	(100%)	0	—	652
1834	845	(98%)	16	(2%)	861
1855	660	(64%)	372	(36%)	1032
1870	721	(59%)	506	(41%)	1227

Source: J.S. Hansen (1966:125–26)

Note: The Norðoyar are the islands of Svínoy, Fugloy, Borðoy, Kalsoy, Kunoy, and Viðoy; together they contained about 12% of the total Faroese population in each of these years

[a]Figures include those for nonagricultural pursuits

elaboration of old norms than on an attempt to create or borrow new ones. Moreover, land-based pursuits were not abandoned. Between 1841 and 1850, for example, the Faroes exported an average of 51 tons of sweaters each year; between 1876 and 1885, the average yearly export of sweaters was 52 tons. By that time, however, the shift from farming to fishing was becoming more than a shift in emphasis. In the same period, the Faroes' average yearly export of klipfish rose from 21 tons to over 2000 tons, and by 1896-1900, to nearly 3900 tons. At the end of the century, fish and fish products accounted for 93.7 percent of all exports by value (E. Patursson 1961:55-57).

It is less easy to generalize about political and cultural developments during the period between the abolition of the Monopoly and the rise of ship fishing, in the 1880s. Perhaps we may say that the Faroes became a more provincial place, where "folkishness" slowly faded despite the villages' continuing vitality, and a certain unease about one's place in the world occasionally surfaced.

After Dahlerup's departure, in 1861, "Faroese politics entered a quiet, conservative stage" (West 1972:98), and although the Løgting proposed several times that its powers be increased, "it is quickly told, that nothing came of these recommendations" (E. Patursson 1966:12). Nor were people interested in Danish politics. Well under one-tenth of the electorate voted in the Folketing elections between 1866 and 1879 (E. Patursson 1965:6; Sammendrag 1918, 4:50).

Meanwhile, the increasing importance of the village as a social unit was reflected in a series of changes in the Faroes' legal system. Grannastevnur (village councils devoted primarily to regulating the joint use of lands) were evidently formally institutionalized in about 1840. "The formalisation of the grannastevna . . . can be seen as . . . providing the

Table 5. Means of support of the Faroese population, 1801-1911

Population supported by	1801	1845	1850	1855	1880	1890	1901	1911
Agriculture	4475 (85.0%)	5305 (68.2%)	5285 (65.0%)	5555 (64.2%)	4611 (41.1%)	4385 (33.8%)	4393 (28.8%)	3315 (18.4%)
Fishing	53 (1.0%)	825 (10.6%)	1266 (15.6%)	1524 (17.6%)	3411 (30.4%)	4864 (37.5%)	6199 (40.2%)	9515 (52.9%)
Crafts and industry	—	503 (6.4%)	?	?	864 (7.7%)	967 (7.5%)	1686 (11.6%)	1871 (10.4%)
Trade and transport	—	12 (0.2%)	?	?	471 (4.2%)	831 (6.4%)	1412 (9.4%)	1435 (8.0%)
Other, don't know	737 (14.0%)	1136 (14.6%)	?	?	1863 (16.6%)	1908 (14.8%)	1620 (10.6%)	1864 (10.4%)
Total	5265	7781	8137	8651	11220	12955	15230	18000

Sources: 1801: estimated from Heinesen (1966:27); 1845: Statistisk Tabelværk 1850, Part IB, Table xi, pp. 338-41; 1850-55: Fólkateljingar í Føroyum 1801-1955, Folketaellingen paa Faeroerne den 1 Oktober 1855, p. 121; 1880-90: E. Patursson (1961:65); 1901: Statistisk Aarbog 1904, p. 177 (Table 105.A.2); 1911: Statistisk Aarbog 1912, p. 185 (Table 147.A.2)

people with the machinery for settling their own difficulties [without appeal to Tórshavn]. The need to provide such machinery arose from the large increase in the number of *óðalsmenn* (private holders of land) and the decrease in the average size of their holdings" (West 1975:56-57). The basic principles of allocating rights of land use remained unchanged, however. Second, a law establishing township (Da. *kommune*) government was extended to the Faroes, in 1872. It made the villages political units governed by elected village councils and provided the institutional machinery for the eventual introduction of medical and other social services. As we have seen, it also provided that each *kommune* be responsible for its children's education. Although the language of instruction was supposed to be Danish, the law unwittingly sanctioned the old pattern of local control over education; since schoolmasters began teaching in Faroese, it eventually helped to strengthen the language's position vis-à-vis Danish. Finally, the decline of the district (*sýsla*) as a social and legal unit was reflected in the abolition of the ancient spring parliaments, in 1896.

Some cultural changes of this period were minor. Hair styles, for example, had long since begun to follow Continental fashions. Graba noted, in 1828, that although most Faroese men had close-cropped hair, "many, especially from Suðuroy, had long, plaited pigtails hanging down to the small of the back, [while] others wore their hair hanging down over the shoulders, sometimes straight but customarily in ringlets or curls" (1848:27). Costume also changed, women's perhaps more rapidly than men's, for we find a German visitor noting, in 1883, that "In Iceland the women wear a national costume; in the Faroes it is the other way around."[8] People's formal names changed when, in 1832, a Danish ordinance was extended to the Faroes requiring "each child to be named at its christening not only with a first name but also with a family or surname (*Stamnavn*) that it had to bear in the future" (J.H.W. Poulsen 1979:190). In other words, the old system of patronymics was formally set aside. Informally, however, Faroese still use a patronymic style based on the preposition *hjá* ("of, at the home of").

More consequential were a linked series of changes in the Faroes' sociolinguistic situation. On the one hand, Faroese remained unchallenged as the language of everyday life. In 1844 Hammershaimb wrote that "the Faroese who [does not speak] his mother tongue upon returning from Denmark" would be treated contemptuously (quoted in Bekker-Nielsen 1978:86). M.A. Jacobsen echoed him in 1921, in words that still hold true: Danish, he said, was "never spoken man-to-man, because whoever wanted to try it would rightly be considered foolishly presumptuous" (1921:34). Faroese even increased its range slightly, becoming the language of trade in the village shops. Meanwhile, Danish remained little challenged as (in effect) the register of Faroese appropriate to religious and political activity, and it "reigned supreme" in the Løgting, "at any rate until 1868."[9] At least as late as the early 1880s, the primacy of Danish in religious affairs was stressed in the way parents taught their children the catechism, asking the questions in Faroese to be sure the children understood, but requiring the responses in Danish, perhaps to be sure that God understood (P.M. Rasmussen 1978:136). Nor was Danish challenged as what Enok Bærentsen called "the cultured language (*kulturmaalet*) with which we stand in connection with the outside world" (*Dimmalætting*, 12 January 1889).

Yet this old pattern of "low" Faroese and "high" Danish was threatened from several directions. At the level of everyday speech, Hammershaimb wrote, in 1854, that in Tórshavn people spoke a "wretched mishmash" and "poke[d] fun at the true, old Faroese." Thus "especially when they come to Tórshavn," young people had "begun to forgo the use of the old forms (e.g., *vær hövum* for *vit hava*, the latter more closely resembling the Danish *vi have*)." Already he had noted examples of villagers imitating Tórshavn speech, and feared that "the language will quickly be completely dissolved" (1854:235 [1969:227]). This did not happen, of course, but when Jakob Jakobsen published the oral literature he had collected in the early 1890s, he cleaned out the many danicisms that he found had crept into spoken Faroese (Jakobsen 1898-1901:ix).

As Jakobsen's editorial strategy suggests, Faroese was also threatened in its literary registers. Hammershaimb had claimed, in 1854, that what "particularly" kept the language alive was "the heroic ballads, which . . . are still composed in Faroese by farmers to this very day, and not seldom in a fairly clean language and quite nicely" (1854:235 [1969:227]). But whereas the more formal occasions when ballads were sung naturally survived (holidays, weddings, whale slaughters, and so forth), the *kvøldseta* passed out of existence. Jakobsen traced its demise, along with a corresponding impoverishment of oral literature, particularly its prose forms, to the advent of free trade: instead of telling stories in the *roykstova*, people gathered to chat in the shops (Jakobsen 1898-1901:viii, xxxii-xxxiv). Moreover, the last great composer of heroic ballads in the old style, the king's farmer J.C. Djurhuus, died in 1853. The tradition survived into the twentieth century in an increasingly attenuated form, but most new verse compositions were *tættir*, satirical ballads dealing with local events and figures. Many of these were in Danish (M. Johannesen 1978:342ff.), suggesting that local society could no longer be wholly comprehended in local terms, particularly when disunity arose among Faroese. The form's satirical element likewise suggests an undercurrent of social tension; and, like the belief that Faroese was a merely local and folkish tongue, its lack of historical and geographical scope suggests a literary correlate of the period's socioeconomic retreat to the villages.

A similar cultural unease is reflected in the spread of the temperance movement and the somewhat later incursion of evangelical religion.

Temperance societies had been in existence, off and on, since 1846. The movement gained impetus when the introduction of free trade made liquor more easily available. One is often told, and sometimes reads, that many farmers and fishermen went deeply into debt in order to buy liquor, sometimes being forced to mortgage their land to merchants. Be that as it may, a Temperance Union was founded in Tórshavn in 1878, in whose hall men might gather for conversation or a congenial game of chess. Drinking did not stop, of course; but a German who had visited the islands in 1877 found on a second trip, in 1882, that the Union's activities had at least checked public drunkenness at Ólavsøka, the holiday marking the start of the Løgting's annual session.[10] In the next decades, several of the "early nationalists" supported the movement (West 1972:245; cf. Mitens 1966:135); in 1907 a partial prohibition was enacted against little open opposition. The consumption of alcohol immediately fell by about two-thirds (Sammendrag 1918, 4:32). Partial prohibition is still partially in force.

Evangelical religion reached the Faroes in the summer of 1865, in the person of William Sloan, a Scottish missionary of the Plymouth Brethren. He later took up full-time residence in Tórshavn, and after years of fruitless proselytizing (in Danish), built a hall there in 1879. One morning in 1880, to the wonder of a town that had somehow not realized Sloan's anabaptist persuasion, a convert was baptized in the harbor (*Dimmalætting*, 6 November 1880). A few more followed (Anon. 1975). But then, although Sloan was personally well liked, "strong opposition . . . arose against him in Tórshavn" (Fossing n.d.:29), and he had to move to Miðvágur. He spent from 1893 to 1897 in Shetland. The Plymouth Brethren, locally called "Baptists" (*baptistar*), gained considerable ground after the turn of the century. Their membership was estimated at 197 in 1911, out of a total Faroese population of 18,000 (*Sammendrag* 1918, 4:5). It has been estimated that today perhaps 7 to 10 percent of all Faroese belong to the "sect" (*sekt*). Other groups now operating as "sects" outside the established Church include the Salvation Army, a few Catholics (see Michelsen 1930), Jehovah's Witnesses, Seventh Day Adventists, the "Free Evangelical Congregation," and the "Philadelphia Congregation." Groups operating as "sects" nominally within the established Church include the YWCA and the YMCA and several branches of Lutheran "Home Mission" (Da. Indre Mission) (Ársfrágreiðing 1980:273-79).

Little or no research has been done on the historical sociology of the temperance and evangelical movements. Christian Matras has suggested (in Trap 1968:187-88) that the one was a response to "unfortunate social conditions" attending the introduction of free trade, while the other reflected "the transition from a patriarchal peasant society to a fishing society." This may be so. It is certainly clear, in a general way, that both represented attempts to live an upright life in a world whose values were shifting underfoot. Since drinking is a male pastime, for example, and, as the proverb says, "Beer is another man" (Hammershaimb 1969 [1891]:321), attempts to control it were surely linked to a concern also expressed in folktales: redefining male roles and, indeed, "the integrity of Faroese life at a time when the traditional economy based on the land was being overtaken by one based on seafaring" (Wylie and Margolin 1981:65). From our present point of view, however, the lack of research on the movements is nearly as interesting as whatever their social history may have been. For although both are ideologically highly charged, raising strong, divided opinion among Faroese, neither was brought within the national-cultural frame of Faroese politics or scholarship. They remain, for the moment, persistently visible but incomprehensible elements of the local scene (Wylie 1983).

The temperance and (especially) the evangelical movements were, of course, also branches of intellectual currents arising outside the Faroes. As such, they contribute to one's general picture of the Faroes' deepening provinciality in the second half of the nineteenth century. The picture is clearer, perhaps, in tourists' reactions to Tórshavn, "the Paris of the archipelago" (Labonne 1887:392). Tórshavn was an extremely unprepossessing place, to say the least, through the 1880s.

"'Could that be a town,'" a Danish visitor might wonder in the 1850s, before coming ashore where an old iron ring fixed in the rocky point of the Tinganes provided practically the only harbor facilities, "'the dark wooden houses, which lie higgledy-piggledy therein?'" (Holm 1855:30; cf. Holm 1860:23ff.) It was, a British visitor commented several years later, "the queerest, quaintest place imaginable" (Clark 1861:320), comprising a few large houses, including the governor's new stone-built, slate-roofed residence; the eighteenth-century church, in whose graveyard another Briton was disappointed to find no runic inscriptions (Forbes 1860:14-15); the half-derelict fort, where one might discover a gentleman of scant military demeanor trimming the sod roof (Forbes 1860:13); the old Monopoly buildings on the Tinganes; and, for the rest, a huddled warren of alleyways twisting between the small, dim, sod-roofed dwellings of fishermen and day laborers, from which peat smoke seeped out to mingle with a pervasive reek of fish. The arabist Richard Burton, dismayed here as he was soon to be in Iceland that no Vikings were in evidence about the place, reported in 1875 that Tórshavn was "one of the 'slowest' places now in existence" (1875:299). A more sympathetic visitor, Caroline Birley, wrote after a trip to the Faroes in the summer of 1889:

There is nothing very striking in the first view of Thorshavn. The houses, all detached, are placed somewhat irregularly, but—save for one short, outstretched tongue of land, covered with buildings—the general effect is that of a semicircular town, dipping low in the centre, and on each side climbing a gentle eminence. On the eastward rise are the well-placed, whitewashed Lutheran church, the imposing official residence of the Amtmand or Danish Governor, and the House of Parliament (Tinghuset), where the legislative chamber . . . holds its assemblies. As we were used to native architecture, and had learnt to look upon slate roofs as ugly, cold, and ostentatious, this last, with deep-red timber walls, rectangular white-sashed windows, broad gables, and thick overhanging verdure, never struck us as insignificant for its purpose; so the shock was wholly unexpected when after proudly displaying its photograph in England, we were met with the response, 'That the house of Parliament! I thought it was a shed!' [1891:226]

There was more to Tórshavn than met the tourist's eye, but even by Faroese standards of the next decades, its cultural amenities were few. In 1878, for example, the provincial library closed down. Founded fifty years earlier, at Christian Tillisch's instigation, by the 1850s it had contained over five thousand volumes, "a quaint medley of all authors of all countries," a British visitor found, but "invaluable to the islanders during their dreary winter" (Forbes 1860:13; cf. West 1972:79). The several institutions Tórshavn did acquire before the mid-1880s suggest, more than anything else, how "slow" a place it was: the bookstore in 1865 and a press in 1870, the temperance hall in 1878, the "Baptist" meetinghouse in 1880, and an apothecary shop and a mutual life insurance company in 1883. The newspaper *Dimmalætting,* a semiofficial paper whose masthead still proclaims it "county news for the Faroes" (*Amtstidende for Færøerne,* in Danish), was founded in 1877. It was written almost entirely in Danish, but from time to time published a few items in Faroese. And in 1861, a high school (Da. *højskole*) was founded. Its teacher-training program, set up in 1870, offered the highest level of education available in the Faroes. The increasing number of Faroese desiring more advanced degrees or training in other subjects went to Denmark, where many of them made their careers.

Another indication of the Faroes' deepening provincialism in the second half of the nineteenth century is the rather sad and isolated air of resident Danes' lives. We have already cited a British tourist's comment that Governor Dahlerup "seemed sadly oppressed with ennui, and to be looking anxiously for the arrival of the steamer which was to take him to Copenhagen and his wife" (Clark 1861:320). A Frenchman, Jules Leclercq, wrote, after a visit in 1882, that

the arrival of the steamer is a holiday for the Danish merchants exiled in this place, which no telegraphic wire links with the rest of the world; on this occasion they raise the flag of their mother country on their houses, and they receive with joy the passengers who bring them news from Europe. One of them, M. Hanson [*sic*], invites us to dine. We enter a comfortable Danish house of irreproachable cleanliness; from the windows one enjoys a magnificent view of the bay of Tórshavn; . . . the wooden walls are decorated with views of the last Paris Exposition. Madame Hanson has the graciousness to bring us flowers, the most precious thing she could offer us in this sad climate. [1883:34]

And in 1889, Caroline Birley was party to an affecting scene in Kvívík. Her guide

decreed that a call on the priest's wife was indispensible, so we walked through the straggling, poverty-stricken village, with the usual odours of fried fish and whaleflesh, and after a short visit the 'minister's lady' put on a cloak, hat, gloves, and black-lace veil elaborately, and showed us round her bright and well-kept garden, in which double-pink campion, London Pride, and globe-flowers were conspicuous. But the absence of trees and shrubs in this small enclosure made it seem but a dreary resort for one who answered our inquiry, 'Do you walk much?' with 'Only in the garden.'[11]

Kvívik may indeed have seemed dreary to the Copenhagen-born "minister's lady," who was probably pleased when her husband was reassigned to a parish in the metropolis the next year. But in Faroese terms, the village was not notably impoverished either materially or culturally. The "odours of dried fish and whaleflesh" meant full larders, and when Hammershaimb had served there, from 1855 to 1862, he had inspired two rural poets in their youth. One, Kvívíks-Jógvan (Jógvan Dánjalsson, 1843-1926) had moved, in 1872, to another village in the parish, but the other, Jóan Petur uppi í Trøð (J.P. [often I.P.] Gregoriussen, 1845-1901), still lived there. He was a leading light in the movement to revitalize Faroese culture that had taken root in Tórshavn a few months before Birley's visit. It is said that he had determined to become a writer when, on a fishing trip to Iceland, he had heard a sermon in Icelandic and had reflected that in the Faroes all sermons were delivered in Danish.

The pace of change accelerated, and the cultural reaction to it became more concerted, when the Faroese "industrial revolution" got under way in the late 1880s. Its dimensions can be summarized quickly, principally from census data on the population supported by various categories of pursuits.[12]

In the 1870s, British fishermen were selling off their sloops, smacks, and schooners in order to equip themselves with steam-powered trawlers. Faroese were able to buy the old sailing vessels second-hand. The first of them, a little sloop called *Fox*, was bought in 1872 by three brothers in Tórshavn. The Faroese fleet grew to 22 ships by 1882, but dwindled to only 14 in 1890. Thereafter it grew rapidly, to 45 ships by 1895, 81 by the turn of the century, and 144 by 1920. Ship fishing quickly eclipsed "rowing out" as a commercial enterprise. As early as the period 1885-1890, the ships accounted for about 22 percent of the average yearly export of salt cod. They accounted for 45 percent ten years later, and for over 70 percent between 1916 and 1920 (E. Patursson 1961:34-37, 45, 81). The shift to ship fishing was hastened by the new British trawlers, which so scoured local waters that inshore fishing became unprofitable. The growing Faroese fleet was thus forced away to Icelandic and other distant grounds.

The census of 1921 introduced a new style of listing occupations, which makes it difficult to trace ship fishing's socioeconomic impact over the whole period up to 1930. However, the general picture is clear enough

Table 6. Means of support of the Faroese population, 1911-30

Population supported by	1911	1921	1930
Agriculture, bosses (*hovedpersoner*)	2031 (11.3%)	1778 (8.3%)	1648 (6.8%)
Fishing, bosses	4083 (22.7%)	6669 (31.2%)	7238 (30.0%)
Agriculture and fishing, bosses	2230 (12.4%)	1163 (5.4%)	479 (2.0%)
Crafts and fishing, bosses	276 (1.5%)	133 (0.6%)	175 (0.7%)
Assistants (*medhjælpere*) in agriculture and fishing	2209 (12.3%)	2418 (11.3%)	2932 (12.1%)
Children at home over 14 years old[a]	980 (5.4%)	654 (3.1%)	418 (1.7%)
Crafts and industry	1671 (9.3%)	2542[b] (11.9%)	3114 (12.9%)
Trade	950 (5.3%)	1490 (7.0%)	1575[c] (6.5%)
Transport	657 (3.7%)	1174 (5.5%)	2078 (8.6%)
Domestic duties (*husgering*)	868 (4.8%)	1000 (4.7%)	2084 (8.4%)
Other, don't know	2045 (11.4%)	2331 (10.9%)	2459 (10.2%)
Total	18000	21352	24200

Sources: 1911-21: Statistisk Aarbog 1924, p. 195 (Table 156.A.2); 1930: Statistisk Aarbog 1933, p. 185 (Table 181.2)
[a]Includes only 5 dependents (*forsøgede*) in 1921 and 17 in 1930
[b]Includes mining (190 persons)
[c]Includes financial institutions

(Table 6); and a more detailed one emerges from figures for the economically active population, which are available from 1901 on (Table 7).

Each ship in the growing fleet needed a crew of about twelve to twenty men.[13] Fishing thus supported more and more people, 9515 of them by 1911, or 52.9 percent of the total Faroese population. Only now did fishing cut into the agricultural labor pool. In 1901, agriculture still supported 4393 people, substantially the same number as in 1801 or, for that matter, in 1701 or 1601. (Now, of course, this kernel of the traditional economy represented only about 29 percent of the total Faroese popula-

Table 7.   Economically active population (*forsøgere*), 1901-30

	Population	
Occupation	*1901*	*1911*
Agriculture, bosses (*hovedpersoner*)	844	862
employees (*funktionærer* and *arbeidere*)	1807	569
Fishing, bosses	1748	2417
employees	559	1665
Crafts and industry, bosses	507	651
employees	362	102
Trade and transport, bosses	149	335
employees	321	220
Other, don't know	1025	1402
Total economically active population	7317	8223
Total population	15230	18000
	1921	*1930*
Agriculture, bosses	574	590
Fishing, bosses	1668	2276
Agriculture and fishing, bosses	338	112
Crafts and fishing, bosses	34	46
Assistants (*medhjælpere*) in agriculture and fishing	2443	2279
Children at home over 14 years old	649	401
Crafts and industry, bosses	436	405
employees	440[a]	865
Trade, bosses	268	256
employees	198	409
Transport	429	634
Domestic duties (*husgering*)	952	2006
Other, don't know	966	985
Total economically active population	8761	11715
Total population	21352	24200

Sources: 1901: Statistisk Aarbog 1904, p. 177 (Table 105.A.2); 1911: Statistisk Aarbog 1912, p. 185 (Table 147.A.2); 1921: Statistisk Aarbog 1924, p. 195 (Table 156.A.2); 1930: Statistisk Aarbog 1933, p. 185 (Table 181.2)
[a]Includes mining (62 persons)

tion.) But by 1911 the number had fallen to 3315, or 18.4 percent of the population. Farmers did not abandon their fields and flocks, for the number of "bosses" in agriculture remained fairly constant. But the number of their employees dropped precipitously, from 1807 to 569. In other words, farmers did without hired hands. Fishing absorbed the labor. Not only did the number of independent fishermen ("bosses") rise from 1748 in 1901 to 2417 in 1911, but the number of mere crewmen ("employees") nearly tripled, jumping from 559 to 1665.

Fishing had, however, long since lost the capacity to support directly *all* the additions to a growing population. In 1880-90, the population supported by fishing had grown by about 42 percent, but as early as the next decade it grew by only about 25 percent. There was greater growth in the secondary sector of the economy, and after the turn of the century a remarkable rise occured in the number of one-man firms. (I am assuming that the number of "bosses" reflects the number of firms.) The number of bosses in crafts, industry, trade, and transport rose from 656 in 1801 to 986 in 1911, while the number of employees fell from 683 to 322.

These were boom times. The period from 1921 to 1930 was one of deepening depression. Remarkably, perhaps, the economy's secondary sector continued to grow; for although a few firms went out of business, the surviving ones expanded. The number of bosses in crafts, industry, and trade fell slightly, from 704 in 1921 to 661 in 1930; but the number of employees in these categories doubled, from 638 to 1275. By 1930, 19.4 percent of the total population was supported by crafts, industry, and trade, and another 6.5 percent by transport.

It is sometimes assumed (J.P. Joensen, personal communication) that the depression of the 1920s and 1930s gave Faroese agriculture a reprieve. Certainly it is clear from the stories people tell about this period that they relied heavily on plots of potatoes and, if possible, a cow and a few sheep. In many villages, fresh enclosures were made from the outfields, and infields were expanded. But this was not agriculture in the traditional sense, nor was it a paying proposition. Erlendur Patursson remarks that "freehold land, which had previously given freeholders an appreciable supplement, was . . . broken apart into small bits by inheritance, so that an individual's income was probably much less than before" (1951:68). The census evidence suggests that the depression accentuated the turn to the sea that had begun a century before. "Agriculture" itself, a category probably by now representing only the most substantial landholders and their families, remained nearly constant in the 1920s. The more marginal category of "agriculture and fishing" dwindled, however; and the number of independent fishermen rose. In 1921 and 1930, about 30 percent of the total population was supported by fishing "bosses." It is possible, moreover, that the censuses' combination of agricultural and fishing "assistants" masks a continuing shift from work on land to work at sea. One must conclude that although the larger farms continued to operate on a reduced scale, agriculture and animal husbandry were now chiefly important only for household subsistence. Otherwise, more people earned a living from fishing and, increasingly, from the secondary occupations spawned by it.

A bit more detail is suggested by anecdotal evidence and the somewhat mysterious census categories of "domestic duties" (*husgering*) and "children at home over 14 years old." The former, an almost entirely female occupation that might almost be translated as "housewives," engaged 952 people in 1921 and 2006 in 1930. It is not entirely clear what to make of this dramatic rise. We cannot simply conclude that more women remained at home as the economy slumped after 1920, for more women held paying jobs in 1930 than in 1921, both absolutely and proportionally. In 1921, 950 women (8.9 percent of the total female population) were employed in agriculture, fishing, crafts and industry, trade, and transport; in 1930, the figure was 1390, or 11.5 percent of the total female population. (The corresponding figures for males were 5793, or 54.3 percent, in 1921, and 7183, or 59.2 percent, in 1930.) However, bearing in mind that the number of children at home fell during this period, what probably happened was that, as one also learns from the stories people tell, boys were shipping out as soon as possible after their confirmation, when they were about fourteen, while their female counterparts left home to seek work in fish-processing firms. They took up "domestic duties" after they had children. If this is so—if, that is, the depression of the 1920s and 1930s kept more adult, married women at home—it may have had a culturally conservative effect as important in its own way as the agricultural economy's long survival as an ideological resource, by preserving women's culturally central position as mistress of the household.

In sum, ship fishing grew dramatically after 1880, constricting the Faroes' traditional "agricultural" base but leaving it more or less intact until after the turn of the century. As a means of support, fishing was by then growing more slowly than the population as a whole. It reached a kind of upper limit, in proportional terms, in 1920. Meanwhile, it fed the expansion of the economy's secondary sector. By these stages, the Faroes' old economic order, based on a single export (wool) and diversified subsistence pursuits, at last gave way to a new one based on another single export (fish) and a diversity of full-time pursuits. The transition, which was essentially complete by 1920, was reinforced by the long depression that followed.

The Faroes also diversified demographically between 1800 and 1920, as a handful of fishing towns and, at last, Tórshavn replaced the villages as centers of population growth. In a former age, when land was the main source of wealth and ships might contain pirates or English fishermen who kidnapped Faroese crewmen, Faroese had found difficult access from the sea a source of security.[14] Now a community's fortunes depended on a good roadstead, preferably with a wide foreshore for drying cod and building warehouses, wharves, and slipways. Several previously well-off communities dwindled. One settlement was entirely abandoned in the

1880s, followed by others in 1910, 1914-15, 1920, and 1930.[15] A few old communities, like Koltur, nearly disappeared. But others held their own or became little towns. Towns also grew up where there had previously been little more than a hamlet or a commonly used landing. Tvøroyri, the most important fishing town, grew up, in the 1880s, around the commercial nucleus established after the Monopoly branch store was set up in an outfield, 1836.;[16] Another major, early fishing town was Vágur, also on Suðuroy, followed, after about 1910, by Klaksvík, in the Norðoyar. Other fishing towns included Vestmanna (on Streymoy). Fuglafjørdur (on Eysturoy, followed after 1920 by the villages around the mouth of Skálafjørður), and Miðvágur-Sandavágur (on Vágar) (E. Patursson 1961:121-27). Most Faroese industry depended directly on the ship fishery and was concentrated in these towns. It was thus in Tvøroyri that the Faroes' first shipyard was built, in 1894. Others followed in Vestmanna (1898), Skáli (on Eysturoy, 1903), Vágur (1913-14), and Klaksvík (1918).

Tórshavn was also a fishing town at first. In 1901, 35 of the Faroes' 87 ships were registered there. But the number fell to 23 out of 146 ships by 1921, by which time it was outranked by Tvøroyri and Vágur and would soon be overtaken by Klaksvík (E. Patursson 1961:122). When Tórshavn got its first drying house for klipfish, in 1920, there were already four in Tvøroyri and many more elsewhere. Nor did Tórshavn boast a shipyard until 1936. Its importance was more as an intellectual, commercial, and political capital and as the hub of a developing communications network than as an industrial center.[17] In the 1890s, it finally began to grow a bit faster than the rest of the Faroes. By 1921 it was a city of 2500 people, nearly 12 percent of the total population.

Tórshavn housed most of the modern institutions the Faroes acquired after about 1890. Even a partial list is long: the literary and political society Føringafelag (1889); its organ, the newspaper *Føringatíðindi*, followed by other periodicals and publishers; a mutual insurance association for sailing vessels (1892); a school of navigation (1893); a Skippers' Association (1896); a Literary Society (1898); the new quarters of the savings bank (1904); the revived national library (1905-6); a new central post office (1906); a trading bank (1906); a Young People's Association (1906), whose members wrote out by hand their journal *Baldursbrá* (1906-12); the telegraph station (1906-8); the residence of the "national doctor" (1907); the remodeled but still very modest Løgting building (1907); a tuberculosis sanitarium outside town (1908; the existing hospital near Tórshavn had been supplemented by hospitals in Klaksvík, in 1898, and Tvøroyri, in 1904, but was not itself extensively rebuilt until 1924); a folk high school (moved in 1909 from Klaksvík, where it had been founded in 1899); and a Ship-Owners' Association (1909), followed by a Fishermen's Union (1911).

The proliferation of such institutions suggests the dimensions of an increasingly pressing cultural predicament facing the Faroes in the 1890s.

Its origins were economic and demographic. The local economy had kept pace with demographic growth. But, by the same token, Faroese society had to accommodate a highly untraditional array of occupations; not only full-time fishermen, craftsmen, and workers, but also a native middle class and, particularly in Tórshavn, teachers, civil servants, bankers, lawyers, journalists, and so forth. Moreover, the traditional mixed economy was now clearly faced with extinction, and with it the distinctive "folkishness" of Faroese culture.

Several elements of this general predicament deserve attention.

First, the need had arisen to establish a form of self-identification consonant not only with modern life but also with traditional expressions of Faroeseness. Jakob Jakobsen stated the problem succinctly in 1901, along with the solution that had already been found for it. Oral literature, he wrote, had maintained the Faroes' "spiritual life"; but now "the thread of oral tradition has broken; it is the *written* word that will replace it and create a new culture for us" by drawing on "*local* circumstances, local historical events" (1957:57, 59; his emphasis). The Faroes' cultural history in the late nineteenth and early twentieth centuries is thus, in large measure, literary history.

Another element of the Faroes' predicament involved the place of the modern, essentially urban elite. I shall argue that members of this rising elite led the cultural revival movement of the end of the nineteenth century without, however, opposing either the traditional local elites or Denmark, Danish, and Danes. The movement gained ground rapidly, in part because it was not at first overtly political.

A third element, which came to the fore in the late 1890s, involved an unexpected consequence of the language's widening application in a period of socioeconomic diversification. For although the language remained a symbol of Faroese unity, it also became a vehicle for *dis*agreement about both internal affairs and the place of Denmark in local life. A final element thus involved a reluctant politicization of part of the cultural movement and an increasing specialization of institutions that articulated Faroese identity. Most notably, the first decade of the new century saw the establishment of local political parties, much of whose rivalry was expressed through opposed opinions of Denmark's place in Faroese society.

CHAPTER SEVEN

Now the Hour is Come to Hand
Culture and Politics, circa 1890-1920

Ideology and reality diverged in the middle of the nineteenth century. In 1846 the Faroes acquired a written language in which little was written. At about the same time, they attained a "national" identity even as they were reduced to a Danish province.

The divergence was of a complicated sort. For one thing, Danish ideals departed from Danish practice. Copenhagen's liberal ideologues of the 1840s succeeded in revising the terms of debate about the Faroes' status, but were unable (and in some cases unwilling) to enact a real separation between them and "Denmark proper." Meanwhile, on the Faroese side of things, a few individuals had embraced the idealization of "folkishness." But as Hammershaimb's unfortunate experience in the Kvívík pulpit suggests, most Faroese did not find their own language ennobling; nor, as Winther's frustrated retirement from politics suggests, did most Faroese entertain the corollary proposition that the Faroes' political future might lie apart from Denmark's. Moreover, the very basis of separatist claims was increasingly undercut after the mid-1880s; for the Faroes grew less "folkish" as the material progress looked forward to by leading Faroese and Danes of all persuasions began to reshape local society.

The question now is: How was Copenhagen's romantic-national ideology of the 1840s domesticated in the Faroes in the 1890s? How was it shaped by changing local realities, and how, in turn, did it reshape them?

The ground had been prepared in two crucial ways. First, as we saw in Chapter Three, Faroese folk literature already performed many of the cultural functions attributed to it. Faroese had found works of language a powerful symbolic means of distinguishing themselves in the aftermath of the Reformation, although they did not, of course, seek to distinguish themselves from Danes politically. Second, as we saw in Chapter Six, the culturally threatening modernization[1] attending the rise of "ship fishing" followed some fifty years of culturally conservative development of an export fishery.

Both these factors were internal to Faroese society. So was the most important immediate factor fostering the domestication of a sense of nationality: the rapidly changing socioeconomic conditions of the 1890s. The process of ideological domestication entailed revising the Faroes' relationship to Denmark; but it was not primarily a reaction to fresh turns of events "down there."

139

The process had two phases. The first, more cultural phase may be said, rather arbitrarily, to have begun dramatically with a public meeting in Tórshavn on Boxing Day, 1888, and to have lasted until the quiet demise of the Society of Faroese (Føringafelag) and its organ, *Føringatíðindi,* at the end of 1901. The second, more political phase involved the formation of two political parties, between 1901 and 1906: the more conservative, "pro-Danish" Union party (Sambandsflokkur) and the opposition Self-Rule party (Sjálvstýrisflokkur).

Hammershaimb remained in Kvívík until 1862, when he moved to the Eysturoy parish. He became dean in 1867, an "amiable, middle-aged man," according to a Norwegian visitor who met him in 1874, "known among the learned of Scandinavia [for having] in his time traveled about his native land and collected legends, folktales, and ballads" (Storm 1874:17). He later recalled his years on Eysturoy as the happiest of his life (Grohshenning and Hauch-Fausbøll 1914, 1:676), but ministering to such a large parish left him little time for scholarly work. Reassigned to a Danish parish in 1878, he retired to Copenhagen twenty years later. He died there in 1909, having revisited the Faroes several times.

Hammershaimb's principal work in the 1880s was the two-volume *Færøsk Anthologi,* which came out in 1891. Its first volume contains a grammar and a description of the language, both in Danish, followed by texts of ballads and other folk literature, together with examples of modern poetry and prose. These include several short translations of biblical material and a series of romantic "pictures of folk life": the *kvøldseta,* an elegant old-fashioned wedding, a fishing trip, and so on. The second volume is a Faroese-Danish glossary, prepared by Jakob Jakobsen. The whole is not only a "linguistic monument," to borrow N.M. Petersen's phrase, but also a scholarly and literary one.

Together with Hammershaimb's earlier work, much of which it incorporates, the *Færøsk Anthologi* is a cornerstone of a strong tradition of what might be called Dano-Faroese scholarship: works by Danes as well as Faroese, written entirely in Danish or using a Danish scholarly apparatus in conjunction with Faroese texts. An earlier piece in this tradition had been Niels Winther's *Færøernes Oldtidshistorie* (1875), a highly romanticized (not to say speculative) chronicle of ancient times, which retains a certain historiographic interest in illustrating "the spirit of the 1840s" (C. Matras 1935:58). Faroese historiography was put on a firmer footing with Niels Andersen's *Færøerne 1600-1709* (1895), essentially a documentary history of the seventeenth century. Andersen was a Dane who had been *sorinskrivari* between 1890 and 1895 and a member of the Løgting between 1893 and 1895. Although poorly received at the time (*Føringatíðindi* criticized it for being unreadable and, unlike Hammershaimb's and Winther's works, insufficiently infused with affection for Faroese "memories, life, and manners"), it helped relieve, as Jakobsen said, some of the darkness of Faroese history.[2] More recent works in the Dano-Faroese historiographic tradition include Anton Degn's indispensable history of the Monopoly (1929) and compilation of data on king's farmers (1945). Degn, a Faroese trained in Copenhagen, became the islands' first official archivist, in 1932. By that time, several collections of documents had also appeared in Faroese translation or with a Faroese scholarly apparatus, including Jakobsen's *Diplomatarium Færoense* (1907) and A.C. Evensen's *Savn til føringa sögu í 16. öld* (1908-14).

Hammershaimb's *Færøsk Anthologi* also exemplified the efforts of Faroese scholars and their Danish colleagues to save Faroese folk literature from oblivion. Svend Grundtvig had become a professor in Nordic philology at Copenhagen and had embarked with his assistant, Jørgen Bloch, on the monumental task of producing a definitive edition of the ballads. He published a programmatic appreciation of studies in Faroese folk literature in 1882, but his untimely death the next year set back the ballads' full publication (Djurhuus and Matras 1951-72). More immediately important was Jakob Jakobsen's own great collection of legends and folktales, *Færøske Folkesagn og Æventyr*, most of the material for which was collected during a year's fieldtrip around the Faroes in 1892-93. Jakobsen, a brilliant linguist who received a doctorate in 1897 for his work on Shetlandic Norn, was the son of the Tórshavn bookseller H.N. Jacobsen (Grønneberg 1981, 1984). *Færøske Folkesagn og Æventyr* came out from 1898 to 1901, with a long introduction and notes in Danish. It was followed, in 1904, by his *Færøsk Sagnhistorie* (or, to translate the full title, "Faroese Legendary History, with an Introductory Survey of the Islands' Popular History and Literature"), in which Jakobsen skillfully pieced together a historical narrative from documentary and folk-literary sources. It too was written in Danish, but together with his folklore collection, it eventually inspired the vernacular genre of "village histories" (*bygdarsøgur*), in which, however, the narrative element is less pronounced.

Hammershaimb's and Jakobsen's folklore collections were not just scholarly exercises, more or less timeless and aimed at an international audience. They were also specifically Faroese cultural monuments, grounding modern Faroese culture in written recollections of traditional life. As such, their appearance was exceedingly timely; for by the 1890s, memorializing the past was felt to be an urgent task, especially, perhaps, in Tórshavn. In 1898, when Jakobsen ended a final collecting tour with a public reading in Tórshavn of some of the tales he had "written"(!), *Føringatíðindi* reported with evident relief that "according to him . . . people in the Faroes knew the land's old legends, the land's customs, and the land's language." When the first installment of *Færøske Folkesagn og Æventyr* reached the Faroes, the next spring, a reviewer proclaimed that the "pithy and engaging" stories "bear proud witness to the spiritual life of the old Faroese." Similarly, when the final installment of Hammershaimb's *Færøsk Anthologi* reached the Faroes, in 1892, a reviewer had written that "this great and difficult work . . . preserves for the future the ballads, songs, stories, and legends concerning Faroese folk customs. Each and every person who wishes to preserve what is old and good must thank . . . Dean Hammershaimb."[3]

As the very existence of Faroese reviews indicates, the preservation in writing of "what is old and good" was supplemented by turning the "land's language" to new uses. The first steps in this direction had been taken in Copenhagen, in 1876, when a dozen Faroese students gathered for a Shrovetide party, for which several of them composed poetry and songs. The gathering quickly became customary and led to the formation, in 1881, of the Society of Faroese in Copenhagen (Føroyingafelag í Keypmannahavn), which provided an institutional outlet for further literary activity. Hammershaimb included three examples of this "new poetry" in the *Færøsk Anthologi,* and the next year, Jakobsen published a collection of fourteen student poets' work (Hammershaimb 1969 [1891]:310-13; Jakobsen 1892).

Not surprisingly, given the age in which these poets wrote, their own ages, and their distance from home, much of their verse is nostalgic and sentimental. Nor is it surprising that it explicitly glorifies the language and the local past as tokens of Faroese identity, an aim more implicitly achieved through a pervasive imagery of cliffs, birds, outfields, and the shore: the marches of the Faroese home world which, as we saw in Chapter Three, also figure prominently in the legends collected by Jakobsen. A better effort than most is Frederik Petersen's "Eg Oyggjar Veit" ("I Know Islands"), which has since been taken over as a national anthem. Petersen, a theology student, later became priest of Sandoy (1880-85) and eventually dean (1900-17) and a leader of the Union party. It begins:

> I know islands that have mountains
> and green pastures,
> and are thatched with light snow
> in wintertime;
> and streams run pretty there,
> and pour in torrents;
> they all want to hurry
> into the blue sea.
> God bless my native land, the Faroes.

Another well-remembered piece is a drinking song by Rasmus Effersøe, called either "Faroes" or "Home." Effersøe, the son of the sheriff of Suðuroy, was an agricultural student who later gained literary distinction as a playwright. Ironically, he was also a leader of the temperance movement.

> Faroese who now gather here,
> let us use the old language!

. . . .
Birds that nest in the mountain peaks
each winter go across the sea;
each spring they must look back
to the nest they love.
Dawn finds the bird on his shelf in the cliff,
though he ranges over sound and fjord,—
Yes, the wild bird teaches us:
'Home is the best place on earth.'

Early Dano-Faroese scholarship and the student verse of the 1870s and 1880s began to erect several sorts of monuments to Faroese culture. But the movement to revitalize the language and to preserve and distinguish Faroese culture did not gain widespread support at home until after the dark afternoon of 26 December 1888, when an overflow crowd braved "nasty weather, rain and wind, [and] disagreeable walking" to attend a meeting at the parliament building in Tórshavn.[4]

The "Christmas Meeting," as it came to be known, had been advertised as a public discussion of ways to "defend the Faroes' language and the Faroes' customs." Its urgent but hopeful tone was set by the first speaker, Enok Bærentsen, a long-time member of the Løgting who had given up a tenancy near Tórshavn to receive a commercial education in Denmark and set himself up as a merchant. Bærentsen claimed that the current language was "not so greatly changed" from that of the Faroes' Norse settlers, whose deeds lived on in the ballads. "Therefore," he proclaimed, "there was still time to do something to save it from destruction." But he feared for the future unless Faroese changed their attitude about the vernacular:

the Faroese language was not coming into its own, and he wished to add that if the language did not come into its own, the Faroese people would not do so either. But the fault was our own [, for] it was considered by many Faroese to be a language which could do well enough for everyday use; and therefore we were also inclined to grasp at all that was foreign and consider that all that came from the outside was exceedingly good. . . . [But] the Faroese language was rich enough to be able to express what lived in the heart and mind of a Faroese.

Rasmus Effersøe agreed: "One must hold on to the Faroese mother tongue, which so fits our special local conditions and which is so tied up with our folk character that we can hardly give it up without at the same time ceasing to be an independent people (*selvstændigt Folk*)."

The same points were made in verse at the meeting's emotional climax: Effersøe's reading of a poem by the young heir to the tenancy at Kirkjubøur, Jóannes Patursson. (Patursson shyly declined to read the poem himself, perhaps the last time he exhibited such a retiring nature.) It begins:

Now the hour is come to hand
in this country
for us to join hands together
in honor of the language.

Urging Faroese to unite in resisting the degradation of the language, it dwells at length on the heroism of the earliest generations of Faroese ("old grandfathers,/Norway warriors") and concludes that if only they could see the present generation preserve the ancient tongue,

Then they would tell us gratefully,
'Thank you, sons and daughters, your
inheritance not forgotten, but truly kept.'

The meeting concluded with the unanimous passage of six resolutions. Religious instruction should be given in Faroese, not Danish; Faroese should be made the language of instruction in the schools as soon as possible; Faroese history should be stressed in history classes; priests should have the right to use Faroese both inside and outside church; Faroese should be fully permitted for use between "the people and the authorities"; and a Faroese folk high school should be founded. It was further resolved that another meeting should be held ten days later, so that more people could attend, especially country folk.

A second meeting was duly held, on 6 January 1889, in the Temperance Union's more spacious quarters. Its stated purpose was to found a club called the Føringafelag, or Society of Faroese. More or less modeled on the Copenhagen club of the same name, its goals were "to bring honor to the Faroese language" and "to get Faroese to unite and go forward in all respects, so that they may rescue themselves (vera sjálvbjargnir)."

The Føringafelag's two-point program may fairly be called the charter of Faroese separatism, just as the Føringafelag itself was the first (and in that respect the most important) institution through which the national-cultural ideology of the 1840s was domesticated. For the time being, however, the movement was more cultural than political. Stressing the unity of the people, its leaders generally sidestepped the potentially divisive issue of replacing Danish with Faroese, at least immediately. As Føringatíðindi pointed out, in 1894, "Of course our language cannot be taken all at once as a church language. There is much to do first, for a language that has lain neglected as long as ours requires a great deal of work before it acquires garments fitting it to pass through the doors of the church" (18 October 1894). Thus, for practical as well as ideological reasons, the Føringafelag's immediate goals were to make Faroese literate in Faroese, to widen the language's use, and to promote a sense of pride in the language and in local culture generally.

The Føringafelag's journal, Føringatíðindi, began coming out the next year. Written entirely in Faroese, Føringatíðindi "can without exaggeration be said to have taught the Faroese nation to read and write its own language" (West 1972:116-17). It was supplemented, in 1891, by a "Faroese ABC and Spelling Book" (Poulsen and Johannessen 1891), put together by two schoolteachers. Noting that publications in Faroese were generally too difficult or too expensive for most people, *Føringatíðindi* recommended the *ABC* ("available, bound in good covers, for 20 *oyrur* in the bookstore in Tórshavn") to its readers and to "those Danes resident here who are interested in learning to read our language" (October 1891).

A few years later, the Føringafelag began promoting its aims by sponsoring *fólkafundir,* or "people's meetings." The first *fólkafundur,* which set the pattern for many more, was held in an outfield near Sandur on Whit Monday, 1894.[5] It had been organized by the Skopun merchant Jóhan Hendrik Poulsen and by Mads Andrias Winther, a native of Sandur, who, having been educated in Denmark, was now serving as the *sorinskrivari's* clerk in Tórshavn. He later became a distinguished writer, a representative of the Self-Rule party in the Løgting, and the sheriff of Sandoy. The day was sunny despite fog on the heights, and warm where a rocky outcropping offered shelter from a chilly northeast wind. *Føringatíðindi* reported that about 250 people assembled "from all the villages of Sandoy [. E]ven the farmer from Stóra Dímun had come, and some people from Tórshavn, Kirkjubøur, Velbastaður, and several other villages."

Winther greeted the crowd, telling them that the meeting had been called to arouse interest in "popular progress (*fólkaligan framburð*)." The priest of Sandoy, Jørgen Falk Rønne, the only Danish priest who was a member of the Føringafelag, led holy services; the crowd picnicked; and Poulsen read a poem composed for the occasion by the Kvívík poet and carpenter Jóan Petur uppi í Trøð. Poulsen gave the first of several speeches, relating what the mother tongue meant for "true, sincere sentiment and enlightenment," and how the Danish language was oppressed "where Danes had come under German rule." "No intelligent Faroese," he went on, according to *Føringatíðindi's* report, "wants to press the Danish language out of the country or lock Faroese out from the enlightenment that can be gained from knowledge in other languages; but the mother tongue must and shall attain its rights before long." Rasmus Effersøe urged: "Now that communications with foreign countries are becoming greater and greater, it is important for Faroese to hold together, to honor themselves and honor their forefathers and *their* way of life above foreign customs, which can weaken body and soul." Jóannes Patursson encouraged his listeners to win back the Faroese people's old equality with "other races in all respects, both at sea and ashore." Effersøe spoke again "about the unity among Faroese, and mentioned that such people's meetings could help to remove old sore points between villages." Finally, Just Jacobsen, the Tórshavn king's farmer and foreman of the Føringafelag,

A *fólkafundur* in session, with Jóannes Patursson addressing the crowd, in a cartoon by William Heinesen (Á. Dahl 1981). By permission of Árni Dahl and the artist.

thanked the meeting's organizers; Poulsen thanked all those who had come; and the crowd dispersed homewards, "singing so that it resounded in the ledges and hillside meadows."

The whole occasion not only advertised the Føringafelag's program explicitly; the program and its implications were also expressed symbolically. In a general way, as we suggested in Chapter Three, the *fólkafundur* was a reclamation of the outfield, the edge of the Faroese home world. The apparently spontaneous singing as people dispersed is particularly interesting in this light, although we are not told what they sang. The obvious parallel is with the hymn singing that traditionally marked the beginning and end of dangerous enterprises such as gathering eggs on the cliffs, the whale slaughter, and fishing trips. As a rule, no hymns were sung in the fields. Perhaps, indeed, since egging, whaling, and fishing took place even beyond the outfields, the singing after the *fólkafundur*, as well as the speeches that had filled it, both recognized and controlled the uncertainty inherent in reclaiming the outermost fringes of the Faroes' cultural universe.[6]

Føringatíðindi, meanwhile, was expanding the language's scope by turning it to untraditional uses. In the paper's pages, readers found world as well as local news, songs and poetry, editorials, letters to the editor, translations of biblical material, book reviews, obituaries, jokes, columns

A view of Tórshavn in 1778, from a watercolor. The Monopoly warehouses can be seen to the right of the church. Føroya Fornminnisavn.

Frederik Barfod, right, a leader
in the pan-Scandinavian movement, and his friend Svend
Grundtvig were among Danish
intellectuals who helped to lay
the foundations of Faroese separatism in the 1840s. Grundtvig
later devoted his scholarly career
to collecting and editing the Faroese ballads. Det Kongelige
Bibliotek, Copenhagen.

The House of Parliament in Tórshavn, wrote a visitor in 1891, had "deep red timber walls, rectangular white-sashed windows, and thick overhanging verdure." Fiske Icelandic Collection, Cornell University. Below, the Danish constitutional convention of 1848, in a painting by Constantin Hansen. The constitution's failure to mention the Faroes led to debates about their cultural and political relations with Denmark between, among others, C.F. Tscherning (in uniform, standing at right) and the constitution's principal author, D.G. Monrad (holding a top hat). Det Nationalhistoriske Museum på Frederiksborg.

The use of small, four-man boats helped to maintain the vitality of Faroese village life during the economic and demographic growth of the nineteenth century. From a photograph taken in Kvívík around 1900. Dansk Folkemuseum, Lyngbye.

The *roykstova*, or kitchen, was the heart of the Faroese home. These late nineteenth-century photographs show a poor family's one-room dwelling and the hearthside of a more prosperous family. Dansk Folkemuseum, Lyngbye.

Tvøroyri, the Faroes' main ship-fishing port, in the late nineteenth century.
Føroya Fornminnisavn.

Knitting as they go, three women set off to the outfields with their milk pails.
A photograph from around the turn of the century. Dansk Folkemuseum, Lyngbye.

The village of Eiði at haying time (Labonne 1887). Harvard University Libraries.

An emblem of Faroese culture. A *grind*-boat's crew poses in Miðvágur, probably in the 1920s. Føroya Fornminnisavn.

of advice on health and agriculture, reports of scientific advances, announcements of cultural events, and so forth. As vernacular journalism spread, Faroese readers might also peruse the temperance journal *Dúgvan* (1894-1928), the newspapers *Fuglaframi* (1898-1902) or *Tingakrossur* (1900-present), the household paper *Oyggjarnar* (1905-8), the short-lived literary, scientific and world-political review *Búreisingur* (1908), or the children's magazine *Ungu Føroyar* (1907-9 and 1914-15), whose educational importance was second only to *Føringatíðini*'s own. As a modern schoolbook says, "There can be no doubt that many, many children and young people learned to read Faroese with *Ungu Føroyar* in front of them" (Á. Dahl 1981:57).

Progress was not, however, so easy as it may seem in retrospect, especially in areas where Faroese would have to supplant Danish. At first, writers found considerable difficulty in creating a vocabulary and a sufficiently high tone for legal, bureaucratic, and especially liturgical purposes. In 1911, when A.C. Evensen brought out a reader of Faroese literature (far more heavily modern, now, than Hammershaimb's collection of twenty years before), he still stressed how much work remained to be done: "Although Hammershaimb could write in 1899: 'The Faroese tongue, which was tied when something special had to be said, is now loosed and can speak and write about everything that comes to the mind or moves the heart' [Hammershaimb 1900:26], we must briefly say that much is lacking. In many spiritual matters our language is unusable. It must still be made supple by many hands before it becomes a cultured language (*kulturmál*)" (1911:461).

But the *Reader* itself suggests how supple the language had already become. It contains not only texts of folk literature, but also transcriptions and translations of ancient documents, pieces of historical scholarship, a great deal of lyric verse and descriptive prose, some passages from the Bible, excerpts from two plays (one of them in verse) by Rasmus Effersøe, the articles of incorporation of the Faroe Bank, and an excerpt from a botanical handbook written by Rasmus Rasmussen, a botanist and the first principal of the Folk High School, who, under the pen name Regin í Líð, published the first Faroese novel, *Babelstornið* ("The Tower of Babel"), in 1909. The status of Faroese as a "cultured language" was secured by a great flowering of literature and scholarship in the 1920s and 1930s. The language's continued vitality may be suggested statistically. In 1980 alone, publications in Faroese included eight newspapers, one monthly newsmagazine, 93 books, and 77 journals and periodical publications, not to mention hundreds of hours of radio broadcasting and a certain amount of television (Ársfrágreiðing 1980:281-86).

Why did Faroese gain ground so rapidly? The answer involves the timing of the language movement's arrival in the Faroes, its ideology, and the social position of its leaders.

By 1890, the Faroes had experienced over half a century of economic and demographic growth. But urbanization had been slight; "modern" institutions were scarce; Danish intrusion was diffuse; and the disruption of village life had been minimal. The shift from farming to fishing profited freeholders and landless folk as well as king's farmers, none of whom found themselves opposed to each other or to the rising mercantile or intellectual elites who now spoke in their name. The vernacular was threatened but not moribund, having quietly replaced Danish as the ordinary language of trade, for example; and it now extended its range to the new fishing ships, which were owned, manned, and skippered by Faroese. Balladry survived, although "the dance relinquished its old setting" in the 1890s (J.P. Joensen 1980:175). Moreover, Danish and Faroese were not opposed. The Faroese had long accepted Danish as their own language of law and religion. In short, the vernacular remained strong enough so that the movement to revitalize it could push into an expanding sociolinguistic frontier that Danish might otherwise have occupied, when the rise of ship fishing inaugurated a period of increasingly rapid industrialization and modernization and the proliferation of the institutional appurtenances of modern life.

This general statement has a sociological correlate and an ideological one. Sociologically, there was considerable continuity between what might be called the provincial elite of the period 1856-1890 and the leadership of the language movement thereafter. Both were disproportionately from Tórshavn and included both merchants and farmers along with sheriffs, teachers, and priests and others with liberal and clerical professions. The data suggest, however, that the former categories lost ground to others (especially teachers), as the movement spread both geographically and socially. Our richest data are provided in a series of subscription and membership lists containing people's occupations along with their names.

The segments of the Faroese population that had actively supported local literary culture at an early date are suggested by the list of forty-eight people who, in 1836, subscribed funds toward the publication of Schrøter's collection of documents (see Table 8). Forty-three of them lived in the Faroes, and of these, nineteen (44 percent) lived in Tórshavn. Predictably, one of Tórshavn's subscribers was a teacher, and two were high officials (the governor and the *sorinskrivari*). One was a sheriff's assistant, and the occupations of three are not given. Curiously, however, the rest were day-laborers, "youths," and several rather lowly employees of the Monopoly. The "rural" subscribers included four sheriffs, four priests, twelve farmers, two artisans (a smith and a joiner), and two men whose occupations are not given. It is not entirely clear what one should make of this rather odd social mixture. The subscribers' list does, however, indicate the early importance of Tórshavn as a cultural center, and the importance elsewhere of scattered elements of the agricultural community along with the old rural elite of sheriffs and priests. It also illustrates how crucial

Table 8.   Local subscribers to Schrøter's collection of documents, 1836

Occupation	Tórshavn	Elsewhere	Total
Royal administrators	2	0	2
Teachers	1	0	1
Day-laborers and "youths" (*ungkarl*)	7	0	7
Monopoly employees	5[a]	0	5
Sheriffs	0	4	4
Liberal and clerical professions	1[b]	4[c]	5
Farmers	0	12[d]	12
Craftsmen, artisans	0	2	2
Don't know	3	2	5
Total	19	24	43

Source: Schrøter 1836: unnumbered prefatory pages.

[a]Includes one cooper, one stocking-inspector, one stockboy, and two porters.

[b]A sheriff's assistant (*kaldsmand*).

[c]All priests

[d]Includes eight freeholders, two king's farmers (with tenancies of 5 and 6 *merkur*), and two men with mixed types of holdings (including tenancies of 6 and 10 *merkur*). The men with tenancies were all getting on in years, having taken over their estates in 1801, 1806, 1808, and 1820 (Degn 1945).

was the role played *after* 1856 by two occupational groups new to Faroese society: merchants and teachers.

The prominence of merchants between 1856 and 1890 is suggested by a list of ninety-four men living in the Faroes who purchased shares of *Dimmalætting* when it was incorporated, in 1877 (see Table 9). Thirty-six of them (38 percent) were merchants, a large figure, considering that at that period perhaps 4 percent of the Faroese population was supported by "trade and transport." Another twenty-five (27 percent) were farmers, and the rest included an undoubtedly high proportion of the Faroes' officials and clerical professionals, along with a smattering of teachers and others. At first glance, *Dimmalætting*'s shareholders seem notably rural, since only twenty-one (22 percent) of its members lived in Tórshavn. At that time, however, Tórshavn contained only 9 percent of the Faroese population, and all six members of *Dimmalætting*'s board of directors lived there.

The student poets of the 1870s and 1880s form a more selective, transitional group (see Table 10). They too came disproportionately from Tórshavn, five of the fourteen (36 percent) having been born there. The data on their fathers' occupations are incomplete, but they included two teachers, a bookseller and a merchant, a sheriff and a priest. One interesting feature of this group of young poets is how few of them made their careers in the Faroes. A further hint of the predicament in which bright

Table 9.   Local shareholders in *Dimmalætting,* 1877

Occupation	Tórshavn	Towns[a]	Villages	Total
Merchants	7	14	15	36
Teachers	2	–	2	4
Sheriffs, officials	5	2	1	8
Craftsmen, artisans	1	1	3	5
Shipmasters	–	1	2	3
Farmers	–	4	21	25
Liberal and clerical	6	1	3	10
Other, don't know	–	–	3	3
Total	21	23	50	94

Source: Dimmalætting, Prøvenummer ("Specimen number"), 8 December 1877
Note: An additional six shareholders lived in Denmark.
[a]Tvøroyri, Klaksvík, Vestmanna, Vágur, Miðvágur; it is, however, rather early to speak of a distinction between "towns" and "villages."

young people of that generation found themselves is given by Charles Edwardes, an English writer who visited the Faroes in (probably) the summer of 1884. Having walked across the ridge from Tórshavn to Kirkjubøur, he met "the farmer's daughter, a young lady of eighteen, who had just finished her education, as the phrase goes, in Copenhagen, and, after greetings, was commissioned to bring wine and cake and cigars. She was a beautiful girl, with dark eyes unusual in this land of Northmen, brilliant complexion, and an elegant figure; but, much as one could not help admiring her, it went against the grain to be waited upon by her with a deference that was yet more humiliating." Edwardes realized that the young lady (she was evidently Jóannes Patursson's younger sister, Súsanna Helena Patursson, called Sannulena) was acting as a Faroese peasant woman should, serving the menfolk their meal; but he reflected, upon leaving, that her "Copenhagen piano and finished education" sorted oddly with the "[simplicity] of speech and manner [of] a peasant's daughter dependent for her education upon nature alone." Sannulena probably felt uncomfortable too, for "Her fair face was crimson when she said 'Goodbye,' and her eyes looked down modestly; but she gripped my hand as tightly as a boy" (Edwardes 1885:126, 130). In 1889 Sannulena wrote a comedy for the Føringafelag's first dramatic presentation, but did not finally make her home in the Faroes until shortly after the turn of the century. She edited a newspaper "for men and women," *Oyggjarnar,* which came out at somewhat irregular intervals between 1905 and 1908, and wrote two books. One was called "Recipes for Each House," the Faroes' first cookbook. Having been ill for many years, she died at Kirkjubøur, in 1916 (Á. Dahl 1981:39-40).

In a sense, the formation of the Føringafelag was a response to the predicament facing a growing number of people like Sannulena Patursson

Table 10.   Student poets in Copenhagen

Name	Place of Birth	Father's Profession	Career
Kristian Bærentsen	Tórshavn	merchant	law, civil service; Governor 1897-1911
Jakob Djurhuus	Klaksvík	} ?	{ ?
Johannes Djurhuus	Klaksvík		?
Rasmus Effersøe	Tvøroyri	sheriff	agricultural officer in Faroes; playwright
Hjalmar Hammershaimb	Nes (Eyst.)	} Dean	{ civil service, law, insurance in Faroes; in Denmark after 1886
Jørgen Hammershaimb	Nes (Eyst.)		?
Billa Hansen	Sandur	?	teacher in Denmark
Jakob Jakobsen	Tórshavn	bookseller	scholar in Denmark
Johan Carl Joensen	Miðvágur	?	civil service; colonial officer in Greenland 1888-1904
Edvard Lützen	Tórshavn	teacher	priest in Greenland and Denmark
Hans Chr. Müller	Tórshavn	?	emigrated to Canada in 1890s
Johan Olsen	Tórshavn	bookkeeper	teacher in Faroes, then in Denmark
J.H.J. Petersen	Saltnes (Eyst.)	} teacher	{ teacher in Faroes
Frederik Petersen	Saltnes (Eyst.)		priest in Faroes; Dean 1900-1917

and the student poets of the 1870s and 1880s: how to fulfill at home the promise of a cosmopolitan education, despite the Faroes' lack of cultural amenities. It is not surprising, then, that all but two of the conveners of the "Christmas Meeting" were from Tórshavn, where the Faroese and cosmopolitan worlds met (see Table 11). Their ages varied (Enok Bærentsen was born in 1831 and H.N. Jacobsen in 1832, while Jóannes Patursson was born in 1866, but all were culturally marginal by virtue of their educations, occupations, or both. Bærentsen had received a commercial education and his firm was a large one; Patursson had been partly educated in Norway and was heir to the Faroes' largest tenancy; Effersøe, who had been trained in Sweden as well as in Denmark, had the singular occupation of agricultural consultant; H.N. Jacobsen was the Faroes' only bookseller; and so forth.

A suggestion of how their ideas spread—and of the reaction to

Table 11.   Conveners of the "Christmas Meeting," 1888

Name	Born	Residence	Profession
Enok Bærentsen	1831	Tórshavn	merchant
Rasmus Effersøe	1857	Tórshavn	agricultural consultant
D. Isaksen	1849	Tórshavn	editor
H.N. Jacobsen	1832	Tórshavn	bookseller
Just Jacobsen	1860	Tórshavn	king's farmer
Chr. L. Johannesen	1861	Toftir (Eyst.)	teacher
Jens Olsen	1860	Tórshavn?	merchant
Jóannes Patursson	1866	Kirkjubøur	king's farmer
S.F. Samuelsen	1852	Tórshavn	quartermaster

them—may be gathered from *Føringatíðindi*'s reports of *fólkafundir* in the mid-1890s. As we have seen, the Sandoy *fólkafundur*, in 1894, was organized by the *sorinskrivari*'s clerk, Mads Andreas Winther, and Skopun's merchant (and leading citizen) Jóhan Hendrik Poulsen. As well as several of the Føringafelag's founders, the speakers or organizers for a second *fólkafundur*, held outside Kaldbak on Midsummer's Day, included a cooper and three king's farmers: Óli við Á, who held 4 *merkur* in Velbastaður; Ólavur á Heygum, who held 9¼ *merkur* in Vestmanna; and Hanus á Bø, who held 10 *merkur* in Kaldbak. A discordant note was struck, however, by one Johannes Bærentsen, a shoemaker, who said "we should speak Faroese but not write and read it," and by Bærent Wang, who held a tenancy of 6 *merkur* in Kaldbak. Wang "wanted to have only Danish in the schools." Another discordant note was struck the following year, on Nólsoy, when a Tórshavn smith attacked Jóannes Patursson by asking "if it wasn't perverse (*rangt*) to support the big land owners." He favored redistributing the land.[7]

The cultural movement of the 1890s was obviously not universally popular. The manner in which Faroese literary culture spread after the turn of the century to embrace the likes of those who spoke out against the Føringafelag's program in 1894-95 is suggested by the membership lists of the Føroya Bókmentafelag, a literary society founded in Tórshavn, in 1898 (see Table 12). Its base in 1899 was in Tórshavn and among merchants. Thirty of its fifty-eight charter members (52 percent) lived in Tórshavn, and twenty-six of the fifty-eight (45 percent) were merchants. Seventeen members (32 percent), including ten merchants, lived in the towns. The Society's membership more than doubled by 1911. It did not lose its earlier core of support, but now only about one-quarter of its members lived in Tórshavn, and only about one-quarter were merchants. Some 39 percent of its members lived in the villages and they included substantially greater numbers of artisans, fishermen, and farmers.

In sum, the Faroes' cultural separatism, which promoted an essentially urban, bourgeois culture, or form of culture, began at the upper fringes of the provincial elite in the late 1880s. At first it received a mixed reception, merchants and the old agricultural elite perhaps favoring it more than did artisans and craftsmen. But eventually it spread, first to the towns and then to the villages, and among the lower ranks of Faroese society.

The language movement's success was also fostered by an ideology enabling it to cut across the latent (or not-so-latent) divisions within Faroese society. As we have seen, two propositions were axiomatic to Romantic Nationalism's Faroese application, at least as Hammershaimb (but not Svend Grundtvig) had understood it. The Faroese language, and hence the Faroese people, were unified; and neither the language nor the people was opposed to Danish or Denmark. Just as, in 1845, Grundtvig had apparently missed Hammershaimb's point that Faroese did not think it strange to have one written language and one spoken one (see Bekker-Nielsen 1978:86), so, in about 1884, Charles Edwardes found it "a trifle strange, considering how little actual advantage they derive from Danish rule, that the Faroese should be so warm in their devotion to the Danish government . . . . I never entered a house in Faroe without seeing a portrait of the Danish king—a steel engraving or a common woodcut daubed with rainbow colors" (1885:127). But this kind of unity with Denmark was deeply embedded in Faroese culture; both by insisting on it and maintaining that the Faroese people and their language were unified as well, the language movement avoided becoming openly politicized during its first, crucial decade.

In the introduction to the *Færøsk Anthologi,* Hammershaimb writes that he had chosen an etymological orthography partly in order to avoid choosing any "particular dialect's sound system [as a base, which] might be an injustice to other dialects' perhaps equally rightful claim for their characteristic sound systems" (1969[1891]:lv). Moreover, the very format of the *Færøsk Anthologi,* as well as that of Jakobsen's *Færøske Folkesagn og Æventyr,* combining Faroese texts with a Danish scholarly apparatus, embodied the assumption that Faroese was "folkish" while Danish was "cultured." To both men, the Faroes' continued cultural and linguistic dependence on Denmark remained axiomatic. The same was true for nearly all the organizers of the "Christmas Meeting." Enok Bærentsen claimed that building up Faroese did not mean dispensing with Danish, "which was the cultured language (*kulturmaalet*) with which we are connected with the outside world." Rasmus Effersøe added: "Our adherence to the mother tongue, which is a link between us and our kinsmen in the three Scandinavian countries, must not be stamped with hatred against Danishness taken as a whole."[8]

There can be little doubt that the movement's success was favored by the insistence that the Faroese need not be at odds with each other or with Danes. But this position was paradoxical to begin with and proved impos-

Table 12. Local membership in the Føroya Bókmentafelag (Faroese Literary Society), 1899 and 1911

Occupation	1899					1911				
	Tórshavn	Towns[a]	Villages	Total	Percent	Tórshavn	Towns[a]	Villages	Total	Percent
Merchants	13	10	3	26	44.8	7	15	9	31	25.6
Teachers	1	1	4	6	10.3	2	4	8	14	11.6
Sheriffs, officials	2	3	2	8	13.8	1	2	1	4	3.3
Craftsmen, artisans	4	1	1	6	10.3	8	6	4	18	14.9
Fishermen, seamen	1	1	0	2	3.4	1	4	12	17	14.0
Farmers	1	1	0	2	3.4	1	3	6	10	8.3
Liberal and clerical	7	0	1	8	13.8	9	4	3	15	12.4
Women (no profession given)	0	0	0	0	—	2	4	1	7	5.8
Other	1	0	0	1	1.7	1	0	3	4	3.3
Total	30	17	11	58		32	42	47	121	
Percent	51.7%	29.3%	19.0%			26.6%	34.7%	38.8%		

Source: 1899: Ársbók 1900: 10-12; 1911: Ársbók 1911: 8-11

Note: Two members lived abroad in 1899. Forty-one members lived abroad in 1911.

[a] Tvøroyri, Vágur, Miðvágur-Sandavágur, Vestmanna, Klaksvík

sible to maintain, as the language was increasingly put to "unfolkish" uses and threatened to invade the territory of Danish. A few cracks in the ideological facade appeared early on. J.C. Joensen, a student poet of the 1880s, wrote that Faroese

> was heard in the Faroes in the mountains and at sea
> from ancient times until this day;
> well may it be banned from church and school,
> but it will return, either soon or late.

In "Now the Hour Is Come to Hand," Jóannes Patursson urged that foreign ways be blown away to the northeast (away from Denmark) "like soap bubbles." When Evensen reached these lines at the Christmas Meeting, the Danish priest of South Streymoy, C.A. Hansen, rose in shock and made as if to leave. Others did not react so strongly, although some were undoubtedly equally opposed to Patursson's view (J. av Skarði 1980:9-10). Nor was such anti-Danishness the official view of the Føringafelag, as Evensen's and Bærentsen's remarks show.

By the turn of the century, however, the Føringafelag's apolitical ideology was on the defensive. For example, the Literary Society's bylaws had to warn potential contributors that "the Society does not support books about how the country or parts of the country should be ruled (politics), or which directly give or demand an answer in favor of (or against) other books (polemics)" (Ársbók 1900:4). During the 1890s, the use of Faroese became an openly political issue, and as the disunity of people's views sharpened, new institutions had to be created to articulate them. The Føringafelag itself broke up in 1901, having become fatally embroiled in a dispute over the orthography of Faroese.

The orthographic dispute was triggered by Jakob Jakobsen. He held a more modern opinion of the desirable relationship between spoken and written languages and was convinced, besides, that Faroese had a very limited future for literary or official purposes. He accordingly proposed a substantial revision of Hammershaimb's orthography, to bring the written language closer to the spoken one. He felt that what the language might lose in orthographic dignity it would gain in ease of comprehension.[9] His proposals, which were published in *Dimmalætting,* in 1889, stopped short of a fully phonetic orthography, but they did favor the dialect of South Streymoy, including Tórshavn. Well aware of his orthography's artificiality, Hammershaimb himself was apparently not unalterably opposed to making a few changes in (Hammershaimb 1969 [1891]:lv-lvi). Others felt more strongly, but the Føringafelag took Jakobsen's proposals under formal consideration between 1892 and 1895. A few minor revisions were accepted, but were largely abandoned in 1898. By that time, the Føringafelag's membership was badly split. Patursson had resigned in 1896; membership dwindled; and in 1901 the club dissolved. "At the last meeting of the Society, most agreed that there was no hope for its life. Absalon á Trøllanesi maintained, however, that they should carry on. But the meeting broke up when Rasmus Effersøe had to leave to act in a play! So undramatically did the Føringafelag pass away" (H.J. Debes 1969). *Føringatíðindi* ceased publication. Briefly, there was once again "greater life among the Faroese in Copenhagen than at home in the Faroes" (Matras 1935:83).

The orthographic issue was not so trivial as it may seem today. Jakobsen was proposing to fix the language in a relatively easy form, resting on an urban base. But the written tongue's still precarious standing as an alternative high language depended precisely on its "difficult" distance from everyday speech, its deliberately countrified, "folkish" air, and its transcendance of dialectal differences. An easy language was simply not respectable enough. One correspondent who favored Hammershaimb's orthography wrote to *Føringatíðindi*, at the height of the debate, that if Jakobsen's proposals were adopted, "then the language will travel a very short path—then it will come no farther than everyday use among us, and [the same result] will befall each part of the club." A return to Hammershaimb's orthography, he concluded, would "return compromise and peace to our club, which the [orthographic] change has divided."[10]

It seems as well, at least in retrospect, that the orthographic debate and other, more minor ones, revealed an unexpected (indeed, unwelcome) consequence of the establishment of Faroese as a high language: its use as a vehicle for *dis*agreement among Faroese. The orthographic debate was the first major modern case of public, sustained, essentially political disagreement among Faroese carried out in their own language; and in it they found, almost despite themselves, the high-principled, bickering style, curiously at odds with the modest matter-of-factness and measured avoidance of open dissension in everyday life, that still characterizes Faroese politics. As the style's oddity suggests, open disagreement is not something that comes easily to Faroese.[11] The Føringafelag undoubtedly passed out of existence largely because its members resigned rather than take sides against each other.

The late 1890s saw the language movement's twin axioms violated. The unity of Faroese faded as the language was turned to novel uses; and, as we shall see, the unity between the Faroes and Denmark became problematic, as Faroese began to encroach on previously Danish territory. It is significant, therefore, that the demise of the Føringafelag coincided with further institutional specialization; the Literary Society, for example, continued to promote an apolitical cultural unity, while an especially "sharp note of controversy" (West 1972:125) appeared in 1901-6 with the rise of political parties, whose rivalry involved differing views of Denmark's place in Faroese society.

The formation of Faroese political parties was triggered by the Danish election of 1901, following which the Left Reform party (Venstre) formed a government, after years of Conservative rule. The Faroes' representative in the Folketing was Jóannes Patursson, who was also elected to the Løgting. He was reelected to the Folketing by a narrow margin in July 1903. There he allied himself with the Left, in hopes of winning greater autonomy for the Faroes. He claimed some official Danish support for his program, which anticipated the present home-rule arrangement. His most important proposals were that: (1) all the Løgting's members should be popularly elected (that is, it should exclude the governor and the dean, who were members ex officio, unless they were elected in their own right); (2) the governor might take part in the Løgting's deliberations, but could not vote unless he himself were elected; (3) no law for the Faroes alone might come into effect unless it were entirely approved by the Løgting; (4) the Løgting should be able to propose laws directly to the Danish administration, not just through the Danish parliament; and (5) the Løgting should control Faroese finances. But the last of these raised the specter of higher taxes. For that reason, as well as for his outspoken anti-Danishness, Patursson was defeated for reelection to the Folketing in 1906, although he retained a seat in the Løgting.

The elections of 1901 and 1903 had been markedly partisan, with an especially clear distinction between Patursson and his more conservative opponents. However, it was not until September 1903, after his reelection to the Folketing, that the Faroes' first political club was formed. Led by Patursson, Jóhan Hendrik Poulsen, Rasmus Effersøe, M.A. Winther, and others, the Faroese Progressive Society (Føroya Framburðsfelag) was at first chiefly a Tórshavn organization but soon extended elsewhere. It put up its first candidate (unsuccessfully) in a town council election in Tórshavn, in 1904. In the Løgting elections of 1905, its candidates lost to still unorganized conservative opponents in the Norðoyar; but they swept South Streymoy, Sandoy, and Suðuroy. (Vágar, Eysturoy, and North Streymoy did not vote that year.)

Following the Folketing elections of 1906, unionist and separatist opinions were more formally institutionalized. The victors formed the Union party; Patursson and his supporters formed the Self-Rule party: *Dimmalætting* became the organ of the Union party, and *Tingakrossur* (founded in 1901) became the organ of the Self-Rule party. Except from 1918 to 1920 (when the Self-Rule party had a two-seat majority) and from 1920 to 1924 (when the two parties were evenly matched), the Union party remained the majority party in the Løgting until 1928. In 1908 the Union party entered upon a curious but long-lived alliance with the Danish Left. However, neither it nor any other Faroese party has ever been a branch of a Danish one.

In cultural matters, the Self-Rule platform was essentially that of the Føringafelag, which it considered still unfulfilled. There was "nothing said against Danish or Danes, [and] equally little about separation from Denmark" (Sjalvstýrisflokkurin n.d.:9). In economic matters, it followed Patursson in favoring local control over local finances. Along with its

Table 13.   Birth dates of party leaders, 1906-24

| | Self-Rule party | | Union party | |
Date of Birth	Number	Percent	Number	Percent
1830-1839	0	—	1	2.7
1840-1849	0	—	2	5.4
1850-1859	3	13.0	3	8.1
1860-1869	3	13.0	10	27.0
1870-1879	14	60.9	9	24.3
1880-1889	3	13.0	10	27.0
1890-1900	0	—	2	5.4
Total	23		37	

Source: Waag (1967)

support for greater use of Faroese in the schools, for example, the Self-Rule party's economic plank nonetheless anticipated a substantial redefinition of the Faroes' subordinate relationship to Denmark (see J. Patursson 1903, 1931).

The Union party accepted the cultural gains of the previous decades, but saw further economic progress as depending on a continued close association with Denmark. It labeled the Self-Rule party "separatist."

What factors influenced the choice of party affiliation among Faroese? Unfortunately, no firm answer can be given. The Faroes' political sociology is a difficult and still largely unexplored field. Its complications include the small size of the population (which makes statistical analysis difficult or doubtful); the large number of parties (at present six, plus a minuscule Communist party); the combination of sometimes disparate communities' electoral returns before 1918; and the fact that, especially in the early days of party politics and especially in country districts, party platforms were probably less decisive than the personal prestige of locally prominent adherents of one party or the other. A start can be made, however, and the last of these complications in part overcome, by considering the socioeconomic characteristics of each party's members of the Løgting in the period between 1906 and 1924. There were sixty such men:[12] fifty-eight elected members, plus two deans (Jákup Dahl and Fr. Petersen), who were ex officio members but who voted regularly with one party or the other. Four factors evidently determined their choice of party: age, occupation, and (at least for the elected members) residence and position in the communities from which they were elected.

Age seems to have been the most decisive factor. The Union leaders' birthdates are well distributed over fifty-seven years, from 1837 to 1894; but the Self-Rule leaders were mostly born in the 1870s (see Table 13).

Table 14.   Age and occupation of party leaders, 1906-24

	Self-Rule party			Union party		
	Age			Age		
Occupation	Born 1870-79	Older or younger	Total	Born 1870-79	Older or younger	Total
Farmers, sheriffs, priests	4	4	8	1	8	9
Merchants, other trade and industry	2	0	2	5	8	13
Teachers, other liberal professions	5	3	8	0	8	8
Crafts and trades	3	1	4	0	2	2
Fishermen	0	0	0	1	2	3
Government functionaries, etc.	0	1	1	2	1	3
Total	14	9	23	9	28	37

Source: Waag (1967)

Of the twenty-three leaders of both parties born in the 1870s, fourteen (61 percent) were members of the Self-Rule party, while only nine (39 percent) were Unionists. By contrast, of the thirty-seven leaders born either before or after the 1870s, twenty-eight (76 percent) were Unionists, while only nine (24 percent) were members of the Self-Rule party. Clearly, the more expressly political aspects of the Føringafelag's program were adopted by men who came of age during the cultural agitation of the 1890s.

Occupation was a second factor determining party affiliation. The largest occupational categories of Self-Rule leaders were teachers and lawyers (eight, or 35 percent), the traditional elite of king's farmers, sheriffs, and priests (eight, or 35 percent), and men engaged in crafts and trade (four, or 17 percent). The largest single category of Union leaders was merchants and others engaged in commerce and industry (twelve, or 33 percent), followed by members of the traditional elite (eight, or 22 percent), and teachers and men with other liberal professions (seven, or 19 percent). The pattern of divisions in allegiance becomes clearer when we correct for age (see Table 14). The Union party was largely led by merchants of all ages, while age divided teachers, members of the traditional elite, and practitioners of crafts and trades into Union and Self-Rule factions. In short, merchants tended to abandon the politicized version of the cultural movement, while other groups found themselves divided by it.

A third factor was residence, the kinds of communities from which the leaders came. Here we must shorten our list of leaders slightly, by excluding the two unelected deans. And we must define several types of

Table 15.   Residence of elected party leaders, 1906-24

Residence	Self-Rule party		Union party	
	Number	Percent	Number	Percent
Tórshavn	5	22.7	8	22.2
Towns[a]	10	45.5	9	25.0
Villages	7	31.8	19	52.8
Total	22		36	

Source: Waag (1967)

[a]Klaksvík, Fuglafjørður, Vestmanna, Miðvágur-Sandavágur, Tvøroyri, Vágur

communities. First, of course, Tórshavn stands in a category by itself. Second, "towns," or "fishing towns," may be defined somewhat arbitrarily as the six communities other than Tórshavn where at least four ships were registered in 1911: Klaksvík, Fuglafjørður, Vestmanna, Miðvágur-Sandavágur, Tvøroyri, and Vágur (E. Patursson 1961:122). The remaining communities were "villages." In these terms, the Self-Rule and Union leaderships were proportionately equally residents of Tórshavn (22 vs. 23 percent). Otherwise, the Self-Rule leadership came disproportionately from the towns (45 percent), while the Union leadership came disproportionately from the villages (53 percent) (see Table 15). The Self-Rule leadership may thus be said to have represented a coalition between Tórshavn and the towns, while the Union party's represented a coalition between Tórshavn and the villages.

A similar conclusion emerges from the voting statistics themselves (see Table 16). The figures suggest not only that the Union party enjoyed greater support in the villages than in the towns, but also that the more remote a village was, the stronger was its Union party support. All this accords well with our earlier observations about the diffusion of adherence to the goals of the language movement.

A related conclusion emerges from consideration of a fourth factor: the party leaders' socioeconomic position in their home communities. No matter where they lived, they were generally prominent figures in local society. A more interesting pattern emerges, however, if we take into account the fact that socioeconomic change had reached different stages in different places. In the villages, where the period from 1906 to 1924 saw the rapid decline of the agricultural economy, we may say that there was an existing establishment of king's farmers, sheriffs, and priests. In the towns, where the deep-water fishery presided over by merchants was supporting increased occupational diversification, the existing establishment consisted of merchants. Tórshavn was the Faroes' political, commercial, and intellectual capital and a fishing center, as well. The line is not always easy to draw, but we may fairly assume that its existing establishment

consisted of lawyers and high government functionaries, substantial merchants, secondary school teachers, and ship owners.

Now the pattern is clear. Party leaders tended *not* to be members of
their communities' existing establishments (see Table 17). Among the
twenty-six village-dwelling representatives, only nine (35 percent) were
king's farmers, sheriffs, or priests. The remaining seventeen (65 percent)
included eight teachers, four merchants, three fishermen, a carpenter, and
a lighthouse keeper. By reason of age, occupation, or both, most of these
men were adherents of the Union party. In the towns, only seven out of
nineteen representatives (37 percent) were merchants. The rest included a
farmer, five sheriffs, two teachers, three craftsmen, and a postman. By
reason of age, occupation, or both, most of these men were adherents of
the Self-Rule party. In Tórshavn, only five out of thirteen representatives
(38 percent) were members of the existing establishment: two teachers at
the folk high school, two lawyers, and a ship owner. All but the last of
these were members of the Self-Rule party. Tórshavn's other representatives (eight, or 62 percent) included an architect, a newspaper editor, two
clerks in merchant firms, a carpenter, a tinsmith, an archivist, and a postman. All but one of these (the tinsmith and poet Nyholm Debess) were
members of the Union Party.

In other words, people everywhere in the Faroes tended to vote the
same way between 1906 and 1924: against the existing establishment. But
because socioeconomic change had reached different stages in the Faroes'
several sorts of communities, because support for Faroese literary culture
had not penetrated all places or segments of society equally, and because
the language movement's politicization had divided the Faroes' elites by
age or occupation or both, the result was not unanimity at the polls.
Rather, it was an institutionalized opposition between two parties whose
differences were expressed partly in terms of opposed views of Denmark's
proper relationship to the Faroes. These views did not only concern Denmark; they also provided a convenient code in which to express views on
other, internal points of difference.

It seems fair to conclude that the Faroes' politicization was more
markedly a reflection of internal developments than of a simple, ideologically motivated alignment for or against Danish governance.[13] Indeed,
the fact that the Union party was "pro-Danish" obscures a most important
point. As we have noted, it and all other Faroese parties have been
uniquely Faroese. In a sense, the formation of exclusively local political
parties, "pro-Danish" though one of them might be, constituted a subtle
but decisive declaration of independence from Denmark. For in 1906, the
Faroes acquired an essential feature of nationhood: a home-grown political
culture to match their recently established literary one.

This is not to say, of course, that the Faroes actually became a nation in
1906. They are not a sovereign state today. Nor is this the place to inves-

Table 16.   Percentages (rounded) of Union party vote, 1906-24

	1906	1908	1910	1912	1914	1916	1918	1920	1924
Four towns and their hinterlands									
Suðuroy									
Tvøroyri	?	?	—	?	—	?	9	24	32
Other northern Suðuroy	?	?	—	?	—	?	49	63	53
All northern Suðuroy	69	82	—	?	—	34	27	40	41
Vágur	?	?	—	?	—	?	54	72	75
Other southern Suðuroy	?	?	—	?	—	?	44	71	78
All southern Suðuroy	92	94	—	?	—	67	50	72	77
Norðstreymoy									
Vestmanna	78	—	?	—	44	—	50	51	58
Other Norðstreymoy	84	—	?	—	52	—	74	74	70
All Norðstreymoy	81	—	80	—	47	—	66	67	67
Norðoyar									
Klaksvík	54	—	51	—	30	—	26	46	48
Other Norðoyar	85	—	71	—	56	—	41	46	57
All Norðoyar	67	—	58	—	37	—	36	46	52
Selected communities and outlying islands									
Sørvágur							90	88	85
Mykines							93	99	97
Klaksvík							26	46	48
Fugloy							53	59	67
Svínoy							53	56	75
Sandur							19	21	20
Skúvoy, St. Dímun							34	50	49

Source: Waag (1967)

Table 17.   Socioeconomic status of elected party leaders in their home communities, 1906-24

	Self-Rule party	Union party	Total Number	%
Tórshavn				
Existing establishment	4	1	5	38.5
Other	1	7	8	61.5
Towns[a]				
Existing establishment	2	5	7	36.8
Other	8	4	12	63.2
Villages				
Existing establishment	5	4	9	34.6
Other	2	15	17	65.4

Source: Waag (1967)

[a]Klaksvík, Fuglafjørður, Miðvágur-Sandavágur, Vestmanna, Tvøroyri, Vágur

tigate in detail what has happened since about 1920. However, it is to suggest that by that time, although the Faroes did not become a nation in political fact, they had essentially acquired a national culture: a shared sense of political and cultural distinctiveness articulated in locally based, locally staffed formal institutions as well as in a set of internationally and locally recognized symbols of nationhood.

We may round off our story by offering a few retrospective remarks on some symbols of Faroese nationhood, by carrying a few series of events up to date, and by suggesting some promising points of comparison between the Faroes and other parts of the world.

The past few chapters have argued that a recognizably Faroese culture survived the demise of its traditional economic base in the late nineteenth and early twentieth centuries. It did so largely through a process of selecting symbols of Faroese "nationality" out of the whole range of elements of the traditional culture and then reelaborating them. The selection was not arbitrary. Potential symbols of "nationality" had to be recognizable as such, abroad as well as at home; their nature had to be such that adherence to them did not imperil economic or civic progress or further social change; and their elaboration required the commitment of local leaders.

The prime symbols of Faroeseness, language and works of language, fitted these criteria admirably. They had sustained local identity since the aftermath of the Reformation and were recognized as emblems of nationality by leading Danes and Faroese alike from the mid-nineteenth century on. Rebuilding the language and extending its range did not entail continued backwardness, despite the fears of Unionists and others. And in the

1890s, they were promoted by a brilliant, articulate, and growing group of leaders who found themselves on the cusp between the local and outside worlds.[14] A further, negative criterion came into play as well. The language movement faced little organized opposition in the 1890s, in large part because it did not immediately invade Danish territory. Thereafter, a potentially serious source of opposition was weakened, if not entirely removed, by the rise to high office of men who sympathized with its goals. Enok Bærentsen's son Christian was the Faroes' first (and only) native-born governor, from 1897 to 1911, for example, and from 1895 on, the deans were Faroese as well.[15]

The same factors underlay the selection and elaboration of other, more minor symbols of Faroeseness. One such symbol is the *grindadráp*, or slaughter of schools of pilot whales, which Kenneth Williamson has called "an integral part of Faeroese nationhood . . . one of the most significant factors in the curious identity of [Faroese] life" (1970:96). I have discussed elsewhere (Wylie and Margolin 1981:95-132) the *grindadráp*'s long history in action and in print as a celebration of Faroese society. Like most writers from Lucas Debes (1673) on, I stressed the hunt's antiquity, its course, the sheriff's method of dividing the spoils, and the rituals accompanying it, including a dance. What is more interesting from our present point of view is how the event was advertised in the late nineteenth century, and the fact that certain of its features were *not* selected as proper elements of the occasion.

The *grindadráp*'s main advertising agent was H.C. Müller, an eminently marginal man: sheriff of South Streymoy from 1843 until his death on Christmas morning, 1897; representative in the Løgting (1852-80), the Folketing (1858-64 and 1887-89), and the Landsting (1864-86); internationally respected amateur ornithologist and zoologist; steamship agent from 1867 on; postmaster from 1870 on; member of the board of directors of the savings bank and of the school board; shopkeeper; and with his "braided cap and frock coat trimmed with buttons bearing the stamp of the royal crown," his occasional trade in photographs, and his parlor crammed with stuffed birds, for nearly half a century a kind of one-man tourist bureau.[16] The British novelist and post-office official Anthony Trollope, who paid the Faroes a fleeting visit in June 1878, wrote that Müller was "in face singularly like Mr. Gladstone, and therefore may be endowed with some of that linguacious capacity for which Mr. Gladstone is so renowned," but regretted that time did not permit what would surely have been a fascinating conversation about postal problems (Trollope 1878:13). Müller was also an aficionado of the *grindadráp*, not only publishing accounts of it abroad (Müller 1883a, 1883b), but also describing it well enough to tourists so that many a traveler's tale of otherwise dubious reliability contains a fair description of the *grindadráp*'s techniques and principles of distribution.

Travelers lucky enough to witness a *grindadráp* for themselves sometimes noted other aspects of the scene as well. An anonymous description of a *grindadráp* in Tórshavn, published in German in 1868, says that while the sheriff was determining the distribution of the spoils, the hunters "talk over the day's adventures with a glass of liquor, and not seldom make too much of a good thing"; many partook of a festive meal of fresh or preserved whale meat and blubber "cooked by the female personnel of the nearby houses and served . . . in a great wooden trough"; and others, "already thoroughly tipsy, pass singing and rejoicing through the streets, while in a few places, for example on the bridge, [they] form groups and perform the national dance—a circle dance with the melody of songs which are struck up by the whole company of dancers under the leadership of a lead singer—in which girls and women soon take part as well" (Anon. 1868:106).

These features of the occasion met various fates. Eating from a trough, or *etingatrog,* was old-fashioned and inelegant even then. At Kirkjubøur in the early 1880s, Edwardes saw "a man on his knees eating fish from a wooden trough" (1885:127), but the custom soon passed away unlamented. The meal after a *grindadráp* may be older than the first time we hear of a whale specially set aside for that purpose, in 1807 (J. P. Joensen 1976:27); it remains a traditional, relatively minor part of the occasion. "It is difficult," Joensen says, "to say how old the dance [after a *grindadráp*] is" (1976:21) suggesting that it "took its special profile after 1835," when Governor Christian Pløyen, himself a fan of both the hunt and balladry, composed a ballad about the *grindadráp* in Danish, which is still sung at *grind* dances. But as late as 1879, Enok Bærentsen lamented that when "the kill and the hauling-ashore are over, the *grind*-men have nothing to do" (*Dimmalætting,* 6 November 1879). Perhaps not until around 1900 did the "national dance" become as important a part of the *grindadráp* as it is felt to be at other times (Reynolds 1923:113). Finally, today's visitor may witness at least as much drinking and rowdiness as did the anonymous German, over a century ago. But like the widespread drinking at Ólavsøka, the national holiday, drinking at the *grindadráp* escaped institutionalization in "the national culture which has been extracted from [the whole of Faroese culture] and overlaid on top of it" (Wylie 1983:39). Drinking may be as "traditional" as dancing; but it is considered reprehensible or incomprehensible, if it is mentioned at all.[17]

Another symbol of nationality was a national holiday. Ólavsøka had medieval roots, but it acquired its modern form in the 1880s and 1890s.[18] Among its features were two dances, one traditionally Faroese in style, the other modern and international. In about 1884, Edwardes found the two dances taking place in adjacent rooms. It was, he remarked, the "daughters of the [Danish] officials . . . with the students of law, medicine, and theology home [from abroad] for the holidays, and with the sons of the more considerable townspeople" who were taking part in the "politer dances" (1892:391). By 1902, the sociology of Ólavsøka dancing had

changed. In the parliament building itself, the governor was now participating in a ballad dance, "and the priest and the doctor and the apothecary
were together in the ring, while the representative to the Folketing lept
bounding among the young folk and sang at the top of his lungs" (Reynolds 1923:123). The governor was Christian Bærentsen; the priest may
have been Frederik Petersen, who was dean; the doctor was Rasmus
Effersøe's brother, Jón; the apothecary was Olav Finsen, the Tórshavn-
born son of one of Bærentsen's predecessors; and the Folketing representative was Jóannes Patursson. All had studied abroad in the 1870s and
1880s.

Another symbol of Faroese identity was what tourists called a "national costume." The Faroese national costume, called "Faroese clothes"
(føroysk klæðir), as opposed to "Danish clothes," is a standardized version
of peasant garb that became fashionable around the turn of the century,
particularly in separatist circles. "At a wedding in Miðvágur in 1888 the
poet and politician Jóannes Patursson wore a frock coat with a tie and high
hat, which would have been unthinkable a few years later, when føroysk
klæðir became his trademark. It has been reported that when the Danish
king visited the Faroes in 1906 the waiters and waitresses were clad in
føroysk klæðir, and this supposedly led many in Tórshavn to procure
the costume for themselves" (J.P. Joensen 1980:157). Today "Faroese
clothes" are worn by a few people on formal occasions.

As elements of the old-fashioned native culture were thus selected and
elaborated to mark the Faroes' cultural claims to nationhood, symbols of
foreign origin were adopted as well. The festivities at Ólavsøka, for example, had begun to incorporate nominally native rowing races in the late
1880s and early 1890s, when rowing out to fish was ceasing to be an
everyday chore. These races were followed by such international contests
as soccer, swimming, and handball matches. Similarly, Ólavsøka featured
agricultural expositions in 1895, 1901, and 1927.

A more expressly political symbol was a flag. The modern Faroese
flag, a red cross with a blue border on a white field, was designed in
Copenhagen in 1919, chiefly by the law student Jens Oliver Lisberg and
the theology student Emil Joensen.[19] Earlier Faroese flags had used the
ancient emblem of the ram or the more recent one of the oystercatcher,
displayed on a blue ground with a red border. They had been flown at
fólkafundir in the 1890s. The new design was a deliberate variation on the
theme of other Scandinavian flags, including Finland's and Iceland's,
which had both been adopted the previous year. First flown at a meeting
of the Copenhagen Føroyingafelag, the new Faroese flag was adopted, in
1920, by a young men's society in Tórshavn. The society and the flag
were called "Merkið" (the sign, banner, or boundary marker), and the
flag's white field was said to "[bring] to mind the clear pure sky and the
breakers along the coasts of the Faroe Isles" (Jepsen 1969:48). It was

briefly flown at the Icelandic Althing's millenary celebrations, in 1930, until the Danish delegates protested. At home, Danish officials and the Union party blocked the Self-Rule party's repeated attempts to "get the flag adopted as a provincial symbol" (West 1972:196). It was first officially recognized by the British on 25 April 1940, when the German occupation of Denmark rendered the Danish flag an ambiguous token of allegiance. The Home Rule Ordinance of 1948 recognized the Faroese flag. April 25 is now Flag Day in the Faroes, an official public holiday.

The Faroese flag faced opposition from Danes as well as some Faroese, since flying it explicitly questioned Denmark's authority. The same is true of the language's incursions into Danish territory after the turn of the century, and there, too, matters were complicated by the politicization of the cultural movement. Since using Faroese in church had been one of the Føringafelag's original goals, the language's path toward full acceptance in ecclesiastical matters is particularly interesting.[20]

The first problem was with the language itself. As *Føringatíðindi* had pointed out in 1894, "a language that has lain neglected for so long requires a great deal of work before it acquires garments fitting it to pass through the doors of a church" (18 October 1894). Frederik Petersen, A.C. Evensen, and others achieved a mixed success translating biblical passages in the decades around the turn of the century, but it was not until around 1920 that Jákup Dahl discovered the proper combination of dignity and fluidity. Dahl came from a prominent Suðuroy merchant family; before turning to the priesthood, he had distinguished himself in the ranks of the Self-Rule party as a teacher outspokenly favoring the use of Faroese in school. He saw many of his translations authorized during his long tenure as dean, from 1918 to 1944: the ritual and service books, in 1930 and 1939, respectively, and the New Testament, in 1937. In 1939, Faroese was approved for use in all ordinary services. The hymnal was authorized in 1956, followed by the whole Bible in 1961, Dahl's translation having been completed by Kristian Viderø.

Another problem was popular resistance to hearing Faroese in church at all, although such conservatism was by no means universal. A.C. Evensen had begun preaching regularly in Faroese, on Sandoy, as early as 1902, with special authorization to do so in Skopun, in 1903 (P.M. Rasmussen 1978:141). The strict limitations surrounding such use were slightly loosened in 1912. On the other hand, as late as "between the wars . . . polls in Tórshavn [showed] a clear majority favoring the retention of Danish" (West 1972:169).

Matters were further complicated by the issue's entanglement in both local politics and Faroese-Danish relations in 1917-18.

In internal politics, the Self-Rule party followed the Føringafelag in insisting that the language of the Church should be the language of the people. The Union party held that the language of the Church should be

Danish, since the Faroese Church was a branch of the established Danish Church. But even the established Church was factionalized, with partisans of the evangelical "Home Mission" (Da. Indre Mission), which had been introduced to the Faroes in 1904, generally favoring or at least tolerating the use of Faroese. Moreover, there was opposition between the Lutheran Church (especially its evangelical branch) and the Plymouth Brethren, who had adopted Faroese as their language after Sloan's death, in 1914. As if all this were not enough, what might otherwise have been a natural alliance between the Self-Rule party and one or both parties of evangelicals was undercut by the latter's militant disapproval of a key symbol of Faroese national identity, the "sinful" old dances (see Fossing n.d.; J. í Lon Jacobsen 1981).

Faroese-Danish relations were going through a particularly troubled phase shortly before 1920, caused in part by the somewhat uneasy coalition between the ruling Left Reform party and the Social Democrats in the Rigsdag. The Faroese Self-Rule party was allied with the coalition, since the Prime Minister, C.T. Zahle, and the Faroes' Folketing representative, Edward Mitens, found each other's support convenient.[21] More openly than was wise, however, Zahle favored the election of Jóannes Patursson to the Landsting, in 1918. He thus incurred the enmity of the governor, Svenning Rytter, who, for his part, favored the Union party more openly than was wise in internal Faroese politics. A crisis in ecclesiastical affairs thus arose in 1917, after the death of the dean, Frederik Petersen. Petersen had been an early leader of the language movement and the head of the Union party. His successor, A.C. Evensen, had been a member of the Self-Rule party, but had been elected to the Løgting as an independent, in 1916. He died, however, after only three months as dean. Acting on Mitens's advice, Zahle now appointed Dahl, who was anathema to Rytter. This further embittered relations between Zahle and Rytter, who, finding his authority impossibly compromised, resigned.

After this crisis, the whole dispute died of its own complexity. Its outcome, the acceptance of Faroese in church, was ultimately decided by two factors: the fact that by the 1920s, men fostered on the linguistic ideals of the 1890s had assumed leadership of the established Church; and the general success of the language movement in other areas, so that by the 1930s most young people had had at least some schooling in Faroese, while everyone was accustomed to hearing the language used on formal occasions.

The Faroes had come a long way in the seventy-five years since Niels Hunderup had informed the Roskilde Assembly that "the Faroese language . . . cannot well be called a language," and Dean Plesner could counter only by regretting the lack of "communal organs on the islands through which the inhabitants can express themselves." Faroese now expressed a diversity of opinions, chiefly in their own language, through "communal organs" ranging from literary associations to a shipowners' association and a fishermen's union and including the Løgting itself, rival parties within it, and competing newspapers tied to the parties. The continued proliferation of such institutions suggests that even a moderately comprehensive social history of the Faroes since, say, 1920, would require a book of its own.[22] We must, however, offer a brief summary of developments since then.

Economically, the period between the world wars was marked by a deep depression, triggered by a drop in the price of fish. Salt cod, one of the Faroes' main exports, fetched an all-time high of 0.80 kr., in 1920; the price fell below 0.19 kr., in 1932, before rising to about 0.29 kr., in the late 1930s. Fishermen's average annual income fell from an all-time high of 528 kr., in 1919, to as low as 136 kr., in 1936; that is, from about $190 to about $30 at contemporary rates of exchange. A few trawlers were bought, and most ships were equipped with auxiliary motors; but mostly the fleet grew older. By 1938, over 60 percent of the ships in the Faroese fleet were at least fifty years old (E. Patursson 1961:83ff., 343ff., 399ff.). Hard times forced people to live from the land as much as possible, but otherwise the "agricultural" economy died away. In 1950 only 1631 people (5.1 percent of the total population) were supported by agriculture, and by 1977 the figure had fallen to 595 (1.4 percent) (Årsberetning 1972:19; Ársfrágreiðing 1980:57). The economy continued to diversify in the 1920s and 1930s, although its mainstay, fishing, remained sufficiently labor-intensive so that in 1930 it still supported directly about 30 percent of the population, or over 7000 people (see Table 7, above).

By the early 1950s, the Faroese fishery was desperately antiquated. The necessary modernization was supported in large part by the formation of a Danish-Faroese lending agency, backed at first by Marshall Plan funds; by the development of onshore processing facilities for fish meal and frozen fillets; by an expansion into new, North American and northern European markets; and by the extension of the fishing limit from three miles to twelve between 1955 and 1964, and to two hundred miles in 1977, in accord with the other North Atlantic nations' agreements in that year. Today the Faroese fleet is as modern as any in the world. It continues to provide over 95 percent of the Faroes' exports by value, but now supports under 20 percent of the population directly and contributes a similar percentage to the GNP. In 1978 the Faroese per capita gross domestic product was $9,063 (Årsberetning 1980).

Demographically, the period since 1920 has seen the birth rate decline from about 30 per thousand to about 18 per thousand, despite a baby boom in the 1940s and 1950s. The death rate has fallen slowly but steadily, from over 10 to under 7 per thousand. Emigration peaked in the late 1920s, early 1950s, and late 1960s, but has now fallen practically to zero. Tórshavn grew a bit more rapidly than the population as a whole in the 1920s and 1930s, and much more rapidly into the 1970s. As of 1980, it had 13,757 inhabitants, or 31.5 percent of the total Faroese population. Recently, however, its primacy as the center of population growth has been challenged by its own suburbs and increasingly suburban neighboring villages, by the region around Skálafjørður, on Eysturoy, and by a number of villages throughout the Faroes, where the extension of the fishing limit has revived a now more and more industrialized inshore fishery (see Table 1, above, and Ársfrágreiðing 1980:46).

Culturally, the 1920s and 1930s witnessed a great flowering of Faroese letters, as a new generation of poets, novelists, playwrights, and scholars came of age. Most are only locally known, but a few have gained an international readership, perhaps most notably William Heinesen, whose best-known novels, however, are written in Danish.[23] The Faroes' continued literary productivity has been supplemented by a growing amount of work in the fine arts. The painters S.J. Mikines, Ingálvur av Reyni, Ruth Smith, and Eyvindur Mohr deserve special mention, as do the sculptors Janus Kamban and Frithjof Joensen. Scholarship has also flourished. Its landmarks since 1920 include the foundation of the literary review *Varðin*, in 1921, the publication of a Faroese-Danish dictionary, in 1928 (much expanded and revised for a second edition, Jacobsen and Matras 1961, and now with a supplement, Jacobsen and Matras 1974), the publication of a Danish-Faroese dictionary, in 1967 (J. av Skarði 1967), and the establishment of the teaching and research institute Fróðskaparsetur Føroya, in 1965, which puts out the learned journal *Fróðskaparrit* (J.P. Joensen 1983).

Political parties have multiplied since 1920, and there have been two readjustments of the Faroes' relationship to Denmark.[24] The Social Democratic party (Javnaðarflokkur) was founded in 1925, elected its first representatives to the Løgting in 1928, and today receives about one-fifth of the total vote. As its name implies, it was (and is) moderately leftist on economic issues, but unionist on the issue of the Faroes' relationship to Denmark. A short-lived, economically rightist party called the Economic party (Vinnuflokkur) held a single seat in the Løgting from 1936 to 1940. In 1939 the old Self-Rule party split when Jóannes Patursson bolted it, on the issue of land reform, to found the People's party (Fólkaflokkur), which incorporated the Economic party and took over perhaps half of the old Self-Rule party's membership. The People's party was (and is) separatist but otherwise conservative. Today it generally receives about one-fifth of the total vote. The "Old Self-Rule party," as it is usually called, receives about one-tenth. Another one-fifth of today's vote is received by the Republican party, which was founded in 1948 in the aftermath of the 1946 referendum on independence. It is socialist and nationalist. Another one-tenth of the vote is received by the Progress and Fishery party (Framburðs- og Fiskivinnuflokkur), as it has been called since 1978 (it was founded, in 1954, as the Progress party). It is economically conservative, but separatist. The final one-fifth of the vote is received by the still union-ist and conservative Union party.

The Faroes' governmental organization and relationship to Denmark were somewhat modified by a law passed by the Rigsdag on 28 March 1923, which came into effect at the new year. It gave the Løgting greater oversight of local finances, stripped the dean and the governor of ex officio membership in the Løgting (although the latter might still take part in its deliberations), and set the Løgting's membership at eighteen, plus up to five "extra seats." These were (and are) allocated on the basis of the total popular vote instead of the vote of each electoral district. The result is a flexible and surprisingly workable electoral system.

World War II brought a more decisive change. German troops occu-pied Denmark on 9 April 1940. Two days later, Winston Churchill an-nounced that Great Britain would "shield the Faroe Islands from all the severities of war and establish ourselves there conveniently by sea and air until the moment comes when they will be handed back to the crown and people of a Denmark liberated from the foul thraldom into which they have been plunged by German aggression" (quoted in West 1972:175-76). The first British forces did not, however, arrive until around noon on the twelfth. The ensuing occupation lasted until 16 September 1945, and was entirely amicable on both sides (see, e.g., Macmillan n.d. and E. Müller 1945). Despite their straitened circumstances, due to the curtailment of imports, Faroese built up considerable foreign-currency reserves by fer-rying Icelandic fish to Britain. Many men were lost to German U-boats, and the Faroes suffered a few air raids, as well.

Among the war's other fruits was the construction of the airport on Vágar, now much enlarged. In 1980 the airport logged over twenty-four thousand departures and an equal number of arrivals, mostly to and from Denmark. There is also regular air service between the Faroes and Ice-land, Norway, and Scotland (Ársfrágreiðing 1980:117).

More significant was the de facto break with Denmark, for by 1945 it was clear to everyone that the Faroes' relationship with Denmark would have to be substantially revised. After protracted negotiations, a referen-dum on independence was accordingly held, on 14 September 1946.

Unfortunately, the referendum produced an enormously confusing re-sult.[25] Of the voting electorate, 48.7 percent favored complete indepen-dence, 47.1 percent favored essentially the present arrangement with Den-mark, and the rest wrote "no" on their ballots. The Løgting declared independence by the slimmest of majorities, but the Danish government dissolved the Løgting, undoubtedly more out of bewilderment than mali-ciousness. Further negotiations ensued, resulting in the present arrange-ment under the Home Rule Act of 1948.

Faroese recognize the Danish king (or queen) as head of state and elect two members to the Folketing (the Danish parliament has been unicameral since 1953). The currency is the Danish *krone* or a Faroese *króna,* defined as equal to it. Denmark is responsible for the Faroes' defense and foreign relations, and the Faroese cannot negotiate independently with foreign states or with such international organizations as the Common Market and NATO.[26] The Danish supreme court is the court of appeal from the Faroese court. The interests of the Danish state in the Faroes are overseen by a High Commissioner (Da. Rigsombudsmand, Fa. Ríkis-umboðsmaður), who is a nonvoting member of the Løgting. The local administration is a three-person committee chosen by the Løgting from among its membership. The chair of this committee, called the Landsstýri, bears the ancient title of *løgmaður.* The Løgmaður also chairs the Løgting, and is in effect the prime minister. Under the terms of the Home Rule Act, the Løgting was empowered to assume exclusive control over a number of areas of government. Other areas would remain under joint Faroese and Danish control, until or unless the Løgting took them over. The Løgting immediately assumed control over taxation, trade regulations, fishing inside territorial waters, and so forth. Since then it has also taken over the postal service, for example. The Faroese language has full rights and is the primary language of schooling; but Danish must be taught "thoroughly" to all pupils.

The Home Rule Act defines in detail the Faroes' current ambiguous nationality within the Danish kingdom. From our present point of view, however, its most significant passage is perhaps its most general one, the preamble, which regally restates the ideological presuppositions of the 1840s: "We, Frederik the Ninth, by God's grace King of Denmark and of the Wends and the Goths, Duke of Slesvig, Holsten, Stormarn, Ditmarsken, Lauenborg, and Oldenborg, do proclaim by these presents: In recognition of the special position which the Faroe Islands occupy within the realm in national, historical, and geographical respects . . . [we affirm that] they comprise within the framework of this law a self-ruling folk society (*Folkesamfund*) in the Danish realm.[27]

CONCLUSION ▰▰▰▰▰▰▰▰▰▰▰▰▰▰▰▰

Specters and Illusions
The World Abroad and the World at Home

▰▰▰▰▰▰▰▰▰▰▰▰▰▰▰▰▰▰▰▰▰▰▰▰▰▰

🜊 When Lucas Debes described the Faroes in 1673, he wished chiefly to bring their plight to the world's attention. Probably few people cared. But Debes included in his book "a splendid collection of uncanny tales both old and new, under the heading 'Of Specters and Illusions of Satan in Feroe,'" and thereby "gained a larger public than he could ever have anticipated" (Seaton 1935:218; see also Helgason 1940); the more so, perhaps, because he insisted that they were not "the meer fancies of melancholly people" (1676:367).

This book, too, may gain a wider audience than Faroese affairs might otherwise attract, by stressing another limited aspect of local life: the rise of a national culture. I have argued, in any case, that like other notable elements of the Faroe scene, including the landscape, the people's folkishness, and their memories of the Viking past, "uncanny tales" and the formulation of a national culture are closely related. Just as tales like "Snæbjørn" were critical to the survival of Faroese culture during the bleak years of the seventeenth and eighteenth centuries, so their boundary-marking function was assumed by the national culture in the increasingly prosperous years of the late nineteenth and early twentieth centuries.

Thus there remain two tasks in conclusion.

First, as A.F. Tscherning predicted, the Faroes have gained "a certain measure of European importance." How, then, does the Faroes' cultural and political development compare to that of other peoples? The problem is that even in Western Europe, the number of comparable peoples is enormous. Not only is the region rich in new nations (five have gained independence in the present century: Iceland, Norway, Finland, Eire, and Malta, not to mention the two Germanies); but its Atlantic reaches abound in peoples who have claimed, or might claim, a heritage at least as distinct as the Faroes': Lapps (all together or variously grouped), Irish (northern or southern, Catholic or Protestant, or all together), Scots (including not only Highlanders and Lowlanders but also Shetlanders, Orcadians, and Hebrideans), Manxmen, Welsh, Flemings, Walloons, Frisians, Bretons, Channel Islanders, Occitans, and Basques on either side of the Pyrenees; and, if we cast our net a bit more widely, Greenlanders, Bornholmians, Ålanders, Tyroleans, Corsicans, Catalans, Canary Islanders, Cape Verdeans, Puerto Ricans, Acadians, Newfoundlanders, Québécois, and the Indians and Eskimos of northeastern Canada.

For the sake of methodological tidiness, however, and lest, having come so far with them, I do the Faroese the injustice of losing them in this motley chorus, I shall limit my comparisons to their two closest neighbors, Iceland and Shetland, and to two crucial points: the pace and timing of the transition from a peasant economy to an industrial one, and the hearing granted culturally based separatist claims in the "mother country." Iceland is a separatist success story. Having begun the nineteenth century underpopulated and even more impoverished than the Faroes and having ended it by modernizing far more rapidly, Iceland was granted its own constitution in 1874, home rule in 1904, and virtual sovereignty in 1918. It became fully independent in 1944. Shetland began the nineteenth century heavily populated and with two large-scale commercial fisheries already in place; but despite a good deal of antiquarian and folkloristic attention, it never experienced any serious separatism.

Our second, more daunting task returns us to the Faroes. Literature and history are important elements of a national culture that, although it marks the Faroes' place in the world, no more covers or comprehends all of Faroese life than did "uncanny tales" or the Faroes' shell of Danishness after the Reformation. How, then, are local literature and historiography Faroese but not necessarily nationally Faroese? How do they represent the world at home as well as mediating between it and the world abroad?

This question is far too complex to address adequately in a few pages. Here its dimensions are only suggested by a few examples of Faroese literary and historiographic sensibility.

By way of setting the parameters for comparing the Faroes to Iceland and Shetland, let us first calculate in a very rough way the carrying capacity of each country's traditional economy, the point beyond which people must find new ways of making a living and beyond which, therefore, social change becomes inevitable.

We have seen that, given the monopoly system and traditional agricultural and fishing techniques, the Faroes could probably support at most around 4500 people. The Faroes' area is 540 square miles, of which about 34 square miles are arable. Virtually the whole land is used as pasturage. This means that they could support about 132 people per square mile of arable land, or about 8.3 people per square mile of arable land plus pasturage. It also suggests that in 1801, when the population stood at 5265, the Faroes were slightly overpopulated and on the brink of social change. In the event, the change did not prove seriously disruptive. The economy could not expand ashore, but the excess population was able to live from the sea, exploiting it in traditional ways for many years. Emigration was slight, for most people could fulfill *Føringatíðindi*'s hope, in an article about emigration to Canada, that "promising people can have a good future for themselves in their homeland" (February 1893). By the end of the century, an increasingly industrialized but still labor-intensive fishery was supporting a newly diversified economy and a native middle class and was fostering the reformulation of Faroese culture in a movement that soon became political as well.

Iceland was *under*populated in 1801. Iceland's total area is 40,437 square miles. Only slightly over 400 square miles are actually arable, however, while the total area of arable land plus fair pasturage is about 10,000 square miles. If, as in the Faroes, each square mile of arable could support 132 people (given very similar crops, techniques, restraints upon trade, and a comparable growing season), this would allow Iceland a maximum population of 52,800, not far off the actual 1703 population of 50,358. Much of Iceland's pasturage is more marginal than the Faroes', however, and inland farms (of which the Faroes had none) enjoyed no easy access to the sea's supplementary resources for subsistence. If we grant Iceland a correspondingly lower figure for people supportable by the total arable land plus pasturage (say 5.0 or 5.5 people per square mile) we again reach a maximum population under traditional circumstances of 50,000 to 55,000. In 1801 the population was only 47,240. Other things being equal, there was room for perhaps 5000 more people in the country.

Other things had not been equal in Iceland in the eighteenth century. The century's calamities included a smallpox epidemic between 1707 and 1709, in which perhaps a third of the population died; chronic famine in the late 1750s, followed by another smallpox epidemic in 1760 and a sheep plague in 1762; and earthquakes and volcanic eruptions off and on, culminating in the disastrous eruption of 1783, when famine and disease followed close upon the loss of farmlands and livestock. The population, which had been creeping stubbornly upward, fell back to 40,623 in 1785. The loosening of trade restrictions, two years later, did little immediate good.

Iceland's socioeconomic development in the nineteenth century thus followed a rather different course from that of the Faroes. Iceland had at first to catch up with its smaller neighbor. Agriculture expanded until about 1880, when it supported over 54,000 people, or 74.3 percent of the population (see Table 18). It had not modernized, however, and since 54,000 people was near the upper limit of what traditional ways could support, the 1880s saw substantial emigration to Canada. Held back, as it were, by a large and largely traditional population, Iceland's economic development thus lagged behind the Faroes'. For one thing, the land was a slightly less limiting resource. The 1880s and 1890s saw some progress with such innovations as rural cooperatives and by supplementing the traditional exports of wool and woolens with ponies, cattle, and sheep. As late as the period from 1901 to 1920, agricultural products accounted for over 20 percent of Iceland's exports by value, more than twice the comparable Faroese figure.

For Iceland, as for the Faroes, the sea eventually proved a far more elastic resource. The Icelandic fishery was also dominated by small boats

Table 18.   Populations of Shetland and Iceland, 1801-1961

	Shetland				Iceland		
Year	All Shetland	Lerwick	% Lerwick	Year	All Iceland	Reykjavík	% Reykjavík
1801	22,379	—	—	1801	47,240	307	0.7
1811	22,915	—	—				
1821	26,145	2224	8.5				
1831	29,392	2750	9.4				
				1835	56,035	639	1.1
1841	30,558	2787	9.1	1840	57,094	890	1.6
1851	31,044	2870	9.2	1850	59,157	1149	1.9
1861	31,579	3143	10.0	1860	66,987	1444	2.2
1871	31,371	3655	11.7	1870	69,763	2024	2.9
1881	29,149	3801	13.0	1880	72,445	2567	3.5
1891	28,241	4216	14.9	1890	70,927	3886	5.5
1901	27,736	4803	17.3	1901	78,470	6682	8.5
1911	27,238	5533	20.3	1910	85,183	11,600	13.6
1921	24,117	5137	21.3	1920	94,690	17,679	18.7
1931	21,229	5118	24.1	1930	108,861	28,304	26.0
				1940	121,474	38,196	31.4
1951	19,102	5450	28.5	1950	143,973	56,251	39.1
1961	17,483	5678	32.5	1960	175,680	71,926	40.9

Sources: Shetland: Cluness 1967:52-3 (somewhat different figures are given for 1851-1971 in the Zetland County Report of the 1971 Scottish Census, Tables 1, 5a, 5b.); Iceland: Tölfræðihandbók 1974, p. 7

until the 1880s; and then after about 1890 by decked sailing vessels. Socially, however, Iceland's fishery was less important. In 1890 it supported only 17.9 percent of the population, compared with 37.5 percent in the Faroes (see Table 19). In both countries, then, the industrialization of the fishery led to further economic diversification and to the growth of Reykjavík and Tórshavn. But Iceland's urbanization was also laggardly by Faroese standards. Not until after 1890 did Reykjavík contain over 10 percent of the total Icelandic population. Thereafter, however, Reykjavík grew much more rapidly than Tórshavn. By 1920 it contained over 15 percent of the Icelandic population, a level Tórshavn did not reach until 1945.[1] Iceland's fishery also developed far more rapidly than the Faroese fishery between the world wars, its growth being hastened by the earlier acquisition of a modern trawler fleet.

In short, Iceland remained more rural than the Faroes until the very end of the nineteenth century. Then it urbanized and industrialized more quickly. We have seen that the rise of Faroese separatism depended partly on the survival of traditional culture as an ideological resource, even while the traditional sector of the economy became relatively less important. Yet Iceland's earlier attainment of separatist goals, despite the more abrupt displacement of an independently viable peasant way of life, leads us to suspect that the actual retention of a living traditional culture is less crucial than the Faroese case may suggest. For Icelanders had a far more potent cultural resource to tide them over. If they had to catch up with the Faroese economically, the Faroese had to catch up with them culturally and politically.

Iceland's great resource was, of course, its literature, particularly the sagas of its heroic age. Since Icelandic (unlike Faroese) had remained a written language after the Reformation, Iceland supported a literary tradition essentially unbroken since well before the country's loss of independence, in 1264. The entire Bible was published in Icelandic in 1584, for example, only thirty-four years after the Danish Bible of 1550, which influenced it and which had in turn been influenced by Luther's earlier German translation. Moreover, as early as the 1780s, virtually all Icelanders were literate in their own language (Tomasson 1975b, 1980:116-20). Iceland was thus uniquely blessed in the matter of an established great tradition popularly adhered to, and it had long partaken of European intellectual movements without, however, leading them.

Yet until the end of the eighteenth century, Icelandic culture, let alone the ancient Icelandic polity, moved neither Icelanders nor Danes so much as the country's starvation and general distress. In 1787, for example, the Iceland trade was partially freed, not in recognition of the country's medieval glories, but in order to help ease its plight; and few lamented the dissolution, in 1801, of the anachronistic and nearly powerless Althing.

By that time, Iceland's place in Scandinavian civilization was changing. Iceland was singularly well served by the liberal, romantic, and antiquarian trends of early nineteenth-century Danish thought and by the growing conviction that nationality was a cultural matter, not just one of allegiance to a crown. As Icelandic culture was felt to embody all that was most noble about the common Norse experience, Icelanders became leading members of the North's intellectual partnership. Where Icelanders had once followed the continental lead, even Danes now looked to Iceland for inspiration. By the middle of the nineteenth century, many Faroese and Norwegians were seeking to emulate Icelanders' linguistic and literary achievements.

The manuscript collecting of Árni Magnússon in the late seventeenth and early eighteenth centuries was of crucial importance in the whole Nordic movement, bringing together as it did for the first time a fully representative collection of the literary production of medieval Iceland. The founding of an [Icelandic] Learned Society (Lærdómslistafélagið) in 1779 and its fifteen volumes of [Icelandic] publications (1781-96) made it possible for Icelanders and other Scandinavians to learn for the first time the nature of their heritage. . . . If [Icelandic] had not fought itself free of [Danish] influence in the late eighteenth and early nineteenth

Table 19. Means of support of the Icelandic population, 1850-1930

Population supported by	1850	1860	1870	1880	1890	1901	1910	1920	1930
Agriculture	48,513	53,523	52,950	54,050	46,670	53,622	45,914	44,220	40,714
	82.0%	79.9%	75.9%	74.3%	65.8%	68.1%	53.9%	46.7%	37.4%
Fishing	4056	6297	6976	8875	12,696	9181	17,377	18,938	24,603
	6.9%	9.4%	10.0%	12.2%	17.9%	11.7%	20.4%	20.0%	22.6%
Crafts, mfg.	741	1005	1184	2110	2837	5100	8518	11,268	16,547
	1.3%	1.5%	1.7%	2.9%	4.0%	6.5%	10.0%	11.9%	15.2%
Trade, transp.	605	1072	1465	2110	3191	4237	7581	12,878	17,527
	1.0%	1.6%	2.1%	2.9%	4.5%	5.4%	8.9%	13.6%	16.1%
Services	2747	2746	2651	2473	2341	2433	3067	3882	5334
	4.6%	4.1%	3.8%	3.4%	3.3%	3.1%	3.6%	4.1%	4.9%
Other	2494	2345	4535	3128	3191	4080	2726	3504	4137
	4.2%	3.5%	6.5%	4.3%	4.5%	5.2%	3.2%	3.7%	3.8%
Total	59,157	66,987	69,763	72,445	70,927	78,470	85,183	94,690	108,861

Sources: 1850: estimated from David (1857:10-11); 1860-1930: estimated from Tölfræðihandbók 1974, Tables II-1 and II-16. (These sources give only the percentages [to three decimal places!] for each category. I have estimated the absolute numbers from these figures and the total population figures for Iceland in each year, given elsewhere. Thus the figures in each column, above, do not always add to the totals for each year, because of rounding.)

centuries, it is highly probable that [Faroese] and [Norwegian] might not have done so either. . . . [Faroese] and [Nynorsk] are fairly direct offshoots of [Icelandic] in a sociolinguistic sense, though not of course linguistically. [Haugen 1976:398, 401]

An old current of Icelandic criticism devoted to the "purity" of the language (in the first instance, that is, to its dissimilarity to Danish) gathered strength, and with the encouragement of such influential figures as Rasmus Rask, an old-fashioned orthography was adopted to replace the Dano-Icelandic one that had long been standard. Icelandic writers went on to build up a self-consciously native modern literary and technical vocabulary.

Meanwhile, Iceland, like the Faroes, was drawn intellectually and politically closer to Copenhagen. Unlike their Faroese counterparts, however, Icelandic leaders immediately found themselves able to argue effectively, in accordance with the "folkish" and history-minded ideology of the metropolis, that their homeland's future state should match its ancient one. The Althing was restored in 1843, at least in name, though not in its old form or at its old site. The Icelanders having refused to recognize the Danish constitutions of 1849 and 1866, Iceland was granted a constitution of its own in 1874, not so coincidentally at the millennium of permanent Norse settlement. Home rule followed in 1904, sovereignty under the Danish crown in 1918, and full independence in 1944.

Icelandic voters approved the moves of 1918 and 1944 by nearly unanimous votes, an interesting but misleading phenomenon, contrasting sharply with the ambiguous outcome of the Faroese referendum of 1946. It is misleading because it accords all too well with the governing myth of Icelandic historiography, that "When liberal trends from abroad reached Iceland in the nineteenth century, it was not an enslaved or ignorant people that held aloft the banner of patriotism, freedom and progress. It was an old, civilized nation desirous of independence" (Gíslason 1973:89; see also Tomasson 1975a, 1980:3-21).

Still-unpublished work by Guðmundur Hálfdanarson promises a more accurate picture of the social origins of Icelandic nationalism. He argues that the events of 1848-49 in Denmark split apart Iceland's political and administrative systems. On the one hand, a highly conservative, not to say reactionary, agricultural elite maintained its dominance over internal Icelandic politics in the Althing. Opposed to them now stood the educated, liberal, royally appointed Icelandic officials, who had previously mediated between Iceland and the Danish government they nominally represented. The gap between these groups was filled, at first very precariously, by a rising Icelandic intelligentsia, based less at home than in Copenhagen, where, led by Jón Sigurðsson, they allied themselves with Danish liberals, if not with the Danish government. The national-cultural ideology they espoused paradoxically appealed both to Iceland's administrative and educated elite (because it offered a way of opposing the Danish government's political illiberalism and the agricultural elite's economic illiberalism) and, more ambiguously, to the agricultural elite (because it offered a way of opposing the economic liberalism of the Danish government and its Icelandic agents). As time went on and agriculture's importance faded, it also appealed, for various other reasons, to Iceland's emerging middle class and previously despised and largely disenfranchised fishermen and laborers.

Iceland's strikingly unanimous rejection of foreign rule allowed direct, open opposition on internal economic and social questions. The Faroese were less divided at first and less unanimous later, for the question of nationhood itself became a primary focus for debate and a ground for internal political differentiation. The reason for this contrast was that the Danish national-cultural ideology of the 1840s was domesticated and politicized in somewhat different social settings, during differently timed courses of socioeconomic development. The Faroes' less distinct, proportionately larger "agricultural elite" of king's farmers helped lead an earlier turn to the sea, and were supported in this by a nascent intelligentsia and middle class, by their liberal Danish allies in Copenhagen, and indeed by the Danish governors. The Faroes' longer, more even, and, until the late 1880s, culturally rather conservative economic growth allowed the cultural separatism of the 1890s to take root relatively unhindered by differences of opinion on economic issues and delayed its politicization until after the turn of the century. Iceland's initially greater cultural visibility in Denmark produced an earlier formal articulation of a national culture, the course of whose adoption at home, however, reflected Iceland's initially slower and then more rapid modernization.

Shetland presents a very different picture. Economic development came much earlier than in Iceland or the Faroes, but it was predicated upon the virtual destruction of traditional rural life. Moreover, it faltered after 1840 and then failed.

It is difficult to calculate the carrying capacity of Shetland's traditional economy. The islands' area is 551 square miles, of which about 31 square miles are arable. Both figures are very close to the Faroes', suggesting a maximum population of from 4000 to 5000. Shetland enjoys a rather longer growing season, however, and had a more regular trade with mainland Britain. Coull (1967:160) reckons that, before the early eighteenth century, the traditional economy could support from 10,000 to 12,000 people. This seems a reasonable, even rather generous figure by Faroese standards. The introduction of the potato in about 1730 must have made a considerable difference, although the crop often failed. In any case, it is clear that the 1801 population of 22,379 (a figure that does not include some 3000 press-ganged "volunteers" in the Royal Navy) betokens a precariously intensive use of the land. It likewise suggests the extent to which

Shetlanders depended on a commercial fishery. In fact Shetland had two commercial fisheries.

Since the early eighteenth century, Shetland landlords had promoted a deep-water, open-boat fishery called the "haaf," carried out by a tenantry that found little profit in it. Like the Faroese fishery's first expansion along traditional lines, the rise of the haaf fostered population growth; but because (unlike the early Faroese fishery) it was the landlords' business rather than a family and village enterprise, it worsened the already unhappy lot of the Shetland peasantry: "The counterpart of more men involved in fishing was increased pressure on the land and subdivision of holdings to such an extent that few could maintain a family" (Coull 1967:161). The haaf nonetheless brought a good deal of rather unevenly distributed prosperity and supported the growth of Lerwick as the islands' commercial center.

In 1839, when Governor Pløyen landed in Lerwick with three Faroese to seek inspiration for reviving the Faroese economy, he often thought sadly, he said, of "the helpless starving town of Thorshavn, when I saw what life and activity the cod fishing, and still more the herring fishing, developed in Lerwick; and how many hands were employed in cooperages, in loading, and unloading vessels, in seafaring, and what a respectable middle class of tradesmen, shopkeepers and skippers of vessels had arisen in the place" (1896:12). But this was Shetland's high-water mark. The haaf had peaked by the middle of the century and dwindled rapidly away in the 1880s. In the 1860s and 1870s, it was replaced, as it were, by a smack fishery; but this, too, declined rapidly in the 1880s. Meanwhile, the development of the herring fishery that had so impressed Pløyen in 1839 was set back the next year by a storm that destroyed many boats (with heavy loss of life) and by the collapse of a Lerwick bank, in 1842. A herring boom began in the late 1870s, but, herring being a notoriously fickle species, it declined rapidly after a record year in 1905.

By that time, Shetland's population had been falling for many years. Population growth had slowed as early as the 1830s, and after about 1840 landowners had begun to find sheep farming more profitable than fishing and started clearing crofters from the land. Land pressure, clearances, erratic fishing, and a series of crop failures led to a great emigration, much of it to the same industrial centers that so impressed Pløyen when he traveled farther into Scotland. After 1861, the population was falling, although Lerwick itself continued to grow.

The haaf was not Shetland's only commercial fishery in 1801, nor were landlords its only upper class. A Greenland whale fishery had been established in the late eighteenth century, underwritten by Lerwick merchants. It did not decline until the 1860s, when the Greenland stocks were becoming exhausted. "In 1874 there were still between 600 and 700 Shetlanders employed on whalers, but in 1888 only seven vessels called at Lerwick to complete their crews, and by 1907 the industry was dead"

(Nicolson 1979:170). A century earlier, according to one observer, merchants and landed "heritors" were embroiled in "endless jealousies" as they vied for crewmen. Landlords argued that "the Greenland trade is prejudicial to the morals of the people and . . . they wish to put a termination to so injurious a system" (Edmonston 1809:69). Their solicitude is doubtful. In fact, they resembled their mercantile rivals more than their tenants or employees. Edmonston regrets the "heritors'" ignoble "spirit of enterprize" and laments their unwillingness to live in the country. It goes almost without saying that they found nothing ennobling about rural ways. Unlike the Faroes' priests and better-off king's farmers, who remained oriented to the land and formed one end of a continuum of poverty and prosperity, Shetland landlords and merchants composed a distinct if divided class of the population, living mostly in Lerwick and oriented to Edinburgh and London.

Shetland's comparatively early economic development thus did not lead to the idealization of traditional peasant culture, much less to the formulation of a national culture inspired by it. For one thing, Shetlandic culture offered less to build on than the Faroes', let alone Iceland's. The old Nordic language, Norn, had almost died out by the early eighteenth century. Fixed expressions (place-names, sayings, snatches of song) survived longer; but what Shetlanders spoke in the 1830s was clearly a dialect of English with a Nordic-flavored vocabulary.[2] Variously combined with other factors, this lack of a distinct difference in language had far-reaching effects. In 1872, for example, both the Danish and British governments passed compulsory education laws. As we have seen, the Danish *kommune* law, as applied to the Faroes, strengthened local control over schooling, posed anew the question of the proper language of instruction, and so tended inadvertently to strengthen the separate standing of the Faroese language. The British Education Act fostered a "growing awareness of the opportunities available in Britain and in English-speaking lands overseas" (Coull 1967:162), which, together with the final breakdown of the subsistence economy, after 1880, and the simultaneous decline of the smack fishery and the haaf, led to the further depopulation of Shetland's country districts.[3]

Moreover, Shetlanders would have had nothing to gain by ennobling local folkways. Copenhagen might be moved by that sort of thing; London was not. Influential Danes were inspired by the antiquity of Icelandic culture, which they were pleased to call in a sense their own; and Faroese might hitch their aspirations to the Icelandic star. It is true that, Scotland's teeth having been drawn after The '45, Englishmen might find romantic appeal in the Scottish Highlands through James MacPherson's Ossianic apocrypha or Robert Burns's poetry or, somewhat later, in the novels of Sir Walter Scott. Still later, Queen Victoria herself played at Scottishness during summers at Balmoral.[4] But Shetland was not part of the Highlands.

More important, the British government could not have recognized "folk-ishness" as a legitimate basis for regional political claims without denying the unity of the United Kingdom. Even Liberal Englishmen found no self-esteem in, say, Irish culture. Ideologically, as well as linguistically and politically, Shetland had dropped out of the Norse world. "While Shetland is an integral portion of the home British empire, participating in her en-lightened laws and policy, her freedom and progress in improvement, to-gether with the good, and also, alas! evil, more or less attendant on our peculiar institutions, Faroe, as respects manners and state of society, is in much the same condition as it has been for a century past at least" (Anon. 1848:180).

This is not to say that Shetland failed to receive its share of antiquar-ian and folkloristic atttention; nor did it fail to develop a literature. But the folklorizing was amateurish by Scandinavian standards and without political import. By and large, even amateur Faroese scholarship is serious and careful. Hammershaimb's early writings deservedly found space in the preeminently respectable journal of the Royal Nordic Ancient Text Society (Det Kongelige Nordiske Oldskrift-Selskab), which enjoyed the crown's patronage. At home, articles by Dr. Jakob Jakobsen (whose cre-dentials were impeccable) do not seem out of place amid the amateur scholarship in the pages of *Dimmalætting* or *Tingakrossur*. But the profes-sionalism of his work in the Shetlands stands in marked contrast to most of the pieces that found space in the main vehicle for notices about Shet-landic folklore, *The Saga-Book of the Viking Club*. This was the journal of the Viking Club, or Orkney, Shetland, and Northern Society, which was founded in London in 1892-93. Its officers sported titles like "Things-Both-Man (*Convener*)" and "Skatt-Taker (*Hon. Treasurer*)," reflecting the overripe romanticism concerning the Viking Age that had recently taken hold in England, but which had only the flimsiest foundation in living regional cultures (cf. Mjöberg 1980).

An early piece of Shetlandic literature (one of its classics, perhaps) is George Stewart's *Shetland Fireside Tales; or, the Hermit of Trosswickness* (1892 [1877]). His aim was not unlike Jakobsen's: to entertain his readers and to recall "the habits, thoughts and feelings of past generations." And Stewart claimed "some satisfaction in believing that his own countrymen will at least appreciate his efforts in trying to preserve, in a written form, some of those familiar tales which once so happily whiled away the long winter nights, and in their present form may still, he hopes, help in some measure to serve the same important purpose[s] of entertainment and rec-ollection."[5] The result is a kind of combination of novel and folktale col-lection, written partly in standard English, partly in dialect. Around the turn of the century, the blind poet and polymath J.J. Haldane Burgess claimed (perhaps even demonstrated) that the Shetland dialect could ex-press fine feelings as well as English could.[6] But not even he claimed that the dialect could or should replace standard English. In the context of British letters, Burgess's work, like these lines by the modern poet Vagaland (T.A. Robertson), is merely wistful:

> Nooadays der very little
>   o da aald wyes left ava.   *at all*
> Tinks du, wid da folk be better
>   if dy cöst da rest awa?
>
> Trowe wir minds wir ain aald language
>   still keeps rinnin laek a tön;   *tune*
> Laek da laverik id hömin,   *skylark in the twilight*
>   sheerlin whin da day is döne;   *singing*
> Laek da seich of wind trowe coarn   *sigh; through*
>   at da risin o da mön.

[Robertson 1975:2; glosses added]

In the context of Scandinavian letters, Faroese verse expressing similar thoughts had some fire to it.

More important, Stewart's confusion of tongues has never been shared by Faroese writers who, even if they use both Faroese and Danish, have taken pains to keep them separate. Nor was any Shetlander moved, so far as I know, to write whole newspapers, histories, liturgies, botanical texts, or a bank's articles of incorporation in "wir ain aald language." Shetlandic literature remained provincial, without pretensions beyond clothing proverbial verities in homely guise. The dialect remained a literary shadow tongue, while Faroese became an alternative standard, recognized, if not widely read, abroad and fully established at home in the numerous formal institutions of modern life. In short, Shetlandic literature suggests at most a small, belated measure of cultural separatism.

Several general conclusions emerge from a comparison between Iceland, Shetland, and the Faroes. First, it is clear that economic growth and a population's increase beyond the level that traditional livelihoods will sustain may motivate some measure of cultural separatism. But this is not a sufficient condition for its success. Its success depends in part on the country's cultural integration under the traditional dispensation; in part on the extent to which the traditional culture can for a time survive economic change; in part on a growing economy's ability to absorb a growing population; and, perhaps most decisively, on whether the new elites thrown up by economic change seek to identify themselves with an ideology glorifying traditional ways. The selection of traditions is crucial. In Iceland and the Faroes, they were chiefly linguistic, literary, and historical traditions, shared by the local population as a whole as well as respected elsewhere in Scandinavia; and they were espoused in such a way as to provide a sense of cultural continuity through a period of continuing socioeconomic change. Elsewhere in the world, the traditions chosen may be, for example, religious, and thus not only uncompromising and ostensibly timeless to begin with, but also upheld by an old elite interested in retaining its primacy in the face of socioeconomic change.

Second, the successful politicization of cultural separatism depends largely on the extent to which demonstrations of cultural distinctiveness can be used as a lever in adjusting relations with the "mother country." Cultural separatism perforce begins as an elite movement at home—the work of poets, journalists, teachers, lawyers, and so forth. It requires an audience of readers or students, for example, and local control over the institutions through which this audience is reached. At least in fairly democratic circumstances like those in the Faroes, separatism's politicization likewise requires a supportive audience of voters and locally controlled institutions (parties) through which popular debate can be articulated. Even if the aims of political separatism are not universally popular (in the Faroes, unlike Iceland, it was evidently a minority movement until the end of the First World War), it may become widely popular if the previous establishment of cultural separatism has settled the terms of debate. Abroad, however, there need not be widespread support for the proposition that, for example, Iceland or the Faroes deserve greater autonomy. What matters more is the support of a few influential figures (in the Faroes' case Rask, Sigurðsson, Rafn, Müller, Petersen, Barfod, the two Grundtvigs, and others) who, disinterestedly or for reasons of their own, are able to articulate separatist goals in terms even their opponents must agree merit a serious hearing.

In other words, the home audience for culturally based claims to a separate political status must become popular; the foreign audience may remain elite. Iceland was the most favored of our three countries in this respect. Its officials' and intellectuals' claims were granted an immediate hearing in Copenhagen and found widespread support in Iceland, as well. The Faroese followed Iceland's path, but first had to discover how to present such home-grown resources as folk literature in a sufficiently refined form. In "unfolkish" Britain, Shetland did not experience any political separatism.

Let us return, in conclusion, to the ambiguous situation in which Faroese find themselves. More than a province like Shetland, they remain less than a sovereign state like Iceland. Economic development in the nineteenth century destroyed much of their traditional culture but fostered its idealization in a national culture that itself legitimized a measure of political autonomy by domesticating a foreign ideology. Faroese separatism thus enacted a complex association between local and international society. At the same time, it maintained a formal sort of cultural continuity by replacing an official Danishness with an official Faroeseness, and by elaborating the latter.

"Official Faroeseness" does not, however, comprehend all of Faroese culture. Indeed, the essential complexity in the Faroes' situation is that, like other "modern," national peoples, the Faroese have acquired many levels of culture, all of which are open to outside influence. Maintaining the integrity of Faroese culture involves mediating external contacts; more crucially, it involves maintaining the continuity between cultural levels.

The process of internal integration is as difficult to describe as its agencies are, for the most part, diffusely institutionalized. Sometimes they even cast an ironic light on the national culture itself. Thus, since formal, national-cultural institutions have never opposed social change; since they have different, sometimes conflicting interests; and since they could not completely control external contact even if they tried, their attempts to stand watch on the borders of the local world may just seem silly. That is one point of a cartoon in a widely popular booklet of sketches and satires put out one Ólavsøka. Similarly, Jóhan Hendrik Poulsen, of the language department at Fróðskaparsetur Føroya, recently told me a joke on himself. He has just brought out a Faroese-Danish/English, Danish/English-Faroese glossary of computer jargon (J.H.W. Poulsen 1985). Its aim is to check Danish and English intrusion into the linguistic frontier opened up by electronic data processing. Most of the Faroese terms are neologisms based on Old West Scandinavian roots. Jóhan Hendrik has been told, he says, that in one firm someone has posted a notice next to the computer: "Here we use only Jóhan Hendrik's words." He chuckles. "*My* words!" To make sure I get the point, he adds, "As if they weren't *Faroese* words." The humor here is typically Faroese. Resting on intimate common knowl- edge of the local scene (everyone knows how confusingly the newspapers interpret the world, and Jóhan Hendrik is the paragon of exaggerated Faroeseness in language), it is amiably but decisively deflating—even self-deflating. Since everyone may laugh at such sallies, they provide one informal means of maintaining a common identity outside the national culture, although with reference to it. So do the widespread drinking and strolling about at Ólavsøka (Wylie 1983).

A similar function is performed in a more subtle way by less ephem- eral cultural artifacts, especially by literary and historical works produced for a local audience. The very existence of such works invites an outsid- er's respect; and if one can read Faroese, they may at first seem quite comprehensible by international canons. But one also senses a naggingly different perspective on the world that, upon inspection, evinces a Faro- eseness broader than that purveyed by the national culture in which they also serve as monuments. We shall conclude with two examples of such texts: "Neytakonurnar" ("the milkmaids"), a famous poem by the scholar and poet Christian Matras, which may be read to illustrate some enduring but implicit differences between Faroese and foreign sensibilities; and Mikkjal Dánjal á Ryggi's *Miðvinga Søga* ("History of the People of Miðvágur"), the earliest and, from a literary point of view, probably the

The Faroese press—an ironic view by Bárður Jákupssen (Hoydahl et al. *Ruskovnurin,* Tórshavn, 1971). Courtesy of the artist.

finest "village history" (*bygdarsøga*). It illustrates, among other things, enduring values pervading all levels of Faroese culture.

Matras, who was born in 1900 in Viðareiði, published his first poetry in 1920, the same year he went off to school in Copenhagen. In 1933 he received a doctorate in Nordic philology for a dissertation on place-names in the Norðoyar. The great works of his scholarly career include the Faroese-Danish dictionary (with M.A. Jacobsen) and the definitive compendium of Faroese ballads (with Napoleon Djurhuus, based on Svend Grundtvig's work). He returned to the Faroes for good in 1965, to take over the linguistics department of the newly founded Faroese Academy (Fróðskaparsetur Føroya). His literary works include a Faroese literary history (1935), numerous translations (of Swift, Burns, Voltaire, and Camus, as well as of Danish writings by his compatriots William Heinesen

and Jørgen-Frantz Jacobsen), and several volumes of verse. His stature is
perhaps comparable to that of Robert Frost in the United States. Matras
also resembles Frost in his intimate depictions of homely scenes, although
his fluid intellectual sensibility is more reminiscent of Robert Lowell or
Langston Hughes. "Neytakonurnar" was published in 1933.

> Now the milkmaids walk back from the outfields
> with pails on their backs and weary in their knees.
> Milk splashes in the pails, and under their soles prickle
> the heather on the heath and the gravel in the streambeds.
> At home the baby lies sleeping.
>
> Now the milkmaids walk back toward the walls,
> walk single file and look like mountain cairns,
> that set off walking when darkness came over the heath.
> Now the gate opens for them, and the broad village path.
> At home the baby lies sleeping.
>
> Now the milkmaids plod bowed through the infield.
> There at home the cat waits in impatient anticipation,
> streaks through the grass, when the milkmaid comes
> with night on her back and pail brimming over.
> At home the baby lies sleeping.
>
> [Matras 1933:20-21]

An American or British reader does not find this sort of pastoralism
entirely alien. The final image of the milkmaid's approach "with night on
her back" while the cat rushes through the grass and the baby lies sleeping
indoors remains vivid even in a rather literal translation; and even if we
can call to mind no very precise picture of cairns and the wooden pails
women carried out to cows in distant pastures, we know many precisely
rendered depictions of similar scenes in our own literatures.

But the poem seems a strangely shallow exercise in this familiar vein.
I believe we miss two things: the resonance of Matras's sociogeographic
imagery and an underlying opposition between society and the individual
that we are accustomed to in our own romantic or neoromantic visions.

As an artifact of Faroese culture, Matras's poem might best be read
as a modern rendition of the nuanced geographical metaphors in
"Snæbjørn": a fugue on the points of passage from the mountains and the
sea to the hearth and the home. As in much Faroese literature, the chief
aesthetic and dramatic tension thus derives from the juxtaposition of the
natural and domestic worlds and from people's movement from one to the
other. To less finely tuned imaginations, the contrast appears more
crudely:

> Out [at sea] they strive each day,
> they suck the bitter smell from the sea,

in the evening they gather in friendship,
it is lovely to dwell in the Faroes.
                                                [Gregoriussen 1928:40]

But in a way no translation of Matras's poem could catch, Faroese "nature" is not the wild, uncultured place *we* make of it, but an intimately and elaborately known setting for human affairs. In a word-for-word translation, for example, the poem's first line is: "Now walk the cow-women from-the-south out-of (*sunnan úr*) outfields." *Sunnan úr* is a local idiom of orientation (presumably from Viðareiði) not only expressing this village's place in the world but also joining it to a highly complex sense of place shared almost unconsciously by all Faroese, which, as it is elaborated over time and space, provides a means of encompassing local knowledge and "coming to terms with change. With the social world as inseparable from the landscape as it is from the past, knowing one's place in the Faroese world seems quite as natural as speaking the language" (Wylie and Margolin 1981:45; see also B. Nielsen 1977).

Such imagery and the sense of place it evinces are pervasive but, as it were, invisible in Faroese culture. Sometimes, common local knowledge of this sort is actively kept implicit. Here is a passage from Jørgen-Frantz Jacobsen's novel *Barbara*, translated from the original Danish and from Matras's Faroese rendition. A boat has set out from Sandavágur.

original	*Matras*
Shortly afterwards they were near Klovning, a broad headland whose outermost part was cloven free from the land and stood stooping out over the sea. Here they set out onto the open Vágaførður and rowed eastward along the high land.	Shortly after that they came near Klovning. They set out onto Vágafjørður and rowed east along the cliff. [Á. Dahl 1981:112]

Matras obviously felt that his Faroese readers would not need to be told that Vágarfjørður is open, or what Klovning looks like. But in deleting the descriptive matter, he has lost much of Jacobsen's point; for the novel deals with figures as heroically fractured from Faroese society as Klovning is from the land. By not forcing a particular, ostensibly foreign vision on the landscape, Matras has in a small way preserved the implicit, internal integrity of local culture.

His translation and his poem about the milkmaids are thus Faroese in several senses. They are elements in the national culture, marking the border between the Faroese and foreign worlds. The poem especially marks significant points of articulation within the Faroese world and the continuity of its internal cultural range. And they escape the national-cultural frame by expressing a broader but not explicitly formulated sense of local identity.

It is perhaps clearer, in this light, why the foreign reader may miss an underlying opposition between society and the individual in Matras's poem. For us, the contrast between nature and human society conventionally provides a way of expressing a deeper opposition between the individual and the collectivity. A retreat *to* nature gives perspective on society and forces a choice, as in Gray's "Elegy," between lonely satisfactions and "the madding crowd's ignoble strife." Matras does not force this choice. We find ourselves less in Gray's darkling churchyard than in his weary plowman's shoes. Two well known poems by Robert Frost offer a similar contrast. Unlike Frost in "The Road Not Taken," Matras's milkmaids have not chosen a way "less traveled by," leading who knows where; they are homeward bound on the path they tread each evening. Of course, like Frost in "Stopping by Woods on a Snowy Evening," Matras's milkmaids "have promises to keep." But these have not been made to seem burdensome by the trip to the outfields, and the milkmaids do not pause for reflection in the dusk. When the baby wakes up, it will want feeding, doubtless with fresh milk; and the cat will have some, too. For Matras's milkmaids, then, it is good to come home to the village at dusk. The retreat is *from* the outlying landscape to the home. To depict the outfields, the mountains, or the sea is not to invalidate the village world, but to make it all the more worthy.[7]

Faroese writers have in general shied away from direct social criticism. Not only do Faroese generally prefer to avoid open criticism of each other in everyday life; but the national culture to which writers contribute has been fundamentally concerned with validating and preserving the integrity of local life. Its establishment involved letting literature express the Faroes' unity, while disunity has been institutionalized in, for example, political parties, where differences are safely coded in terms of desirable relations with Denmark. As a result, much Faroese writing seems curiously shallow to a foreign reader. To take two examples older than Matras's poem: in Símun av Skarði's play *Vár*, the heroine worries briefly about village gossip, but it has little or no effect on the resolution of the plot; and in Regin í Líð's novella "Minnisvarðin," the youths gathered in a shop in the opening scene serve only as a wry kind of chorus. They help to characterize the main characters, but do not drive them to their fate. In neither case is the conflict between the individual and the social system, which the gossippers might have been used to represent (S. av. Skarði 1904; í Líð 1912 [1906]:1-9). In sum, the continuity of Faroese culture beyond its official frame is insured by concentrating on individuals and on the natural setting in which they carry out their pursuits. The social system remains out of focus, especially insofar as it shapes patterns of dissension among its members.

The same lack of focus is even more striking in Faroese historiography. Far from providing, as our own does, a means of sustained critical inquiry into the changing nature of local society, it eschews even generalizations

and renders local life in overwhelmingly fragmented detail. This is particularly true of histories written for a local audience, most notably the "village histories," which began to come out in the 1940s, and their successors.[8] These are closely based on oral sources, and here we find ourselves
plunged, like an anthropologist in the field, into the heart of Faroese "nationality"—the traditional village world as Faroese appreciate it, through
seemingly interminable, disjointed recitations of apparently pointless an-
ecdotes about each house and the people who have lived there since time
not-quite-immemorial.

Two features of this sort of historiography deserve our attention: the
value attributed to their work by the *bygdarsøgur*'s compilers, and the
enduring values of local life repeatedly expressed in the stories they relate.
Noteworthy in both areas is the maintenance of cultural continuity over
time and between the levels of organization of Faroese society. We shall
concentrate on a single text: Mikkjal Dánjalsson á Ryggi's *Miðvinga Søga*
("History of the People of Miðvágur").

Á Ryggi was born in Miðvágur in 1879. He went to school in Denmark for two years and spent a teaching career in the hamlets of Gásadalur
and Bøur, from 1920 until 1945. He wrote poetry and schoolbooks and
was a regular contributor to *Tingakrossur*. He took a leading role in local
politics, serving in the Løgting from 1924 to 1927, as a member of the
Self-Rule party. He died in 1956, after a long bout with tuberculosis. He
began collecting legends about Miðvágur in around 1915, when the Tórshavn young men's club Sólarmagn (fd. 1895) asked him to collect and
map the village's place-names. Consulting with old men, he found that
even without his asking, they told stories about the names or the places
they pointed out to him. The book is a collection of dozens of these stories, arranged chronologically for each homestead, followed by a score of
shorter or more disconnected tales. Á Ryggi appends five tales from Jakobsen's collection, a list of the priests of Vágar since about 1538, and two
genealogical tables. The whole is accompanied by detailed learned notes,
drawn from documentary sources. Most of the stories describe events datable to the late seventeenth through the eighteenth centuries, although,
like Jakobsen's tales, they almost never give dates and seldom refer by
name to nonlocal figures or events. Fewer of them concern semisupernatural figures.

Writing at a time when the traditional culture was as much on its last
legs as his informants were on theirs, he says: "From them I learned much
about bygone times, and I would have learnt more had I thought to ask
more. From them I learned good Faroese expressions. Their manner of
speech was straightforward, accurate, and pithy; the language sounded
dignified and beautiful in their mouths, just as it must have sounded some
three hundred years ago. I would like to be able to thank them—but they
are dead, nearly all of them" (1940:8). In other words, a chief value of
Miðvinga Søga, like that of other national-cultural monuments, is its erec-

tion of the language and its works of recollection as symbols of continuity with the past. As Louis Zachariasen (1945:32) put it in a discussion of Faroese nationality, "Faroese language and customs were a heritage just as lands were."

Á Ryggi is significantly ambivalent about the value of the tales themselves as factual accounts. Three generations ago, he says, "both learned and unlearned men believed such stories were truthful. Nowadays the learned have little confidence in them" (1940:6-7). He has checked their historicity in documentary sources wherever possible, and then "those times I perceive that the storytellers have gone astray, I have put it in the notes in the back of the book. I think these [occasions] have been much rarer than could have been expected; but now each man can judge" (1940:7).

This is interesting on several counts. First, the distinction between "learned and unlearned men," which was new to Faroese society, although not entirely alien to it (the storytellers themselves were learned in their own way), has been reproduced in the format of the book. The continuity between the modern learned, the traditionally learned, and the unlearned is somewhat precarious, but it is maintained by á Ryggi's avoidance of imposing a particular shape on what "each man" knows. His historiographic strategy thus parallels Matras's literary strategy in translating *Barbara*.

Relatedly, á Ryggi leaves no doubt that knowledge of the past was in fact well organized; but he does not tell us how.

Storytellers are many, but their stories match each other well—something can differ in a small way, and something can be forgotten, but mostly the account is the same—nearly always. The same story—especially when it is ancient—was often related by the best storytellers with the same expressions and turns of phrase, indeed most of it at times with the same words—undoubtedly those words they had heard . . . from even older storytellers. A few men given to garrulity had the habit of stretching [the stories] out and coming in with something of their own, but then the manner of expression changed, becoming their own customary manner, and then I became suspicious. Then if I asked other storytellers, the answer was; 'I haven't heard that.' [1940:6]

Insofar as á Ryggi does undertake to organize the traditional organization of knowledge, he follows as closely as possible what was undoubtedly one of its guiding principles: an arrangement by homesteads, which embeds both his and his informants' sense of time's passage in a relatively unchanging social space.

Finally, the sentences just quoted suggest that the stories had traditionally been told in a more or less fixed form. Á Ryggi also suggests that they were told in a more or less fixed setting.

These stories are all [but one] written down as they were told (*eftir mannamunni*); they are *roykstova* stories.

I have heard many of them several times. On winter evenings much was related for amusement's sake, but what we children and young people liked best was when someone began to tell about old things from our village. The listeners were keen, and the tellers no less keen; they lived in history [or: in the story, *í søguni*], and they seemed scarcely to notice what was happening indoors. When I was nearly grown up I thought about writing down the stories, but [until about 1915] this came to no more than a thought. [1940:11]

A further value of *Miðvinga Søga* was thus to fix in writing the old oral form in which the stories had traditionally been fixed, and to replace the *kvøldseta* with the book itself, or perhaps more accurately, with the acts of writing it and reading it. As David Margolin has argued (Wylie and Margolin 1981:70-71), fixing folk-literary genres in writing allowed their didactic and integrating functions to be "taken over by professional works and institutions," letting the old genres survive "to symbolize a modern culture in which they themselves are obsolete." At the cost of losing a certain continuity of form and occasion, *Miðvinga Søga* preserves its sources' content along with the basic structure (now complicated by the addition of a "learned" level) of formal and informal modes of expression.

To a foreign reader, a work like *Miðvinga Søga* seems a queer, unsatisfactory sort of historiography. It makes more sense as a complicated kind of written ritual designed to preserve continuities in time, space, language, forms of expression, the organization of knowledge, and social organization, and between the national and traditional cultures.

But what of the stories themselves? How do they complement the form in which á Ryggi presents them? Most obviously, perhaps, they resemble the tales Jakobsen collected by using rather formal language to embed a sense of continuity over time in detailed evocations of the village's geographic and social space. "Each man" or woman who plays a leading role is carefully characterized and identified by residence. It is assumed that the audience already knows enough about the local scene to make sense of the stories, but sometimes extra geographical or genealogical details are added, to relate the old setting to the new one. A story datable to the mid-1740s begins: "[In the homestead of] Niðri í Tøðu [in the hamlet of] í Húsi lived a woman named Elsba. Some foundation stones of her house can still be seen, but now the manure-heap wall of [the homestead] uttar í Húsum has been laid over them. Elsba was renowned for having second sight and giving good counsel, as well" (1940:79). Similarly, a story about a certain Ata, who died in 1853, according to á Ryggi's notes, ends with a genealogy given in conventional form:

Ata's son was named Jógvan. He was an exceptional shepherd and a renowned fisherman. But he never went to the cliffs—Ata had forbidden him to do so. He was the first Jógvan innan fyri Á who died in bed. His sons were Jesar, who was the farmer at uppi í Stovu on Hestur, and Sámal and Jóhannes. Jesar's son was Jógvan, who was the farmer at uppi í Stovu; he drowned off Hestur. Sámal's sons were Jógvan, Ólavur, Haraldur, and Andrias. Jóhannes' sons were Niklas,

Jógvan, and Hans Dánjal. Hans Dánjal and two of Niklas's sons drowned in the bay at Miðvágur. [1940:81]

During my fieldwork, I was given endless genealogies like this, and they often find their way into print, for example in J.S. Hansen's series about the Norðoyar, *Tey Byggja Land,* "They Build the Country" (J.S. Hansen 1971, 1973, 1975, 1978a, 1978b, 1980, 1981).

Faroese clearly delight in such enumerations, but the foreigner is soon exasperated by the multiplicity of detail. Yet in the end, searching for an underlying order, one is struck by another aspect of the stories' repetitiousness: their kaleidoscopic variation on the single theme of balancing individualism and cooperativeness. We may suggest that the articulation of these values is an enduring characteristic of Faroese culture, and that it complements á Ryggi's national-cultural historiographic strategy.

The stories particularly stress the value of cooperation in the face of external threats and uncertainties, whether human or natural in origin. At a level of social and geographic organization embracing the whole village or perhaps the whole island, one of the oldest stories in the collection relates how the men of Miðvágur "and maybe other men of Vágar with them" took advantage of the lay of the land to defeat some marauding Icelanders. (Á Ryggi dates this incident to 1445, when an Icelandic bishop tried to sieze the Faroese bishopric [1940:109, 156-57; cf. Øssursson 1963:26-28].) At the level of neighboring villages, an undatable story tells how the people of Miðvágur and Sandavágur simply divided in half a great driftwood log that had come ashore on the border between their lands (1940:112). At the level of neighboring farms or homesteads, a story datable to the mid-seventeenth century tells how their owners, who were brothers, combined some of their holdings rather than quarrel about unmarked sheep (1940:51-52). At the level of a single homestead (and of a figure marginal to the village as a whole), a related story tells how a half-blind cripple helped to foil a gang of sheep thieves (1940:52). At the level of a single farm's crew of milkmaids, we hear how "one time in the old days" a half-witted woman whom the others often made fun of helped them all get back home in a fog. "'Yes!' said the old farmer, 'so learn that no one should despise the simple-minded; they often prove themselves better than the intelligent do'" (1940:75-76). Cooperation within a family is assumed; but if it fails, the result can at least be seen as ridiculous. Once, in the late eighteenth century, there were two brothers, Rubbekkur and Janus, and they "were both of them rogues." Janus had a farm in Bøur. "Rubbekkur often traveled to Bøur and was put up by Janus, and they never got along well. One time they quarreled about a shotgun until they broke it in half, so that one held the stock and the other the barrel, and then they used them to hit each other with" (1940:65).

Another amusing story is likewise datable to the late eighteenth century. It illustrates the role of humor in marking social boundaries and, more interestingly, the value of cooperation when an individual moves between sociogeographic levels, in this case by going courting in Kirkjubøur. One day a Miðvágur farmer named Rasmus, an "exceptionally strong man," was sitting with his girlfriend in Kirkjubøur, when a bull broke out of its stall. The Kirkjubøur farmhands herded it as far as the infield wall, but it was too angry to do anything more with. Rasmus told the girl he should go help them. She said he had better not: "'The men of Kirkjubøur are so mocking.'" He replied that he would brave that, went out, and threw the bull. "Rasmus was wearing white stockings; he looks down at his legs and says quietly, 'He mussed my stockings.' Then the men of Kirkjubøur weren't mocking" (1940:39).

Why all the emphasis on cooperation? From one point of view, cooperative effort is clearly a way of dealing with common threats and life's inevitable uncertainties, and of maintaining continuity both within and between levels of social organization. It makes even a dim-witted milkmaid or a half-blind cripple or a man come a-courting from the next island a valued member of local society. *Miðvinga Søga* is also a cooperative work, undertaken in the face of a threat to the continued coherence of Faroese life: a collaboration between old and new, local and national, oral and written, unlearned and learned, and, more concretely, between an author who was marginal to local society, his several aging, once-central informants, and a diffuse future readership. The book as well as the stories it contains celebrate cooperation as an enduring value in Faroese culture; in fact, as the essence of its ability to endure.

From another point of view, cooperation checks another prized value: self-reliant individualism. As some of the examples given above may suggest, the stories generally give sharp characterizations of their main actors. A story datable to the late 1760s, for example, begins by noting that its heroine was "tremendously strong," and goes on to relate how, when she was "much with child," she once carried another woman's milk pails, as well as her own, in from a distant outfield (1940:41-42). The plot of another, slightly later story is set up as follows:

At Sárhús in [the hamlet of] við Kirkjar lived a man who was called Sára's Man. He was the strongest man in Miðvágur at that time.

In Búðatoft there lived at the same time a man who was called Jógvan's Boy. He was beastly, a glutton for food and drink, and a slugabed; but he was held to be strong. [1940:96]

In the end, Jógvan's Boy has to be carried home by Sára's Man, much the worse for drink, after causing such a commotion in the village that the men had to come home from church to protect their houses.

Jógvan's Boy is an extreme case. But clearly it is bad to be covetous, argumentative, hard-drinking, or otherwise unable or unwilling to cooperate with others. It is good to be strong and self-reliant, or, in a word, *raskur,* an untranslatable term of high praise in Faroese meaning strong, bold, resourceful, capable, and clever. Obviously, however, a *raskur* person is not necessarily a cooperative one, and his place in local society may be rather precarious. Significantly, then, a common genre of stories concerns the socialization of a *raskur* hero.

One story in this vein concerns the exceptionally *raskur* farmhand of a man named Heini. The story is particularly rich in geographical detail and social-organizational nuance, and, like Matras's poem, may almost be read as a reversal of the first part of "Snæbjørn," recounting a return to the village from the cliffs. Significantly, the farmhand is not named until the end of the story, when he acquires a homestead nickname appropriate to his new status. He was courting Heini's sister, but Heini was dead set against the match. One day a blizzard overtook Heini's crew at sea. They were forced from one point to another along the cliff-bound coast, until at last they found a spot where they could get ashore and haul up the boat. More and more exhausted, they made their way up through the snow to the very edge, where an overhanging drift blocked the way. They lost hope for their lives, but the *raskur* farmhand pushed on, found a likely spot, and broke through the drift with a mighty effort. When the men came up onto more level ground, "the farmer proclaimed, 'Now you have done a man's work, now you will also have a man's desire.' When he came home and had seated himself well he called his sister to him. 'Now shall be yes what was no before,' he says, and then lays her hand in the farmhand's hand.—They married and lived at niðri á Kletti, and thus he has been called Klettur Man" (1940:33-34).

The story neatly resolves the tension between cooperation and individualism. Like Rasmus in Kirkjubøur, the Klettur man proves himself worthy of assuming a new social status by demonstrating his mastery of two prime values in the face of an uncertain fate. Both statuses (hired hand and independent householder) are contained within the village, whose people certify his reputation.

The values themselves endure outside the frame of the national culture. But at the time á Ryggi was writing, and even more so today, natural uncertainties have diminished, pursuits are more various and generally call for less cooperation or *raskur*-ness, and, perhaps most important, a person's standing may not be certified by his or her fellow villagers alone, but by agencies outside the village or even outside the Faroes. Given the Faroes' increasing socioeconomic diversification, how can a schoolteacher like á Ryggi be socialized; or, today, a doctor, a cabdriver, a snackbar operator, an electrician, or a fish-factory manager, let alone a scholar or bureaucrat in Tórshavn?

The proliferating agencies that do certify such figures' competence help to integrate local culture and society formally, insofar as they are specifically, officially Faroese. But national-cultural institutions also help to maintain such fundamental values as individualism and cooperativeness by *avoiding* tasks and attitudes we probably take for granted in analogous American institutions. Faroese historiography and social science, for example, do not serve as vehicles for social criticism; nor are they divided into organized schools of thought supporting opposed views. Just as Matras avoided translating Jacobsen's vision of geographical features, and just as á Ryggi let "each man . . . judge" the relative worth of oral tradition and documentary evidence, so Faroese scholarship has generally remained content to publish reams of facts, figures, and documents. But even summaries are uncommon and perfunctory; analysis is rare; and explicitly differing interpretations are left to politicians, who, for their part, are far more critical of each other than of Faroese society. The point, after all, is to get along.

These impressions concern the most formal levels of Faroese culture. We may wonder, still, how Faroese get along from day to day in ordinary life. In the villages, what institutions actively promote collective adherence to established values, especially now that the *kvøldseta* has vanished, for example, and (wherever clubs have not been formed to preserve it) ballad dancing has almost completely succumbed to young people's interest in pop music and to evangelicals' opposition to all dancing? What solutions do villagers find to the problem of coming to terms with social change? To what extent do they use national-cultural institutions to maintain the continuity of local life, and to what extent do they skirt the national-cultural frame? One may hypothesize that the evangelical movement is not an entirely aberrant response to social change. (Accustomed to equating evangelical religion with reactionary, even xenophobic politics, an American may find surprising the moderate, social-democratic progressiveness and internationalist bent of many Faroese evangelicals.) The movement is perfectly "Faroese" in using reverent, uncritical readings of old texts to deny that the passage of time makes any fundamental difference, and to certify one's individual worth. But it is "un-Faroese" in choosing an outlandish text (the Bible, not local legends); in expressing individual worth without reference to one's integration in village society (it is more important to be saved than to be *raskur* or cooperative); and in essaying a formal, comprehensive sort of direct social criticism. In other words, evangelical religion may perform a task avoided by secular institutions.[9]

These, however, are essentially preliminary formulations of ethnographic speculations, leading us into the present and away from the business of this book.

Miðvinga Søga depicts an older state of affairs: the village world as its inhabitants knew it, the world from which Faroese students departed for Copenhagen in the late nineteenth and early twentieth centuries. It was a doomed world, changing from within even as the Faroes were more and more closely drawn into the Danish orbit. Yet it had remained vital enough so that an increasingly pressing question arose, particularly in the new upper reaches of Faroese society: How might the Faroes' "individuality" be preserved as the islands attained a "measure of European importance"?

We have argued that the Faroese were able to attain the difficult double end of maintaining cultural continuity and promoting socioeconomic change because an old-fashioned way of life that had survived the Reformation beneath a covering Danishness was little affected by agricultural reform movements in the eighteenth century and was, if anything, revitalized in the nineteenth century by a shift from farming to fishing as the basis of the export economy. Meanwhile, the dismantling of a medieval political and administrative system formally incorporated the Faroes into Denmark, and the introduction of free trade led to the rise of a new mercantile and intellectual elite. Adopting a Danish ideology, members of this elite led a culturally separatist movement, in the 1890s, which took on political shape after the turn of the century. One result has been the creation of a national culture that is as much (and as little) a part of the local scene as the "specters and illusions" discussed by Debes in the aftermath of the Reformation. Then, increasing Danish hegemony had entailed using works of language to renegotiate the contract with nature; now, works of language used natural and other symbols to renegotiate the contract with Denmark.

Finally, the national culture was not designed to hinder further social change; nor, by the same token, is it all of Faroese culture. Certainly it deserves further study, as do other national cultures and their fit with local ones.

> Now I have written the stories
> that bygone men told to me;
> now *you* write in other villages,
> each in his own place.
>
> Let us lay
> stones on good foundations,
> draw into the light of day
> the forefathers' life and lineage.
>
> Life at sea, on the cliffs, in the village,
> within gable and threshold,
> and hate's odium, honor's virtue—
> may the story witness them well.
>
> Write down and listen to
> what wise men proclaim;
> then may the fogs dwindle
> which hide the Faroes' history.
>
> á Ryggi [1940:8–9]

Governance and Governors

▬▬▬▬▬▬▬▬▬▬▬▬▬▬▬▬▬▬▬▬▬▬▬▬▬▬▬▬

🖼 In the second half of the seventeenth century, Christoffer von Gabel (1655-70) and his son Frederik (1670-1708) held the Faroes as an enfeoffed tax farm and mercantilist colony.

In 1655 the elder Gabel was granted a monopoly over the Faroe trade, abrogating a twenty-year agreement made with the "Iceland Company," in 1649. At first he paid 1000 *rigsdaler* a year for all the Faroes' income, but in 1661 he was granted the income without payment for his and his son's lifetimes. At the same time, his and, prospectively, his son's feudal overlordship was confirmed. The following year, the old Iceland Company was abolished, and Gabel's trade monopoly was confirmed. Trading privileges were rented out to Jonas Trellelund in 1656-69 and then briefly to his brother Evert, or Eberhardt, Trellelund.

In 1671 Christian V reconfirmed the Gabels' feudal overlordship. From 1670 to 1674, the younger Gabel managed the trade himself, but from 1675 to 1680, it was rented out to the former bailiff, Johann Heidemann, and to one Simon de Petkun. In 1680 Gabel managed the trade with others and after 1685, alone. Like his father, Frederik von Gabel received the Faroes' income, except that from 1683 to 1699, he was granted 2000 *rigsdaler* a year instead.

The elder Gabel was styled Commander of the Faroes (*Befælingsmand over Færøerne*). The younger was styled Governor of the Faroes (*Gouvernør over Færøerne*).

Frederik von Gabel's heirs briefly retained his privileges, after his death on 21 June 1708. The following year, the overlordship was abolished. In 1709, then, oversight of the Faroes' finances was passed to the Northern Norwegian Bureau of the Finance Office (*Nordenfjeldske norske Renteskrivekontor*) within the Exchequer (*Rentekammer*). This arrangement lasted until 1771.

In that year, in accordance with Struensee's attempt to streamline the Danish administration, three offices (*kamre*) were created out of the combined Exchequer and General Customs Office (*Generaltoldkammer*): the Danish Office for Denmark, the Faroes, and overseas Danish possessions; the Norwegian Office for Norway and Iceland; and the German Office for Slesvig, Holsten, Oldenborg, and Delmenhorst. With the reestablishment of the Exchequer, in 1773, after Struensee's fall, Faroese, Icelandic, and Greenlandic affairs were briefly placed under its Trondhjem Bureau and then under a special Icelandic, Faroese, and Greenlandic Financial Bureau, which in turn was part of the West Indian and Guinean Exchequer and General Customs Office (*Vestindisk-guineisk Rente- samt General-toldkammer*). As of 1781, this bureau was placed within the Exchequer. In 1789 it was united there with the Bergen Financial Bureau, which, after 1804, was called the Second Northern Norwegian Bureau (*Anden norske nordenfjeldske*). With the loss of Norway and the dissolution of the Norwegian Financial Bureaus, a special Financial Bureau for Icelandic, Faroese, and Greenlandic affairs was set up, in 1814.

Meanwhile, direct management of the Faroe trade had been combined with those of the Iceland and Finmark trade, in 1777, and of the Greenland trade, in 1781. Of the company's four managers, one had special responsibility for the Faroes. Trade with Iceland and Finmark was partially freed, in 1786-87. The intention was to free the Faroe trade as well. This did not come to pass, because of Faroese protests, and in 1791 a new price schedule was worked out. It was then intended to abolish the monopoly in 1796. Again Faroese protested, and, in 1798, "The Faroese and Greenlandic Trade Commission" was established. A continuation of the royal monopoly was promised in 1821. The monopoly was finally abolished as of 1 January 1856.

The Faroes' administrative apparatus had also changed after Frederik von Gabel's death. In 1709 the Faroes were placed in the province (*stift*) of Sjælland, while the more immediate administrative functions were taken over by a committee consisting of the *løgmaður* (as foreman), the bailiff (Da. *landsfoged, foged;* Fa. *fúti*), and Naval Lieutenant Rasmus Juel. The bailiffs in this period (1709-20) were also charged with the local management of the Faroe trade. Thereafter a special manager was appointed.

From 1720 to 1775, the Faroes were combined in a single province with Iceland. Its chief administrator bore the title of Provincial Commander of Iceland and the Faroes (*Stiftsbefællingsmand over Island og Færøerne*). These administrators did not live in the Faroes. They were:

Peter Raben (1720-27)
Kristian Güldencrone (1728-30)
Henrik Ochsen (1730-50)
Otto Manderup Rantzau (1750-68)
Kristian Leberech von Proeck (1768-69)
Lauritz Andreas Thodal (1770-75).

From 1776 to 1816, the Faroes were again incorporated in Sjælland province, whose chief administrative officer bore the title of Provincial Governor of Sjælland Province and the Faroes (*Stiftsamtmand over Sjællands Stift og Færøerne*). As of 1777, this office was administratively tied to the Customs Office, while trade was under the Exchequer. The provincial governor was, as it were, his own subordinate so far as the Faroes were concerned, since he was also governor of the Faroes (*Amtmand over Færøerne*). The provincial governors in this period were:

Henrik Adam Brockenhuus (1776-87)
Gregers Kristian von Haxthausen (1787-90)
Johan Heinrich Knuth (1790-1802)
Frederik Hauch (1802-10)
Verner Jasper Andreas Moltke (1810-16).

They were resident in Copenhagen.

In 1816 the offices of Provincial Governor and Governor were divided. The Governorship was made permanent in 1821. The provincial governors from 1816 to 1848 were:

Kristoffer Schøller von Bülow (1816-21)
Frederik von Lowzow (1821-31)
Frederik Kristian Julius Knuth (1831-50)

The governors resided in the Faroes. They were:

Emilius Marius Georgius von Löbner (1816-28)
Christian Ludvig Tillisch (1828-30)
Frederik Ferdinand Tillisch (1830-37)
Christian Pløyen (1837-48).

In 1848 responsibility for Faroese affairs was transferred from the Exchequer to the Icelandic Department (*Islandske Department*). This department was at first within the Ministry of the Interior (*Indenrigsministeriet*), then (1855-58) within its replacement, the Common Ministry of the Interior (*Fællesindenrigsministeriet*), and then (1858-74) within the Ministry of Justice (*Justitsministeriet*). When a separate ministry was created for Iceland, in 1874, Faroese affairs were transferred to the Second Department of the Ministry of Justice, except that ecclesiastical and schooling affairs were the responsibility of the Ministry of Religion (*Cultusministeriet*).

The Faroes' governors since 1849 were:

Carl Emil Dahlerup (1849-61)
Peter Holten (1862-65)
Hannes Christian Steingrim Finsen (1871-85)
Lorentz Høyer Buchwaldt (1885-96)
Christian Bærentsen (1897-1911)
Svenning Rytter (1911-18)
Victor Stahlschmidth (1918-20)
Elias Olrik (1920-29)
Hjalmar Ringberg (1929-36)
Carl Aage Hilbert (1936-45)
Cai Andrias Vagn-Hansen (1945-48).

Of these, only Bærentsen was Faroese. The office of Governor was abolished in 1948. Since then, the highest representative of the Danish government in the Faroes has been the High Commissioner (Da. *Rigsombudsmand på Færøerne;* Fa. *Ríkisumboðsmaður*).

From 1852 until 1924, the governor was a member and ex-officio chairman of the Løgting.

From 1816 to 1865, the governor served as commandant of the Tórshavn garrison. This had been Løbner's post as early as 1801, when he was acting governor. For a list of commandants, see Heilskov (1919). The post was abolished in 1865.

Since medieval times, the Faroes had had a bailiff (Fa. *fúti*), whose subordinates were the sheriffs (Fa. *sýslumenn*) in each district. The bailiffs were generally Danish or Norwegian; the sheriffs have always been Faroese. Until 1655, the bailiff was the highest royal officer in the country. Thereafter, he was subordinate to others. In the nineteenth century, he collected rents from king's farms and served (in American terms) as a combination police chief and district attorney. The bailiffs from 1579 to 1886 were:

> Mads Poulsøn (1579-81)
> Søren Christensøn Flue (1582)
> Mikkel Ibsøn (1583-84)
> Niels Skinkel til Gierskov (1584)
> Lyder Augustinssøn (1586-87)
> Mads Batzersøn (1588-91)
> Mogens Nielssøn (1592-93)
> Søren Nielssøn (1593-94 and 1598)
> Strange Madssøn (1597 and 1599-1619)
> Mads Christensøn Gullandsfar (1620-44)
> Hans Selmer (1645-47)
> Christen Madssøn (1648-55)
> Baltzer Jacobsen (1655)
> Johan Heideman (1656-64)
> Søren Pedersøn Skougaard (1664-74)
> Christopher Heideman (1675-80)
> Hans Willumsøn (1680-1708 or -1709)
> Jørgen Kristian Klein (1708- or 1709-15)
> Didrik Markussen (1715-20)
> Jørgen Frantz Hammershaimb (1723-65)
> Wenzel Hammershaimb (1765-1815)
> Hans Wilhelm Meyer (1816-29)
> Chr. Pløyen (1830-37)
> Jacob Andreas Lunddahl (1837-52)
> ? Randropp (1852-57)
> H. Chr. S. Finsen (1858-71)
> ? Brendstrup (1872-1886)

A final official has been the *sorinskrivari*. As explained in the text, the *sorinskrivari* was at first the recording secretary of the Løgting. In the seventeenth century, he assumed judicial functions, which he still holds. The *sorinskrivarar* from the late sixteenth century until 1890 were:

Niels Andrasson (?) (before 1584?)
Gabriel Mitens (1584-1620 or -1621)
Jacob Jacobsøn (?) (ca. 1622-23)
(unknown) (1624-26)
(office perhaps vacant) (1627-28)
Jacob Pederssøn Morsing Gullsmed (1629-39)
Jacob Willumssøn Hannemand (1640-45)
Hans Madssøn (1646)
Nils Jacobssøn (1647-69)
Peder Sørensen Broberg (1670-74 and 1677-94)
Hans Joensen, pro tempore (1675-76)
Morten Mortensen (1694-1705)
Friderich Severinsen Skougaard (1705-51)
Frederik Jonassen (1751-53)
Peder Samuelsen Weyhe (1760-75)
Peder Pedersen Weyhe (1775-82)
Joen Pedersen Weyhe (1782-?)
? Olsen (1790-1815)
Sören Sevel (1816-18)
Johan Peter Gorm (1819-32)
Niels Hunderup (1832-41)
Georg Fleming von Tillisch (1842-49)
Gerhardt Sigvart Rehling (1849-57)
Emil Lauritz Frederik Kock (1857-66)
Nicolai Reimer Rump (1866-71)
Harald Emil Høst (1871-78)
Lorentz Høyer Buchwaldt (1878-85)
Albert Ludvig Chr. Thrane (1885-90)

As recounted in the text, a high court called the Løgting had evidently been founded in Tórshavn soon after the Faroes' Norse settlement. It survived, although increasingly circumscribed in its functions, until 1816. Its chairman was called the løgmaður. The løgmenn from 1555 to 1816 were:

Guttorm Andersen (1555-72)
Joen Heinesen (1572-83)
Isak Guttormsen (1583-88)
Peder Jacobsen (1588-1601)
Thomas Simonsen (1601-8)
Zacharias Thormodsen (1608-28)
Joen Justinussen (1628-53)
Joen Poulsen (1654-55 and 1661-77)
Baltzer Jacobsen (1655-61)
Jacob Joensen (1677-79)
Johan Henrik Weyhe (1679-1706)
Samuel Pedersen (1706-52 [-1755])

Hans Jacobsen Debes ([1750-] 1755-72)
Thorkild Fieldsted (1769-72)
Jacob Bentzen Hveding (1772-86)
Johan Michael Lund (1786-[1805] 1806)
Jørgen Frantz Hammershaimb ([1805] 1806-16).
Except for Baltzer Jacobsen (1655-61), the *løgmenn* were all Faroese,
until 1769. Except for Hammershaimb (1806-16), they were Norwegians
or Danes thereafter.

For the period before 1709, the above account follows wherever possible
E. Joensen (1953, 1958, 1961, 1969), L. Zachariasen (1952, 1961), and
Degn (1939, 1945), along with N. Andersen (1895) and miscellaneous
other sources (e.g., Heilskov 1915, 1919). The reader is referred to L.
Zachariasen (1952) for a detailed account of administrative changes between 1708 and 1710. Thereafter, I have followed chiefly J. Bloch (1895),
Joensen, Mortensen and Petersen (1955), and Holmgaard (1964) (see also
Erslev 1923 and Sachs 1921), along with, e.g., Trap (1879). I have also
had access to the *Kongelig Dansk Hof- og Statscalender* for 1818, 1822,
1823, 1825, 1827, 1828, 1830, 1831, 1833, 1834, 1835, 1841, 1859,
and 1860.

I have made no attempt to regularize the spelling of proper names.
The reader is warned that various sources give somewhat different dates
for officials' periods in office.

Another crown official was a doctor. For holders of that position, see
Carøe (1917).

A convenient and exhaustive summary of the Faroes' ecclesiastical
establishment, from the earliest times through 1963, will be found in
Øssursson (1963). For a brief but dense ecclesiastical history and a detailed enumeration of the Faroese priesthood since 1849, the reader is
referred to Nedergaard (1951).

For summaries of ministerial minutes and discussions concerning the
Faroes between 1848 and 1912, see Harald Jørgensen (1954-62).

Notes

INTRODUCTION. *TERRA INCOGNITA* ⎯⎯⎯⎯⎯⎯

1. The post-Viking, pre-Reformation North has, however, received a good deal of scholarly attention, which is now growing and slowly being organized. For a recent description of the Viking and Hanseatic maritime empires, see Scammell (1981); for a survey of Iceland's commerce in the late Middle Ages, see Gelsinger (1981:181-94).

2. The shelf of anthropologically interesting works about the Faroes was, of course, longer than I first imagined; and it is growing longer. For recent bibliographies, see J.P. Joensen (1978, 1980).

3. A review of the rapidly expanding literature on this problem is beyond the scope of this book. For classic accounts from, respectively, a cultural-anthropological and a sociological point of view, the interested reader is referred to Redfield (1960) and Deutsch (1953). For more recent, theoretical anthropological formulations, see Geertz (1980), Spicer (1971; cf. Castile and Kushner 1981), Ward (1965), Wilson (1973, 1974; cf. Emmet 1964), and Wolf (1982). Anderson (1983) combines anthropology and political science. For recent studies of the use of historical and folkloristic symbols in defining regional identities, see Hobsbawm and Ranger (1983), Manning (1983), and Whisnant (1983). A recent bibliography of such studies will be found in Gusfield and Michalowicz (1984).

For an outline in English of the traditional Faroese economy and the islands' relations with the outside world, see J.P. Joensen (1982b); for more detailed accounts (in Swedish) see J.P. Joensen (1980, 1981). Anthony Jackson (1979:63) concludes an account of socioeconomic change in the Faroes by saying that a "combination of nationalism and material progress has enabled the Faroese to cope with the problems facing a small group of people trying to compete for a place in the world scene." "Custom," moreover, has helped to bridge "the discrepancies that the change in economy has forced upon their social structure." He does not, however, provide a very satisfactory account of why material progress fostered "nationalism," nor of how or why *some* customs have been retained and given a new form.

4. Farologists (if that may be a word) will also note that since this book was drafted, a number of important contributions to Faroese social history have been published. Most of them became available to me too late to use in revising the manuscript, although I have wedged in a few references here and there.

The reader is particularly referred to Hans J. Debes's history, in Faroese, of the "nationalist movement" (H.J. Debes 1982).

Isaksen (1983) has edited a valuable and engaging little collection of newspaper articles from the crucial period from 1901 to 1905, supplementing the facsimile editions of *Búreisingur* (1969), *Fuglaframi* (1972), and *Føringatíðindi*

206 NOTES TO PAGES 7-10

(1969). J.P. Joensen (1982a) provides a carefully edited, invaluable documentary and oral history of everyday activities and the domestic economy during the "ship fishing" era of the late nineteenth and early twentieth centuries. A slightly expanded, Danish version of this book is due to appear soon.

Two books now partly fill the vacuum of works about Faroese evangelical movements. Høj (1984) gives an informal account, in Faroese, of the Home Mission's work in several communities. Hansen (1984) offers a scholarly study, in Danish, of the Plymouth Brethren and Home Mission up to 1918. This otherwise extremely useful work is unfortunately marred by an emphasis on theological matters, recalling Björnsson's (1971) study of Icelandic marriage patterns, and by an unrealistic presupposition that the evangelical movements impinged upon a quite static, homogeneous culture.

Krogstrup and Lund (1983) offer an account, in Danish, of recent political trends in the light of continuing economic development. Erlendur Patursson (1976-1981) has extended to the post-war period his compendious history of the Faroese fishery (E. Patursson 1961).

An English-Faroese dictionary has at last come out, edited by Jóhannes av Skarði (1984).

As this book goes to press, the most recent collection of statistical data is Ársfrágreiðing (1983).

1. ANOTHER SET OF SMALL ISLANDS ⸻⸻⸻

1. Tierney (1967:74-77). On textual and other problems in this famous passage, see Tierney's notes (ibid., pp. 115-16). There was no archeological evidence supporting Dicuil's mention of an Irish settlement until 1968-71, when paleobotanical research by Jóhannes Jóhansen suggested that an area near Tjørnuvík was inhabited in the early seventh century, presumably by Irish; "but if so, they were here about a hundred years before the time Dicuil names" (Jóhansen 1971:157). On some tentative legendary recollections of Irishmen, see Jakobsen (1904:18-19).

The name "Faroes" means "sheep islands," and from Dicuil's comment it seems that the Norsemen must have found sheep there when they arrived. The oldest breed of Faroe sheep was evidently small and dark, resembling that still found on St. Kilda. The last of these were killed off on Lítla Dímun in 1868.

2. See S. Dahl (1958, 1961, 1965, 1970a, 1970b), Dahl and Rasmussen (1956), C. Matras (1956), and Small (1967-68) for archeological evidence. See MacGregor (1984) for a summary of place-name evidence from Shetland and the Faroes. On the Faroes' Norse settlement generally, see e.g., Marcus (1956), Trap (1968:188ff.), Young (1979:5-38), and scattered references in standard accounts of the Viking Age (e.g., Foote and Wilson 1970; G. Jones 1968a). For modern scholarship on the Icelandic saga evidence, see Foote (1964, 1965, 1970) and Halldórsson (1961).

3. For English translations of *Færeyinga saga*, see Johnston (1975), Powell (1896), Press (1934), and Young and Clewer (1973).

4. Hammershaimb (1891:379-81), Jakobsen (1898:xxvii-xxxii; 1904:26-27); but cf. Young (1979:67).

5. Jakobsen (1907:24). Young (1979:39) dates this ordinance to 1271. The following paragraphs rest largely on L. Zachariasen (1961:9-21, 314-59).

6. Strictly speaking, the Seyðabræv was not issued by the crown, but by Hákon Magnússon, who was lord over the Faroes and Shetland. Hákon succeeded to the throne a year later on the death of his brother King Eirík. For an English translation of the Seyðabræv, see Young (1979:140-53).

7. For legends of Kálvur lítli, see Jakobsen (1898-1901:57-62) and Hjalt (1953:19-21, 176); for commentary see Jakobsen (1898-1901:477-79; 1904:31; 1907:49-50), Øssursson (1963:24-25), and Zachariasen (1961:389). An English translation of the letter will be found in Young (1979:166).

8. The population estimate is Degn's (1932), and is the best we are likely to have, given the skimpy evidence. Other estimates range as high as twelve thousand (Djurhuus 1963:29) or even twenty thousand (Winther 1875:23), but these seem to be the products of wishful thinking, arrived at by applying a presumed mortality of 60-80 percent to the much later but apparently stable population of four to five thousand.

For traditional evidence of the Black Death in the Faroes, see, e.g., Hammershaimb (1891:373-77), Jakobsen (1898-1901:46 and note; 1904:38-39), and P. Petersen (1968:198). The best-known owner of extensive lands in the Faroes after the Black Death is remembered as "The Lady of Húsavík" (*hústrúin í Húsavík*). On her see, e.g., Hammershaimb (1891:373-77), Jakobsen (1904:32-38), and Davidsen (1970).

9. Guttesen (1971:136); see also Jakobsen (1907:14) and Young (1979:143, 149-50). This requirement, which probably reflects earlier customs, certainly had the effect of checking population growth. It seems also to have been aimed, however, at limiting the settlement of outlying lands by the poor. Young (1979:100-101) maintains that "Prior to 1200, the land was held by farmers who farmed their lands with the help of thralls. However, slavery was . . . abolished in about that year, but when released, these persons became known as 'good-for-nothings'. Between 1200 and 1298, a number of the freed thralls saved half a year's supply of food and then tried to set up their own houses and small-holdings in remote areas. Presumably they earned this money by working as farm labourers. However, the creation of new small-holdings was virtually prohibited by the provisions of the *Sheep Letter* which required a man to own at least three cows before he could set up house on his own. The only other people allowed to set up house on their own were those who were unable to find any other means of livelihood with which to support themselves. The result of the restriction on small-holdings was that people who could have started such holdings were, in general, compelled to work as farm labourers."

10. Jakobsen (1907:24-25); see also Joensen, Mortensen, and Petersen (1955:7) and Young (1979:139).

2. CHURCH, KING, COMPANY, AND COUNTRY ⸻

1. Documents concerning the Reformation and the seventeenth century have been published in various languages in N. Andersen (1895), Degn (1929, 1933, 1935, 1937a, 1938a, 1938b, 1938c, 1945), Evensen (1908-14), E. Joensen

(1953, 1958, 1961, 1969), Joensen, Mortensen, and Petersen (1955), Niclasen (1945), P.J. Nolsøe (1963-70, vol. 1), P. Petersen (1968), the *Tillæg* ("Supplement") to the *Forslag og Betænkninger afgivne af den Færøske Landbokommission* (Copenhagen, 1911; hereafter referred to as *Tillæg*), etc. While most of these works are strictly speaking secondary sources, some (e.g., Andersen's account of the period 1600-1709) share with many Faroese historical works such a predilection for quoting their sources at length that they are very close to being primary sources. Lucas Debes's description of the Faroes is of course invaluable (1673; English translation 1676); see also Friis (1881), Resen (1972), and Tarnovius (1950). Any student of the period must be heavily indebted, as I am, to Louis Zachariasen's study of "The Faroes as a Legal Society, 1535-1635" (1961).

2. For modern studies of the history of fishing and other "sea limits" around the Faroes, see D. Nolsøe (1963) and E. Patursson (1961).

3. Herring fishing is treated at some length in the laws of Magnus Lagabøter (Taranger 1970:143ff.). For detailed discussions of trespass, see P. Petersen (1968).

4. A *mørk* is divided into sixteen *gyllin;* a *gyllin* is in turn divided into twenty *skinn*. The *gyllin* appears to have been a Hanseatic unit that came to the Faroes in the late fifteenth century (L. Zachariasen 1961:392-96). *Merkur, gyllin,* and *skinn* were also monetary or quasi-monetary units, a barrel of barley, for example, being reckoned at 2 *gyllin* 8 *skinn,* according to the price schedule of 1691 (West 1972:37). A *mørk* of land can vary greatly in size. Degn suggests (e.g., 1945:244) that a *mørk* might be generally definable as the pasturage necessary for eighty of the old breed of sheep or forty of the new. For discussions, see, e.g., Bærentsen (1911:466n), Degn (1930), Lunddahl (1911:430ff.), P. Petersen (1968:191), and L. Zachariasen (1961:381-96). At the end of the nineteenth century, a *mørk* was redefined for tax purposes as 1000 kr. in land.

5. It is difficult to calculate rent rates. There were five kinds of rents: 1) on land (Da. *jordlejen*), reckoned on the basis of the amount (or value) of cultivated infield, and varying from place to place from about 10 *skinn* per *mørk* to about 20 *skinn* per *mørk*, or about 3-6 percent of the assessed value of the land; 2) on sheep (Da. *faarelejen*), reckoned on the basis of the number of sheep assessed for each holding, at one-half lambskin and three-fifths of a cask of tallow for each sheep; 3) on cattle (Da. *smørlejen*), reckoned on the basis of the number of cows assessed for each holding, at 1 wey (about 40 pounds) of butter per cow (this tax was not paid on Suðuroy or in the Norðoyar); 4) on other livestock and equipment (Da. *inventarieleje*), at ⅛ *gyllin* per item; and 5) on each *mørk* of rented land (Da. *aagave*), at ½ *gyllin* per *mørk*, paid every three years, or about 1 percent of the land's assessed value per year. Tenants paid in addition a fee for entering upon their leases; the amount varied from time to time. All these were paid in kind until 1856. From 1868 to 1899 the whole system was put on a cash basis, such that the combined rents were about 7 percent of an estate's assessed value (Degn 1945: unnumbered prefatory pages; see also P. Petersen 1968:142ff.).

Concerning the distinction between rich and poor farmers, Arnbjørn Mortensen (1954:5) notes that "Between 1604 and 1613-1614 there is a gap in the rent rolls, and when they start up again the distribution of holdings is something quite different [from what it had been in 1584]—a change occurred, certainly gradual at first, with the result that 30 years after 1584 the land came into fewer hands, and that to a great extent new names have come to stand in the places we have considered in this article." Mortensen goes on to give the following statistical picture of Faroese society in 1584 (pp. 30ff.). There were 436 farmers: 266 king's farmers, 120 freeholders, and 50 who worked holdings belonging to or leased from others. The first two categories may be broken down as follows:

(1) with holdings of 1 *mørk* or less (average holding, 0.6 *m*): king's farmers only, 80; king's farmers and freeholders, 7; (2) with holdings of 1-4 *m* (average holding, 2.3 *m*): king's farmers only, 87; king's farmers and freeholders, 10; (3) with holdings of more than 4 *m* (average holding, 10.4 *m*): king's farmers, 66; king's farmers and freeholders, 14; (4) freeholders only (average holding, 7.4 *m*), 120.

The total here of 384 does not include two priests, though it does include the five others, insofar as they were landholders in their own right. The high figure for the freeholders' average holding is due largely to the fact that Mortensen has included in this category the several large estates owned by foreign noblemen and institutions (*aðalsjørð*), most of which passed into Faroese hands in the seventeenth century.

6. See N. Andersen (1895:407-12), Jakobsen (1898-1901:479-80), and L. Zachariasen (1961:356-57).

7. The office of *løgmaður* was elective, but apparently it was common until nearly the end of the sixteenth century for a *løgmaður* to be succeeded by his son. Andras Guttormsson was *løgmaður* from 1531 to 1544, and was followed by his son Guttormur Andrasson, from 1544 to 1571. Jón Heinason was *løgmaður* from 1572 to 1583, but was followed by Guttormur Andrasson's son Ísakur, 1583-88. A confused period followed, but for more than a century after 1629, it seems to have been usual for a *løgmaður* to be succeeded by his son-in-law (see Figure 6). This remarkable almost-matrilinearity may represent a successful local attempt to preserve as nearly as possible the earlier pattern of patrilinearity at a time when the Danish crown was trying to rationalize succession of state offices. It is surely related, too, to the general crisis in Faroese government around 1620. It certainly reflects as well the importance of the *svágur* relationship (SiHu, WiBr, DaHu; DaHu may also be called *mágur*) in the Faroese kinship system, and the woman's crucial standing as mistress of the household and joiner of patrilineal *ættir* ("lineages"). It has its analogue in folklore in the evidently very popular Ashlad tales, in which a poor boy becomes heir to the throne by marrying the king's daughter. From 1769 through the end of the eighteenth century, the *løgmenn* were foreigners. (On the Ashlad, see Wylie and Margolin 1981:47-72. On Faroese kinship terminology, see Wylie 1974:259ff.) For a remarkable example of quasi-matrilineal succession to the ministry in a Danish parish, see H.G.A. Jørgensen (1937:255-56).

8. Jens Christian Svabo's brother Samuel Christopher Hansen Svabo succeeded their father as priest on Vágar.

A few priests' sons made names for themselves in the outside world. Jónas Bronck (or Brunck) was the son of Mortan Jespersen Bronck, who had probably been Bishop Riber's chaplain just after the Reformation, and who was parish priest of South Streymoy from 1541 to 1590. Jónas seems to have gone to school at Roskilde, in Denmark, in 1619, but then found his way to Holland, where he joined an expedition to New Amsterdam. The Bronx is named after him.

9. West (1972:39); see also Joensen, Mortensen, and Petersen (1955).

Figure 6.   Descent of Løgmenn, 1531-1769

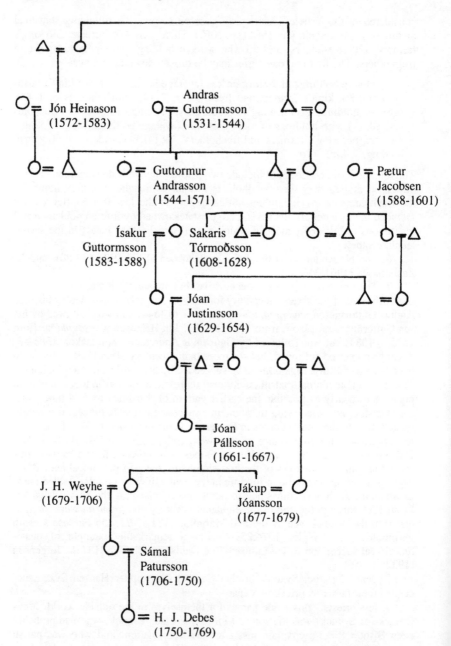

Note: A certain Tummas Símunarson was *løgmaður* from 1602 to 1608. Baltzer Jakobsen, a foreigner, was *løgmaður* from 1654 to 1661. From 1769 through the end of the eighteenth century, the *løgmenn* were foreigners.

3. OUTSIDE THE WALL _____

1. Lucas Debes, who was much concerned to represent the Faroese as a pious people, also notes that "For all their household sitting for the most part at home in Winter, they exercise themselves continually in Singing of Psalms" (1676:339).

Until the late nineteenth century, servants and others were required to perform set amounts of labor during each period of the day and evening (*setningar*); on these, see R. Joensen (1963).

2. *Kvæðir* and *tættir* are memorized word for word; they are not orally recomposed by each singer. For a discussion of the possibility of oral-formulaic structures in *kvæðir,* see O'Neill (1970); for a more "literary" approach to ballad composition, see Conroy (1979); for an ethnomusicological study of balladry today, see Luihn (1980). For authoritative general discussions of the provenance and performance of ballads, see, e.g., C. Matras (1958, 1968). The standard collection of ballads is Djurhuus and Matras (1951-72).

3. For studies in English of the pilot-whale hunt (*grindadráp*) and associated customs, see J.P. Joensen (1976), Williamson (1945; 1970:95-119), and Wylie and Margolin (1981:95-132).

On the *grindadráp* in the century following the Reformation, see L. Zachariasen (1961:88-96). On laws and customs otherwise, see especially Müller (1883a, 1883b) and P. Petersen (1968), and the various editions and translations of the Seyðabræv (in English, Young 1979:140-51).

4. One major episode in "Óli Jarnheysur" has Óli throw overboard a woman Mikkjal had let on he would marry, though he was really only interested in her lands. This partly reflects Mikkjal's well-attested land hunger and the notoriously vexed relations between him and his wife (see S. av Skarði 1922). It may also reflect another bloodless killing, in which the real-life Óli figured. His name was Ólavur Jóansson, and he worked for Mikkjal. One day in 1617, he lost his temper at one of Mikkjal's maidservants, struck her on the side with "a little piece of barrel stave, and the woman died right away in the same hour," despite all attempts to revive her. No mark being found on her body, the court ruled that she was responsible for her own death because she had sworn at Ólavur when he struck her. His innocence was proven in a trial by ordeal: in the presence of the *løgrættumenn* (one of whom was Ólavur Larvasson), he laid his hand on the corpse, which did not begin to bleed. The maidservant's brother declined to press murder charges, saying that a final accounting must rest with God (E. Joensen 1953:47-48). Trial by ordeal was never a strictly legal proceeding under Norse law, though it seems to have been used in the Faroes from time to time in the sixteenth and seventeenth centuries. Its use in this case may reflect the rather uncertain status of Faroese law after 1604 (L. Zachariasen 1961:26-27; see also N. Andersen 1895:200-201).

5. *Føringatíðindi* reported in December 1894, that a blue whale had drifted ashore; but I believe this was after Jakobsen had made his collection. On the great whales, see á Ryggi (1927).

The name "Kolbein" also appears in the folktale of the Giant's Wedding (Jakobsen 1898-1901:247ff.) as the name of the giant whose daughter a farmer's son wants to marry (see also Wang 1931).

6. On Mikkjal and Magdalena, see N. Andersen (1895:376-77), Heilskov (1915:255-58) Jakobsen (1898-1901:488-90; 1904:62-63), S. av Skarði (1922),

and L. Zachariasen (1961:290-309). Zachariasen corrects Andersen's statement that Magdalena's father became bishop of Bergen. On Ólavur Larvasson and Marjun, see also Hammershaimb (1891, 1:327-30), Jakobsen (1898-1901:37-44, 204-5, 472-73), and L. Zachariasen (1961:312-13). According to one of Jakobsen's informants, Marjun's and Ólavur's father was himself from Øravík but his wife came from Strendur. This informant also claimed that it was Ólavur's half-brother Hanus who stuck his ax in the whale's back, though both men were in the boat at the time.

7. For a similar dating of the legend, see Jakobsen (1898-1901:470-71). Jakobsen surmises that "Snæbjørn" may have transferred to this period some undocumented, far older case of assault on a judge (1904:56). On Jákup Hálvdansson, see N. Andersen (1895:237, 434-36), Degn (1945:244ff.), L. Zachariasen (1961:47-48, 127-29, 343, 359), and E. Joensen (1953:225, 286-87, 376-78, 382-83).

For an interesting comparison, see an undatable but probably very old Sandoy tale recounted by Hjalt (1953:155). On his way to the Suðuroy spring parliament, the bailiff demands immediate passage from two brothers in Sandur. They decline, the currents being unfavorable. A fight ensues. One brother kills the bailiff's dog, and the bailiff kills him with a staff.

8. For a study of nicknaming habits in the Faroes, see Wylie (1974).

9. These birds would most likely have been ravens or crows, and this must have been in the late spring or early summer, after lambing time but before the sheep were driven in for shearing. Svabo (1959:227) says that "in Hvalba one drove sheep . . . on the 28th of June"; Graba (1848:55) witnessed shearing in Hvalba on June 14.

10. Gannets and bottle-nosed whales are collectively taken and distributed; driftwood belongs to whoever owns the stretch of shore where it is stranded. Significantly, it is the driftwood, the only individually owned of the three gifts, that "no longer comes" in both "Snæbjørn" and the Mykines tale about Óli and Tórur (see P. Petersen 1968:34-40, 55-60; Bjørk 1959; and Nørrevang 1979).

11. Faroese did not entirely escape the temptation to adhere to a religion more or less of their own devising. According to Lucas Debes (1963 [1673]: 166ff.; 1676:385ff.), in January 1667, a sick young man on Eysturoy believed that he was visited by an angel, later identified as St. John the Baptist, who cured him, taught him a special prayer, and later announced portents and said that Saturday should be the sabbath. For over a year this cult had a certain following, particularly among servants.

4. A GREAT DEAL OF FUSS FOR AN OMELET

1. For a more detailed outline of administrative arrangements, see the Appendix.

2. For a study of the negotiations leading to this partial revision of the price schedule, see Korsgaard (1979).

3. Nólsoyar Páll (or Poul Nolsøe) was born on Nólsoy, in 1766. As a young man, he sailed with Ryberg's ships and then with those of the Monopoly. He sailed more widely from about 1791 to 1798. Returning to the Faroes in 1800 to become a king's farmer on Borðoy, he at once became interested in the possibil-

ities of ship fishing around the Faroes. In 1804 he launched the *Royndin Fríða*, a small schooner he, his brothers, and some friends had rebuilt from the wreckage of a ship that had drifted ashore. Having fished for a year, Páll attempted, between 1805 and 1807, to trade with the continent on his own, but he ran afoul of the Monopoly and Tórshavn officialdom.

Páll was also a poet of no mean talent. His best remembered poem is "The Ballad of the Birds" (*Fuglakvæði*), in which he pictures himself as the oyster catcher, who warns other birds of the approach of birds of prey, i.e., government authorities. The *Fuglakvæði* was composed in the winter of 1806-7.

In 1808, as famine threatened, Páll was allowed to seek grain supplies abroad, but the *Royndin Fríða* was captured and damaged by the British. The British authorities, however, hearing of the Faroes' distress, provided him with a new ship, the *North Star*. Páll sailed from London with a cargo of grain in November, but the ship was lost at sea with all hands.

For accounts in Danish and English of these rather confused years, see Heilsen (1969) and West (1969; 1972:49-70); for a full-length biography of Nólsoyar Páll and a collection of his poetical works, see Jakobsen (1912). An oral biography is given by S. Jacobsen (1936).

4. It is difficult or impossible to know exactly how many tenants (as opposed to tenancies) there were, partly because so many men had the same names. Tenancies were sometimes jointly held, and sometimes a farmer held more than one. At a guess, there were fewer tenants than tenancies, but nearer the same number in the eighteenth century than in the sixteenth and seventeenth centuries (see Mortensen 1954).

The figure of 1100 *merkur* does not include beneficed land or, for example, the *løgmaður*'s estate on Vágar. It does include a small amount of mortgaged land (*pantajørð*).

5. Mortensen (1954:35-37) reckons that each 3 *merkur* needed one man to work it. A holding of six *merkur*, for example, would require one hired hand plus the farmer. However, judging from the sheriffs' reports of 1775 (*Tillæg*, pp. 137-40) and other data, it appears that most holdings in this range were worked mostly by family labor. Mortensen's estimate of one man per 3 *merkur* is, he says, a modern one, which probably means that it is inflated by eighteenth-century standards. In the middle of the nineteenth century, the period to which many modern notions of "traditional" Faroese customs refer, farmers employed exceptionally large numbers of hired hands (see Chapter Six, below).

6. *Tillæg*, p. 135; Degn (1945:216ff). Neither man is said to have had freeholdings. Although neither is said to have had a wife, both probably did.

7. The redistribution was not uniform all over the Faroes. Most changes occurred on Streymoy and Eysturoy, where most of the largest estates were. The pattern of holdings on these islands thus came more to resemble those of Sandoy and the Norðoyar, where estates were of mixed but generally smaller size. The priest's and *løgmaður*'s estates excepted, Vágar was largely freehold. Suðuroy's tenancies were mostly very small. A number of these parcels were combined in the eighteenth century, but the average Suðuroy tenancy increased only from 1.9 *merkur* in 1700 to 2.4 *merkur* in 1800.

Since the priests' land was not divided, another result of the redistribution of holdings was the greater relative prominence of priests.

8. The sheriffs of these districts reported in 1775 that there were in all 385

servants in their districts (*sýslur;* the Sandoy district includes Skúvoy and Stóra Dímun; the Streymoy district includes Nólsoy, Hestur, and Koltur; and the Vágar district includes Mykines.) Of these, 309 (162 men and 147 women) worked outside Tórshavn and on the two farms based in Tórshavn (see Figure 7A). It was evidently the general practice for young men and women to enter service in their teens and early twenties. Women married (and so left service) in their late twenties, men in their late twenties and early thirties. This left, however, a substantial residue of people who remained in service and never married. As the *amtmand* reported in his summary memorandum of 13 March 1776, farmers did not like to hire married people as servants (*Tillæg,* p. 97).

The Tórshavn servant population was generally younger and included fewer men (32) than women (44). Most of the men worked for artisans or for Ryberg or the Monopoly, or were soldiers at the fort; most of the women were maidservants in the homes of Danish officials and their widows (see Figure 7B).

As well as servants' ages, the sheriffs (perhaps rather incompletely) noted their marital status and physical condition. In the countryside, seven servants were married, one was widowed, and eighteen were infirm, feeble-minded, or otherwise incapable of working full-time. In Tórshavn, none were married, and four were infirm or incapacitated.

The sheriff of Streymoy noted that seven servants (six men and one woman) were in the process of changing jobs at the time he wrote his report. In Tórshavn itself, he mentioned at least thirty-eight "loose and idle" people (sixteen men and twenty-two women, including "full grown" and "half grown" girls and boys). It is not clear how he meant to classify several more, including two or three widows, three or four soldiers, and the wife of a man who, although he had his own "poor dwelling" and "two small children," and was "young and a hard worker," was "incapable of supporting himself." The sheriff mentions fourteen "loose and idle" people in the countryside (seven men and seven women). Five of these were children living at home, and four were engaged to be married.

These figures do not include people listed as members of the immediate families of the farmers for whom they worked. The sheriffs' reports are published in *Tillæg,* pp. 131-40.

It is remarkable that, although sexual activity was denied to so large a part of the population for so much of their lives, homosexuality was unheard of. There were apparently a few women of questionable morals. In most years in the seventeenth century, cases of whoring, primarily from Streymoy, came before the Løgting (L. Zachariasen 1961:55-63), and in 1775 the sheriff of Sandoy complained of an unmarried woman from Vágar living in Dalur, "about 40 years old, with a daughter of 10 years. Her means of livelihood are to my mind, and so far as I know, not quite legal" (*Tillæg,* p. 135). Otherwise, Panum was told in 1846, by "an official intimately acquainted with conditions [that] onanism is probably not rare on the Faroe Islands. . . . Although the facts that circumstances frequently do not permit marriages that are wished for, and that debauchery with the other sex often appears dangerous to the prudent Faroese, yet it seems to me not unlikely that the disposition which the unconscious impress of nature produces in the inhabitants may develop a sort of predisposition to this vice, which, too, again both develops an attending disposition to mental disease and becomes a powerful occasional factor in its evolution. Yet it is impossible, of course, to decide

Figure 7.   Age Structure of Servant Population, 1775

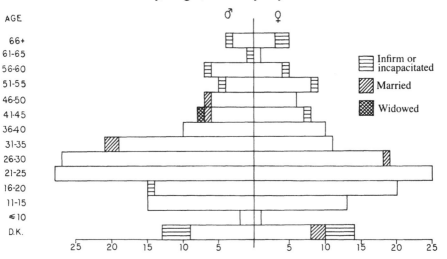

A.   Sandoy, Vágar, and Streymoy outside Tórshavn

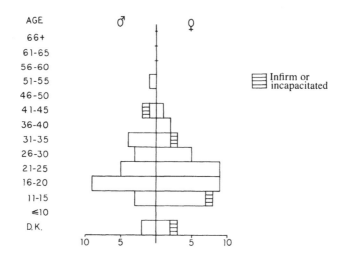

B.   Tórshavn

whether this vice is more general on the Faroes than in Denmark" (Panuin 1940:18).

9. Korsgaard (1979, 1982) has recently argued that the price schedule had created a place for virtually landless full-time knitters in Faroese society in the late seventeenth and early eighteenth centuries; the ordinance of 1777 forced them back into service with substantial farmers.

10. For recent studies of Danish diplomatic attempts to balance political and economic interests between 1775 and 1800, see Feldbæk (1971, 1977).

11. Another possible export product was low-grade coal. Coal deposits on Suðuroy had been investigated as early as 1626, but the first serious attempt to mine them (by an English company) was not made until 1733. Nothing much came of this or subsequent attempts. Because coal was not listed in the price schedule, Faroese were not prohibited from trading in it on their own, and in 1805 Nólsoyar Páll took advantage of this loophole in the monopoly laws to carry cargoes of coal to Bergen and Copenhagen. Unfortunately, there were no such loopholes in the import schedule, and he was unable to take on a return cargo. In general, coal was not exploited in the eighteenth century because of shipping costs; and besides, the merchants said, only three ships a year called in the Faroes, and they already had full cargoes! (Landt 1810:71ff; see also J. Rasmussen 1958; Svabo 1959:238-40; Trap 1968:10; and L. Zachariasen 1961:377).

12. The documents quoted below will be found in *Tillæg*, pp. 83-141.

13. Begging and almsgiving were explicitly allowed in the Seyðabræv, and Lucas Debes pointed out, in 1673, that "none would willingly have the reputation of niggardness, whence it comes, that the poor Countrymen live near as well, as those that live on the Kings Farms; so that they are all almost equally rich in mony; only the Farmer hath his Sheep and Cattle more than the other" (1676:260). Debes exaggerates the equality of Faroese, but it was (and is) a characteristic they insist upon, and one that did distinguish them from Danes at the time.

14. Those without a craft, in his estimation, may have included the soldiers of the Tórshavn garrison, of which there were about thirty.

15. These 8 *merkur* of infield had been split off in 1555 from 8 *merkur* of outfield now belonging to Steigagarður. The infield had been split up and was held in tenancies. Hveding lost the case when it came before the high court in Copenhagen, in 1780 (Degn 1937a:202-3).

Jacob Bentzen Hveding (1736-1819) was the Faroes' *løgmaður* from 1772 until 1786. He then occupied a similar position in Stavanger, until the *lagting* there was abolished, in 1797. Hveding, who was born in Trondheim, belonged to a family (probably of Danish origin) that had been prominent in North Norway since the late seventeenth century (Bloch 1944:331, 1968:273-78; Castberg 1941:52; Thomle 1882:138n).

16. This idea may have been the bailiff's, Wenzel Hammershaimb, whose father and predecessor, J.F. Hammershaimb, had proposed something similar, in 1723 (Korsgaard 1979:119).

17. There seems to have been an effort made around this time to discourage individuals from holding scattered tenancies, on only one of which they could be resident. The *sorinskrivari*, Peder Samuelsen (Weyhe) (1715-75) had grown up at Steigagarður while his father, Samuel Pedersen (Lamhauge) (1676-1755) was *løgmaður*, from 1706 to 1755. In 1726, his grandfather having died the year

before, Peder Samuelsen fell heir to the large estate at Lamba. This estate was divided in half in 1764. Peder Samuelsen kept one-half, while his second son took over the other. His eldest son, Peder Pedersen (173?-82) became his assistant, in May of 1775, and succeeded to the post of *sorinskrivari* when he died, in October. Peder did not, however, take over his father's half of the Lamba estate, which passed to another of his brothers, in January of 1776. Peder had married to Hvalvík, on Streymoy, where, in October of 1776, he took over his father-in-law's tenancy (Degn 1945:79-81, 175-76; Heilskov 1915:259, 263).

18. See notes 9 and 16, above. Struensee had also attempted some projects with state-supported industry in Copenhagen.

19. Later in 1777, for example, it was proposed that "competent newly married commoners" be enabled to get a piece of land to work, or some other legal occupation. Hveding and the bailiff, W. Hammershaimb, received the idea coolly, and the commission they suggested be set up to look into the matter never met. In 1787 the Exchequer proposed making leaseholds freehold. Nothing came of this, either (*Tillæg*, pp. 83-86).

5. WHAT BETTER THING?

1. For a glimpse of a governor at work, see Graba (1848). Among their other duties, the governors attended the spring parliaments, or *várting*, in each district. These survived until 1896.

2. Ri.2.L:875. References in this form are to the published proceedings of the Rigsdag: Ri (for *Rigsdagstidende*), followed by the session number, the house (L for Landsting, F for Folketing), and the column number.

3. Sometime before 1831, Nólsoyar Páll's brother Jacob Nolsøe, with whom Rask corresponded, wrote but failed to publish a Faroese grammar, now lost, in which he followed Rask's earlier suggestions and proposed an Icelandicized form of writing Faroese. This influenced Rask's thinking, but the writing system was not refined or even used except, to some extent, by Jacob Nolsøe's son Napoleon Nolsøe. Rask had also advised the priest of Suðuroy, J.H. Schrøter, on the orthography for a Faroese version of *Færeyinga saga* (Rafn 1832). On Rask's interest in Faroese, see Skårup (1964).

4. On Schrøter's correspondence, see Degn (1937b) and West (1970a).

5. Quoted in Bekker-Nielsen (1978:85); see also Djupedal (1964a, 1964b) and C. Matras (1936). See C. Matras (1971) for an account in English of Hammershaimb's role in creating the modern Faroese orthography.

6. References in this form are to the published proceedings of the Roskilde Assembly (*Tidende for Forhandlingerne ved Provindsialstænderne for Sjællands, Fyens og Lollands-Falsters Stifter samt for Færøerne*): Ro (for Roskilde), followed by the date and column number.

7. The whole question of how, in this period, information about the Faroes reached Denmark outside official channels deserves investigation. Much news undoubtedly traveled through the clergy. Schrøter kept up a voluminous international correspondence; but one also wonders for example, whether A.F. Tscherning's "pro-Faroese" views in 1850 were influenced by whatever correspondence accompanied his wife's commission to paint an altarpiece, in 1842, for the church

in Miðvágur, where her friend Jens Engelstedt served as priest from 1839 to 1850 (á Ryggi 1940:120).

We may remark, parenthetically, that most Danes' misapprehension of the Faroes' linguistic situation in the mid-nineteenth century was not entirely baseless. For one thing, the vocabulary of Faroese Danish naturally incorporated many, probably Icelandic-sounding archaisms and danicized versions of peculiar local terms describing the landscape, agricultural and fishing practices, and so forth. The phonology of Faroese Danish was (and to some extent still is) odd as well, being based on that of the Danish spoken by priests two hundred years before. Moroever, resident Danes probably mistook for Faroese, and so imitated, the "wretched mishmash" (Hammershaimb 1854:235 [1969:227]) of heavily danicized Faroese—a kind of half-formed pidgin—that Faroese used to make themselves understood by Danes, especially in regular interaction with them in Tórshavn.

8. Hammershaimb's letter is published in Bekker-Nielsen (1978:83-87), along with Niels Winther's letter, also signed "A Faroese" (1978:87-100).

9. Ro.1844:1724; Ro.1846:414, 467-74, 2184, 3567-71.

10. Grundtvig (1845), republished in Bekker-Nielsen (1978:11-79). References to this work in the following pages are to Bekker-Nielsen's edition.

11. The German spelling is derogatory.

12. The advertisement appeared in *Dannevirke*, on 23 April. It is reprinted in C. Matras (1951:13), along with several satirical replies and N.M. Petersen's more substantial one from the 13 May 1845 issue of *Fædrelandet* (1951:15-18). According to Matras, Petersen evidently thought so little of his letter that he failed to include it in his collected works. The following paragraphs draw heavily on C. Matras (1951).

13. The written language Petersen and Munch envisaged, and Sigurðsson and Hammershaimb created, amounts, in modern terms, to "a reconstruction of what is conceivably an older stage of [Faroese], prior to the diphthongization of its long vowels, the lengthening and diphthongization of many of its short vowels, the loss of its final and medial *ð* and *g*, the merger of its unstressed *i* and *u*, and the development of its hiatus consonants (*Verschärfung*). At the same time, it is to a large extent a morphophonemic orthography, since it permits the writing of a word like *dagur* day nom. (gen. *dags,* dat. *degi,* acc. *dag*) so that the base *dag-* appears in each form (with i-umlaut in the dat.), while Svabo wrote the same forms *dēavur, dags, dëi, dēa* as they are actually pronounced" (Haugen 1976:402).

14. But Alexander Weihe, a Faroese student who never made much of his talents (he died in great poverty, in Copenhagen, in 1870), published several small pieces between 1846 and 1851 using an idiosyncratic writing system (Weihe 1850).

15. Denmark's political parties at this time were the National Liberals (who formed the government), the Conservatives, and the Farmer's Friends (*Bondevenner*). Generally speaking, opposition to the Faroese electoral bill was led by members of the *Bondevenner,* although others (such as A.C. Ørsted, in the Landsting) likewise opposed it. National Liberals generally supported the bill, in part no doubt because it was, after all, a government bill, but also because they opposed the dismemberment of the kingdom. Except for Ørsted, Conservatives took little part in the debate.

16. The bill's expeditious course through the Rigsdag may be followed in the *Rigsdagstidende* for 1850-51. On 17 October 1850, the foreman of the Landsting announced that the Minister of the Interior, H.M. Rosenørn, would introduce an election bill for the Faroes (Ri.2.L:108). Rosenørn did so the next day, a Friday, giving a little speech (Ri.2.L:131ff.) outlining its rationale. His remarks summarized a long addendum to the printed version of the bill (Ri.2.Anhang XX:211ff.), which he recommended to the honorable members' attention. On Monday, the Landsting referred the bill to committee, which in due course produced two reports (Ri.2.Anhang B XI:69ff.), a majority one endorsing the bill (subject to several minor changes), and a minority one signed only by Ørsted, which argued that the bill was unconstitutional. The highlights of the bill's first reading, on 14 November, were a powerful speech by Ørsted and a lengthy rebuttal by Rosenørn. The second reading, on the nineteenth and twentieth, was less eventful; and after the third reading, on the twenty-seventh, when Ørsted again declared it unconstitutional, the bill passed on a voice vote, 35 to 2, and was sent along to the Folketing. The Folketing's deliberations involved sharper debate at each reading, but were otherwise even more expeditious than those of the upper house. No committee was formed, and no amendments were offered. Introduced on 5 December, the bill received its first reading on the eleventh and twelfth, its second reading on the eighteenth, and its third on the twenty-first. Then it was passed by the comfortable margin of 51 to 20, with 27 absences and abstentions.

For a summary, see Steining (1953:108-18).

17. The nationalist leader Jóannes Patursson elaborated on this point many years later (1903; 1939:60-68).

18. Wylie and Margolin (1981:89-90). For an account of Faroese schools and schooling between 1845 and 1854, see P.J. Nolsøe (1950). For biographies of Faroese teachers, see Føroya Lærarafelag (1976).

19. For a dramatic oral history of the election, see R. Rasmussen (1954).

20. For a summary of the background, course, and consequences of this debate, see Steining (1953:119-29). The bill's course through the Rigsdag may be followed in the *Rigsdagstidende* for 1851-52 (Ri.3.F:1174, 1598-1605, 1690-92, 1710, 1889-1918, 2343-45, 2611-12, 3645, 3647-3706, 3847-63, 4500, 4939-46; Ri.3.L:2596-2600, 2764-72, 2877-80; Ri.3.Anhang XXXIII and LXXIII; and Ri.3.Anhang B XL).

21. One liberal feature of Tillisch's bill and the law that grew out of it was a provision charging the Løgting, when it first met, to propose changes in the law. The Løgting accordingly suggested several changes, including increasing the number of elected members from sixteen to eighteen, enlarging the franchise and simplifying property qualifications, and reducing the elected members' terms from six years to four. The Rigsdag readily accepted these proposals. For a convenient point-by-point comparison of the original law and the modified one and a summary of the Løgting's reasons for proposing the modifications, see Ri.5.Anhang IX.

22. Dahlerup is not fondly remembered in the Faroes. But an English yachtsman who called there in the summer of 1860 wrote: "The Danish Governor resides at Thorshaven. He spends three months only in the year there; the rest he passes at Copenhagen, where he has a seat in the parliament. We found him a pleasant, middle-aged man, talking a polyglot of English, French, and Danish. He seemed sadly oppressed with ennui, and to be looking anxiously for the arrival

of the steamer which was to take him to Copenhagen and his wife" (Clark 1861:320).

For extracts about Dahlerup from a contemporary journal, see H.D. Matras (1951).

6. THE TRANSITION FROM MONOPOLY ────────────

1. Clark (1861:320-21). Recent research by a medical historian suggests, however, that the Faroese population had not been so isolated as is generally held (H.D. Joensen 1981).

2. Trevelyan (1835:155-56). For a description of what was grown in Faroese gardens at this period, see Martins (1842-55).

3. On the pilot-whale hunt (grindadráp) see J.P. Joensen (1976) and Wylie and Margolin (1981:95-132). 18,488 whales were taken between 1840 and 1850, and between 1841 and 1850, almost exactly half of the Faroes' exports of "fish and fish products" was train oil, most of it tried from the whales (Degn 1929:19, 145). Pilot whales have not, however, generally provided an export item. On their periods of plenty and scarcity, see Joensen and Zachariassen (1982).

4. Degn (1929); E. Patursson (1961:14). For accounts of the Klaksvík branch store, see J.S. Hansen (1960:2-4) and Heilsen (1969:116-20). An earlier breach in the Monopoly system occurred in 1844, when the Frederikshavn merchant A.W. Skipsted was granted permission to set up a commercial fishing operation in the Faroes. Despite a promising start in 1845, the Tórshavn-based company lost money in 1846 and received permission to set up shops there and elsewhere that might sell vinegar, sugar, tobacco, cigars, clothing, and various alcoholic beverages. One of its main products was train oil tried from fish-livers or from the heads of pilot whales. Skipsted took out merchant's papers in 1856, and for many years his was one of the largest firms in the Faroes (Joensen, Mortensen, and Petersen 1955:145-52).

5. For a contemporary assessment of the Faroe trade from a historical point of view, see Nathanson (1832); for a somewhat later assessment of the fishery's possibilities, see Rye (1866); and for modern treatments, see Degn (1929:84-87), E. Patursson (1961:56-57), and Joensen, Mortensen, and Petersen (1955). A collection of booklets, articles, and letters from the 1840s about the Faroe trade will be found in E. Joensen (1970).

6. Graba's description is misleading in a few minor particulars. Halibut, for example, was one of several species reckoned as sjálvsdráttarfiskar, "that is, fish that a participating fisherman caught and received as his share from the undivided portion of the catch" (E. Patursson 1961:16, 21).

7. For an amusing modern example of a foreigner being drawn into the Faroese style of crew recruitment, see Severin (1978:131-34). On Faroese kinship terms, see Wylie (1974). Otto Blehr (1963) has posited a kinship-based system of crew recruitment resting on the supposed existence of something he calls a "kith"; in a later article (1964), he goes on to speculate on this basis about the social correlates of economic change in the Faroes. I believe both articles are tendentious. For a critique of Blehr and a study of manning practices and patterns on Faroese sailing ships, see J.P. Joensen (1975). In another book, I hope to deal at some length with crew recruitment and, in general, "familiarity" as a principle

of social organization in a Faroese village from the late nineteenth century on (see also Wylie 1974).

8. Keilhack (1885:225). It was not until around the turn of the century that a conventionalized version of peasant garb became established as a "national costume."

9. Wylie and Margolin (1981:78-79); E. Patursson (1965:60). I do not know why 1868 should have been a turning point. For some years thereafter, Faroese was uncommon enough in the Løgting so that an 1887 obituary for Jóan Pauli Poulsen, who served there from 1869 to 1872, found it notable that "what he said was clear and steady—always in Faroese" (*Dimmalætting,* 15 October 1887).

10. Von Geyr-Schweppenburg (1900). On drinking at Ólavsøka, see Wylie (1983); on drinking and prohibition generally, see Blehr (1976), Joensen, Mortensen, and Petersen (1955:151), and Støðisútbúgvingin (1973).

11. Birley 1891:323. On the priest, I.P. Dall, and his wife, Alma Dorthea, see Nedergaard (1951, s.v. Skt. Stefans Kirke, Copenhagen). For other reactions to Kvívík, see Colding (1933) and especially Landt (1820). Landt enlarged the garden there.

12. The data must be read with some caution. I know of no evidence one way or the other, but it is possible that the recorded decline of "agriculture" and rise of "fishing" and other pursuits in part reflect an increase in the latter categories' prestige, so that they were more likely to be reported to census takers. Even so, the figures' general trend is overwhelming.

13. For a full study of this fishery, see J.P. Joensen (1975); see also Joensen, Mortensen, and Ravnsfjall (1983).

14. Charles Forbes was told, in the late 1850s, that British fishermen still made a habit of stealing sheep (1860:19-20).

15. R. Joensen (1966). Two more have been abandoned since then; and Stóra Dímun, once one of the richest farms in the Faroes, is now inhabited only in the summer. Two families live on Koltur.

16. On Tvøroyri and Suðuroy's four other new settlements, see R. Jensen (1952). On Klaksvík, see J.S. Hansen (1960, 1980, 1981). Trap (1904:870, 879) gives the following figures for the populations of Froðba township (*sókn;* including Tvøroyri) and Vágur township (including Klaksvík):

	Froðba	Vágur	Tórshavn	Other Faroes
1801	121	158	554	4432
1840	210	244	714	6146
1860	338	285	823	7376
1890	650	534	1303	10468
1901	933	647	1656	11994

Between 1860 and 1890, Froðba and Vágur together grew by about 90 percent, Tórshavn by about 58 percent, and the rest of the Faroese population by about 29 percent. Between 1890 and 1901, Froðba and Vágur together grew by about 33 percent, Tórshavn by 27 percent, and the rest of the Faroese population by about 15 percent.

17. The modern communications network began to take shape in 1896, when the J. Mortensen company, in Tvøroyri, initiated regular steam ferry runs to and from Tórshavn. In 1908 a new dairy and margarine plant in Tórshavn began pro-

viding regular service with the villages bordering Skálafjørður and the straits between Streymoy and Eysturoy. By the end of the 1930s, all the Faroes' larger
communities and many smaller ones were linked by regular sailings. The Faroes'
first real road was built between Skopun and Sandur in the 1920s, as part of a
government-financed scheme to improve the islands' primitive or nonexistent harbor facilities. This scheme's principal beneficiary was Tórshavn, a poor natural
port. Another form of communication was provided by a telephone network,
which began with a private line between Vestmanna and Tórshavn, in 1905. It
was taken over by the state the following year. Every village had at least one
telephone by the 1920s. A common pattern in these developments was for privately initiated enterprises to be taken over by the state. The trend toward state
control was encouraged by a series of legal reforms in 1924, which granted the
Løgting far greater control over local finances and public works.

The passage of mail and travelers had previously been assured by *skjútsur,* a
compulsory ferry duty. *Skjútsur* was formally abolished in 1922 for all but priests,
and in 1936 for them as well.

For convenient overviews of these matters, see Trap (1968:120-29) and Joensen, Mortensen, and Petersen (1955:117-19, 122-30).

7. NOW THE HOUR IS COME TO HAND ⎯⎯⎯⎯⎯⎯⎯⎯

1. By "modernization," I mean the process by which the Faroes became
demographically more urban, economically more industrialized, and socially
more highly differentiated. A cultural correlate of modernization is, of course,
the proliferation of full-time specialists in "knowledge, belief, art, morals, law,
custom, and any other capabilities and habits acquired by man as a member of
society" (Tylor 1958 [1871]:1).

2. *Føringatíðindi,* 6 February 1896; Jakobsen (1957:58).

3. *Føringatíðindi,* 17 November 1898; 4 May 1899; May 1892.

4. J. av Skarði (1980:9). The advertisement quoted below appeared in *Dimmalætting,* 22 December 1888. The following accounts of what was said at the
meeting are taken, unless otherwise noted, from *Dimmalætting,* 12 January 1889.

5. The following account is based on the report in *Føringatíðindi,* 7 June
1894, except that the estimate of attendance is from *Føringatíðindi,* 17 May
1894.

6. P.M. Rasmussen (1978:79); see also Hammershaimb (1969 [1891]:389-
429) and J.P. Joensen (1980:165ff.). The singing also clearly provided ritual clo-
sure for the meeting, by echoing the hymns sung during the service at its start.
During the meeting itself, the speeches and poetry were explicitly devoted to
reclaiming the Faroese past.

7. *Føringatíðindi,* 5 July 1894, and 4 July 1895. The data on tenancies are
from Degn (1945). Interestingly, the Self-Rule party split on the issue of land
reform in 1939, when Patursson opposed granting uncultivated crown lands to
landless fishermen and others.

8. *Dimmalætting,* 12 January 1899. Note the somewhat different views of
Faroese. Effersøe was stressing its symbolic importance in defining the Faroes'
membership in the Nordic world. Bærentsen was taking the more "practical" view

that Faroese was a local language, while Danish was the language of contact with the outside world.

9. Some idea of how different Faroese looks on the page in the two orthographies may be gathered from a glance at the first verse of Petersen's "Eg Oyggjar Veit":

Hammershaimb (modern)

Eg oyggjar veit, sum hava fjøll
og grøna líð,
og taktar eru tær við mjøll
um vetrartíð;
og áir renna vakrar har
og fossa nógv
tær vilja allar skunda sær
í bláan sjógv.
Gud signi mítt føðiland Føroyar.

Jakobsen (1892:7)

E åiggjar vait, sum häva fjödl
o grøna ly,
o taktar ero tär vi mjödl
um vetrarty;
o ájir rænna väkrar här
o fåssa nægv;
tär vilja adlar skunda sär
y blåan sjægv.
Gud signe mytt føjeland Förjar.

In 1890, *Føringatíðindi* commented in a front-page editorial that Jakobsen's renditions of Faroese "remind one of the boy who had drawn a scribble on a slate and wrote underneath, 'This will be a horse'" (December 1890).

A collection of Jakobsen's orthographic proposals (which changed somewhat over the years) may conveniently be found in Jakobsen (1957:23-43, 48-54). For the proposals as they were made to the Føringafelag, see *Føringatíðindi*, January 1893 and 2 January 1896.

10. *Føringatíðindi*, 21 January 1897. Unlike most letters to the editor, this one is signed. Its author was Absalon Guttormsen, of Trøllanes (at the northern tip of Kalsoy), where he was the king's farmer at Útistova, an estate of 5½ *merkur*. He was born in 1830 or 1831 and entered upon his tenancy in 1857 (Degn 1945:122-23; J.S. Hansen 1978b:185-86).

11. See Wylie (1974, 1982). The same is true of other Scandinavians. For a Norwegian example of the difficulties of open conflict in a society where it is held that "no man should have more privileges than his fellows" (Barnes 1954:40), see Hollos (1976); for a suggestion of the sociolinguistic consequences, see Blom and Gumperz (1972).

12. Women's suffrage was enacted in all of Denmark, including the Faroes, in 1915. Women first voted in a Løgting election in 1918, but the first woman was not elected to the Løgting until 1964.

13. There is an interesting multiple contrast here between the Faroes, Nor-

way, and Denmark. Øyvind Øresund has argued that in Norway in the 1870s, "the dominant sections of the peasantry gravitated towards the ordinary middle class, rather than towards [the] pre-industrial rural masses. . . . [P]easant politics were reformulated in a coalition with the liberal-democratic middle class." By contrast, the Danish peasantry at the same time found itself mobilized in opposition to a Right composed of a consolidated "capitalist aristocracy—rural and urban" (1976:209-10).

The chief differences between the Faroes and the continental nations were, of course, that the Faroese countryside became "mobilized" a generation later, during an economic boom brought about by the industrialization of the fishery, and that, except to some extent for the early Self-Rule party under Jóannes Patursson, a "peasant party" has never existed in the Faroes. Nevertheless, it can be said in general that in internal politics, the Faroese have tended to follow the Norwegian pattern of alliances between rural elites and the urban (Tórshavn) intelligentsia and middle class. But insofar as the Faroese are part of the Danish electorate, they have tended to follow the Danish pattern. In the early twentieth century, for example, the locally "rightist" but in Danish terms rural Union party was allied with the Danish Left. A similar pattern had emerged around 1850, when the Danish "Farmer's Friends" championed the cause of their (in Danish terms) peasant but (in local terms) middle-class or otherwise elite Faroese friends. The apparent oddity of this state of affairs derives, of course, from the fact that, depending on your point of view, the Faroes are either their own nation or part of the Danish one.

14. The sociolinguistic concomitant of their creation of a new, high register of Faroese to replace Danish was the redefinition of Danish as an outside language (Wylie and Margolin 1981:91). This redefinition was not formally completed until 1948, but the trend was undoubtedly under way in the 1890s, as Faroese came into increasingly regular contact with speakers of other outside languages, chiefly English. In 1899, for example, a (probably) Irish tourist commented that "English was not only understood but spoken by all" on Suðuroy (Anon. 1899:386). This is not to say that outsiders appreciated how much a part of the wide world the Faroese felt themselves to be. It was the same tourist who exulted in his discovery of a *terra incognita* (see Introduction).

15. In 1963 the Faroes were raised to the status of a subbishopric (Da. *vicebispedømme*).

16. The quotation is from Leclercq (1883:31). On Müller, see his obituary in *Føringatíðindi*, 6 January 1898, and Degn (1945:20).

17. This account does not mention something I have been told was traditional in the "old days" (meaning, in this case, the 1920s): "contests of strength in which men tried to throw each other by grabbing and tugging at one another's sleeves and shoulders" (Wylie and Margolin 1981:98).

18. I have argued elsewhere (Wylie 1983) that the festivities at Ólavsøka developed largely through a process of establishing a core of "traditionalistic" (if not strictly speaking traditional) activities, around which "modern" ones then safely proliferated. Ballad dancing at Ólavsøka is not mentioned before 1855, for example (Holm 1855:37; see also H.M. Debes 1977:38-41; Hammershaimb 1969 [1891]:xliii-xliv; and Ri.3.F:1892-93, 1899, 3657, 3677, 3659-60, for accounts of the period around 1850, although by 1877, it was felt that "there should be dancing on St. Olaf's eve" (von Geyr-Schweppenburg 1900:51). By 1888, the

occasion was felt to belong "as is well known, to the privileged dancing times" (*Dimmalætting*, 14 July 1888). At the same time, certain features of the older Ólavsøka were abandoned, while others (like men's drinking and couples' strolling the streets and visiting) escaped formal institutionalization. An analogous process took place as regional holidays began to proliferate around the now traditionalistic core of Ólavsøka itself. The first of these were Jóansøka for Suðuroy (after 1925) and the Norðoyastevna for the Norðoyar (after 1936) (J.P. Joensen 1980:186).

19. Like that of West (1972:193-97), this account follows Jepsen (1969) and Mitens (1966:237-52).

20. Other areas where Faroese came into conflict with Danish included the schools and the courts. Schooling in Faroese had long been a goal of the Føringafelag, for as *Føringatíðindi* noted, in 1894, "Faroese is so dwindled in the Faroes that many people believe it would be right and correct for Danish to rule in all organizations. To open people's eyes—as they say—that this is a mistake, a knowledge must go out from the schools which can get people to love their language, and which shows them that home-made clothing is more becoming than borrowed feathers" (18 October 1894). A critical moment came in 1912, when a regulation was issued requiring that Danish be the language of instruction for older students. One teacher (and later historian, Self-Rule politician, and chairman of the telephone company), Louis Zachariasen, openly defied the regulation until he was forced to resign. Other teachers quietly ignored the law. Despite many appeals and much negotiation, the Løgting was not able until 1938 to ensure the equal status of Faroese and Danish in the schools. Faroese has been the language of instruction since 1948.

Court testimony in Faroese was first permitted in 1924, but the Union party insisted, on constitutional grounds, that official documents must be in Danish. Faroese gained equal standing with Danish in 1944, when the tie with Denmark was broken and separatist opinion was in the ascendant. Meanwhile, Faroese had also "won its way to acceptability in a number of minor fields. From 1920, the telephone directory appeared in Faroese. From 1925, the language became acceptable for postal and telegraphic purposes. From 1927 onwards, the deliberations of the Løgting were recorded in it—and so on" (West 1972:171).

21. Mitens had been born Edward Mortensen; he changed his name in 1923.

22. Although not a social history, the last seven chapters of John West's *Faroe* (West 1972:126-261) remain the best general account in English for the period up to about 1970.

23. For English translations of modern Faroese prose, see Brú (1970), Brønner (1972), and W. Heinesen (1971, 1974, 1980, 1981, 1983). For critical studies in English, see W. Jones (1974b) (the Danish edition [1974a] is slightly revised and expanded) and Brønner (1973).

24. The following description of party platforms in terms of ranges of positions on economic and "national" issues follows West (1972:204), who provides this useful scheme:

Economic Issues	*National Issues*
Left wing	Separatist wing
Republican party	Republican party
Social Democratic party	Progress party

Self-Rule party	People's party
Union party	Self-Rule party
People's party	Social Democratic party
Progress party	Union party
Right wing	Unionist wing

It seems to me, however, that each of the major parties, at least, might also be characterized according to a primary concern with either economic or ideological ("national") issues. The major "ideological parties" have been the Self-Rule party, until 1939, the People's party, and the Republican party. The major "economic parties" have been the Union party and the Social Democratic party. Shifts in voting patterns tend to occur *within* these categories. In 1940, for example, the People's party drew votes from the Self-Rule party, while in 1950, the Republicans in turn drew votes from the People's party. On the economic side, the Social Democrats drew votes from the Union party between 1928 and 1936 (cf. Sjálvstýrisflokkurin n.d.:13).

The sizes of the economic and ideological electorates have been fairly constant and fairly even, but a certain amount of free play has been provided by minor parties offering compromise positions. There have been three such parties: the Self-Rule party, since 1940, the short-lived Economic party, in the mid-1930s, and the Progress party (now the Progress and Fishery party).

It appears to me that the terms of political debate have been dominated alternately by ideological or economic issues, according to economic trends. Heightened concern with ideological matters has coincided with the periods of economic growth up to 1920 and during and after the Second World War, while economic concerns have been more important recently and during the depression between the wars.

For a summary of party platforms, see Ársfrágreiðing 1980:32-39.

25. The referendum was, as much as anything, a Danish attempt to cut the Gordian knot of Faroese politics. Its background was as follows. In 1943 the People's party captured twelve of the Løgting's twenty-five seats. The rest were divided between the Social Democrats (five) and the Unionists (eight). After the elections of November 1945, the People's party remained one vote shy of a majority, with eleven out of twenty-three seats; but because it was the most popular single party, its leader, Thorstein Petersen, was chosen by the Løgting to lead an all-party committee that was sent to Copenhagen to discuss constitutional changes.

The People's party and the Social Democrats were opposed to a referendum in the first place. The Union party wanted one, because it felt that the people would not vote for independence. The Danish government wanted one, perhaps partly for that reason, but also in order that some clear expression of the people's will might emerge. The government view prevailed, and the heart of the problem became the formulation of the referendum questions. Petersen favored putting four questions on the ballot, ranging from secession to an arrangement much like the existing one. The government proposed asking a single pair of questions: did voters want secession from Denmark, or did they want a status defined by a government proposal that represented a compromise between the Unionists and the Social Democrats? The government proposal essentially foreshadowed the Faroes' status today.

The voting produced Byzantine complications, including: the low voter turn-out (only about two-thirds of the electorate voted); the vote itself (a narrow plurality favored secession, but a small but decisive number of voters simply wrote "no" on their ballots); the "no" votes (advocated by the People's party to protest the formulation of the questions); the formulation of the questions (most Faroese would undoubtedly have prefered a wider choice); and the secessionists' claim that the turnout was so low because the referendum was held in September (when many fishermen, who were inclined toward secession, were away at sea).

At this point, one Social Democrat in the Løgting bolted to the People's party, thereby giving the Løgting a majority favoring secession. The other parties protested, and the king dissolved the Løgting. New elections were held in November, resulting in a twenty-seat Løgting. The Unionists retained six seats; the Social Democrats lost two of their six to the previously unrepresented Self-Rule party, which had allied itself with them; and the People's party lost three of its eleven seats. Thus of the Løgting's twenty members, only the eight People's party representatives favored secession. Further negotiations with Denmark resulted in the Home Rule Act of 1948.

Nationalists now believe that the Danish government cheated the Faroes of a perfectly legitimate move to independence in 1946. Others argue that nationalism was a minority position and that, despite the referendum's indecisiveness, the final outcome was a status most Faroese found acceptable.

For a legalistic explication of the nationalist position, see Mentunargrunnur Studentafelagsins (1966); for a "revisionist" interpretation of the referendum vote, see Bærentsen and Jacobsen (1971); and for a sustained inquiry into relations between Denmark and the Faroes between 1945 and 1948, see Harder (1979). Discussions leading to the referendum are published in Upprit 1946. The Republican party's manifesto, as it were, is Erlendur Patursson's *Føroysk Stjórnarmál* (1945).

26. Denmark followed Great Britain into the Common Market in 1973. Fearing for the fishing grounds upon which their livelihood depends, the Faroese declined to follow suit. A special agreement regulates Faroese trade with the Common Market.

27. The Home Rule Act was officially published in *Dansk Lovtidende 1948*, Afdeling A I:255-60. For a detailed summary in English and German, see Veiter (1961).

"*Folkesamfund*" defies easy translation. It may mean "folk," "popular," "ethnic," "minority," or even "national" society.

CONCLUSION: SPECTERS AND ILLUSIONS ────────────

1. Coincidentally, perhaps, there seems to be a correlation between Scandinavian separatist achievements and a country's population reaching 15 percent urban: Iceland between 1910 and 1920 (independence under common monarchy with Denmark, 1918), the Faroes in 1945 (referendum on independence, 1946), Norway shortly before 1865 (nationalist agitation and a radical parliament), and Finland shortly before 1910 (general strike, 1905). Sweden was, of course, already a sovereign state; it became 15 percent urban in the late 1870s, a period of

agricultural crisis leading to tariff reforms. Denmark was already over 20 percent urban by 1800.

2. For evidence of the survival of Norn in Shetland, see J. Stewart (1974) and Jakobsen (1928); on traditional culture in Shetland generally, see Fenton (1978); on its Scandinavian elements, see Baldwin (1978).

3. Dr. Coull states that, compared with Shetland's, the Faroes' emigration was inhibited partly by "the greater degree of readjustment required in language and way of life at the destination" (1967:163). This is surely an overstatement. All adult Faroese could (and can) speak Danish and were (and are) literate in it. Moreover, modern evidence suggests that in letters home, for example, emigrants to Copenhagen often minimize the considerable linguistic problems they do face there, which are thus not appreciated in advance by potential emigrants (M. Andersen 1971).

4. For studies of the invention of Scottishness and similar trends in Victorian Britain, see Hobsbawm and Ranger (1983).

5. G. Stewart (1892:iii–iv). Compare Niels Winther's justification for studying Faroese history, relying partly on oral sources: "[Finding] the civic development of the Faroese people left much to be desired . . . I assumed . . . that when the Faroese were initiated into the past's memorable events, there would awake among them a national consciousness without which any people allows itself to remain a plaything for a sometimes harmful foreign influence; and . . . a fundamental knowledge of their forefathers' activities would possibly become not only a powerful spur for them to defend their precious memories, but also a mighty means of breaking the yoke under which they have sighed all too long" (1875: iii–iv).

6. It may have been Burgess, a fan of the Viking Age, who gave new life to the moribund custom of Up-Helly-Aa by making its central activity the parading and burning of a mock longship. Linklater (1971:186) says that the longship first appeared in 1886; Nicolson (1978:153) says 1889.

7. An exception proving the rule is William Heinesen, whose most important works are in Danish. In his case and others', writing in Danish is the functional equivalent of a retreat to nature in our own romantic tradition, allowing one to keep local society in better focus and at a little distance. In terms of Danish literature, of course, writing about the Faroes at all offers a critical perspective on metropolitan Danish society.

8. I myself may be overgeneralizing here. Faroese historians naturally make general statements about Faroese society and the course of events, although less frequently than one might hope. However, critical assessments of local life are exceedingly rare, particularly if there is a question of opposition between local groups or classes. Generalizations of all sorts occur most often in discussions of the Faroes' relationship with Denmark. Danish rule itself is commonly criticized.

Four classic *bygdarsøgur* are those by Hjalt (1953) for Sandur, J. Patursson (1966) for Kirkjubøur, J.C. Poulsen (1947) for Hestur, and á Ryggi (1940) for Miðvágur. The last two are of a high literary quality. More recent works in a similar vein include Johansen's memoir of village life at the turn of the century (1970; arranged by activities—"agriculture," "peat," "haying," and so forth), Johannesen's description of Kalsoy (1976; arranged geographically, with an accompanying section of legends in no particular order), and J.S. Hansen's (1971, 1973, 1975, 1978a, 1978b, 1980, 1981) series of books on the Norðoyar, *Tey*

Byggja Land (arranged by island, parish, village, and homestead, and then genealogically). See also Andreasen (1977), Clementsen (1981), and Pedersen (1960).

For a bibliography of recent collections of folktales, see Nyman (1981).

9. Compare Park's hypothesis that in Norway "religiosity and moderation in politics are alternative expressions of the same ideology" (Park 1972:19).

References

⊠ This bibliography is alphabetized as usual in English, except for the last three letters: Æ, Ø or Ö, and Å or AA. No distinction is made between D and Ð, or between accented and unaccented vowels.

I. YEARBOOKS AND GOVERNMENT PUBLICATIONS _____

Ársbók 1900. *Ársbók Førja Bókafelag. Firsta Ár.* Tórshavn.

Ársbók 1912. *Ársbók 1: Hitt Føroyska Bókmentafelagið.* Tórshavn.

Ársfrágreiðing 1980. *Ársfrágreiðing fyri Føroyar 1980.* Tórshavn: Føroya Landsstýri and Ríkisumboðsmaðurin í Føroyum.

Ársfrágreiðing 1983. *Ársfrágreiðing fyri Føroyar 1983.* Tórshavn: Føroya Landsstýri and Ríkisumboðsmaðurin í Føroyum.

Búreisingur: Føroyskt tíðskrift. 1969. Facsimile edition, Tórshavn: Offset-Prent/ Emil Thomsen.

Fólkateljingar í Føroyum, 1801-1955. Collection of photocopied reports in Landsbókasavn, Tórshavn.

Fuglaframi 1898-1902. 1972. Facsimile edition, Tórshavn: Bókagarður and Off- set-Prent/Emil Thomsen.

Føringatíðindi 1890-1906. 1969. Facsimile edition, Tórshavn: Offset-Prent/Emil Thomsen.

Kongelig Dansk Hof- og Statscalender. Statshaandbog for det danske Monarchie. 1818-60. Copenhagen: Bianco Luno.

Ri.2.F. *Rigsdagstidende: Forhandlingerne paa Folkethinget, Anden Session 1850.* Copenhagen: Bianco Luno.

Ri.2.L. *Rigsdagstidende: Forhandlingerne paa Landsthinget, Anden Session 1850.* Copenhagen: Bianco Luno.

Ri.3.F. *Rigsdagstidende: Forhandlingerne paa Folkethinget, Tredie Session 1851.* Copenhagen: Bianco Luno.

Ri.3.L. *Rigsdagstidende: Forhandlingerne paa Landsthinget, Tredie Session 1851.* Copenhagen: Bianco Luno.

Ri.5.F. *Rigsdagstidende: Forhandlingerne paa Folkethinget, Femte Session 1853.* Copenhagen: Bianco Luno.

Ri.5.L. *Rigsdagstidende: Forhandlingerne paa Landsthinget, Femte Session 1853.* Copenhagen: Bianco Luno.

Ro.1844. *Tidende for Forhandlingerne ved Provindsialstænderne for Sjællands, Fyens og Lollands-Falsters Stifter samt for Færøerne i 1844.* Copenhagen and Roskilde: Bianco Luno.

Ro.1846. *Tidende for Forhandlingerne ved Provindsialstænderne for Sjællands,*

Fyens og Lollands-Falsters Stifter samt for Færøerne i 1846. Copenhagen and Roskilde: Bianco Luno.

Sammendrag 1918. *Sammendrag af Statistiske Oplysinger om Færøerne. Danmarks Statistik: Statistiske Meddelelser, 4 Række, 56 Bind, 4 Hæfte.* Copenhagen: Det Statistiske Department.

Statistisk Tabelværk 1850. *Statistisk Tabelværk, Ny Række, Förste Bind indeholdende en detaillert fremstilling af folkemængden i Kongeriget Danmark i aaret 1850.* Copenhagen: Statens Statistiske Bureau.

Statistiske Aarbog 1904. *Danmarks Statistik (Statistique du Danemark): Statistiske Aarbog 9de Aargang 1904 (Annuaire Statistique 9me Année 1904).* Copenhagen: Statens Statistiske Bureau.

Statistiske Aarbog 1912. *Danmarks Statistik (Statistique du Danemark): Statistiske Aarbog 17de Aargang 1912 (Annuaire Statistique 17me Année 1912).* Copenhagen: Statens Statistiske Bureau.

Statistiske Aarbog 1924. *Danmarks Statistik (Statistique du Danemark): Statistiske Aarbog 1924 (Annuaire Statistique 1924).* Copenhagen: Det Statistiske Department.

Statistiske Aarbog 1933. *Danmarks Statistik (Statistique du Danemark): Statistiske Aarbog 1933 (Annuaire Statistique 1933).* Copenhagen: Det Statistiske Department.

Tillæg. 1911. *Tillæg til forslag og betænkninger afgivne af Den Færøske Landbokommission nedsat i henhold til lov av 13. Marts 1908.* Copenhagen: J.H. Schultz.

Tölfræðihandbók 1974. 1976. *Tölfræðihandbók 1974 (Statistical Abstract of Iceland 1974): Hagskýrslur Íslands (Statistics of Iceland),* vol. 2, no. 63. Reykjavík: Hagstofa Íslands.

Upprit 1946. *Upprit av munnliga orðaskiftinum í donsk-føroysku sendinevndini í Keypmannahavn, januar-mars 1946.* Tórshavn: Bókaprent.

Zetland County Report. *Census 1971: Scotland. County Report: Zetland.* General Register Office, Edinburgh: Her Majesty's Stationery Office.

Årsberetning 1972. 1973. *Årsberetning 1972.* Rigsombudsmand på Færøerne, Tórshavn (mimeograph).

II. OTHER

Andersen, Maria. 1971. *Føroyskur gentur í Keypmannahavn.* Copenhagen: Hitt føroyska studentafelagið.

Andersen, Niels. 1895. *Færøerne 1600-1709.* Copenhagen: G.E.C. Gad. Reissued 1964, edited by John Davidsen. Tórshavn: Justinssen.

Anderson, Benedict. 1983. *Imagined communities: Reflections on the origin and spread of nationalism.* London and New York: Verso Editions and Schocken Books.

Andreasen, Poul. 1977. *Úr Vágs søgu.* Klaksvík: privately printed.

Anon. 1848. Fowling in Shetland and Faroe. *Chambers's Edinburgh Journal* 10 (246, new series):180-83.

———.1868. Der Grindefang auf den Faröer-Inseln, von einem Augenzeugen. *Die Gartenlaube 1868* (7):104-7.

————.1899. Iceland and the Faroe Islands. *Dublin Review* 125(251)[n.s., no. 32]:385-401.

————.1975. Teir ymsir trúarðbólkarnir: Soleiðis varð brøðra-samkoman til í Føroyum. *Nú* 2(9) [unpaginated].

Baldwin, John. 1978. *Scandinavian Shetland: An ongoing tradition?* Edinburgh: Scottish Society for Northern Studies.

Barnes, J.A. 1954. Class and committees in a Norwegian island parish. *Human Relations* 7:39-58.

Bekker-Nielsen, Hans, ed. 1978. *Svend Grundtvig: Dansken paa Færøerne— Sidestykke til Tysken i Slesvig* [1845]. C.C. Rafn-Forelæsning no. 5. Odense: Odense Universitetsforlag.

Birley, Caroline. 1891. In the Faroes. *Good Words* 32:264-68, 320-25.

Bjørk, E.A. 1959. Strandarætturin í Føroyum. *Fróðskaparrit* 8:66-102.

————. 1961. Óðalsrætturin í Føroyum. *Fróðskaparrit* 10:110-36.

Björnsson, Björn. 1971. *The Lutheran doctrine of marriage in modern Icelandic society.* Oslo and Reykjavík: Universitetsforlaget and Almenna Bókafélagið.

Blehr, Otto. 1963. Action groups in a society with bilateral kinship: A case study from the Faroe Islands. *Ethnology* 2(3):269-77.

————.1964. Ecological change and organizational continuity in the Faroe Islands. *Folk* 6(1):29-33.

————. 1976. Social drinking in the Faroe Islands: The ritual aspect of token prestations. *Ethnos* 39(1-4):53-62.

Bloch, Jørgen. 1895. *Stiftamtmænd og amtmænd i kongeriget Danmark og Island 1660-1848.* Copenhagen: Rigsarkivet.

Bloch, K. 1944. Utdrag av rikpreken over sogneprest til Dverberg hr. Niels Olufssøn Bye, med endel oplysinger om nordlandsslekterne Bye og Brønlund. *Norsk Slekthistorisk Tidsskrift* 9(4):321-33.

————. 1968. Nordlandslekterne Hveding og Bloch. *Norsk Slekthistorisk Tidsskrift* 21(4):273-315.

Blom, Jan-Petter, and Gumperz, John J. 1972. Social meaning in linguistic structure: Code-switching in Norway, in *Directions in sociolinguistics: The ethnography of communication.* Edited by John J. Gumperz and Dell Hymes, pp. 407-34. New York: Holt, Rinehart and Winston.

Blöndal, Sigfús, ed. 1908. *Æfisaga Jóns Ólafssonar Indíafara samin af honum sjálfum (1661).* Vol. 1. Copenhagen: Hitt Íslenska Bókmentafélagið and S.L. Möller.

Boissevain, Jeremy, and Friedl, John, eds. 1975. *Beyond the community: Social process in Europe.* The Hague: European-Mediterranean Study Group of the University of Amsterdam.

Brú, Heðin. 1970. *The old man and his sons.* Translated and with an introduction by John West. New York: P.S. Eriksson.

Brønner, Hedin, trans. and ed. 1972. *Faroese short stories.* Translated from the Faroese and the Danish with an introduction and notes by Hedin Brønner. Library of Scandinavian Literature vol. 16, general editor Erik J. Friis. New York: Twayne Publishers and The American-Scandinavian Foundation.

————. 1973. *Three Faroese novelists: An appreciation of Jørgen-Frantz Jacobsen, William Heinesen, and Heðin Brú.* The Library of Scandinavian Studies, vol. 1. New York: Twayne.

Burton, Richard F. 1875. *Ultima Thule; or, a summer in Iceland*. 2 vols., London and Edinburgh: William P. Nimmo.

Butterfield, Herbert. 1973. *The Whig interpretation of history*. Harmondsworth: Penguin. (Original edition 1931, London: Bell.)

Bærentsen, C. 1911. Ejendomsforholdene i bygden Sand, in Tillæg, pp. 463-582.

Bærentsen, Håkon, and Jacobsen, Ole. 1971. Folkeafstemningen 14. September 1946 på Færøerne: Et kapitel af Nordens nyere politiske mytologi. *Fra Færøerne/Úr Føroyum* 6:20-37.

Carus-Wilson, E.M. 1954. *Medieval merchant venturers, collected studies*. London: Methuen.

Carøe, K. 1917. Landkirurger og fysici på Færøerne 1584-1916. *Personalhistorisk Tidsskrift* 38 (7th series, vol. 2):47-51.

Castberg, A. St. 1941. Torsten Povelsen-Østenes og hans efterslekt. *Norsk Slekthistorisk Tidsskrift* 9(1):39-52.

Castile, George Pierre, and Kushner, Gilbert, eds. 1981. *Persistent peoples: Cultural enclaves in perspective*. Tucson: University of Arizona Press.

Clark, John Willis. 1861. Journal of a yacht voyage to the Faroe Islands and Iceland, in *Vacation tourists and notes of travel in 1860*. Edited by Francis Galton, pp. 318-61. Cambridge (England) and London: MacMillan and Co.

Clementsen, Ólavur. 1981. *Søga og skemt av Sandi*. Tórshavn: Klovin.

————. 1983. *Skopun 150 ár*. Tórshavn: Klovin.

Cluness, Andrew Thomas, ed. 1967. *The Shetland book*. Lerwick: Zetland Education Committee.

Colding, J.H. 1933. Ein trupul ferð til Føroya í 1789. *Varðin* 13:129-37.

Conroy, Patricia. 1979. Ballad composition in Faroese heroic tradition: The case of "Hernilds kvæði." *Fróðskaparrit* 27:73-101.

Coull, J.R. 1967. Demographic trends in the Faroe and Shetland Islands. *Transactions of the Institute of British Geographers* 41:159-66.

Dahl, Árni. 1980. *Bókmentasøga I: Frá landnámi til Hammershaimb*. Klaksvík: Fannir.

————. 1981. *Bókmentasøga II: 1876-1939*. Klaksvík: Fannir.

Dahl, J. 1938. Føroya seinasti biskupur: Eitt 400-ár minni. *Varðin* 18 (5-6):158-62.

Dahl, Sverri. 1958. Toftarannsóknir í Fuglafirði. *Fróðskaparrit* 7:121-46.

————. 1961. Bústaður í Eingjartoftum, Sandavági (Settlement in Eingjartoftir, Sandavágur). *Fróðskaparrit* 10:53-76.

————. 1965. Víkingabústaður í Seyrvági. *Fróðskaparrit* 14:9-23.

————. 1970a. Um ærgirstaðir og ærgistoftir. *Fróðskaparrit* 18:361-68.

————. 1970b. The Norse settlement of the Faroe Islands. *Medieval Archaeology* 15:60-73.

Dahl, Sverri, and Rasmussen, Jóannes. 1956. Víkingaaldargrøv í Tjørnuvík. *Fróðskaparrit* 5:153-67.

Dahl-Krosslíð, Jákup. 1902. Skúlaskapur í Føroyum. *Búreisingur: Føroyskt tíðskrift*, pp. 37-54. (Facsimile edition, 1969, Tórshavn: Emil Thomsen.)

Dalsgaard, Jóannes. 1964. Nær fingu vit eplini? *Varðin* 36(1-2):31-33.

Dansk-Færøsk Samfund. 1958. *Færøerne*. 2 vols. Copenhagen: Dansk-Færøsk Samfund, Dansk-Færøsk Kulturfund, and Det Danske Forlag.

David, C.N. 1857. *Folketællingen paa Island, Oct. 1, 1855*. *Meddelelser fra det Statistiske Bureau* 4 (May 1857). Copenhagen: B. Luno and F.S. Muhle.

Davidsen, John. 1970. Hústrúin í Húsavík. *Fróðskaparrit* 18:69-76.

Debes, Hans. 1769. *Kort underretning om inbyggernes handels-maade paa Færøe, samt forsøg til handelens muelige forbedring samme steds*. Copenhagen: Nicolaus Møller.

Debes, Hans Jacob. 1969. Formæli: Tjóðskaparrørslan og *Føringatíðindi*. Unpaginated foreword to *Føringatiðindi* [facsimile edition]; Tórshavn: Emil Thomsen.

———. 1982. *Nú er tann stundin . . . : Tjóðskaparrørsla og sjálvstýrispolitikkur til 1906—við søguligum baksýni*. Tórshavn: Føroya Skúlabókagrunnur.

Debes, Hans M. 1977. *Søgur úr gomlum døgum*. Tórshavn: Stabbin.

Debes, Lucas. 1673. *Færoæ et Færoa reserata* [etc.]; Copenhagen: Mattias Jørgensen. Republished 1963, with an introduction by Einar Joensen. Tórshavn: Einars Prent og Forlag.

———. 1676. *Færoæ et Færoa reserata: that is a description of the islands and inhabitants of Foeroe . . .* , englished by J[ohn] S[terpin], doctor of physic. London: W. Isles.

Degn, Anton. 1925. Rettelser og tilføjelser I. *Personalhistorisk Tidsskrift* 46(8th series, vol. 4):96.

———. 1929. *Oversigt over fiskeriet og monopolhandelen paa Færøerne 1709-1856*. Tórshavn: Varðin.

———. 1930. Marken som værdienhed paa Færøerne. *Historisk Tidsskrift* 1 (10th series):68-78.

———. 1932. Hvat kann rómaskatturin í Føroyum siga okkum? *Varðin* 12(5-6):129-33.

———. 1933. Kongs-, ognar-, og prestajørð í Føroyum. *Varðin* 13(3-4):65-83.

———. 1935. Nøkur brot úr søgu "Dalsgarðs." *Varðin* 15(1-2):20-31.

———. 1937a. Nøkur gomul áður óprentað brøv o.a. Føroyum viðvíkjandi. *Varðin* 17(7-8):193-209. (Corrections, ibid., p. 256.)

———. 1937b. Presturin J.H. Schrøter sigur frá loynihandli og øðrum í Suðuroy. *Varðin* 17(1-2):34-47.

———. 1938a. Nøkur gomul áður óprentað brøv [etc.]; *Varðin* 18(1-2):24-39.

———. 1938b. [same title] *Varðin* 18(5-6):129-50.

———. 1938c. [same title] *Varðin* 18(7-8):193-214.

———. 1939. Um løgmannin Johan Heinrich Weyhe. *Varðin* 19(4):219-30.

———. 1945. *Færøske kongsbønder 1584-1884*. Tórshavn.

Deutsch, Karl W. 1953. *Nationalism and social communication: An inquiry into the foundations of nationality*. Cambridge (Mass.): M.I.T. Press.

Djupedal, Reidar. 1964a. Kring J.H. Schröters omsetjing av Matteus-Evangeliet, 1823. *Fróðskaparrit* 13:235-62.

———. 1964b. Litt om framvoksteren av det færøyske skriftmålet, in *Skriftsspråk i utvikling: Tiårsskrift for norsk språknemnd 1952-1962*. Edited by Alf Hellevik and Einar Lundeby, pp. 144-86. Oslo: J.W. Cappelen.

Djurhuus, Hans Andreas. 1963. *Føroya søga*. 3rd ed., Tórshavn: H.N. Jacobsens Bókahandil.

Djurhuus, N., and Matras, Christian, eds. 1951-1972. *Føroya kvæði: Corpus carminum Færoensium a Sv. Grundtvig et J. Bloch comparatum*. 6 vols. Copenhagen: Einar Munksgaard (vols. 1-3), Akademisk Forlag (vols. 4-6), and Universitets-Jubilæets Samfund (all vols.).

Edmondston, Arthur. 1809. *A view of the ancient and present state of the Zetland*

Islands [etc.]. 2 vols. Edinburgh and London: John Ballantyne and Longman, Hurst, Rees, and Orme.

Edwardes, Charles. 1885. A walk in the Faroes. *Macmillan's Magazine* 53(314):121-31.

———.1892. St. Olaf's day in the Faroes. *Chambers's Journal* 69, pt. 102 [July 1892]:378-81.

Emmet, Isabel. 1964. *A North Wales village: A social anthropological study.* London: Routledge and Kegan Paul.

Erslev, K.R. 1923. *Rigsarkivet og hjælpmidlerne til dets benyttelse: En oversigt.* Copenhagen: Nielsen & Lydiche.

Evensen, A.C., ed. 1908-14. *Savn til føroyinga søgu í 16. öld.* Tórshavn: Hitt Føroyska Bókmentafelagið.

———, ed. 1911. *Lesibók.* Tórshavn: Hitt Føroyska Bókmentafelagið.

Feldbæk, Ole. 1971. *Dansk neutralitetspolitik under krigen 1778-1783: Studier i regeringens prioriteten af politiske og økonomiske interesser.* Københavns Universitet, Institut for Økonomisk Historie, Publikation nr. 2. Copenhagen: Københavns Universitets Fond til Tilvejbringelse af Læremidler and G.E.C. Gad.

———. 1977. The Anglo-Danish convoy conflict of 1800. *Scandinavian Journal of History* 2:161-82.

Fenton, Alexander. 1978. *The northern isles: Orkney and Shetland.* Edinburgh: John Donald.

Foote, Peter G. 1964. *Færeyinga saga,* chapter forty. *Fróðskaparrit* 13:84-98.

———. 1965. *On the Saga of the Faroe Islanders.* London: H.K. Lewis.

———. 1970. On legal terms in *Færeyinga saga. Fróðskaparrit* 18:159-75.

Foote, Peter G., and Wilson, David M. 1970. *The Viking achievement: A survey of the society and culture of early medieval Scandinavia.* New York and Washington: Praeger.

Forbes, Charles S. 1860. *Iceland: Its volcanoes, geysers, and glaciers.* London: John Murray.

Fossing, Henrik. n.d. Færøernes kirkehistorie fra ca. 1900-1946. Unpublished student term paper in theology/church history. [Tórshavn?: Fróðskaparsetur Føroya?]

Friis, Peder Claussøn. 1881. *Norigis Bescrifuelse,* in *Samlede skrifter af Peder Claussøn Friis.* Edited by Gustav Storm. 4 vols. Kristiania (Oslo): Den Norske Historiske Forening and A.W. Brøgger.

Føroya Lærarafelag 1976. *Lærarafólk í Føroyum 1870-1976.* 2nd edition. Tórshavn: Føroya Lærarafelag.

Gad, Finn. 1979. "La Grönlande, les Isles Ferröe et l'Islande non comprises": A new look at the origins of the addition to Article IV of the Treaty of Kiel of 1814. *Scandinavian Journal of History* 4:187-205.

Gade, Peter Nielsen, and Lyngbye, Hans Christian. 1820. Færøeske oldsager. A. Om den gamle kirkemuur ved Kirkeboe paa Færøe. *Antiquariske Annaler* 3:266-74.

Geertz, Clifford. 1980. *Negara: The theatre state in Bali.* Princeton: Princeton Univ. Press.

Gelsinger, Bruce E. 1981. *Icelandic enterprise: Commerce and economy in the middle ages.* Columbia: Univ. of South Carolina Press.

von Geyr-Schweppenburg, A. 1900. *Meine Reise nach den Färöern*. Paderborn: J. Esser.

Gíslason, Gylfi Þ. 1973. *The problem of being an Icelander, past, present and future*. Translated by Pétur Kidson Karlsson. Reykjavík: Almenna Bókafélagið.

Graba, Carl Julian. 1848. Reise nach Färö, in *Reisen nach Färö, Island, Sibirien, und den Nord-Polarländern*. Edited by Fr. Heinzelman, vol. 2, part 1, pp. 1-64. Leipzig: August Weichart. First published 1830, Hamburg: Perthes & Vesser.

Graubard, Stephen R. 1984. Preface to the issue, "*The Nordic enigma.*" *Dædalus* 113(1):v-xiii.

Gregoriussen, J.P. (Jóan Petur uppi í Trøð). 1928. *Yrkingar*. With an introduction by M.A. Jacobsen. Tórshavn: Varðin.

Grohshenning, Max, and Hauch-Fausbøll, Th. 1914. *Danmarks Præstehistorie 1884-1911*. 2 vols., Copenhagen: Dansk Genealogisk Institut.

Grundtvig, Svend. 1845. *Dansken paa Færøerne, Sidestykke til Tysken i Slesvig*. Copenhagen: C.A. Reitzel. Reprinted in Bekker-Nielsen (1978), pp. 11-79.

―――. 1882. Meddelelse angående Færøernes litteratur og sprog. *Aarbog for Nordisk Oldkyndighed og Historie* 82:357-72.

Grønneberg, Roy. 1981. *Jakobsen and Shetland*. Lerwick: Shetland Publishing Company.

―――. 1984. Jakob Jakobsen and his Shetland correspondents, in *Essays in Shetland history*. Edited by Barbara E. Crawford, pp. 224-33. Lerwick: Shetland Times.

Graae, G. Fr. A. 1901. Gamle minder. Edited by Th. Graae. *Personalhistorisk Tidsskrift* 22 (4th series, vol. 4):1-38.

Gusfield, Joseph R., and Michalowicz, Jerzy. 1984. Secular symbolism: Studies of ritual, ceremony, and the symbolic order in modern life. *Annual Review of Sociology* 10:417-35.

Guttesen, Rolf. 1971. Útlitið fyri áhaldandi vøkstri í fólkatali Føroya. *Fróðskaparrit* 19:132-46.

Halldórsson, Ólaf. 1961. Um landnám Gríms Kambans í Føroyum. *Fróðskaparrit* 10:47-52.

Hammershaimb, Venceslaus Ulricus. 1846. Færøiske trylleformularer. *Annaler for Nordisk Oldkyndighed og Historie 1846:* 347-65. Reprinted in facsimile in Hammershaimb (1969), pp. 9-27.

―――, ed. 1851. *Færöiske kvæder*. 2 vols., Copenhagen: Det Nordiske Litteratur-Samfund and Brødrene Berlings Bogtrykkeri.

―――. 1854. Færøsk sproglære. *Annaler for Nordisk Oldkyndighed og Historie 1854:* 233-316. Reprinted in facsimile in Hammershaimb (1969), pp. 223-308.

―――, ed. 1891. *Færøsk anthologi*. 2 vols., Copenhagen: S.L. Møller (Møller & Thomsen). Facsimile edition 1969, Tórshavn: Hammershaimbsgrunnurin.

―――. 1900. Hitt Føroyska Bókafelagið, in *Ársbók 1900*, pp. 21-27.

―――. 1969. *Savn úr* Annaler for Nordisk Oldkyndighed og Historie *og* Antiquarisk Tidsskrift. Tórshavn: Offset-Prent/Emil Thomsen.

Hamre, Håkon. 1944. *Færøymålet i tiden 1584-1750*. Skrifter utgitt av det Norske Videnskaps-Akademi i Oslo: II: Hist.-Filos. Klasse, no. 2. Oslo: Jacob Dybswad.

Hansen, Gerhard. 1984. *Vækkelsesbevægelsernes møde med færingernes enheds-*

kultur: En analyse ca. 1850-1918. Annales Societatis Scientiarum Færoensis supplementum X. Tórshavn: Føroya Fróðskaparfelag.

Hansen, J. Símun. 1960. *Havið og vit. l. partur: Norðoyggja skipa- og handilssøga*. Klaksvík: privately printed.

———. 1966. *Havið og vit. 2. partur: Minniligir dagar*. Klaksvík: privately printed.

———. 1971. *Tey byggja land. 1. partur: Fugloyar sókn*. Klaksvík: privately printed.

———. 1973. *Tey byggja land. 2. partur: Svínoyar sókn*. Klaksvík: privately printed.

———. 1975. *Tey byggja land. 3. partur: Viðareiðis sókn*. Klaksvík: privately printed.

———. 1978a. *Tey byggja land. 4. partur: Kunoyar sókn*. Klaksvík: privately printed.

———. 1978b. *Tey byggja land. 5. partur: Húsa- og Mikladals sókn*. Klaksvík: privately printed.

———. 1980. *Tey byggja land. 6. partur. Klaksvíks sókn*. Klaksvík: privately printed.

———. 1981. *Tey byggja land. 7. partur. Klaksvíks sókn, seinna helvt*. Klaksvík: privately printed.

Harder, Kirsten. 1979. *De dansk-færøske forhold 1945-48*. Odense: Odense Universitetsforlag.

Haugen, Einar. 1976. *The Scandinavian languages: An introduction to their history*. Cambridge, Mass.: Harvard University Press.

Heilsen, Henning. 1969. John Gudmundsen Effersøe. *Personalhistorisk Tidsskrift* 89(15th series, vol. 3):109-23.

Heilskov, Chr. 1915. Af den "Heinesenske" slægts saga, med en inledning om færøsk personalhistorie. *Personalhistorisk Tidsskrift* 36(6th series, vol. 6):248-82.

———. 1919. Kommandanter paa Færøerne 1632-1865. *Personalhistorisk Tidsskrift* 39(7th series, vol. 3):88-102.

Heinesen, Jens Pauli, ed. 1966. *Føroyar í dag (Færøerne i dag)*. Tórshavn: Norrøna Felagið.

Heinesen, William. 1971. *The lost musicians*. Translated from the Danish by Erik J. Friis. New York: Twayne Publishers and The American-Scandinavian Foundation.

———. 1974. *The kingdom of the earth*. Translated from the Danish and with an introduction by Hedin Brønner. New York: Twayne Publishers and The American-Scandinavian Foundation.

———. 1980. *Arctis: Selected poems*. Translated by Anne Born. Findhorn, Moray (Scotland): Thule.

———. 1981. *The tower at the end of the world: A poetic mosaic novel of my earliest youth*. Translated by Maja Jackson. Wellingborough, Northamptonshire: Thorsons.

———. 1983. *Winged darkness and other stories*. Translated by Hedin Brønner. New York: Irvington.

Helgason, Jón. 1931. Tvey gomul føroysk skrift. *Varðin* 11(3-4):65-84.

———. 1940. *Lucas Debes*. Føroyingafelags hefti Nr. 2. Copenhagen: Føroyingafelagið.

Helle, Knut. 1968. Anglo-Norwegian relations in the reign of Håkon Håkonsson (1217-63). *Medieval Scandinavia* 1:101-14.

Hjalt, Edward. 1953. *Sands søga*. Tórshavn: Varðin.

Hobsbawn, Eric, and Ranger, Terence, eds. 1983. *The invention of tradition*. Cambridge (England): Cambridge University Press and Past and Present Publications.

Hollos, Marida. 1976. Conflict and social change in a Norwegian mountain community. *Anthropological Quarterly* 49(4):239-57.

Holm, P.A. 1855. En dag i Thorshavn. *Folkekalender for Danmark 1855:* 29-37.

———. 1860. *Skildringer og sagn fra Færøerne*. 2nd edition, expanded. Copenhagen: K. Schønbergs.

Holmgaard, Jens. 1964. *Rentekammeret I: Danske og norske afdelinger 1660-1848*. Vejledende arkivregistraturer XII. Copenhagen: Rigsarkivet.

Hoydahl, Kjartan; Jacobsen, Bárður; Dalsgarð, Jens; and Guttesen, Rolf, eds. 1971. *Ruskovnurin 1971*. Tórshavn.

Høgnesen, Róland Waag. 1966. Tá ið Føroyar komu upp í donsku stættatingini. *Fróðskaparrit* 15:91-95.

Høj, Chr. 1984. *Brot úr Heimamissionssøguni*. Gøta: Heimamissionsforlagið.

Isaksen, Finnbogi. 1983. *Tilburðir í okkara øld. 1. 1901-1905*. Klaksvík: Frøi.

Jackson, Anthony. 1979. Socio-economic change in the Faroes, in *North Atlantic maritime cultures: Anthropological essays in changing adaptations*. Edited by Raoul Anderson, pp. 31-64. The Hague, Paris, and New York: Mouton.

Jacobsen, Jógvan í Lon. 1981. *Føroyskur dansur í Eysturoynni í 20. øld fram til Eysturoynni Dansifelag (1969)*. Undergraduate thesis, Tórshavn: Fróðskaparsetur Føroya (mimeograph).

Jacobsen, M.A. 1921. *Úr bókmentasøgu okkara*. Tórshavn: "Færø Amtstidende"s Bogtrykkeri.

———. 1939. Nicolai Mohr. *Varðin* 4:112-18.

Jacobsen, M.A., and Matras, Christian, eds. 1961. *Føroysk-donsk orðabók (Færøsk-dansk ordbog)*. 2nd edition, revised and expanded, Tórshavn: Føroya Fróðskaparfelag.

———, eds. 1974. *Føroysk-donsk orðabók (Færøsk-dansk ordbog): Eykabind (Supplementsbind)*. Prepared by Jóhan Hendrik W. Poulsen. Tórshavn: Føroya Fróðskaparfelag.

Jacobsen, Sanna. 1936. Um Nólsoyar Páll og ætt hansara. Edited by Poul Johannesen. *Varðin* 16(3-4):104-22.

Jacobsen, Steinbjörn. 1974. *Kjökr: Yrkingar*. Tórshavn: Steplið.

Jakobsen, Jakob, ed. 1892. *Føriskar vysur irktar og sungnar äv Føringun y Kjøpinhavn (1876-92)*. Copenhagen: S.L. Møller.

———, ed. 1898-1901. *Færøske folkesagn og æventyr*. 2 vols. Copenhagen: Samfund til udgivelse af gammel norsk litteratur. Republished in 3 vols., 1964-1972, Tórshavn: H.N. Jacobsens Bókahandil.

———. 1904. *Færøsk sagnhistorie, med en indledende oversigt over øernes almindelige historie og litteratur*. Tórshavn and Copenhagen: H.N. Jacobsens Forlag and Vilhelm Priors Hofboghandel.

———, ed. 1907. *Diplomatarium Færoense: Føroyskt fodnbrævasavn. I: Miðalaldarbrøv upp til trúbótarskeið, við søguligun rannsóknun*. Tórshavn and Copenhagen: H.N. Jacobsens Bókahandil and Vilhelm Prior.

240   REFERENCES

————. 1912. *Poul Nolsöe: Lívssøga og irkingar.* Tórshavn and Copenhagen: H.N. Jacobsens Bókahandil and Vilh. Prior.

————. 1928. *An etymological dictionary of the Norn language in Shetland.* London and Copenhagen: David Nutt and Vilhelm Prior.

————. 1957. *Greinir og ritgerðir.* Tórshavn: H.N. Jacobsens Bókahandil.

í Jákupsstovu, Jákup. 1972. *Kor fiskimanna í Føroyum (Wage determination and working conditions for fishermen in the Faroe Islands).* Tórshavn: Marius Ziska.

Jensen, Albert C. 1972. *The cod.* New York: Crowell.

Jensen, Rikard. 1952. Fimm nýggjar niðursetubygdir. *Varðin* 30(1-2):45-59.

Jepsen, Bodil. 1969. The Faroese flag/Det færøske flag/Die färöische Flagge. *Welcome to the Faroes/Velkommen til Færøerne/Willkommen auf den Färöern* 1969:45-49.

Joensen, Einar, ed. 1953. *Tingbókin 1615-54.* Tóshavn: Landskjalasavnið.

————, ed. 1958. *Løgtings- og vártingsbókin 1655-1666.* Tórshavn: Landskjalasavnið.

————, ed. 1961. *Løgtingsbókin 1666-77.* Tórshavn: Landskjalasavnið.

————, ed. 1969, *Vártings- og løgtingsbókin 1667-1690.* Tórshavn: Landskjalasavnið.

————, ed. 1970. *Carl Adolf Muhle, Carl Mogensens Færøske krønikke: Skriv og blaðgreinir om kongaliga handilin somu tíð eru skoytt uppí/Med tillæg af samtidig piece samt avisartikler vedr. den kongelige fæøske handel.* Tórshavn: Einars Prent.

Joensen, Høgni Debes. 1981. Sambandið føroyinga og útlendinga ímillum: Hugleiðingar um viðurskiftini frá 1273 til 1856. *Fróðskaparrit* 28-29:210-45.

Joensen, Jákup Sverre, and Zachariassen, Petur. 1982. Grindatøl 1584-1640 og 1709-1978: Statistics for pilot whale killing in the Faroe Islands 1584-1640 and 1709-1978. *Fróðskaparrit* 30:71-102.

Joensen, Jóan Pauli. 1975. *Færøske sluppfiskere: Ethnologisk undersøgelse af en erhvervsgruppes liv.* Skrifter från Folkelivesarkivet i Lund, nr. 17. Also published as Annales Societatis Scientiarum Færoensis, supplementum 6.

————. 1976. Pilot whaling in the Faroe Islands. *Ethnologia Scandinavica* 1976:1-42.

————. 1978. Føroysk fólkamentan: Bókmentir og gransking. *Fróðskaparrit* 26:114-49.

————. 1980. *Färöisk folkkultur.* Lund: LiberLäromedel.

————. 1981. Tradition och miljö i färöiskt fiske, in *Tradition och miljö: Ett kulturekologiskt perspektiv.* Edited by Lauri Hanko and Orvar Löfgren, pp. 95-134. Lund: LiberLäromedel.

————. 1982a. *Fiskafólk: Ein lýsing av føroyska húshaldinum í slupptíðini.* Tórshavn: Føroya Sparikassi.

————. 1982b. Man and the physical environment, in *The physical environment of the Faroe Islands (Monographicae Biologicae,* vol. 46). Edited by R.K. Rutherford, pp. 125-41. The Hague and Boston: W. Junk.

————. 1983. Um ikki at flyta annan fótin fyrr enn hin stendur tryggur: Ein stutt søgulig lýsing av Føroya Fróðskaparfelag og Fróðskaparsetri Føroya. *Fróð skaparrit* 31:11-35

Joensen, Jóan Pauli; Mortensen, Andras; and Ravnsfjall, Jógvan. 1983. Føroyar í slupptíðindi: Frágreiðing um eina fólkalívsfrøðiliga innsavning. *Fróð-skaparrit* 31:94-103.

Joensen, Jóhan K.; Mortensen, Arnbjørn; and Petersen, Poul. 1955. *Føroyar undir fríum handli í 100 ár: Minnisrit um frígeving Føroya handla 1 januar 1856*. Tórshavn: Føroya Landsstýri.

Joensen, Robert. 1963. Eitt sindur um setningar. *Fróðskaparrit* 12:61-82.

———. 1966. Hvussu gomul er bygdin. *Varðin* 38(1-2):26-31.

Johannesen, Marius. 1976. *Eitt sindur um Kalsoynna og nakrar sagnir knýttar at henni*. Tórshavn: Grønalið.

———, ed. 1978. *Tættir*. Tórshavn: Grønalið. Published separately in 5 vols., 1966-1978, Tórshavn: Tingakrossur (vols. 1-3) and Grønalið (vols. 4-5).

Jóhansen, Jóhannes. 1971. A paleobotanical study indicating a pre-Viking settlement in Tjørnuvík, Faroe Islands. *Fróðskaparrit* 19:147-57.

Johansen, Sámal. 1970. *Á bygd fryst í tjúgundu øld*. Tórshavn and Vágur: H.N. Jacobsens Bókahandil.

Johnston, George, trans. 1975. *The Faroe Islanders' saga*. Ottowa: Oberon.

Jones, Gwyn. 1968a. *A history of the Vikings*. New York: Oxford University Press.

———. 1968b. *The legendary history of Olaf Trygvasson (The W.P. Ker Memorial Lecture delivered in the University of Glasgow, 6th March 1968)*. Glasgow: Jackson, Son, and Co.

Jones, W. Glyn. 1974a. *Færø og kosmos: En indføring i William Heinesens forfatterskab*. Copenhagen: Gyldendal.

———. 1974b. *William Heinesen*. Twayne's World Authors Series, no. 282, general editor Sylvia Bonnan; Denmark, edited by Leif Sjöberg. New York: Twayne.

Jørgensen, H.G.A. 1937. *Sognepræst og præstegaard: Dansk præstegaardsliv gennem 1000 aar*. Copenhagen: G.E.C. Gad.

Jørgensen, Harald, ed. 1954-1962. *Statsrådets forhandlinger, 1848-1912*. 12 vols. Copenhagen: Rigsarkivet.

Keilhack, Konrad. 1885. *Reisebilder aus Island*. Gera: A. Reisewitz.

Korsgaard, Peter. 1979. Fyriskipanin frá 3.5.1724 om handil í Føroyum og kærurnar um hana. *Fróðskaparrit* 27:113-29.

———. 1982. "Beaucoup de bruit pour une aumellette": Skerjingin í rættinum at ganga í hjúnarlag í Føroym eftir fyriskipanini frá 21.5.1777. *Fróðskaparrit* 30:59-70.

Krogstrup, Hanne, and Lund, Yvonne Barnholdt. 1983. *Færøernes erhvervspolitik*. Aalborg: Aalborg Universitetsforlag.

Labonne, Henri. 1887. L'Islande et l'archipel des Færoer. *Le Tour du Monde* 54(2nd semester 1887):385-416. Republished 1888, Paris: Hachette.

Landt, Jørgen. 1800. *Forsøg til en beskrivelse over Færøerne*. Copenhagen: Tikjøbs. Republished 1965, Tórshavn: Einars Prent.

———. 1810. *A description of the Feroe Islands[. . .]translated from the Danish*. London: Longman, Hurst, Rees and Orme.

———. 1820. Jørgen Landts breve om hans rejse til Færøe 1792. *Magazin for Rejseiagttagelser* (edited by R. Nyerup) 1820(vol. 1):119-28. Copenhagen: Fr. Brummer.

Leclercq, Jules. 1883. *La terre de glace: Féröe—Islande: les geysers—le mont Hekla*. Paris: Plon.

242 REFERENCES

í Líð, Regin (Rasmussen, Rasmus). 1912. Minnisvarðin, in *Glamlýsi: Smásögur*, pp. 1-41. Tórshavn: Hitt Føroyska Bókmentafelagið. First published 1906.
Linklater, Eric. 1971. *Orkney and Shetland: An historical, geographical, social & scenic survey.* 2nd edition. London: Robert Hale.
Lockwood, W.B. 1964. *An introduction to modern Faroese.* Copenhagen: Munksgaard.
Luihn, Astri. 1980. *Føroyskur dansur: Studier i sangtradisjoner på Færøerne.* Trondheim: Rådet for folkemusikk og folkedans.
Lunddahl, J.A. 1911. Nogle bemærkninger om de færøske landboforhold, in *Tillæg*, pp. 421-62.
Lyngbye, Hans Christian. 1820a. Færøeske oldsager. B. Efterretning om adskillige oldsager og mærkværdiheder paa Færøe. *Antiquariske Annaler* 3:274-305.
———. 1820b. Noget om Færøerne, især om de der brugelige bryllupsskikke. *Magazin for Rejseiagttagelser* (edited by R. Nyerup) 1820(vol. 1):203-34. Copenhagen: Fr. Brummer.
———. 1822. *Færøiske qvæder om Sigurd Fofnersbane og hans æt.* Randers: S. Simenhoff.
MacGregor, Lindsay J. 1984. Sources for a study of Norse settlement in Shetland and Faroe, in *Essays in Shetland History.* Edited by Barbara E. Crawford, pp. 1-17. Lerwick: Shetland Times.
Macmillan, Kenneth. n.d. *A brief history of the 12th Battalion of the Cameronians (Scottish Rifles) June 1940-November 1943 and something of what happened after disbandment.* No place of publication given.
Manning, Frank E., ed. 1983. *The celebration of society: Perspectives on contemporary cultural performance.* Bowling Green and London, Ontario: Bowling Green University Popular Press and the Congress of Social and Humanistic Studies (University of Western Ontario).
Marcus, G.J. 1956. The Norse emigration to the Faroe Islands. *English Historical Review* 71:56-61.
Martins, Charles Frédéric. 1842-55. Essai sur la végétation de l'archipel des Féröe, comparée à celles des Shetland et de l'Islande meridionale, in *Voyages de la commission scientifique du nord, en Scandinavie, en Laponie, au Spitzberg, et au Féröe, pendant les années 1838, 1839, et 1840 sur la corvette la Recherche, commandée par m. Fabvre.* Edited by Paul Gaimard. 12 vols. Paris: A. Bertrand. Reprinted in *Géographie Physique* 2:353-450.
Matras, Christian. 1933. *Heimur og heima.* Tórshavn: Dimmalætting.
———. 1935. *Føroysk bókmentasøga.* Copenhagen: Føroya Málfelag.
———. 1936. Tá ið Schrøter ætlaði at týða Nýggja Testamenti. *Varðin* 16(181-87).
———. 1951. Det færøske skriftsprog af 1846. *Scripta Islandica (Isländska Sällskapets Årsbog)* 2:5-23.
———. 1956. Gammelfærøsk ærgi, n., og dermed beslægtede ord. *Namn och Bygd* 44:151-67.
———. 1958. Sproget, in Dansk-Færøsk Samfund (1958), pp. 70-82.
———. 1968. Litteratur: I. Folkedigting, in Trap (1968), pp. 174-76.
———. 1969. *Føringatíðindi og móðurmálið.* Unpaginated introduction to *Føringatíðindi* [facsimile edition]. Tórshavn: Emil Thomsen.
———. 1971. V.U. Hammershaimb (1819-1909). *Arv: Tidsskrift för Nordisk Folkminnesforskning (Journal of Scandinavian Folklore)* 27:23-33.

Matras, H.D. 1951. Dahlerupsakin. *Varðin* 29(4):213-22.

Mentunargrunner Studentafelagsins. 1966. *Heimastýri sjálvstýri*. Copenhagen: Mentunargrunnur Studentafelagsins.

Michelsen, Anna Cathrine. 1930. Katolikkarnir í Havn. *Varðin* 10(5-6):159-66.

Mitens, Edward. 1966. *Eg minnist—Lögtingsmaður 1916-1939*. Tórshavn: H.N. Jacobsens Bókahandil.

Mjöberg, Joran. 1980. Romanticism and revival, in *The northern world: The history and heritage of northern Europe, AD 400-1100*. Edited by David M. Wilson, pp. 225-38. New York: Harry N. Abrams.

Mortensen, Arnbjørn. 1954. Fólkatalið og ognarbýtingin um 1600, við jarðabókini 1584 sum grundarlag. *Fróðskaparrit* 3:7-59.

Müller, A.C. 1883a. *Oplysning om grindefangsten på Færøerne*. Copenhagen: Naturhistorisk Forening.

———. 1883b. Whale-fishing in the Faroe Isles, in *Fish and fisheries: A selection of prize essays of the International Fisheries Exhibition, Edinburgh 1882*. Edited by Daniel Herbert, pp. 1-17. Edinburgh and London: William Blackwood and Sons.

Müller, Eiden. 1945. *Fem aar under Union Jack, Færøerne 1940-1945: Atlanterhavsøerne under den britiske okkupation*. Copenhagen: Gyldendahl.

Munch, P.A. 1845. Om indførelsen af en forbedret retskrivning i vort folkesprog. *Den Constitutionelle* nos. 181, 184, 186 (30 June; 3 and 5 July 1845). Reprinted (1873) in *P.A. Munch: Samlede Afhandlinger*. Edited by Gustav Storm, vol. 1, pp. 148-59. Christiania (Oslo): Alb. Cammermeyer.

Nathanson, M.C. 1832. *Udforligere oplysinger om handels- og finants-væsnet i Christian den 7des og Frederik den 6tes Regjeringstide* [etc.]. Copenhagen: C.A. Reitzel.

Nedergaard, Paul, ed. 1951-56. *Personalhistoriske, sognehistoriske og statistiske bidrag til en dansk præste og sognehistorie (kirkelig geografi) 1849-1949*: vol. 1 (1951), *Københavns stift (med Færøerne, Grønland og udlandspræster);* vol. 3 (1956), *Fyns stift*. Copenhagen: O. Lohses Forlag.

Niclasen, Poul. 1945. *Færøerne i krønikker og foredrag*. Copenhagen: Bianco Luno.

Nicolson, James R. 1978. *Traditional life in Shetland*. London: Robert Hale.

Nielsen, Bjørgfinnur. 1977. Kanning av staðarhjáorðum og fyrisetningum í samband við staðanøvn í Sandoynni. Unpublished dissertation, Fróðskaparsetur Føroya, Tórshavn.

Nielsen, H. Hjorth. 1914. Kongelige resolutioner 1815-1847 faldne paa ansøgninger om giftermaalstilladelser fra hærens officerer of ligestillede. *Personalhistorisk Tidsskrift* 35(7th series, vol. 5):1-48.

Nolsøe, Dánjal, 1963. Fiskimarkið. *Fróðskaparrit* 12:112-39.

Nolsøe, Páll J. 1950. Skúlaviðurskifti á bygd 1845-1854. *Varðin* 27(1):28-64.

———. 1963-70. *Føroya siglingarsøga*. 7 vols. Tórshavn: privately published.

Nyman, Åsa. 1981. Färöiska folksagor upptecknade efter 1950. *Fróðskaparrit* 28-29:110-13.

Nørrevang, Arne. 1979. Land tenure, fowling rights, and sharing of the catch in Faroese fowling. *Fróðskaparrit* 27:30-49.

Oakley, Stewart, 1972. *A short history of Denmark*. New York and Washington: Praeger.

O'Neill, Wayne. 1970. The oral-formulaic structure of the Faroese *kvæði*. *Fróðskaparrit* 18:59-68.

Panum, Peter Ludvig, 1940. *Panum on measles: Observations made during the epidemic of measles on the Faroe Islands in the year 1846*. Translated by Ada Sommerville Hatcher. New York: Delta Omega Society.

Park, George K. 1972. Regional versions of Norwegian culture: A trial formulation. *Ethnology* 11(1):3-24.

Patursson, Erlendur. 1945. *Føroysk stjórnarmál*. Tórshavn: H.N. Jacobsens Bókahandil.

———. 1961. *Fiskiveiði fiskimenn*. 2 vols. Tórshavn: Einars Prent.

———. 1965. *Føroya søga III: Úr einaveldi í amtsveldi: Stórnarviðurskifti 1834-1854*. Tórshavn: Søguútgávan.

———. 1966. *Føroya søga IV: Undir amtsveldinum: Stjórnarviðurskifti 1854-1939*. Tórshavn: Unga Tjóðveldið.

———. 1976-81. *Fiskivinna og fiskivinnumál 1940-1970*. 3 vols. Tórshavn: Føroya Fiskimannafelag.

Patursson, Jóannes. 1903. *Færøsk politik: Nogle uddrag og betragtninger*. Copenhagen: Alexander Brandt.

———. 1931. *Færøsk selvstyre: Færingerne, et nordisk mindretal, et norrønt folk*. Tórshavn: Tingakrossur.

———. 1939. *Føroya søga I: Úrdráttur úr stjórnarlaginum*. Tórshavn: H.N. Jacobsens Bókahandil.

———. 1966. *Tættir úr Kirkjubøar søgu*. Tórshavn: Varðin.

Pedersen, Pól A. 1960. *Um Mikladals bygd*. Tórshavn: privately printed.

Petersen, Poul. 1968. *Ein føroysk bygd*. Tórshavn: privately printed.

Petersen, Sámal, 1972. Tingstaðurin á Tinganesi. *Fróðskaparrit* 20:71-88.

Phillpotts, Bertha S., ed. and trans. 1923. *The life of the Icelander Jón Ólafsson traveller to India* [etc.]. *Vol. 1: Life and travels: Iceland, England, Denmark, White Sea, Faroes, Spitzbergen, Norway 1593-1622*. Works issued by the Hakluyt Society, second series, no. 53. London: Hakluyt Society.

Pløyen, Christian. 1896. *Reminiscences of a voyage to Shetland, Orkney and Scotland in the summer of 1839*. Translated by Catherine Spence. 2nd edition. Lerwick: T. & J. Manson. (First published 1840, in Danish, Copenhagen.)

Poulsen, Jóan Christian. 1947. *Hestsøga*. Tórshavn: Varðin.

Poulsen, Joen, and Johannessen, Christian Ludvig. 1891. *Förisk ABC og lesingabók*. Tórshavn: Föringafelag. (Facsimile edition, 1972. Tórshavn: Skúlablaðið.)

Poulsen, Jóhan Hendrik W. 1979. Om brug af stednavne i færøske familienavn, in *Språkform och språknorm* (Skrifter utgit av Svenska Språknämnden, nr. 67), pp. 190-96. Lund: Berling.

———, ed. 1985. *Nøkur teldorð: Føroysk-Dansk/Ensk, Dansk/Ensk-Føroysk*. Tórshavn: Málstovnur Føroya Fróðskaparfelags.

Powell, F. York, trans. 1896. *The tale of Thrond of Gate: Commonly called Færeyinga saga*. London: D. Nutt.

Power, Eileen. 1941. *The wool trade in English medieval history, being the Oxford lectures*. London: Oxford University Press.

Press, Mrs. Muriel A.C., trans. 1934. *The saga of the Faroe islanders*. London: J.M. Dent & Sons.

Rafn, Carl Christian. 1832. *Færeyínga saga eller Færøboernes historie i den islandske grundtext med færøisk og dansk oversættelse.* Copenhagen: Jens Hostrup Schultz.

Rasch, Aage. 1964. *Niels Ryberg, 1725-1804: Fra bondedreng til handelsfyrste.* Skrifter udgivet af Jysk Selskab for Historie, Sprog og Litteratur, nr. 12. Aarhus: Universitetsforlaget.

Rask, Rasmus Kristian. 1811. *Vejledning til det islandske eller gamle nordiske sprog.* Copenhagen: J.R. Thiele.

Rasmussen, Jóannes. 1958. Kolanøgdin í Suðuroy (The coal resources on Suðuroy, Faroe Isles). *Fróðskaparrit* 7:102-14.

Rasmussen, P.M. 1978. *Tættir úr Føroya kirkjusøga.* Tórshavn: Føroya Skúlabókagrunnur.

Rasmussen, Rasmus. 1954. Fyrsta fólkatingsvalið. *Varðin* 31:(2):55-59.

————. 1968. *Føroysk fólkamenning.* Copenhagen: Føroyska Studentafelagið.

Redfield, Robert. 1960. Peasant society and culture, in *The little community and peasant society and culture.* Chicago: University of Chicago Press.

Resen, Peter Hansen. 1972. *Peder Hansen Resen: Atlas Danicus, Færøerne.* Færoensia: Textus et investigationes, vol. 9. Edited by Christian Matras. Copenhagen: Munksgaard.

Reynolds, Hans. 1923. *Færøyane: Hjaa gamalt norskt folk.* 2nd edition. Nidaros (Trondheim): G. Krogshus.

Robertson, M., ed. 1975. *The collected poems of Vagaland.* Lerwick: The Shetland Times.

Rye, D.H. 1866. *Betænkning om fiskeriforholdene paa Færøerne, afgiven til Justitsministeriet.* Copenhagen: I.H. Schultz.

á Ryggi, Mikkjal Dánjalsson. 1927. Stórhvalur og stórhvalaveiði. *Varðin* 7(5-6):117-35.

————. 1940. *Miðvinga søga.* 2nd edition, corrected, 1965. Tórshavn: H.N. Jacobsens Bókahandil.

Sachs, Aage. 1921. *Den danske centraladministration, udgivet i anledning af den Danske Kancellibygnings 200 aars dag.* Copenhagen: V. Pios Boghandel and Poul Bronner.

Scammell, G.V. 1981. *The world encompassed: The first European maritime empires, c. 800-1650.* Berkeley and Los Angeles: University of California Press.

Schrøter, Johann Hendrik. 1823. *Evangelium Sankta Matteussa aa førisk o dansk.* Randers: Det Danske Bibelselskab.

————, ed. 1836. *Samling af kongl. anordninger og andre documenter, Færøerne vedkommende, tilligemed en afhandling.* Copenhagen: at the author's expense, by S.L. Møller.

————. 1849-51. Færöiske folkesagn. *Antiquarisk Tidsskrift 1849-1851*:142-70.

Seaton, Ethel. 1935. *Literary relations of England and Scandinavia in the seventeenth century.* Oxford: Clarendon.

Severin, Tim. 1978. *The Brendan voyage.* Drawings by Tróndur Patursson. London: Hutchinson of London.

Sjálvstýrisflokkurin, n.d. [1981?] *Sjálvstýrisflokkurin 75 ár: Brot úr søga sjálvstýrisflokksins.* Klaksvík: Klaksvíkar Prentsmiðja.

av Skarði, Jóhannes, ed. 1967. *Donsk-Føroysk orðabók (Dansk-Færøsk ordbog).* Tórshavn: Føroya Fróðskaparfelag.

————. 1980. *Jólafundurin 1888—or eitt sindur um høvuðsmennirnar í Føroy-*

ingafelag í Føroyum. Tórshavn: Føroya skúlabókagrunnur. First published 1964, *Varðin* 36(3-4):128-36.

————, ed. 1984. *Ensk-Føroysk orðabók.* Tórshavn: Føroya Fróðskaparfelag.

av Skarði, Símun. 1904. Vár, in *Tveir Sjónleikir,* pp. 29-84. Tórshavn: Prentsmiðju "Fram"s.

————. 1921. Lucas Debes í rættartrætu við kommandantin og fútan. *Varðin* 1(4):75-87.

————. 1922. Lambahjúnini Mikkjal og Magdalena. *Varðin* 2:130-49.

————. 1923. Frá siðaskiftatíðini í Føroyum. *Varðin* 7(3):169-89.

Skårup, Poul. 1964. *Rasmus Rask og færøsk.* Færoensia: Textus et Investigationes, vol. 6. Edited by Christian Matras. Copenhagen: Ejnar Munksgaard.

Small, A. 1967-68. The distribution of settlement in Shetland and Faroe in Viking times. *Saga Book of the Viking Society for Northern Research* 17:145-55.

Spicer, Edward H. 1971. Persistent cultural systems. *Science* 174(4011):795-800.

Steining, Jørgen. 1953. Rigsdagen og Færøerne, in *Den danske Rigsdag 1849-1949, udgivet af Statsministeriet og Rigsdagens Præsidium.* Vol. 6: *De sønderjydske landsdele, Færøerne, Grønland, Danmark og Island: Det interparlamentariske arbejde,* pp. 103-201. Copenhagen: J.H. Schultz.

Stewart, George [of Leith]. 1892. *Shetland fireside tales, or The hermit of Trosswickness.* 2nd edition. Lerwick: T. and J. Manson. First edition 1877, Edinburgh.

Stewart, John. 1974. Norn in Shetland. *Fróðskaparrit* 13:158-75.

Storm, Gustav. 1874. *Minder fra en Islandsfærd.* Christiania (Oslo): J.W. Cappelen.

Støðisútbúgvingin. 1973. *Støðisrit um rúsdrekka.* Edited by Jógvan Dahl and others. [Tórshavn]: Støðisútbúgvingin.

Svabo, Jens Christian. 1959. *Indberetninger fra en rejse i Færøe, 1781-1782.* Edited by N. Djurhuus. Copenhagen: Selskabet til Udgivelse af Færøske Kildeskrifter og Studier.

Sørlie, Michael. 1965. *En færøsk-norsk lovbok fra omkring 1300. En studie i Færøys språkhistorie.* Tórshavn; and Bergen and Oslo: Mentunargrunnur Føroya Løgtings; and Universitetsforlaget.

Taranger, Absalon, ed. and trans. 1970. *Magnus Lagabøters landslov.* 4th printing. Oslo, Bergen, and Tromsø: Universitetsforlaget.

Tarnovius, Thomas. 1950. *Ferøers beskrifvelser av Thomas Tarnovius.* Færoensia: Textus et Investigationes, vol. 2. Edited by Håkon Hamre. Copenhagen: Ejnar Munksgaard.

Thomle, E.A. 1882. Gravskrifter fra Stavanger domkirke. *Personalhistorisk Tidsskrift* 3(1st series, vol. 3):122-62.

Tierney, J.J., ed. and trans. 1967. *Dicuili liber de mensura orbis terrae.* Scriptores Latini Hibernae 6. Dublin: Dublin Institute for Advanced Studies.

Tolkien, J.R.R. 1963. *Beowulf:* The monsters and the critics, in *An anthology of Beowulf criticism.* Edited by Lewis E. Nicholson, pp. 51-103. Notre Dame: University of Notre Dame Press. First published 1936, in *Proceedings of the British Academy* 22:245-95.

Tomasson, Richard F. 1975a. Iceland as "The first new nation." *Scandinavian Political Studies* 10:33-51.

————. 1975b. The literacy of the Icelanders. *Scandinavian Studies* 47:66-93.

————. 1980. *Iceland: The first new society.* Minneapolis: University of Minnesota Press.

Trap, J.P. 1879. *Statistisk-topografisk beskrivelse of Kongeriget Danmark.* 2nd. edition, part 6. Copenhagen: O.H. Delbanco, G.E.C. Gad, Gyldendalske Boghandel, and C.C. Lose.

————. 1904. *J.P. Trap, Kongeriget Danmark: Første bind: Aarhus, Vejle, Ringkjøbing, Ribe og Færø amter.* 3rd. edition, revised. Edited by H. Weitemeyer. Copenhagen: G.E.C. Gad.

————. 1968. *Trap, Danmark. Bind 13: Færøerne.* 5th edition. Edited by Niels Nielsen, Peter Skautrup, Therkel Mathiassen, and Jóannes Rasmussen. Copenhagen: Gad.

Trevelyan, Sir Walter Claverly. 1835. On the vegetation of the Faroe Islands. *Edinburgh New Philosophical Journal* 18(35):154-64.

————. 1853. Faroe Islands. *Edinburgh New Philosophical Journal* 54(108):380.

Trollope, Anthony. 1878. *How the "Mastiffs" went to Iceland.* London: Virtue and Co.

Tylor, Edward Burnett. 1958. *The origins of culture.* New York: Harper and Bros. First published 1871, as Chapters 1-10 of *Primitive culture.* London: J. Murray.

Veiter, Theodor. 1961. Die Färöer und ihre autonomie. *Europa Ethnica* 18(2):55-76.

Wang, Hans. 1931. Kolbein og Galti. *Varðin* 11(5-6):182-83.

Ward, Barbara. 1965. Varieties of the conscious model: The fishermen of South China, in *The relevance of models for social anthropology.* Edited by Max Gluckman and Freg Eggan. A.S.A. Monographs 1. General editor Michael Banton, pp. 113-37. London and New York: Tavistock Publications and Frederick A. Praeger.

Weihe, Alexander [Alexander Veya]. 1850. *Førjaríman íð er ógviliga vökur spildurnýj ríma um Førjar og Føringa.* Copenhagen: S.L. Möller.

West, John F. 1969. Brillumanninum til verju. *Fróðskaparrit* 17:139-54.

————. 1970a. The English letters of Pastor Schrøter. *Fróðskaparrit* 18:17-26.

————, ed. 1970b. *The journals of the Stanley Expedition to the Faroe Islands and Iceland in 1789. Vol. 1: Introduction and diary of James Wright.* Tórshavn: Føroya Fróðskaparfelag.

————. 1972. *Faroe: The emergence of a nation.* London and New York: C. Hurst and Co. and Paul S. Eriksson.

————. 1975. How old is the Faroese *grannastevna? Fróðskaparrit* 23:48-59.

————, ed. and trans. 1980. *Faroese folk-tales and legends.* Illustrated by Barður Jákupsson. Lerwick: Shetland Publishing Co.

Whisnant, David E. 1983. *All that is native and fine: The politics of culture in an American region.* Chapel Hill and London: University of North Carolina Press.

Williamson, Kenneth. 1945. The economic and ethnological importance of the caaing whale, *Globiocephalus melaena* Traill, in the Faeroe Islands. *Northwestern Naturalist* 20:118-36.

————. 1970. *The Atlantic islands: A study of the Faeroe life and scene.* 2nd edition. With an epilogue by Einar Kallsberg. London: Collins.

Wilson, Peter J. 1973. *Crab antics: The social anthropology of English-speaking Negro societies in the Caribbean.* New Haven and London: Yale University Press.

————. 1974. *Oscar: An inquiry into the nature of sanity.* New York: Random House.

Winther, Niels. 1875. *Færøernes oldtidshistorie.* Copenhagen: K. Schønberg.

Wolf, Eric R. 1982. *Europe and the people without history.* Berkeley, Los Angeles and London: University of California Press.

Wylie, Jonathan. 1974. *I'm a stranger too: A study of the familiar society of the Faroe Islands.* Unpublished doctoral dissertation, Harvard University.

————. 1978. *The Faroese Reformation and its consequences.* Papers on European and Mediterranean Societies no. 10, Anthropologisch-Sociologisch Centrum, Universiteit van Amsterdam. Amsterdam: Universiteit van Amsterdam.

————. 1979. *Astérix ethnologue:* Anthropology beyond the community in Europe. *Current Anthropology* 20(4):797-98.

————. 1982. The sense of time, the social construction of reality, and the foundations of nationhood in Dominica and the Faroe Islands. *Comparative Studies in Society and History* 24(3):438-66.

————. 1983. Ólavsøka, the Faroese national holiday. *Ethnos* 48(1-2):26-45.

Wylie, Jonathan, and Margolin, David. 1981. *The ring of dancers: Images of Faroese culture.* Foreword by Einar Haugen. Philadelphia: University of Pennsylvania Press.

Waag, Einar. 1967. *Val og valtøl 1906-1966.* Klaksvík: privately published.

Young, G.V.C. 1979. *From the Vikings to the Reformation.* Douglas, Isle of Man: Shearwater Press.

Young, G.V.C., and Clewer, Cynthia R., trans. 1973. *The Faroese saga freely translated with maps and genealogical tables.* Belfast: Century Services.

Zachariasen, Louis. 1945. Føroysk tjóðmenning. *Varðin* 25(1):32-36.

————. 1952. Brot úr Føroya søgu. *Varðin* 30(3-4):81-198.

————. 1961. *Føroyar sum rættarsamfelag 1535-1655.* Annales Societatis Scientiarum Færoensis, supplementum IV. Tórshavn: Fróðskaparfelag.

Zachariasen, Ulf. 1964. Jakob Jakobsen og ritgerðir hansara. *Fróðskaparrit* 13:261-68.

Øresund, Øyvind. 1976. The transformation of Scandinavian agrarianism: A comparative study of political change around 1870. *Scandinavian Journal of History* 1:201-13.

Øssursson, Janus. 1963. *Føroya biskupa-, prósta-, og prestatal.* Tórshavn: Mentunargrunnur Føroya Løgtings.

Index

◙ This index is alphabetized as usual in English except that æ, ø, and aa are treated as the last three letters of the alphabet. No distinction is made between ð and d, between þ and th, or between accented and unaccented vowels.

kommune law, 109, 127, 182
Kongelig Nordisk Oldskriftselskab, 102, 183
Koppen, Thomas, 18, 25
í Króki, Jóannes, 94
Kvívík, 9, 131
Kvívíks-Jógvan (Jógvan Dánjalsson), 132
kvæðir, 43, 211 n.2
kvøldsetur, 41-42, 128, 193, 197

labor. *See* hired hands; servants
labor shortages, 74, 76, 77, 81
lagting, 90, 216 n.15
Lampe, Mads, 25
land measurement, 31, 208 n.4
Landsting, 105, 106, 110
Landt, Jørgen, 92, 221 n.11
land tenure, 13-24, 23, 31-34; changing patterns of, 74, 77, 87, 127, 135, 207 n.9, 208-9 n.5, 213 n.7, 216-17 nn.17, 19
land use, 31, 174; in Iceland, 175; in Shetland, 180. *See also* infield; outfield
land value, 208 n.4
language, Danish: use of in religion, 24-26, 93, 100, 127; in law, 25, 100, 225 n.20; in education, 95, 99-100, 109, 127, 172, 225 n.20; in international affairs, 128, 153, 223 n.8; in literature, 128, 228 n.7; Faroese phonology of, 218 n.7
language, English, 224 n.13
language, Faroese: history of, 5, 24-25, 92-103, 127; dialects in, 24, 101; in oral and written literature, 41-64, 92-94, 98, 100-101, 102, 128, 132, 138, 139, 142-44, 147, 170, 186-96; orthography of, 92, 95, 100-102, 155-56, 217 n.3, 218 n.13, 223 n.9; in religion, 94, 95, 99, 100-101, 112, 144, 167-78; in education, 95-97, 109, 127, 144, 168, 172, 225 n.20; in law, 99, 225 n.20; in politics, 99, 107-8, 127, 155, 167-68, 221 n.9; grammar of, 102, 140, 217 n.3; in commerce, 127, 148; in national culture, 142-47, 156, 163-64, 186, 192; in journalism, 144, 147, 150; in science, 147; in social criticism, 190; in historiography, 191-96
language, Icelandic: grammar of, 92-93; orthography of, 93; as symbol, 93, 103, 177-79; 184-85; in literature, 177; in religion, 25, 177. *See also* sagas
language, Latin, 24
language, Norwegian, 102
law: foundation of, 36; ecclesiastical and secular, 36-37. *See also* judicial system;

Seyðabræv; Stóridómur
legends, 35, 43-61, 191-96; legal themes in, 46-47; fights in, 194, 212 n.7. *See also* folk literature; storytelling
Lerwick, 181
Liber de mensura orbis terræ (Dicuil), 7
libraries, 131, 137
í Líð, Regin. *See* Rasmussen, Rasmus
lighthouse, 68
Lisberg, Jens Oliver, 166
Literary Society, 137, 154
literature, oral, categories of, 43
Lowell, Robert, 188
Lunddahl, J.A., 110, 202
Luther, 8
Lutheran "Home Mission," 129
Lutheranism, 20, 168
Luxdorph, 85
von Løbner, E.M.C., 67, 86, 201
løgmenn, 9, 11, 13, 172, 200, 203-4; plan to eliminate office of, 79; succession to office of, 209 n.7
løgrættumenn, 11, 13
Løgting, 9, 11, 13, 36, 111, 125, 157, 171-72; and smuggling, 28-29; abolition of, 67, 90; reconstitution of, 91, 104, 107, 108, 110; and political parties, 158; changes in, 219 n.21

Madssøn, Strange, 28-29, 202
Madvig, J.N., 105
magazines. *See* periodicals
Magdalena (wife of Mikkjal Jónsson), 48, 211-12 n.6
magic: in legends, 49; formulas for, 102
Magnús Hákonarson, 11, 17
Magnus Lagabøter, 32, 36, 47, 208 n.3
Magnússon, Árni, 177
Magnusson, Hakon, 207 n.6
Magnus the Good, 10
mail service, 137, 222 n.17
Margaret of Denmark, 17-18
marriage, 34, 214-16 n.8; restrictions on, 14, 36, 69, 70, 76, 81, 84; repeal of restrictions on, 115. *See also* population growth: control of
Marshall Plan, 169
masturbation, 214-16, n.8
Matras, Christian, 129, 186-90
men, position of, 57, 129-30, 196
merchants, 118, 119, 149, 152, 159-61; Danish, 131, 220 n.4; in Shetland, 181-82
Merkið, 166
merkur. *See* land measurement
Middle Ages, 11, 13, 15
middle class, 5, 22, 138, 224 n.13

Lightning Source UK Ltd.
Milton Keynes UK
UKHW012129141222
413932UK00001B/69